T0178083

Lecture Notes in Computer Science   13835

Founding Editors

Gerhard Goos
Juris Hartmanis

The series Lecture Notes in Computer Science (LNCS), including its subseries Lecture Notes in Artificial Intelligence (LNAI) and Lecture Notes in Bioinformatics (LNBI), has established itself as a medium for the publication of new developments in computer science and information technology research, teaching, and education.

LNCS enjoys close cooperation with the computer science R & D community, the series counts many renowned academics among its volume editors and paper authors, and collaborates with prestigious societies. Its mission is to serve this international community by providing an invaluable service, mainly focused on the publication of conference and workshop proceedings and postproceedings. LNCS commenced publication in 1973.

Jeremy Singer · Yehia Elkhatib ·
Dora Blanco Heras · Patrick Diehl · Nick Brown ·
Aleksandar Ilic
Editors

Euro-Par 2022:
Parallel Processing
Workshops

Euro-Par 2022 International Workshops
Glasgow, UK, August 22–26, 2022
Revised Selected Papers

 Springer

Editors
Jeremy Singer (iD)
University of Glasgow
Glasgow, UK

Yehia Elkhatib (iD)
University of Glasgow
Glasgow, UK

Dora Blanco Heras (iD)
University of Santiago de Compostela
Santiago de Compostela, La Coruña, Spain

Patrick Diehl (iD)
Louisiana State University
Baton Rouge, LA, USA

Nick Brown (iD)
University of Edinburgh
Edinburgh, UK

Aleksandar Ilic (iD)
Universidade de Lisboa
Lisbon, Portugal

ISSN 0302-9743   ISSN 1611-3349 (electronic)
Lecture Notes in Computer Science
ISBN 978-3-031-31208-3   ISBN 978-3-031-31209-0 (eBook)
https://doi.org/10.1007/978-3-031-31209-0

This Springer imprint is published by the registered company Springer Nature Switzerland AG
The registered company address is: Gewerbestrasse 11, 6330 Cham, Switzerland

Preface

The International European Conference on Parallel and Distributed Computing (Euro-Par) is an annual, international conference in Europe, covering all aspects of parallel and distributed processing. These range from theory to practice, from small to the largest parallel and distributed systems and infrastructures, from fundamental computational problems to fully-fledged applications. It also covers architecture, compiler, language, and interface design and implementation, as well as tools, support infrastructures, and application performance aspects.

The Euro-Par conference is complemented by a workshop program, where workshops dedicated to more specialized themes, to cross-cutting issues, and to upcoming trends and paradigms can be easily and conveniently organized. In addition to workshops, the second edition of the Euro-Par PhD Symposium was also organized at the Euro-Par 2022 conference, with the aim of gathering doctoral students in broadly defined areas related to parallel and distributed processing.

The 28th Euro-Par Workshops and PhD Symposium were held in Glasgow between August 22–23, 2022, following the well-established format of its predecessors. The 28th Euro-Par Workshops and PhD Symposium were organized by the University of Glasgow, with support from Heriot Watt University, the University of Edinburgh and the University of Stirling.

Overall, ten workshop proposals were submitted. The following five workshops were co-located with the Euro-Par 2022 edition, namely:

1. Workshop on Algorithms, Models and Tools for Parallel Computing on Heterogeneous Platforms (HeteroPar)
2. Workshop on Asynchronous Many-Task Systems for Exascale (AMTE)
3. Workshop on Domain Specific Languages for High-Performance Computing (DSL-HPC)
4. Workshop on Distributed and Heterogeneous Programming in C and C++ (DHPCC++)
5. Workshop on Resiliency in High Performance Computing in Clouds, Grids, and Clusters (Resilience)

After a careful revision process, and from a total of 35 submitted workshop papers, 24 papers were accepted, resulting in an acceptance rate of 69%. Each workshop had an independent program committee, which was in charge of selecting the papers. The workshop papers received three reviews per paper on average. These proceedings include 3 papers accepted at AMTE, 3 from DSL-HPC, 11 from Hetero-Par, and in the Miscellaneous section 1 paper each from DHPCC++ and from Resilience.

The Euro-Par PhD Symposium received 10 submissions from five countries, with each submission being reviewed by three technical program committee members of the

Euro-Par PhD Symposium. After the thorough peer-reviewing process, seven submissions were accepted for presentation at the Euro-Par 2022 PhD Symposium, of which six are included as extended abstracts in these proceedings.

This volume contains the papers and extended abstracts presented at the Euro-Par 2022 Workshops and PhD Symposium, divided into five track sections (corresponding to three larger workshops, a miscellaneous chapter aggregating contributions from smaller workshops, and the PhD Symposium.

The success of the Euro-Par Workshops and PhD Symposium depends on the work of many individuals and organizations. We therefore thank all the organizers and reviewers for the time and effort that they invested. We would also like to express our gratitude to the members of the Euro-Par 2022 Organizing Committee and the local staff. Lastly, we thank all participants, panelists, and keynote speakers of the Euro-Par Workshops and PhD Symposium for their contribution to a productive meeting. It was a pleasure to organize and host the Euro-Par Workshops and PhD Symposium 2022 in Glasgow.

August 2022   Jeremy Singer
                                                                       Yehia Elkhatib
                                                                  Dora Blanco Heras

Organization

Steering Committee

Full Members

Luc Bougé (Chair)	ENS Rennes, France
Fernando Silva (Vice-chair)	University of Porto, Portugal
Dora Blanco Heras (Workshops Chair)	CiTIUS, University of Santiago de Compostela, Spain
Henk Sips (Finance Chair)	Delft University of Technology, The Netherlands
Massimo Torquati (Artifacts Chair)	University of Pisa, Italy
Maciej Malawski (Virtualization Chair)	AGH University of Science and Technology, Krakow, Poland
Marco Aldinucci	University of Turin, Italy
Christos Kaklamanis	Computer Technology Institute, Patras, Greece
Paul Kelly	Imperial College, London, UK
Thomas Ludwig	University of Hamburg, Germany
Tomàs Margalef	University Autonoma of Barcelona, Spain
Wolfgang Nagel	Dresden University of Technology, Germany
George Papadopoulos	University of Cyprus, Cyprus
Francisco Fernández Rivera	CiTIUS, University of Santiago de Compostela, Spain
Krzysztof Rzadca	University of Warsaw, Poland
Rizos Sakellariou	University of Manchester, UK
Leonel Sousa	University of Lisbon, Portugal
Domenico Talia	University of Calabria, Italy
Phil Trinder	University of Glasgow, UK
Felix Wolf	Technical University of Darmstadt, Germany
Ramin Yahyapour	GWDG, Göttingen, Germany

Honorary Members

Christian Lengauer	University of Passau, Germany
Ron Perrott	Oxford e-Research Centre, UK
Karl Dieter Reinartz	University of Erlangen-Nürnberg, Germany

General Chair

Phil Trinder   University of Glasgow, UK

Workshop Chairs

Jeremy Singer   University of Glasgow, UK
Dora Blanco Heras   University of Santiago de Compostela, Spain

PhD Symposium Chair

Yehia Elkhatib   University of Glasgow, UK

Submissions Chair

José Cano   University of Glasgow, UK

Publicity Chairs

Anna Lito Michala   University of Glasgow, UK
Patrick Maier   University of Stirling, UK

Web Chair

Michel Steuwer   University of Edinburgh, UK

Virtual/Local Chairs

Rob Stewart   Heriot Watt University, UK
Lauritz Thamsen   University of Glasgow, UK
Syed Waqar Nabi   University of Glasgow, UK

Artifact Chairs

Hans-Wolfgang Loidl   Heriot Watt University, UK
Wim Vanderbauwhede   University of Glasgow, UK
Massimo Torquati   University of Pisa, Italy

Contents

Misc

PhD Symposium

AMTE

Asynchronous Many-Task Systems
for Exascale (AMTE)

Workshop Description

The workshop, Asynchronous Many-Task systems for Exascale (AMTE) 2022, was held on August 23rd in conjunction with the 28th International European Conference on Parallel and Distributed Computing (Euro-Par) as a hybrid event in Glasgow, UK. The workshop explored the advantages of task-based programming on modern and future high-performance systems. It gathered developers, users, and proponents of these models and systems to share experiences, discuss how they meet the challenges posed by Exascale system architectures, and explore opportunities for increased performance, robustness, and full-system utilization.

The workshop was organized by Patrick Diehl, Steven R. Brandt, Zahra Khatami, and Parsa Amini. The keynote was given by Bryce Adelstein Lelbach (NVIDIA) and the invited talk by Elliot Ronaghan (HPE).

This chapter comprises selected contributions of attendees from this event. The contributed papers range from optimization of asynchronous many-task runtime systems to applications. This workshop has shown that AMTs are widely used in academia, industry, and national laboratories, and researchers are working to address some challenges posed by Exascale system architectures.

Organization

Steering Committee

Parsa Amini   Halpern-Wight Inc., USA
Steven R. Brandt   Louisiana State University, USA
Patrick Diehl   Louisiana State University, USA
Zahra Khatami   NVIDIA, USA

Program Committee

Jeff Hammond   NVIDIA
Hartmut Kaiser   Center for Computation & Technology at
                            Louisiana State University, USA
Markus Rampp   Max Planck Computing & Data Facility,
                            Germany
Patricia Grubel   Los Alamos National Laboratory, USA
Bita Hasheminezhad   NASA Ames Research Center, USA
Pedro Valero-Lara   Oak Ridge National Laboratory, USA
H. Metin Aktulga   MSU College of Engineering, USA
Keita Teranishi   Sandia National Laboratories, USA

Quantifying Overheads in Charm++ and HPX Using Task Bench

Nanmiao Wu[1]([✉])[iD], Ioannis Gonidelis[1], Simeng Liu[2], Zane Fink[2][iD],
Nikunj Gupta[2], Karame Mohammadiporshokooh[1], Patrick Diehl[1][iD],
Hartmut Kaiser[1][iD], and Laxmikant V. Kale[2][iD]

[1] Center of Computation & Technology, Lousiana State University, Baton Rouge,
USA
{wnanmi1,igonid1,kmoham6,patrickdiehl,hkaiser}@lsu.edu
[2] Department of Computer Science, University of Illinois at Urbana-Champaign,
Champaign, USA
{simengl2,zanef2,nikunj,kale}@illinois.edu

Abstract. Asynchronous Many-Task (AMT) runtime systems take
advantage of multi-core architectures with light-weight threads, asynchronous executions, and smart scheduling. In this paper, we present
the comparison of the AMT systems Charm++ and HPX with the main
stream MPI, OpenMP, and MPI+OpenMP libraries using the Task
Bench benchmarks. Charm++ is a parallel programming language based
on C++, supporting stackless tasks as well as light-weight threads asynchronously along with an adaptive runtime system. HPX is a C++ library
for concurrency and parallelism, exposing C++ standards conforming
API. First, we analyze the commonalities, differences, and advantageous scenarios of Charm++ and HPX in detail. Further, to investigate
the potential overheads introduced by the tasking systems of Charm++
and HPX, we utilize an existing parameterized benchmark, Task Bench,
wherein 15 different programming systems were implemented, e.g., MPI,
OpenMP, MPI + OpenMP, and extend Task Bench by adding HPX
implementations. We quantify the overheads of Charm++, HPX, and the
main stream libraries in different scenarios where a single task and multi-task are assigned to each core, respectively. We also investigate each
system's scalability and the ability to hide the communication latency.

Keywords: Asynchronous Many-Task (AMT) · Charm++ · HPX ·
Task Bench

1 Introduction

Asynchronous Many-Task (AMT) systems emerge as an effective solution to the
demands of adaptive applications. However, by utilizing the fine-grained parallelism, AMTs tend to generate runtime overheads which inhibits performance
and counteracts their benefits. We are mainly interested in systems that expose

© The Author(s), under exclusive license to Springer Nature Switzerland AG 2023
J. Singer et al. (Eds.): Euro-Par 2022 Workshops, LNCS 13835, pp. 5–16, 2023.
https://doi.org/10.1007/978-3-031-31209-0_1

distributed execution, which is the prevalent technique for massive computational experiments. Many options exist in the realm of parallel runtime systems, *e.g.* Uintah [1], Chapel [2], Legion [3], and PaRSEC [4]. For a more detailed survey of various AMTs, we refer to [5]. **This research focuses on Charm++ [6] and HPX [7] since both systems provide a similar underlying programming model.**

Charm++ delivers a highly abstracted environment for productivity bound to a flexible and performant execution paradigm. On the other hand, HPX provides a C++ standards conforming API and extends the standard parallel facilities by providing asynchronous and distributed components. Our goal is to objectively quantify the overheads of those two systems by evaluating measurements from intrinsic benchmark implementations characteristics. Further comparisons are presented against MPI and OpenMP for distributed and within-node parallel execution, respectively. For that, we utilize Task Bench, a unified benchmarking solution that evaluates these systems under a common ground.

Task Bench was proposed by Slaughter et al. [8] as a standardized solution that unifies the benchmarking process of various existing concurrency frameworks. It provides a backend benchmarking kernel that is exposed through a parameterized interface. Once Task Bench is implemented in a given programming system, it enables a straightforward comparative analysis with every other system in the Task Bench pool. Task Bench has already been implemented for Chapel [2], Dask [9], MPI, OmpSs [10], OpenMP, PaRSEC, Realm [11], Regent [12], Spark [13], StarPU [14], Swift/T [15], TensorFlow [16] and X10 [17]. This makes it suitable for our goal of a fair comparison of two different systems under a common ground. The centralized results enable a direct comparison of the performance of each system in a wide spectrum of tasking paradigms that model various execution schemes corresponding to real world experiments like the stencil pattern, the FFT pattern etc. We extend this work [8] by adding HPX implementations, and reproducing the same results for Charm++ and HPX with using MPI, OpenMP and MPI+OpenMP as a common denominator for the comparisons. Our results reflect those of the original authors and are accompanied by elaborate remarks.

The three major contributions of our work are:

1. This is the first work comparing Charm++ and HPX using the same benchmark. Different HPX implementations with respect to the Task Bench library are implemented, namely HPX local and HPX distributed, in order to fairly compare HPX with Charm++ against the mainstream MPI, OpenMP, and MPI+OpenMP. The optimizations of HPX implementations to minimize the overheads are further introduced.
2. The commonalities, differences, and advantageous scenarios of Charm++ and HPX, are analyzed in detail. The performance results further validate the analysis.
3. The overheads of Charm++ and HPX, along with several other programming systems, are quantified in terms of shared-memory parallelism and

distributed-memory parallelism, in various scenarios wherein a single task and multi-task are assigned to each core, respectively.

The paper is structured as follows: Sect. 2 introduces the existing state-of-the-art performance evaluations. In Sect. 3 Charm++ and HPX are briefly introduced and the similarities and differences are discussed. In Sect. 4 we briefly introduce the ingredients of Task Bench used in this work. Section 5 summarizes the improvements to further reduce the overhead. Section 6 shows simulations in various scenarios without/with overdecomposition. Finally, Sect. 7 concludes the work.

2   Related Work

Many existing works evaluate the performance of task-based parallel programming models. In what follows, we consider studies focusing on mini-apps: simple applications designed to represent the performance characteristics of full-fledged applications.

Karlin et al. [18] evaluate the performance and productivity characteristics of several traditional and task-based parallel programming models using the LULESH [19] mini-application for shock hydrodynamics. In [20], the authors implement a block eigensolver in OpenMP [21] and OpenACC [22] to assess the performance portability of these models. The Parallel Research Kernels [23–26] are a suite of mini-applications and microbenchmarks designed to assess the performance of different parallel systems and programming models. The authors in [27] implement a stencil mini-application in Legion [28] and MPI, observing similar weak-scaling performance between Legion and MPI. In [29], the mini-application and communication microbenchmark performance of Python ports of established programming models Charm++ and MPI is compared. An extensive study at Sandia National Laboratory [30] compares 3 many-task programming models on qualitative and quantitative metrics.

While studies based on mini-application performance provide insight into the performance and programmability of different programming models, the $\mathcal{O}(m \cdot n)$ complexity of implementing m mini-applications in n frameworks makes it onerous to comprehensively evaluate even a few programming models on a range of benchmarks. Section 4 describes another approach to facilitate such comparisons.

3   Asynchronous Many-Task Systems

3.1   Charm++

Charm++ is a parallel programming language based on C++. Unlike the bulk-synchronous and process-centric approach taken by MPI, Charm++ implements a migratable-objects programming model. The basic unit of object in Charm++ is called a *chare* which is typically a class in C++. Functions in a *chare* can group logically-related execution and communication tasks, supporting data-encapsulation and locality. Users can designate some methods as *entry methods* for a *chare* class which are the methods that can be invoked by other, potentially remote, *chares* asynchronously. With the object-oriented approach, Charm++ supports overdecomposition, where the user can define multiple collections ("arrays") of *chares* corresponding to the domain of the problem. Charm++ applications typically partition the domain into finer grains than the amount of available execution units (*e.g.* cores). The location of individual *chares* is controlled dynamically by Charm++'s adaptive runtime system (aRTS). On each core (or node, in some configurations), a user-space scheduler is used to asynchronously but non-preemptively execute the set of available method invocations. This data-driven execution allows Charm++ applications to adaptively overlap communication and computation. By leveraging migratability of *chares*, the aRTS supports dynamic load-balancing, as well as other capabilities such as fault-tolerance, shrinking or expanding the set of nodes assigned to a job in the middle of execution, power/energy/thermal optimizations etc.

3.2 HPX

HPX is a C++ Standard Library for parallelism and concurrency [7]. HPX is implemented as a lightweight user-level task manager running on top of kernel threads. It is widely known that thread creation and destruction managed by the operating system are expensive and reserve lots of memory. For that reason, HPX creates one thread per core and binds each of them to one of the cores. Therefore, the performance can be improved since there is no kernel-level interruption when the tasks are running. HPX is the first implementation of an advanced parallel execution model [31], which essentially resolves critical issues that prevent effective usage of new HPC systems: Starvation, Latency, Overheads, and Waiting for Contention. The HPX asynchronous programming model exposes a C++ standard API entirely conforming to interfaces as defined by C++11/C++14/C++17/C++20 and adds on top of the latest C++ standard by providing distributed and heterogeneous computing scenarios, which makes HPX portable and uniformly usable for local and remote parallelism. HPX aligns with the ongoing C++ standardization proposal with a goal of providing a uniform interface, in particular, related to parallelism and concurrency. HPX is widely used for applications that utilize both shared and distributed memory. PeriHPX [32] is an example of using HPX for shared-memory parallelism, and Octo-Tiger [33] is one example of using HPX for a distributed memory application.

3.3 Commonalities and Differences

Both Charm++ and HPX are highly performant and feature rich AMTs that leverage asynchrony, overdecomposition, and migratability. These features are either implicitly or explicitly exposed to the user. For instance, Charm++ supports built-in migrations while HPX implements user assisted migrations. Furthermore, they bring different interpretations and consequently implementation details on certain key concepts. Charm++ defines a "Processing Element" (PE) that can be an OS thread or a process. Each *chare* is assigned to a PE by keeping it anchored to PEs to enhance locality of the computation. Note that *chares* can move to another PE according to load-balancing strategies to minimize communication or achieve more balanced load distribution. Multiple *chares* are assigned to a PE and user-level scheduler schedules entry method executions non preemptively based on availability of data (messages). On the other hand, HPX keeps the notion of locality explicit and the user needs to assign parallel execution to occur on a certain locality or locally if no locality is provided. Moreover, they both support threading, including features like thread suspension and resumption. While any parallel execution on HPX is run on an HPX thread, Charm++ threading is mainly utilized only in specially designated threaded entry methods that use blocking primitives (such as access to *futures*) that can otherwise block the scheduler if not run on a thread. The default entry methods are not threaded, and can be considered as stack-less tasklets. Finally, Charm++ implements continuations by utilizing callbacks, while HPX utilizes C++ conforming *futures* that can retrieve the underlying computation result.

While both AMTs are feature rich, there are a few key areas in which Charm++ is advantageous. As HPX utilizes HPX threads for any parallel execution, it suffers from the overheads of the threading subsystem and further overheads of the networking interface. Charm++ schedules over each PE individually, *i.e.* anchoring each *chares* to a particular PE (and thereby to a core) except when load-balancing, enhances locality and allows lock-less interaction between entities assigned to the same PE. Furthermore, Charm++ supports load-balancing, automatic checkpoint-restart, and multiple communication protocols. Similarly, HPX supports load-balancing by enabling work-stealing scheduling policy, and supports explicit checkpoint, restart techniques, and several communication layers, *e.g.* TCP, MPI, and libfabrics, with others currently under work.

HPX provides some clear advantages over Charm++ as well. Given HPX exposes an ISO C++ conforming API, porting any standard C++ application to HPX is a mere search and replace. Porting to Charm++ requires careful restructuring of the program. Furthermore, HPX supports all the C++17 parallel algorithms along with various execution policies. An application developer can use these execution policies to achieve NUMA aware parallelism, explicit vectorization of loops, asynchronous algorithm execution, and much more. Charm++ requires the user to explicitly implement some of these features in their code. Given that HPX allows tracking of all function parameters and associated data either as a constant *lvalue* reference or as *rvalue* references, the overheads associated are minimal. Charm++'s parameter marshalling and related copying overheads, resulting in higher overheads in the single node shared-memory setting.

Thus, Charm++ and HPX have similarities and differences, with multiple performance-oriented trade-offs based on the machine and programming model.

4   Task Bench

Task Bench is a parameterized benchmark for evaluating runtime system performance. Notably, Task Bench benchmarks are defined by task graphs expressing communication and task dependency patterns common in real-world applications. This task graph representation enables the evaluation of n systems for m benchmarks with $O(m+n)$ implementation effort, rather than the $O(m \cdot n)$ effort required by other benchmark suites. This dramatically reduces the programming effort required to evaluate new systems and benchmarks.

While *strong* and *weak* scaling have been the prevalent solutions for performance measurement, they both have the potential to yield misleading results. Strong scaling cannot isolate system overheads from application cost while weak scaling could hide the system overheads if large problem size is being used [8]. Task Bench uses METG (*Minimum Effective Task Granularity*) as a metric, which essentially indicates the scaling capabilities of the system on-target. METG exposes how high the computing performance (FLOP/s) can be maintained as the amount of work per task gets smaller. The reasoning behind METG is that for large problem sizes, all systems are expected to behave (almost) optimally. Conversely, for small problem sizes, parallelism becomes challenging. In this work, we use the same choice of 50% as the Task Bench paper [8] to compare the smallest average task granularity such that each system reaches at least 50% peak efficiency. We briefly introduce the ingredients of Task Bench used in this paper. For more details, we refer to [8].

5   Improvements

5.1   Charm++

Charm++ has organically grown over 20+ years, along with many applications and research projects, such as fault tolerance and energy management. As a result, the most general implementation tends to have accumulated overheads. Especially for running fine-grained benchmarks, it is useful to select build-time options carefully. The following briefly describes relevant options:

- **Eight-Byte Message Priority:** Charm++ supports arbitrary-length bit-vector message priorities, complicating the message receive path. A build option to use eight-byte message priorities simplifies it.
- **Simplified Scheduling Path:** We further simplify the message delivery path in Charm++ with these additional changes: no message priorities, no idle detection, and no condition-based or periodic callbacks.
- **Intranode IPC via Shared Memory:** By default, Charm++ uses the NIC for inter-process communication within a node. We assess the performance impact of shared-memory communication within a node.

While we use the Charm++ implementation of Task Bench presented in [34], with the default build here, we provide some data with different build options to evaluate their impacts on fine-grained performance in Sect. 6.3.

Table 1. Left column: Compilers and libraries used to compile all systems. **Right** column: Hardware details of the rostam nodes.

Software				Hardware	
gcc	11.2.0	hwloc	2.6.0	CPU	AMD EPYC 7352 24-Core
boost	1.78.0	OpenMPI	4.1.2	Memory	16 GB DDR-4 memory
gperftools	2.9.1	cmake	3.22.0	Interconnect	200Gb/s EDR Infiniband

5.2 HPX

For HPX, two implementations are available, one is HPX local and another is HPX distributed. Their similarity is that a scheduling facility that is based on top of the current C++ Standard execution proposal [35], called executor, is deployed on both of them. Utilizing such an executor, HPX implementations benefit from retaining the spawning threads alive by allocating existing work to these threads. Further, such executor offers more ability and flexibility, *e.g.* users can determine the priority of worker threads, the stack size of the work threads, and enable or disable work-stealing policy. Note that work-stealing policy is advantageous when we consider overdecomposition, wherein each worker thread has a set of work in queue and the worker thread that finishes its local work can steal the work from currently active worker threads. HPX local and HPX distributed are also different. HPX local relies on HPX local facilities and does on-node computation, while HPX distributed depends on equivalent distributed facilities and manages communication on top of parallelization.

6 Experiments

All experiments were conducted on Buran nodes of the Rostam cluster. The hardware and software details are shown in Table 1. In Sect. 6.1 the overheads of Charm++, HPX, and other systems are measured when considering the scenario where the runtime overhead is dominant, and one computational task is assigned to each core. In Sect. 6.2, overdecomposition is adopted where more than one computational tasks are assigned to each core. We investigate the fine-grained performance of Charm++ in Sect. 6.3, where we use POSIX shared memory for intra-node communication, as described in Sect. 5.1. Each run is 1000 time steps long. Each data point has run 5 times, and a confidence interval with 99% confidence level is shown for the variance in the 5 runs.

6.1 Performance of a Single Task on Each Core

To characterize the performance limited by runtime overhead, the number of tasks is set to the number of total cores.

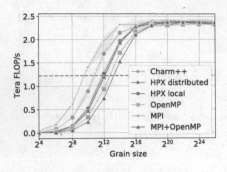
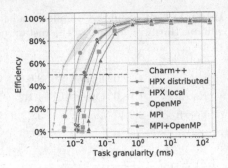

(a) Tera FLOP/s vs grain size.   (b) Efficiency vs task granularity

Fig. 1. Stencil pattern, 1 node (48 cores), 48 tasks.

Figure 1a presents the TeraFLOP/s reached with a compute-bound kernel, varying the grain size. Note that the time for each vertex to execute such a kernel with a grain size of one is 2.5 ns. Almost all systems achieve peak Tera FLOP/s, *i.e.* 2.44×10^{12}, when the grain size is large enough. Figure 1b shows the efficiency of each system responding to the peak Tera FLOP/s vs. task granularity. Task granularity is measured by: wall time × number of cores / number of tasks. Figure 1 shows METG of each system, which is the intersection of its efficiency curve and the 50% efficiency red dashed line in Fig. 1. To calculate METG, we first measure the peak Tera FLOP/s and get the efficiency percentage of each system responding to the peak Tera FLOP/s. For more details about METG, we refer to [8]. For the shared-memory system, *i.e.* OpenMP and HPX local, we observe that HPX local performs better than OpenMP. For the distributed-memory system, we find that MPI has the smallest METG, 3.9 μs. METGs of other systems for this scenario are listed in the first column of Table 2.

Table 2. METG (μs) of each system for the stencil pattern without/with different overdecomposition, using 1 node.

System	single task per core	8 tasks per core	16 tasks per core
Charm++	9.8	37.8	84.1
HPX distributed	19.3	39.2	54.1
HPX local	22.4	54.5	77.9
MPI	3.9	6.1	7.6
OpenMP	36.2	36.9	41.8
MPI+OpenMP	50.9	152.5	258.6

6.2   Performance of Overdecomposition

To quantify the performance of overlapping communication with computation, the total size of tasks is set to N times the number of total cores, such that each core processes N tasks. In this subsection, N is set to 8 and 16, respectively.

Table 2 lists METGs of each system for the stencil pattern with/without overdecomposition, using one node, respectively. For all systems, MPI achieves the smallest METG for these three scenarios.

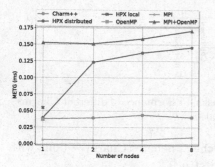
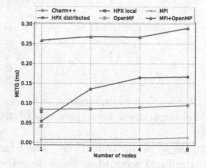

(a) Stencil pattern, overdecomposition 8 (8 tasks per core).

(b) Stencil pattern, overdecomposition 16 (16 tasks per core).

Fig. 2. METG of each system with varying number of nodes for different overdecomposition. METG is short for Minimum Effective Task Granularity, is an efficiency-constrained metric for runtime-limited performance, introduced in Task Bench paper [8].

Figure 2 presents METGs of each system with varying number of nodes. Lower is better because a lower METG indicates a smaller task granularity required to achieve at least 50% overall efficiency. Flat is ideal because a flat line implies that the communication topology does not affect METG by increasing the number of nodes. We observe that Charm++ and MPI have lower and flat trends, while HPX distributed and MPI+OpenMP have higher and rising tendencies. For shared-memory parallelism, OpenMP has smaller METGs than HPX local for both scenarios.

6.3   Fine-grained Charm++ performance

In Fig. 3, we evaluate the performance impact of the different build options meant for fine-grained applications described in Sect. 5.1, which were not used in the above experiments. `Default` is the standard Charm++ build used above. `Char. Priority` denotes a build using eight-byte message priorities; `SHMEM` denotes the build that uses shared-memory for intra-node communication. `Combined` is a

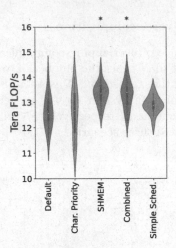

Fig. 3. Stencil pattern, 8 nodes, 384 cores, 384 tasks. Performance of different Charm++ build configurations for a grain size of 4096 iterations.

build using all optimizations, and `Simple Sched.` denotes Charm++ built with the simplified scheduling path described in Sect. 5.1.

We find that `SHMEM` and `Combined` yield an average throughput increase of 5.7% and 5.3%, respectively Using eight-byte message priorities and a simplified scheduling path did not yield a significant increase in throughput. Consequently, we find that scheduling overhead is not substantial even at this grain size, and that communication latency dominates. To further explore the performance impact of scheduling, additional investigation with different Task Bench dependency patterns is required.

7   Conclusion and Outlook

This work is the first work comparing Charm++ and HPX using the same benchmark. Using Task Bench enabled us to study the overheads introduced by the two AMTs compared to the more traditional approaches. The asynchronous scheduling using light-weight threads as in HPX or stackless tasks as in Charm++ incurred some costs. We seen, for larger grain sizes, the overhead was negligible. However, for smaller grain sizes, the overhead was observed. To conclude, the overheads of fine-grained parallelism was not inherent to the programming models, and benchmark studies like this one was expected to lead to further optimizations to reduce or eliminate the gap with respect to MPI.

This study has shown that there is potential for improvement for both AMTs for smaller grain sizes. Here, we need to investigate the differences with respect to MPI and do some profiling with the tools provided by both AMTs. For distributed HPX, we plan to try different libraries for communication, *e.g.* libfabric and LCI. For Charm++ the support for active messaging in the communication layer (such as UCX) will be tested. As a next step, a comparison with other AMTs would be interesting.

References

1. Davison de, J., Germain, St., et al: Uintah: a massively parallel problem solving environment. In: Proceedings the Ninth International Symposium on High-Performance Distributed Computing, pp. 33–41 (2000)
2. Chamberlain, B., et al.: Parallel programmability and the chapel language. Int. J. High Perform. Comput. Appl. **21**, 291–312 (2007)
3. Bauer, M., et al.: Legion: expressing locality and independence with logical regions. In: Proceedings of the International Conference on High Performance Computing, Networking, Storage and Analysis, pp. 1–11 (2012)
4. Bosilca, G., et al.: Parsec: exploiting heterogeneity to enhance scalability. Comput. Sci. Eng. **15**(6), 36–45 (2013)
5. Thoman, P., et al.: A taxonomy of task-based parallel programming technologies for high-performance computing. J. Supercomput. **74**(4), 1422–1434 (2018)
6. Acun, B., et al.: Parallel programming with migratable objects: Charm++ in practice. In: Proceedings of the International Conference for High Performance Computing, Networking, Storage and Analysis (2014)
7. Kaiser, H., et al.: HPX-the c++ standard library for parallelism and concurrency. J. Open Sourc. Softw. **5**(53), 2352 (2020)
8. Slaughter, E., et al.: Task bench: a parameterized benchmark for evaluating parallel runtime performance. In: Proceedings of the International Conference for High Performance Computing, Networking, Storage and Analysis. IEEE (2020)
9. Rocklin, M.: Dask: parallel computation with blocked algorithms and task scheduling, pp. 126–132 (2015)
10. Duran, A., et al.: Ompss: a proposal for programming heterogeneous multi-core architectures. Parallel Process. Lett. **21**, 173–193 (2011)
11. Treichler, S., et al.: Realm: an event-based low-level runtime for distributed memory architectures. In: Conference Proceedings, PACT, August 2014
12. Slaughter, E., et al.: Regent: a high-productivity programming language for HPC with logical regions, pp. 1–12 (2015)
13. Zaharia, M., et al.: Spark: cluster computing with working sets. In: Proceedings of the 2nd USENIX Conference on Hot Topics in Cloud Computing, USA, USENIX 2010, p. 10 (2010)
14. Augonnet, C., et al.: StarPU: a unified platform for task scheduling on heterogeneous multicore architectures. In: Sips, H., Epema, D., Lin, H.-X. (eds.) Euro-Par 2009 Parallel Processing, pp. 863–874. Springer, Berlin, Heidelberg (2009). https://doi.org/10.1007/978-3-642-03869-3_80
15. Wozniak, J.M., et al.: Swift/t: Large-scale application composition via distributed-memory dataflow processing. In: 2013 13th IEEE/ACM International Symposium on Cluster, Cloud, and Grid Computing 2013, pp.95–102 (2013)
16. Abadi, M., et al.: TensorFlow: large-scale machine learning on heterogeneous distributed systems (2016)
17. Charles, P., et al.: X10: an object-oriented approach to non-uniform cluster computing. In: Proceedings of the 20th Annual ACM SIGPLAN Conference on Object-Oriented Programming, Systems, Languages, and Applications, pp. 519–538. ACM, New York, NY, USA (2005)
18. Karlin, I., et al.: Exploring traditional and emerging parallel programming models using a proxy application. In: 2013 IEEE 27th IPDPS, May 2013, pp. 919–932 (2013)

19. Lulesh programming model and performance ports overview. Technical report, LLNL-TR-608824, December 2012
20. Rabbi, F., Daley, C.S., Aktulga, H.M., Wright, N.J.: Evaluation of directive-based GPU programming models on a block eigen solver with consideration of large sparse matrices. In: Wienke, S., Bhalachandra, S. (eds.) WACCPD 2019. LNCS, vol. 12017, pp. 66–88. Springer, Cham (2020). https://doi.org/10.1007/978-3-030-49943-3_4
21. Dagum, L., Menon, R.: OpenMP: an industry standard API for shared-memory programming. Comput. Sci. Eng. IEEE **5**(1), 46–55 (1998)
22. Wienke, S., et al.: OpenACC – first experiences with real-world applications. In: Kaklamanis, C., Papatheodorou, T., Spirakis, P.G. (eds.) Euro-Par 2012 Parallel Processing, pp. 859–870. Springer, Berlin, Heidelberg (2012). https://doi.org/10.1007/978-3-642-32820-6_85
23. Van der Wijngaart, R.F., Mattson, T.G.: The Parallel Research Kernels. In: 2014 HPEC, September 2014, pp. 1–6 (2014)
24. Van Der Wijngaart, R.F., et al.: Using the parallel research kernels to study PGAS models. In: 2015 9th International Conference on Partitioned Global Address Space Programming Models, September 2015, pp. 76–81 (2015)
25. Van der Wijngaart, R.F., Georganas, E., Mattson, T.G., Wissink, A.: A new parallel research kernel to expand research on dynamic load-balancing capabilities. In: Kunkel, J.M., Yokota, R., Balaji, P., Keyes, D. (eds.) ISC High Performance 2017. LNCS, vol. 10266, pp. 256–274. Springer, Cham (2017). https://doi.org/10.1007/978-3-319-58667-0_14
26. der Wijngaart, R.F., et al.: Comparing runtime systems with exascale ambitions using the parallel research kernels. In: Kunkel, J.M., Balaji, P., Dongarra, J. (eds.) ISC High Performance 2016. LNCS, vol. 9697, pp. 321–339. Springer, Cham (2016). https://doi.org/10.1007/978-3-319-41321-1_17
27. Raut, E., et al.: Porting and evaluation of a distributed task-driven stencil-based application. In: Proceedings of the 12th International Workshop on Programming Models and Applications for Multicores and Manycores. Virtual Event Republic of Korea, pp. 21–30. ACM, February 2021
28. Bauer, M., et al.: Legion: Expressing locality and independence with logical regions. In: Proceedings of the International Conference on High Performance Computing, Networking, Storage and Analysis. Washington, DC, USA, IEEE (2012)
29. Fink, Z., et al.: Performance evaluation of python parallel programming models: Charm4py and mpi4py. In: 2021 IEEE/ACM 6th ESPM2 (2021)
30. Baker, G.M., et al.: ASC ATDM Level 2 Milestone# 5325: Asynchronous Many-Task Runtime System Analysis and Assessment for Next Generation Platforms. Technical report, Sandia National Lab (2015)
31. Kaiser, H., et al.: HPX: an advanced parallel execution model for scaling-impaired applications, pp. 394–401. Los angeles, USA (2009)
32. Diehl, P., et al.: An asynchronous and task-based implementation of peridynamics utilizing HPX-the c++ standard library for parallelism and concurrency. SN Appl. Sci. **2**(12), 1–21 (2020)
33. Marcello, D.C., et al.: octo-tiger: a new, 3D hydrodynamic code for stellar mergers that uses HPX parallelization. Mon. Not. R. Astronom. Soc. **504**(4), 5345–5382 (2021)
34. Slaughter, E., et al.: Task Bench: A Parameterized Benchmark for Evaluating Parallel Runtime Performance. arXiv:1908.05790, November 2020
35. Dominiak, M., et al.: P2300r4 std::execution (draft proposal) (2022). www.openstd.org/jtc1/sc22/wg21/docs/papers/2022/p2300r4.html

A Portable and Heterogeneous LU Factorization on IRIS

Pedro Valero-Lara(✉)[iD], Jungwon Kim[iD], and Jeffrey S. Vetter[iD]

Oak Ridge National Laboratory, Oak Ridge, USA
{valerolarap,vetter}@ornl.gov, kimj@ieee.org

Abstract. Here, the IRIS programming model is evaluated as a method to improve performance portability for heterogeneous systems that use LU matrix factorization. LU (lower-upper) factorization is considered one of the most important numerical linear algebra operations used in multiple high-performance computing and scientific applications. IRIS enables the separation of the algorithm's definition from the tuning by using tasks + dependencies. This considerably reduces the effort required to achieve performance portability on heterogeneous systems. One IRIS code can use different settings depending on the underlying hardware features. Different configurations are evaluated on two different heterogeneous systems to achieve important speedups for the reference code with minimal changes to the source code.

Keywords: IRIS · Tasking · Heterogeneity · Performance portability · CPU · GPU · LU factorization

1 Introduction

This paper describes performance portability on different heterogeneous systems using the IRIS programming model[1] for LU (lower-upper) matrix factorization. Iris is a task + dependency-based programming model in which each task can encapsulate almost any kind of current parallel code (e.g., OpenMP, CUDA, HIP, OpenACC) and targets almost any current parallel computer architecture (e.g., CPUs, graphics processing units [GPUs], digital signal processors [DSPs], field-programmable gate arrays [FPGAs]).

---

[1] https://iris-programming.github.io/.

J. Kim—Now at NVIDIA.

Notice: This manuscript has been authored by UT-Battelle, LLC under Contract No. DE-AC05-00OR22725 with the U.S. Department of Energy. The publisher, by accepting the article for publication, acknowledges that the U.S. Government retains a non-exclusive, paid up, irrevocable, world-wide license to publish or reproduce the published form of the manuscript, or allow others to do so, for U.S. Government purposes. The DOE will provide public access to these results in accordance with the DOE Public Access Plan (http://energy.gov/downloads/doe-public-access-plan).

J. Singer et al. (Eds.): Euro-Par 2022 Workshops, LNCS 13835, pp. 17–31, 2023.
https://doi.org/10.1007/978-3-031-31209-0_2

We use LU factorization as a motivating case study given its importance in multiple high-performance computing (HPC) applications [1–3], but the ideas explored in this paper can also be effectively applied to other HPC applications. LU factorization is also one of the most important benchmarks [4,5] used to evaluate the performance of HPC systems.[2] Parallel LU factorization is composed of four major and completely different operations that must be computed on blocks of different shapes and sizes, and the size of these blocks are different along the computation. All these factors make LU factorization a challenging case study for performance portability on heterogeneous systems—for which the best target architecture of each application component is unclear.

To make performance portability on heterogeneous systems simpler, we separate the algorithm design from the tuning. While the algorithm is described by using tasks + dependencies on top of IRIS, the tuning consists of choosing the target/code for each of the tasks, which enables us to use one code for multiple platforms.

The rest of the paper is organized as follows: Sect. 2 presents the main characteristics of the IRIS programming model, Sect. 3 introduces the LU factorization case study, and Sect. 4 outlines the effort to implementation a portable and heterogeneous LU code using IRIS. The performance study is described in Sect. 5. Finally, related work is summarized in Sect. 6, and future directions and conclusions are presented in Sect. 7.

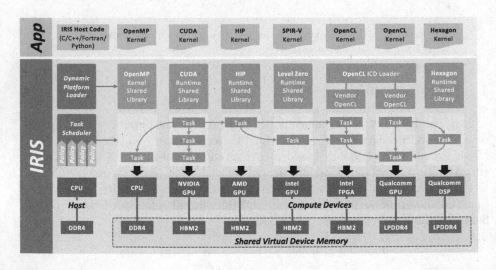

Fig. 1. The IRIS architecture.

---

[2] https://www.top500.org/.

2   IRIS Programming System

As a programming system for extremely heterogeneous architectures, IRIS [6] enables application developers to write portable applications across diverse heterogeneous programming platforms, including CUDA, HIP, Level Zero, OpenCL, and OpenMP (Fig. 1). IRIS orchestrates multiple programming platforms into a single execution/programming environment by providing portable tasks and shared virtual device memory.

IRIS provides a task-based programming model in which a task is a scheduling unit. A task runs on a single device but is portable across any compute device in a system. A task can contain zero or more commands, and there are four types of commands: (1) host-to-device memory copy, (2) device-to-host memory copy, (3) kernel launch, and (4) host. Because a task can have a dependency on other tasks, it cannot start until the prerequisite tasks complete. Therefore, writing an IRIS application means building directed acyclic graphs of tasks. Each task has a target device selection policy when it is submitted. This policy is specified by the programmer, and it can be a device number, device type (e.g., CPU, GPU, FPGA, DSP), or a built-in policy provided by IRIS (e.g., greedy, random, locality-aware, profile).

To achieve application portability and flexible task scheduling with effective data orchestration, IRIS provides shared virtual device memory across multiple, disjointed physical device memories. IRIS automatically transfers data across multiple devices to keep memory consistency across tasks. Therefore, all compute devices can share memory objects in the shared virtual device memory, and they can see the same content in the memory objects.

3   LU Factorization

Decomposing a matrix A into lower and upper triangular matrices (i.e., the LU factorization) is used to more easily solve systems of linear equations:

$$Ax = LUx = B. \tag{1}$$

LU factorization plays a key role in many computational science applications. However, it is also computationally expensive, which motivated us to develop a new LU factorization implementation on top of the IRIS programming model to provide performance portability on different modern heterogeneous systems.

One of the most common ways to parallelize this type of operation is to decompose the matrix into tiles by defining the dependencies between the tiles and the operations to be computed on each tile. This can be accomplished through tasking [7–9].

The LU factorization on a tiled matrix (Fig. 2) consists of (1) factorizing the first tile of the diagonal to obtain the L (dark-green) and U (light-green) matrices of the tile; (2) computing several TRSMs (light-blue) by using the L matrix for the corresponding row and the U matrix for the corresponding column; and (3) computing the so-called *update* step (dark-blue) by multiplying (i.e., general matrix multiply [GEMM]) the result of the set of TRSMs and updating the tiles in the rest of the matrix. We compute the next tile of the diagonal and the next two steps until the entire matrix is computed.

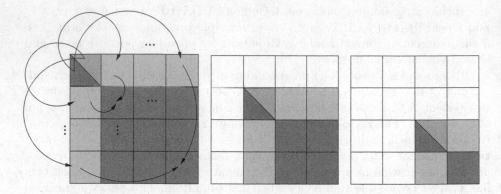

Fig. 2. LU decomposition.

Although the state-of-the-art routine for LU factorization involves pivoting, we developed a non-pivoting version for two reasons: (1) the pivoting is not necessary on well-conditioned matrices, and (2) we want to analyze the performance of the proposed optimizations without the influence of pivoting for the sake of performance analysis. Additionally, although using pivoting to solve linear systems of equations is commonly accepted, we found multiple problems in which the matrices were well conditioned, which made expensive operations such as pivoting unnecessary. For this reason, multiple implementations in reference libraries do not use such a technique. Examples include PLASMA [9], LASs [7], Intel's MKL,[3] NVIDIA's cuSolver [10] and cuSparse [11], FISHPACK [12,13], and SuperLU [14].

4   Implementation

Figure 3 shows the pseudocode for the IRIS-implemented LU factorization. At this *algorithm level*, we declare the different memory spaces and tasks and dependencies among them and describe the algorithm to be computed. As shown, every task can be computed on a CPU, a GPU, or both depending on the optimizations and ideas we want to explore. These optimizations do not require code modifications at the algorithm level, but they are conducted internally in each of the tasks at the *implementation level*. Although the algorithm is described/implemented at the algorithm level in an architecture-agnostic way, the implementation level (set of tasks) attempts to obtain the maximum performance on the target architecture. One of the benefits of using IRIS is that one algorithm-level code can have multiple and different implementation levels with each optimized for a specific heterogeneous platform.

[3] https://software.intel.com/en-us/mkl-developer-reference-c-mkl-getrfnpi.

```
1   int SIZE= 16384; int TILE_SIZE = 512; int num_tiles = SIZE/TILE_SIZE
2   A = malloc(SIZE*SIZE);
3   //Creation of the IRIS graph
4   iris_graph graph;
5   iris_graph_create(&graph);
6   //Creation of the IRIS memory space
7   iris_mem A_iris, B_iris0, B_iris1, C_iris;
8   iris_mem_create(                 TILE_SIZE * TILE_SIZE, &A_iris);
9   iris_mem_create(        TILE_SIZE * (SIZE-TILE_SIZE), &B_iris0);
10  iris_mem_create(        TILE_SIZE * (SIZE-TILE_SIZE), &B_iris1);
11  iris_mem_create((SIZE-TILE_SIZE) * (SIZE-TILE_SIZE), &C_iris);
12  //Creation of the IRIS tasks pointers
13  iris_task *getrf     = malloc(num_tiles*sizeof(iris_task));
14  iris_task *trsm_top  = malloc(num_tiles*sizeof(iris_task));
15  iris_task *trsm_left = malloc(num_tiles*sizeof(iris_task));
16  iris_task *gemm      = malloc(num_tiles*sizeof(iris_task));
17  //Creation of the IRIS tasks parameters
18  struct *getrf_params      = malloc( num_tiles * sizeof(getrf_params);
19  struct *trsm_top_params   = malloc( num_tiles * sizeof(getrf_params);
20  struct *trsm_left_params  = malloc( num_tiles * sizeof(getrf_params);
21  struct *gemm_params       = malloc( num_tiles * sizeof(getrf_params);
22  for ( d = 0; d < num_tiles; d++){
23      //---GETRF TASK---
24      //Creation of the getrf[d] task
25      iris_task_create_perm(&getrf[d]);
26      //Initialization of getrf task's parameters
27      getrf_params[d].M     = TILE_SIZE;
28      getrf_params[d].LDA   = TILE_SIZE;
29      ...
30      getrf_params[d].A_cpu = &A[( (d * TILE_SIZE) * LDA ) + ( d * TILE_SIZE )];
31      getrf_params[d].A_gpu = A_iris;
32      //Initialization of the task
33      iris_task_host(getrf[d], getrf_task, &getrf_params[d]);
34      //Queue task into the graph
35      iris_graph_task(graph, getrf[d], iris_default, NULL);
36      //---TRSM-TOP TASK---
37      n = d + 1
38      iris_task_create_perm(&trsm_top[d]);
39      //Defining dependencies of the trsm-top tasks
40      iris_task_depend( trsm_top[d], 1, &getrf[d]);
41      trsm_top_params[d].M       = TILE_SIZE;
42      trsm_top_params[d].LDA_cpu = SIZE;
43      trsm_top_params[d].LDA_cpu = TILE_SIZE;
44      ...
45      trsm_top_params[d].A_cpu   = &A[( (d * TILE_SIZE) * LDA ) + ( d * TILE_SIZE )];
46      trsm_top_params[d].A_gpu   = A_iris;
47      trsm_top_params[d].B_cpu   = &B[( (n * TILE_SIZE) * LDA ) + ( d * TILE_SIZE )];
48      trsm_top_params[d].B_gpu   = B_iris0;
49      iris_task_host(trsm_top[d], trsm_task, &trsm_top_params[d]);
50      iris_graph_task(graph, trsm_top[d], iris_default, NULL);
51      //---TRSM-LEFT TASK---
52      m = d + 1
53      iris_task_create_perm(&trsm_left[d])
54      iris_task_depend( trsm_left[d], 1, &getrf[d]);
55      trsm_left_params[d].M       = TILE_SIZE;
56      trsm_left_params[d].LDA_cpu = SIZE;
57      trsm_left_params[d].LDA_cpu = TILE_SIZE;
58      ...
59      trsm_left_params[d].A_cpu   = &A[( (d * TILE_SIZE) * LDA ) + ( d * TILE_SIZE )];
60      trsm_left_params[d].A_gpu   = A_iris;
61      trsm_left_params[d].B_cpu   = &B[( (d * TILE_SIZE) * LDA ) + ( m * TILE_SIZE )];
62      trsm_left_params[d].B_gpu   = B_iris1;
63      iris_task_host(trsm_left[d], trsm_task, &trsm_left_params[d]);
64      iris_graph_task(graph, trsm_left[d], iris_default, NULL);
65      //---GEMM TASK---
66      iris_task_create_perm(&gemm[d]);
67      brisbane_task gemm_dep[] = { trsm_top[d], trsm_left[d] };
68      iris_task_depend( gemm[d], 2, gemm_dep);
69      gemm_params[d].M       = SIZE - ( m * TILE_SIZE);
70      gemm_params[d].LDA_cpu = SIZE;
71      ...
72      gemm_params[d].A_cpu   = &A[( (d * TILE) * LDA ) + ( m * TILE )];
73      gemm_params[d].B_cpu   = &A[( (n * TILE) * LDA ) + ( d * TILE )];
74      gemm_params[d].C_cpu   = &A[( (n * TILE) * LDA ) + ( m * TILE )];
75      gemm_params[d].A_gpu   = B_iris1;
76      gemm_params[d].B_gpu   = B_iris0;
77      gemm_params[d].C_gpu   = C_iris;
78      iris_task_host( gemm[d], gemm_task, &gemm_params[d] );
79      iris_graph_task(graph, gemm[d], iris_default, NULL);
80  }
81  iris_graph_submit(graph, iris_default, 1);
```

Fig. 3. LU factorization code using IRIS.

The implementation of our LU factorization consists of four different tasks (Fig. 4): (1) GETRF, in which we compute a no-pivoting LU factorization on the top-left corner matrix TILE; (2) TRSM-top, in which we compute the level-3 BLAS TRSM routine by using the lower side of the LU factorization computed in the previous task as the input matrix (A in Fig. 4) and the rectangular tile located at the right of the LU matrix as the output matrix (B in Fig. 4); (3) TRSM-left, in which we compute the same level-3 BLAS operation used in the previous task but on a different part of the matrix by using the upper side of the LU matrix computed by the first task (GETRF) as input and a set of square tiles located under the lower side of the LU matrix as output (B_0, B_1, B_2, and B_3 in Fig. 4); and (4) GEMM, in which we compute a matrix-matrix multiplication by using the output of the two previous tasks as input and the remaining matrix parts as output. We compute all the previous tasks until the entire matrix is computed (Figs. 2 and 4 [left]).

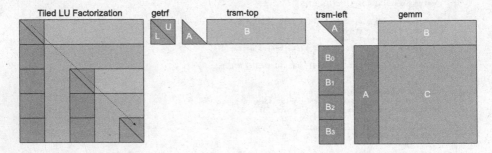

Fig. 4. Tasks of the LU decomposition implementation.

4.1   Memory Management

Our goal is to maximize the use of both the CPU and the GPU. In general, problems with larger tile sizes achieve relatively higher performance during computation. Knowing this, instead of using square tiles (Fig. 2), we decided to use rectangular tiles when possible. The only exception is the TRSM-left task/operation (Fig. 4), in which the rectangular tile is divided into a set of square tiles. This decomposition, which is carried out internally in the TRSM-left task at the implementation level, is necessary because this particular operation requires the vertical dimensions of both A (input) and B (output) matrices to be the same.[4]

In our code, we use one pointer (A in Fig. 3) to allocate the matrix to be factorized. Additionally, we create four different memory spaces that correspond to the memory computed (tiles) from each of the tasks. This way we can define the two-level memory space, one used at the algorithm (IRIS) level (A pointer) and one used at the implementation (task) level (A_iris, B_iris0/1, and C_iris).

---

[4] http://www.netlib.org/lapack/explore-html/db/def/group_complex_blas_level3_gaf33844c7fd27e5434496d2ce0c1fc9d4.html.

4.2 Tasking

As we described above, the idea is to maximize the use of both the CPU and the GPU. To do that, apart from carrying out the matrix decomposition illustrated in Fig. 4, we use multithreaded (CPU and GPU) computations to exploit the parallelism at both the algorithm and the implementation levels.

In our code, basically every task corresponds to one LAPACK or BLAS routine. As parameters, we need the same parameters that are described in the standard specification of these math libraries, so we can then see the tasks as a wrapper to a standard linear algebra library. For convenience, we implemented a different C structure data type per LAPACK or BLAS routine, which is then used to pass the arguments from the algorithm level to the implementation level.

Although it is well known that LU factorizations do not perform well for small matrices on GPUs, it is difficult to know which platform (i.e., CPU or GPU) is best suited for the rest of the tasks. This is particularly challenging when the workload and number of operations (i.e., size of the tiles) in each of the tasks change along the execution. Another important factor to consider is the differences of the components in our heterogeneous systems and the connections between them. Fortunately, in IRIS, one task can be run on either the CPU or the GPU; in other words, we can decide which architecture to use depending on the size of the tile or other factors. We implemented several approaches for each of the tasks using CPU-only, GPU-only, and CPU-GPU methods (Fig. 5).

Next, we explain the main characteristics of the different implementations of each task.

GETRF. The computation of the LU (no pivoting) factorization is carried out on the CPU. Although, we do not perform a GPU computation in this task, we can make some computationally expensive memory transfers between CPU and GPU, such as transferring the B matrices used by the TRSM tasks (TRSM-top and TRSM-left in Fig. 4) while LU factorization is being computed. So, we have two different implementations: (1) one in which we only compute the LU factorization on the CPU and (2) one in which we simultaneously compute the LU factorization, perform the CPU-to-GPU memory transfers for B matrices used by TRSM tasks, and perform the CPU-to-GPU transfer of the factorization output because this is also used by TRSM tasks.

TRSM-Top. Three different variants of TRSM-top were implemented: (1) a CPU version in which we make use of the TRSM routine within the CPU vendor libraries (e.g., IBM ESSL on Summit and Intel MKL on Oswald), (2) a GPU version in which we compute both a cuBLAS call for the TRSM computation and CPU-GPU memory copies for the input (from CPU to GPU) and output (from GPU to CPU), and (3) an optimization of the GPU version in which we compute a cuBLAS TRSM call and a GPU-CPU memory copy to transfer the result of the cuBLAS routine from GPU to CPU. In the last implementation, we do not carry out the CPU-to-GPU communication because this is performed in the GETRF task.

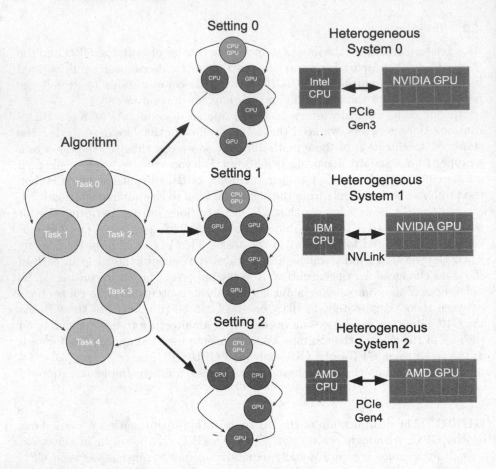

Fig. 5. The IRIS algorithm-implementation partition.

TRSM-Left. Two different versions of TRSM-left were implemented here: (1) a CPU implementation in which we compute the TRSM routine of the IBM ESSL library on Summit and the Intel MKL library on Oswald and (2) a GPU code in which we compute the CPU-GPU memory copies necessary to transfer the input to GPU memory and the output to CPU memory after computing the cuBLAS TRSM routine on the GPU.

4.3   GEMM

We implemented three different variants of GEMM: (1) a CPU code that uses CPU vendor libraries; (2) a GPU code in which the C matrix is transferred from CPU/GPU to GPU/CPU before/after the GPU computation of GEMM (cuBLAS), the A matrix is transferred from CPU to GPU before the computation, and the B matrix (output of TRSM-top) is already in GPU memory; and (3) an optimized GPU implementation in which only the A matrix is transferred from CPU to GPU before the computation of GEMM on the GPU, and the

Table 1. Summit and Oswald hardware specifications.

Name	Summit	Oswald
CPU Architecture	IBM Power 9	Intel Xeon E5-2683 v4
Frequency	3,800 MHz	2,100 MHz
Cores	22	32
Memory	512 GB	256 GB
Compiler	GCC 8.3.1	GCC 11.1.0
LAPACK/BLAS	ESSL	MKL
GPU Architecture	NVIDIA (Volta) V100	NVIDIA (Pascal) P100
Frequency	1,455 MHz	1,126 MHz
CUDA Cores	5,120	3,584
SM/CU Count	80	60
GPU-to-CPU Comm	NVLink 2.0 (50 GB/s)	PCIe Gen3 (16 GB/s)
Shared Memory	up to 96 KB per SM	64 KB per SM
L1	up to 96 KB per SM	64 KB per SM
L2	6,144 KB (unified)	4,096 KB (unified)
Memory	HBM2 16 GB	HBM2 12 GB
Bandwidth	900 GB/s	549 GB/s
Compiler	NVCC v11.0.221	NVCC v11.0.194
BLAS	cuBLAS	cuBLAS

top-left tile of the C matrix is transferred from GPU to CPU after the computation of GEMM. In the last implementation, we transfer the whole matrix to be factorized from CPU to GPU at the very beginning of the execution. Although this can be time consuming, it is only done once and has important implications for the overall performance (see Sect. 5).

5 Performance Analysis

This section describes the performance analysis of our code and the different variants/optimizations implemented. For a test case, we used a $16,384 \times 16,384$ matrix with a tile size of 512×512. We used two different heterogeneous systems for our analysis—Summit and Oswald (see Table 1 for the hardware features).

5.1 GETRF

For the GETRF task, we used Intel MKL's *LAPACKE_mkl_dgetrfnpi* routine on Oswald, whereas we used our own code on Summit because the IBM ESSL library does not have a routine for the non-pivoting LU factorization. In terms of performance, the optimized vendor library (i.e., Intel MKL on Oswald) achieved much better performance (about 48 GFLOP/s) compared to our own implementation on Summit (15 GFLOP/s). However, as we describe below, this did not have a significant impact on the overall performance.

When overlapping communication with computation (i.e., to transfer the B matrix used by TRSM tasks and the output of the factorization from CPU to GPU), we see a fall in performance when compared to the CPU-only implementation, and we achieve an overall performance of 11 GFLOP/s on Summit and 42 GFLOP/s on Oswald.

5.2 TRSM-top

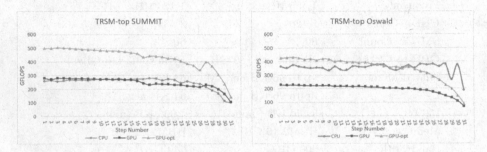

Fig. 6. TRSM-top performance.

Figure 6 illustrates the performance reached by the TRSM-top task on Summit and Oswald. As expected, the GPU-optimized implementation reaches the highest performance on both systems, at least in the first steps. On Summit, the performance of this implementation is considerably higher than the other two implementations—about $2\times$ higher in some cases. In fact, this is the fastest implementation for all steps on Summit. On Oswald, the performance of the GPU-optimized implementation is higher than the CPU implementation (second fastest implementation) in the first steps; however, the CPU implementation is the faster one in the last steps, in which the computational cost and parallelism of computing TRSM is much lower. Although Summit has a much faster CPU-GPU connection (NVLink), a larger number of CPU cores and a more similar performance (GFLOP/s) between CPU and GPU makes the CPU implementation on Oswald faster than the GPU-optimized implementation for the last steps.

As shown, although the GPU-optimized implementation is the best choice for Summit, Oswald benefits from a heterogeneous approach (task) in which the GPU-optimized implementation is used during the first steps of the algorithm, and the CPU implementation is computed in the last steps.

5.3 TRSM-Left

Although we use the same level-3 BLAS operation from the previous task, we achieve very different performance results owing to the different matrix decomposition required by this operation. Again, as we can see in Fig. 7, the performance varies significantly depending on the target platform. While the performance of the GPU implementation is lower than that of the CPU implementation on Oswald, we see the opposite scenario for Summit, where the GPU implementation is considerably faster than the CPU implementation.

As was the case for the TRSM-top task, we also need a different configuration here depending on the target platform.

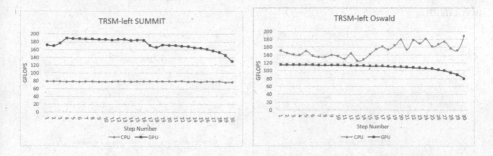

Fig. 7. TRSM-left performance.

5.4 Join TRSM-Top and TRSM-Left

For Oswald, we can see that although the GPU implementation is better for TRSM-top, the CPU implementation is the better choice for TRSM-left. Because both tasks are totally independent, this opens an opportunity for better performance on Oswald by computing both tasks in parallel using the more suitable implementation for each task. As shown Fig. 8, joining both tasks enables significant speedup.

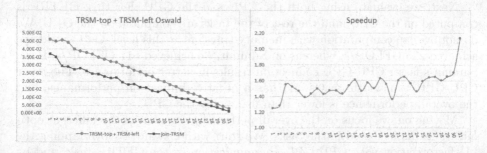

Fig. 8. Left: Time (s) of TRSM-top + TRSM-left and join-TRSM. Right: Join-TRSM speedup.

5.5 GEMM

Unlike the other two tasks, for GEMM we see the same behavior in both heterogeneous systems (Fig. 9). The GPU-optimized implementation has proven to be the fastest implementation in both systems and is 6×–8× faster than the second-fastest approach. As expected, the performance decreases along the execution; this can be seen in the other tasks too, in which the computational cost and the parallelism are much lower in the last steps than in the first steps of the algorithm.

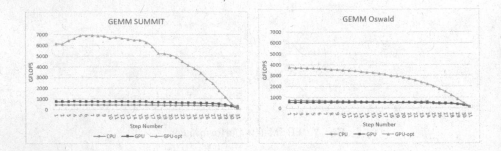

. **Fig. 9.** GEMM performance.

5.6 Overall Performance

Here, we evaluate the overall performance for the different task implementations, and we start with the CPU-only implementations. On Oswald, we achieved an overall performance of 340 GFLOP/s, whereas on Summit we achieved 120 GFLOP/s. The relatively poor performance on Summit is from our implementation of the GETRF task.

Next, we evaluate using both the CPU and the GPU. For this, GETRF is computed on the CPU, and the rest of the tasks are computed on the GPU. We do not overlap computation with memory transfers at this level. On Oswald, we achieved 225 GFLOP/s, whereas on Summit, we achieved 511 GFLOP/s. Here, Summit's faster CPU-GPU connection results in better performance. The lower CPU-GPU bandwidth on Oswald has a negative impact on performance, and the overall performance is lower than using only the CPU.

Moving on, we focus on the overall performance impact of the different optimizations implemented in the tasks. We start with Oswald. By overlapping the LU factorization with CPU-GPU communication in the GETRF task, and by using the GPU to compute the TRSM-top task, we increased performance to 235 GFLOP/s. Also, by running TRSM-left on the CPU instead of the GPU, we achieved 275 GFLOP/s. As shown in Fig. 9, the most important optimization consists of moving the whole matrix from CPU to GPU at the very beginning. Using the GPU-optimized implementation in the GEMM task, we increased the overall performance to 652 GFLOP/s. Finally, we conducted the last optimization, which consists of joining TRSM-left (computed on the CPU) and TRSM-top (computed on the GPU), which increased the overall performance to 700 GFLOP/s.

Next, we focus on Summit. By overlapping the LU factorization with the CPU-GPU communication in the GETRF task, we increased the overall performance to 546 GFLOP/s. As shown in Fig. 7, using the CPU is not faster than using the GPU for TRSM-left. With that in mind, the optimizations on Oswald for TRSM tasks are not beneficial on Summit, but computing both tasks on the GPU is better. Finally, using the GPU-optimized implementation of the GEMM task increases the overall performance considerably—achieving 1,972 GFLOP/s.

6   Related Works

Recently, we have seen important progress toward performance portability. Some examples are the C++ template metaprogramming libraries Kokkos [15] and RAJA [16]. These libraries can build different binaries that target different architectures from one source code. However, they cannot use more than a single architecture at a time.

Using CPUs and GPUs for HPC codes has been widely studied [13,17,18]. Since OpenMP 4.0, it is possible to use GPU offloading in OpenMP codes. Valero-Lara et al. [19] used OpenMP 4.5 to implement a heterogeneous version of the TRSM level-3 BLAS routine and achieved good performance on one node of Oak Ridge National Laboratory's Summit supercomputer. One important reference for heterogeneous linear algebra codes is the MAGMA [20] library. MAGMA, offers multiple heterogeneous implementations for several LAPACK routines. Unfortunately, there is not an implementation for our test case.

In contrast, our work focuses on the potential benefits of using IRIS for performance portability on heterogeneous HPC architectures. To the best of our knowledge, this is the first time that a portable and heterogeneous LU factorization code (i.e., IRIS) has been implemented and analyzed.

7   Final Remarks and Future Directions

The difference in current and upcoming heterogeneous systems hinders implementation of HPC codes. By using IRIS, we not only make this effort more affordable, but we can also implement portable and heterogeneous HPC codes by separating the algorithm design from the implementation. First, we described our algorithm using tasks + dependencies. After that, we had to decide which code to use in each of the tasks. A specific and different setting must be used depending on the target platform. In this paper, we were able to optimize one of the most important HPC algorithms, the LU factorization, on two different heterogeneous platforms with minimal modifications to the code.

However, a more thorough and computationally expensive study is required to evaluate which code/implementation should be used in each of the tasks. In the future, we plan to implement alternatives that enable one to compute the setting in an automatic and computationally cheaper manner. We also want to extend this effort to other HPC applications and heterogeneous systems.

References

1. Bellavia, S., Morini, B., Porcelli, M.: New updates of incomplete LU factorizations and applications to large nonlinear systems. Optim. Methods Softw. **29**(2), 321–340 (2014). https://doi.org/10.1080/10556788.2012.762517
2. Eickhoff, K.M., Engl, W.L.: Levelized incomplete LU factorization and its application to large-scale circuit simulation. IEEE Trans. Comput. Aided Des. Integr. Circuits Syst. **14**(6), 720–727 (1995). https://doi.org/10.1109/43.387732
3. Luciani, X., Albera, L.: Joint eigenvalue decomposition of non-defective matrices based on the LU factorization with application to ICA. IEEE Trans. Signal Process. **63**(17), 4594–4608 (2015). https://doi.org/10.1109/TSP.2015.2440219
4. Kudo, S., Nitadori, K., Ina, T., Imamura, T.: Implementation and numerical techniques for one eflop/s HPL-AI benchmark on fugaku. In: 11th IEEE/ACM Workshop on Latest Advances in Scalable Algorithms for Large-Scale Systems, ScalA@SC 2020, Atlanta, GA, USA, 13 November 2020, pp. 69–76. IEEE (2020). https://doi.org/10.1109/ScalA51936.2020.00014
5. Gan, X., et al.: Customizing the HPL for china accelerator. Sci. China Inf. Sci. **61**(4), 042 102:1-042 102:11 (2018). https://doi.org/10.1007/s11432-017-9221-0
6. Kim, J., Lee, S., Johnston, B., Vetter, J.S.: IRIS: a portable runtime system exploiting multiple heterogeneous programming systems. In: Proceedings of the 25th IEEE High Performance Extreme Computing Conference, ser. HPEC 2021, pp. 1–8 (2021)
7. Valero-Lara, P., Catalán, S., Martorell, X., Usui, T., Labarta, J.: slass: a fully automatic auto-tuned linear algebra library based on openmp extensions implemented in ompss (lass library). J. Parallel Distributed Comput. **138**, 153–171 (2020)
8. Valero-Lara, P., Catalán, S., Martorell, X., Labarta, J.: BLAS-3 optimized by ompss regions (lass library). In: 27th Euromicro International Conference on Parallel, Distributed and Network-Based Processing, PDP 2019, Pavia, Italy, 13–15 February 2019, pp. 25–32. IEEE (2019)
9. Dongarra, J.J., et al.: PLASMA: parallel linear algebra software for multicore using openmp. ACM Trans. Math. Softw. **45**(2), 16:1-16:35 (2019)
10. Valero-Lara, P., Martínez-Pérez, I., Sirvent, R., Martorell, X., Peña, A.J.: NVIDIA GPUs scalability to solve multiple (batch) tridiagonal systems implementation of cuThomasBatch. In: Wyrzykowski, R., Dongarra, J., Deelman, E., Karczewski, K. (eds.) PPAM 2017. LNCS, vol. 10777, pp. 243–253. Springer, Cham (2018). https://doi.org/10.1007/978-3-319-78024-5_22
11. Valero-Lara, P., Martínez-Pérez, I., Sirvent, R., Martorell, X., Peña, A.J.: cuThomasBatch and cuThomasVBatch, CUDA routines to compute batch of tridiagonal systems on NVIDIA GPUs. Concurr. Comput. Pract. Exp. **30**(24), e4909 (2018)
12. Valero-Lara, P., Pinelli, A., Favier, J., Matias, M.P.: Block tridiagonal solvers on heterogeneous architectures. In: IEEE 10th International Symposium on Parallel and Distributed Processing with Applications, ser. ISPA 2012, pp. 609–616 (2012)
13. Valero-Lara, P., Pinelli, A., Prieto-Matias, M.: Fast finite difference Poisson solvers on heterogeneous architectures. Comput. Phys. Commun. **185**(4), 1265–1272 (2014)

14. Demmel, J.W., Gilbert, J.R., Li, X.S.: An asynchronous parallel supernodal algorithm for sparse gaussian elimination. SIAM J. Matrix Anal. Appl. **20**(4), 915–952 (1999)
15. Trott, C.R., et al.: Kokkos 3: programming model extensions for the exascale era. IEEE Trans. Parallel Distributed Syst. **33**(4), 805–817 (2022). https://doi.org/10.1109/TPDS.2021.3097283
16. Beckingsale, D., Hornung, R.D., Scogland, T., Vargas, A.: Performance portable C++ programming with RAJA. In: Hollingsworth, J.K., Keidar, I. (eds.) Proceedings of the 24th ACM SIGPLAN Symposium on Principles and Practice of Parallel Programming, PPoPP 2019, Washington, DC, USA, 16–20 February 2019, pp. 455–456. ACM (2019)
17. Valero-Lara, P., Jansson, J.: Heterogeneous CPU+GPU approaches for mesh refinement over lattice-boltzmann simulations. Concurr. Comput. Pract. Exp. **29**(7), e3919 (2017)
18. Valero-Lara, P., Igual, F.D., Prieto-Matías, M., Pinelli, A., Favier, J.: Accelerating fluid-solid simulations (lattice-boltzmann & immersed-boundary) on heterogeneous architectures. J. Comput. Sci. **10**, 249–261 (2015)
19. Valero-Lara, P., Kim, J., Hernandez, O., Vetter, J.S.: Openmp target task: tasking and target offloading on heterogeneous systems. In: Chaves, R., et al. (eds.) Euro-Par 2021. LNCS, vol. 13098, pp. 445–455. Springer, Cham (2021). https://doi.org/10.1007/978-3-031-06156-1_35
20. Tomov, S., Dongarra, J., Baboulin, M.: Towards dense linear algebra for hybrid GPU accelerated manycore systems. Technical report, 2008-01 (2008)

Halide Code Generation Framework in Phylanx

R. Tohid[1]([envelope]) [ORCID], Shahrzad Shirzad[1], Christopher Taylor[2], Sayef Azad Sakin[3], Katherine E. Isaacs[3], and Hartmut Kaiser[1]

[1] Center for Computation and Technology, Louisiana State University, Baton Rouge, USA
{mraste2,sshirz1,hkaiser}@lsu.edu
[2] Tactical Computing Labs, Muenster, USA
ctaylor@tactcomplabs.com
[3] SCI Institute, University of Utah, Salt Lake City, USA
{sayefsakin,kisaacs}@sci.utah.edu

Abstract. Separating algorithms from their computation schedule has become a de facto solution to tackle the challenges of developing high performance code on modern heterogeneous architectures. Common approaches include Domain-specific languages (DSLs) which provide familiar APIs to domain experts, code generation frameworks that automate the generation of fast and portable code, and runtime systems that manage threads for concurrency and parallelism. In this paper, we present the Halide code generation framework for Phylanx distributed array processing platform. This extension enables compile-time optimization of Phylanx primitives for target architectures. To accomplish this, (1) we implemented new Phylanx primitives using Halide, and (2) partially *exported* Halide's thread pool API to carry out parallelism on HPX (Phylanx's runtime) threads. (3) showcased HPX performance analysis tools made available to Halide applications. The evaluation of the work has been done in two steps. First, we compare the performance of Halide applications running on its native runtime with that of the new HPX backend to verify there is no cost associated with using HPX threads. Next, we compare performances of a number of original implementations of Phylanx primitives against the new ones in Halide to verify performance and portability benefits of Halide in the context of Phylanx.

Keywords: AMT · Phylanx · Halide · HPX · DSL

1 Introduction

In recent years there has been a massive shift towards heterogeneous computing systems as impacts of Moore's law [1] and Dennard scaling [2] have been dwindling. As a consequence, high performance code has become increasingly more complex and expensive to maintain, while less portable. A common approach to

J. Singer et al. (Eds.): Euro-Par 2022 Workshops, LNCS 13835, pp. 32–45, 2023.
https://doi.org/10.1007/978-3-031-31209-0_3

address these issues is separating the algorithm from the scheduling of the computation, i.e., the order of computations and memory accesses. This has resulted in a growing interest in developing domain specific languages (DSLs), code generation frameworks, and runtime systems which all aim at such separation, albeit at different levels of abstraction:

Domain specific languages support high-level abstractions and provide APIs that are closer to domains nomenclature. DSLs are categorized into internal and external languages. External DSLs are stand-alone with custom semantics, and syntax, while internal DSLs are embedded in a host language [3]. External DSLs are typically more expressive and readable [4], but are costly to implement. Internal DSLs, on the other hand, are cheaper to develop but carry over drawbacks of the host language. Internal DSLs also share their Intermediate Representation (IR) with the host language which may further limit their applicable optimizations [5].

DSLs benefit from the prior knowledge on the data characteristics and computational traits of applications in a particular domain in order to utilize optimizations that may not be valid in general. DSLs must still be able to identify the parallelism in the application, and generate optimized code for the target platforms in order to achieve heterogeneous parallelism [6], requiring a deep understanding of hardware architecture, parallelism, and scheduling on developer's part [6].

Code Generation Frameworks. The complexity of new architectures has increased the already exorbitant cost of developing and maintaining handwritten high-performance code. This has led to the emergence of code generation frameworks like Halide which are capable of automatically generating code for multiple architectures while being far less error-prone. The code generation frameworks are great tools for scheduling computations, and managing the associated data for achieving performances on par to highly-tuned handwritten code. It is worth mentioning, though, realizing potentials of such frameworks requires a fair amount of knowledge about the architecture, and application requirements. Also, such frameworks usually target a particular runtime and may cause performance degradation in other environments.

Runtime systems, including asynchronous runtime systems (AMTs), carry out the execution model of the program. Runtime systems facilitate parallelism and concurrency at thread level, and provide functionalities to dynamically adjust execution for the best performance. Their scope of effectiveness, however, is limited to operations rather than larger tasks such as algorithms, or applications.

While each of the above can independently improve the performance, using all together may have adverse effects on overall performance—e.g., Halide's native runtime and HPX competing for resources could be a source of performance degradation. In this work we have taken an overarching solution that avails the combined benefits of all these approaches in a single environment by:

– implementing HPX backend for Halide.

– introducing a new Phylanx plugin which allows seamless interaction with Halide-generated code.
– demonstrating benefits of HPX performance analysis suite for Halide applications in general and in Phylanx in particular.

The remainder of this paper is organized as follows. Section 2 gives an overview of related existing solutions. Section 3 briefly discusses the underlying technologies in the extended Phylanx software stack. Next, Sect. 4 elaborates on how we improved performance portability in Phylanx through Halide. Finally, in the results Sect. 5, we evaluate the effectiveness of Halide's HPX backend and it's benefits in the context of Phylanx. We conclude by sharing learned lessons, and outlining the future work Sect. 6.

2   Related Work

In this section we review several solutions for each DSL, code generation frameworks, and AMT approaches.

2.1   Domain Specific Languages (DSLs)

The Delite Compiler Framework and Runtime [6], based on Scala language, was developed in order to produce heterogeneous, and parallel domain specific languages. Delite developers take a hybrid approach to balance between internal and external DSL implementations [6] by utilizing the concept of Language Virtualization [5,7]. The Delite compiler creates an IR from the DSL, applies the relevant optimizations, automatically generates codes for different compute kernels, and forms the Delite execution graph (DEG), which is then scheduled to be executed with an execution plan [5]. Delite also provides code generators for frequently used parallel patterns to assist application developers. The OptiML [8] machine learning DSL is developed based on Delite Compiler Framework and Runtime.

STELLA (STEncil Loop LAnguage) [9] is a DSL for solving partial differential equations on structured grids and mostly used in weather and climate simulations. STELLA utilizes C++ template meta-programming to generate optimized loop nests for several backend architectures.

Osuna et al. [10] developed Dawn as a DSL compiler toolchain for climate and weather applications. They use GTClang [11] as the DSL frontend, which is integrated in C++ through Clang compiler. In this DSL, first the model is considered sequentially, and a parallel representation of the model is created afterwards based on the identified data dependencies [10].

2.2   Code Generation Frameworks

The developers of CHiLL [12], based their framework on empirical optimizations. They automatically generate code for several combinations of possible optimizations and run a subset of the application on the target platform to identify the best-performing variant [12]. Their framework is capable of performing complex code transformations such as imperfect loop nest transformations [12]. Tiwari et al. [13] extended this work by using Active Harmony [14] in order to facilitate parallel search.

Baghdadi et al. [15] developed TIRAMISU, a polyhedral framework, to generate high performance code on different hardware architectures. Tiramisu's IR represents the polyhedral model of the loop nests. Tiramisu uses this representation to effectively apply multiple transformations at once, and generate high performance code for a wide range of target architectures [15].

2.3 AMT Runtime Systems

Charm++ [16] is a parallel programming system in which the computation is divided into *"migratable"* objects called *chares* and are left to the runtime to decide when and where to execute them. The execution model of Charm++ is based on *message-driven* execution which facilitates overlapping communication with computation [17].

Legion [18] is developed as a data-centric model in which the runtime identifies data locality and dependencies between the tasks, and performs the necessary movements and transformations to achieve high performance. Legion focus is more on GPUs

3 Enabling Technologies

Phylanx is built on top of many existing open source libraries with the aim of creating a suite for developing, profiling, and analyzing array-based applications. In this section, we discuss these enabling technologies used to develop Phylanx and extend its usability.

3.1 HPX

Internally, Phylanx IR is a HPX task graph running on the HPX thread pool [19]. HPX is an open-source (licensed under Boost Software License) C++ high-performance asynchronous many-task (AMT) runtime system for parallelism and concurrency. HPX provides a uniform API for parallel and distributed computation allowing threads to run both locally, and remotely– the latter per active messages called *parcels* [20]. Here we highlight a few HPX facilities used in Phylanx to carry out parallel operations and improve concurrency.

hpx::async. In order to boost opportunities for global parallelism and concurrency, Phylanx follows the asynchronous programming pattern using HPX's *async* syntax. Any Phylanx program is a tree of asynchronous functions evaluated by HPX threading system. This allow the non-blocking async functions start executing as soon as their input is ready and not blocked by the slower statements that may appear before them in the program. Once the evaluation starts, as long as there are resources available on the system, any number of functions can run in parallel, resulting in improved system throughput.

hpx::future. Similar to C++ *std::future* class template, provides a placeholder for the result of an asynchronous operation. Each Phylanx function returns a *future* object. The value of the object can be queried explicitly by the user through the *eval* method or may be evaluated implicitly once its value is needed by another function depending on it. *future* is essential for non-blocking evaluation of HPX execution tree.

hpx::for_loop. HPX's Parallel Algorithms module provides a catalog of C++20 standard conforming algorithms including the *for_loop* which implements functionality over a range specified by integral or iterator bounds. The *for_loop* iteratively applies the input operation following the execution policy set by the user. The HPX Halide runtime (Sect. 4) relies on this construct to execute parallel loops. This approach provides performance better or on par with popular multiprocessing libraries such as OpenMP [21] without requiring any directives by the user. In addition, the profiling information will be readily available and visualizable through APEX (Sect. 3.3) and Traveler (Sect. 3.4).

3.2   Halide

HPX abstracts away many complexities of lower-level APIs for parallelism and concurrency. However, benefiting from the modern architectures to the fullest extent also requires global organization of the computation and the associated data movements. This issue is more pronounced on heterogeneous systems like the state-of-the-art HPC resources. Phylanx relies on the automatic code generation capabilities provided by Halide to overcome complications posed when developing and maintaining high-performance applications.

Halide separates program schedule, i.e., managing the intermediate storage and the order of computation, from the algorithm. Halide allows programmers to define the algorithm with a range of possible organization constraints and generates code with performance equal or better than hand-tuned code. Halide is also capable of generating code for multiple architectures including CPU and GPU from the single source.

3.3   APEX

APEX [22] (Autonomic Performance Environment for eXascale) is a performance measurement library for distributed, asynchronous multitasking runtime systems. APEX collects data though inspectors using the dependency chain in HPX's execution tree to produce traces–instead of the call stack.

The synchronous module of APEX uses an event API and event listeners. APEX can collect performance measurements both synchronously, and asynchronously. APEX's synchronous module will start, stop, yield, or resume timers whenever an event occurs. These timers can also capture hardware metrics using the PAPI [23] library. The asynchronous measurement involves periodic, or on-demand interrogation of OS, hardware, or runtime states and counters.

APEX also supports performance profiling of runtime tasks. The profile data contains the number of times each task was executed, and the total time spent executing that type of task. APEX is integrated with the Open Trace Format 2 (OTF2) [24] library capturing full event traces including event identification and start/stop times. In HPX applications, all tasks are uniquely identified by their GUID (globally unique identifier) and the GUID of their parent task. These GUIDs are captured as part of the OTF2 trace output.

3.4   Traveler

We use Traveler to visualize performance data collected by APEX. Traveler [25] is a visualization platform for parallel performance data. Traveler is built on web technologies and all visualized data is readily available through the web browser. Traveler provides interactive access to performance data at multiple levels of abstraction supporting charts such as time series, histograms, source code, and Gantt charts.

Additionally, Traveler supports aggregated execution graphs as more commonly analyzed to understand AMT execution. In the context of Phylanx, Traveler is capable of visualizing three kinds of data: (1) OTF2 trace data including task traces (optionally annotated with PAPI counters), and extra dependency information through APEX, (2) execution graph data generated by Phylanx, and (3) raw source code.

4   Performance Portability in Phylanx

Phylanx is an asynchronous array processing platform built on top of the HPX runtime system. Previous works have shown the performance-portability of Phylanx in both shared-memory [26], and distributed [27–29] settings. Phylanx has also been tested on container technologies such as Singularity [30] and Docker [31], and run on Agave/Tapis [32] science gateway through the Jet-Lag [28,33] interactive environment.

So far, however, Phylanx has relied on two of the three performance optimizing solutions discussed above Sect. 1, namely, the domain knowledge, and the HPX runtime system. This has been made possible through: (1) the low-level PhySL representation, and (2) the Python frontend.

Internally, all the algorithms and operations of the Phylanx platform are implemented in PhySL (Phylanx Specialization Language). PhySL runs on HPX thread pool to exploit fine-grain parallelism, and concurrency. It benefits from constraint-based synchronization, through *asyn* and *future* constructs, in order to maximize throughput and also to improve opportunities for overlapping computation and communication. The frontend, on the other hand, seamlessly manages data between Python and PhySL making low-level functionalities available in python via the *decorator* design pattern.

In this paper we introduce the automatic code generation approach, through Halide, to improve performance portability of Phylanx. This was done in two steps: first, we developed a custom HPX runtime for Halide (Sect. 4.1), and next, implemented a new Phylanx plugin to enable interoperability between Phylanx and Halide object files (Sect. 4.2).

4.1 HPX Runtime for Halide

Halide's native runtime provides a highly tuned thread pool to optimize for the types of contention patterns that its pipelines encounter. However, to avoid interference with HPX running Phylanx tasks, we exported Halide's thread pool to HPX.

Halide has minimal runtime requirements, solely requiring a memory allocation, and threading implementation. It allows individual pieces of the runtime to be overridden either through weak linking (on supported platforms), or explicitly by calling functions that overwrite a set of function pointers. In order to guarantee support for both Unix-like and Windows platforms, we have overwritten the parallel loop function pointers to replace the default thread pool implementation, using HPX *for_loop* with the parallel execution policy. The HPX runtime is available to Halide in both just-in-time (JIT) and ahead-of-time (AoT) modes. Listing 1.1 shows an example of how one can use HPX's parallel loop construct in the JIT context. Similarly, for the case of ahead of time compilation, we have partially exported Halide's thread pool API, overriding Halide's default runtime. In this case, the user just need to correctly link their Halide applications and have HPX threads carry out the tasks.

4.2 Halide Integration in Phylanx

Interoperability of Phylanx *primitives* (Phylanx functions) and Halide runtime requires (1) compatibility of threading systems of the two platforms and (2) seamless exchange of data between the two. Here, we explain how these are achieved.

Runtime Compatibility. Although it is possible to use JIT compilation 1.1, Phylanx relies on Halide's generators (ahead-of-time compilation scheme) to avoid runtime overheads. This approach allows us to compile Halide objects during Phylanx compilation and requires no changes to the Halide code. The only requirement is linking Halide libraries against the HPX runtime. As a result, all Phylanx and Halide tasks are scheduled and carried out by HPX runtime, avoiding resource competition between the two platforms.

```
int hpx_parallel_loop(void *ctx, int (*f)(void *, int,
    uint8_t *),
    int min, int extent, uint8_t *closure)
{
    hpx::for_loop(hpx::execution::par,
```

```
        min, min + extent,
        [&](int i) { f(ctx, i, closure); });
    return 0;
}

int main(int argc, char **argv) {
    // construct the 'brighten' algorithm in Halide ...
    Func brighten;
    // override the default parallel loop
    brighten.set_custom_do_par_for(
            &hpx_parallel_loop);
    // ...
    // call the function as usual
    output =
        brighten.realize({input.width(),
                          input.height(),
                          input.channels()});
    return 0;
}
```

Listing 1.1. Example of using `hpx::for_loop` to carry out Halide's parallel loops with JIT compilation.

Data Management. Phylanx data objects are built on top of blaze [34] and blaze_tensor [35] while Halide works with *halide buffers*. Fortunately, both libraries support a generic and convenient approach for exchanging data with third-party libraries by exposing a buffer view. These views provide direct access to the underlying raw data in each object. The Halide plugin implements the interface between the two by passing the pointers to the data, allowing copy-free interoperability. The similar scheme is used for exchanging the data between Phylanx and NumPy [36] arrays. Therefore, data can be seamlessly accessed across all these three platforms.

```
from phylanx import Phylanx
import cv2
import numpy

@Phylanx
def py_harris(img):
    return harris(img)

img = cv2.imread("rgba.png")
data = numpy.asarray(img)

new_img = py_harris(data)

cv2.imwrite('result_hpx.png', new_img)
```

Listing 1.2. Seamless integration of a Halide application, `harris`, in Phylanx.

Listing 1.2 is an example of Phylanx and a Halide application interacting through the new Halide plugin for Phylanx. The implementation of the `harris` function is taken from Halide repository[1] and wrapped as a primitive through the Phylanx plugin for interfacing with Halide. This example demonstrates how the data can be seamlessly shared by NumPy, Phyalnx, and Halide.

Finally, it is worth noting that, since the whole pipeline runs on HPX, all the benefits of APEX and Traveler are at the user's disposal in the entire platform, see Fig. 1.

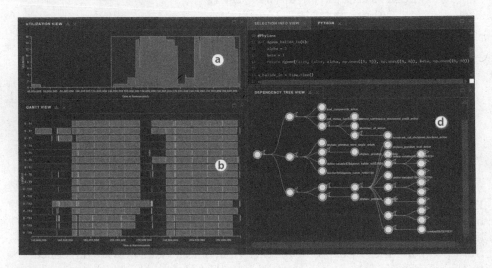

Fig. 1. Phylanx profiling, and performance analysis suite which is now available to Halide application with HPX runtime. The Utilization View (a) shows the utilization of the runtime threads, the Gantt View (b) Shows the scheduling of individual threads, (c) shows the source code, and the Dependency Tree (d) shows the task graph associated to the code [37].

5 Results

In this section we show the empirical results gathered from running a number of Halide applications using HPX thread pool in the context of Phylanx package. We first compare performances of the native runtime and HPX in Halide application. Next, study the data interfaces between Phylanx, NumPy and Halide buffers.

---

[1] https://github.com/halide/Halide/tree/master/apps/harris.

5.1   System Setup

All the experiments were conducted on the Rostam [38] cluster at the Center for Computation and Technology at LSU. Rostam consists of 53 nodes with a wide range of architectures. Table 1 provide the specifications of the nodes used in this work. All applications used the latest version of all software libraries at the time of the experiment. Table 2 summarizes all the versions and commits used for the experiments.

Table 1. Specifications of the Maedusa and Kamand nodes on the Rostam cluster used for experiments in this paper.

Node	CPU	RAM	Number of Cores
Medusa	Intel Skylake	96 GB	40
Kamand	AMD Rome	512 GB	128

Table 2. Specifications of the libraries used in the experiments.

Library	Version	Commit
HPX	1.8.0	0db6fc565c
Blaze	3.9.0	89ee9476df
Phylanx	0.1	295b5f82cc
Halide	12.0.0	085e11e0dc

5.2   Experiments

In order to evaluate the effectiveness of the HPX runtime for Halide, we tested our framework for a convolution arithmetic kernel, as well as IIR Blur and non-local mean algorithm. We adopted all these algorithms from Halide's GitHub repository and compared the performance of the native runtime against HPX. We carried out the experiments on two of the Intel's SkyLake, and AMD's Rome architectures. Figures 2, and 3 show the performance comparison of the two runtimes on each of these architectures. We observed matching scaling patterns on both architectures across all our tests. Although in some cases HPX is slower for smaller number of threads, that gap between the execution times closes as the number of threads increases.

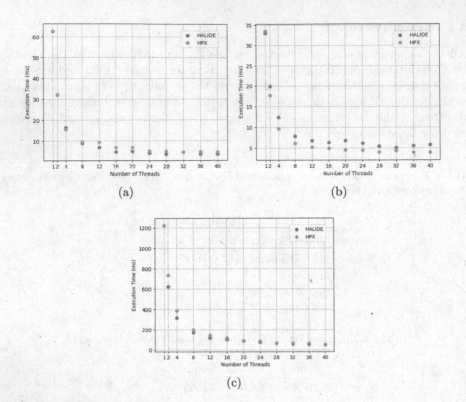

Fig. 2. (a) Convolution layers, (b) IIR Blur, and (c) Non-Local Means run on Intel SkyLake. Both Halide's native runtime and HPX scale similarly.

We further examined the performance of the Halide's HPX runtime in the Python environment to test interoperability of the Halide, NumPy and Phylanx data buffers. Listing 1.2 is an example of a Phylanx primitive, `harris`, that is called from python, demonstrating the compatibility of the two platforms.

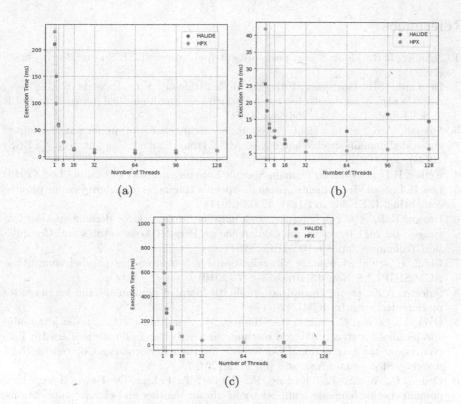

Fig. 3. (a) Convolution layers, (b) IIR Blur, and (c) Non-Local Means running on AMD Rome. Showing comparable performance for Halide's native vs HPX.

6 Conclusion

Separation of algorithms from the scheduling of their computation has been shown effective in removing challenges of programming on heterogeneous systems and the associated portability issues. There are several established approaches, including DSLs, code generation frameworks, and runtime systems to provide such abstractions. In this work, we extended the Phylanx array processing platform to enable code generation using Halide, complimenting the HPX runtime, to better support performance portability. In addition, the HPX-APEX-Traveler pipeline provides excellent tools for analyzing Halide code. The pipeline facilitates measuring and visualizing the performance data without requiring any changes in the application code. To the best of our knowledge, HPX runtime for Halide is the first of its kind to outperform Halide's native runtime.

References

1. Schaller, R.R.: Moore's law: past, present and future. IEEE Spectr. **34**(6), 52–59 (1997)
2. Dennard, R.H., Gaensslen, F.H., Yu, H.-N., Rideout, V.L., Bassous, E., LeBlanc, A.R.: Design of ion-implanted mosfet's with very small physical dimensions. IEEE J. Solid-State Circ. **9**(5), 256–268 (1974)
3. Sujeeth, A.K., et al.: Delite: a compiler architecture for performance-oriented embedded domain-specific languages. ACM Trans. Embed. Comput. Syst. (TECS) **13**(4s), 1–25 (2014)
4. Kelker, R.D.: Clojure for Domain-Specific Languages. Packt Publishing Ltd. (2013)
5. Lee, H.J., et al.: Implementing domain-specific languages for heterogeneous parallel computing. IEEE Micro **31**(5), 42–53 (2011)
6. Brown, K.J., et al.: A heterogeneous parallel framework for domain-specific languages. In: 2011 International Conference on Parallel Architectures and Compilation Techniques, pp. 89–100. IEEE (2011)
7. Chafi, H., et al.: Language virtualization for heterogeneous parallel computing. ACM SIGPLAN Not. **45**(10), 835–847 (2010)
8. Sujeeth, A.K., et al.: Optiml: an implicitly parallel domain-specific language for machine learning. In: ICML (2011)
9. Gysi, T., Osuna, C., Fuhrer, O., Bianco, M., Schulthess, T.C.: Stella: a domain-specific tool for structured grid methods in weather and climate models. In: Proceedings of the International Conference for High Performance Computing, Networking, Storage and Analysis, pp. 1–12 (2015)
10. Osuna, C., Wicky, T., Thuering, F., Hoefler, T., Fuhrer, O.: Dawn: a high-level domain-specific language compiler toolchain for weather and climate applications. Supercomputi. Front. Innov. **7**(2), 79–97 (2020)
11. Osuna, C., Thuering, F., Wicky, T., Dahm, J., et al.: Meteoswiss-apn/dawn: 0.0. 2 (2020)
12. Chen, C., Chame, J., Hall, M.: Chill: a framework for composing high-level loop transformations. Technical report, Citeseer (2008)
13. Tiwari, A., Chen, C., Chame, J., Hall, M., Hollingsworth, J.K.: A scalable auto-tuning framework for compiler optimization. In: 2009 IEEE International Symposium on Parallel & Distributed Processing, pp. 1–12. IEEE (2009)
14. Tapus, C., Chung, I.H., Hollingsworth, J.K.: Active harmony: towards automated performance tuning. In: SC 2002: Proceedings of the 2002 ACM/IEEE Conference on Supercomputing, pp. 44–44. IEEE (2002)
15. Baghdadi, R., et al.: Tiramisu: a polyhedral compiler for expressing fast and portable code. In: 2019 IEEE/ACM International Symposium on Code Generation and Optimization (CGO), pp. 193–205. IEEE (2019)
16. Kale, L.V., Krishnan, S.: Charm++ a portable concurrent object oriented system based on C++. In: Proceedings of the Eighth Annual Conference on Object-Oriented Programming Systems, Languages, and Applications, pp. 91–108 (1993)
17. Kale, L.V., Bhatele, A.: Parallel Science and Engineering Applications: The Charm++ Approach. CRC Press (2019)
18. Bauer, M., Treichler, S., Slaughter, E., Aiken, A.: Legion: expressing locality and independence with logical regions. In: SC 2012: Proceedings of the International Conference on High Performance Computing, Networking, Storage and Analysis, pp. 1–11. IEEE (2012)

19. Kaiser, H., et al.: HPX-the C++ standard library for parallelism and concurrency. J. Open Source Softw. **5**(53), 2352 (2020)
20. Wagle, B., Kellar, S., Serio, A., Kaiser, H.: Methodology for adaptive active message coalescing in task based runtime systems. In: 2018 IEEE International Parallel and Distributed Processing Symposium Workshops (IPDPSW), pp. 1133–1140. IEEE (2018)
21. Dagum, L., Menon, R.: OpenMP: an industry standard API for shared-memory programming. IEEE Comput. Sci. Eng. **5**(1), 46–55 (1998)
22. Huck, K.A., et al.: An autonomic performance environment for exascale. Supercomput. Front. Innov. **2**(3), 49–66 (2015)
23. Mucci, P.J., Browne, S., Deane, C., Ho, G.: PAPI: a portable interface to hardware performance counters. In: Proceedings of the Department of Defense HPCMP Users Group Conference, vol. 710. Citeseer (1999)
24. Eschweiler, D., Wagner, M., Geimer, M., Knüpfer, A., Nagel, W.E., Wolf, F.: Open trace format 2: the next generation of scalable trace formats and support libraries. In: Applications, Tools and Techniques on the Road to Exascale Computing, pp. 481–490. IOS Press (2012)
25. Traveler-integrated (2021). https://github.com/hdc-arizona/traveler-integrated
26. Tohid, R., et al.: Asynchronous execution of python code on task-based runtime systems. In: 2018 IEEE/ACM 4th International Workshop on Extreme Scale Programming Models and Middleware (ESPM2), pp. 37–45. IEEE (2018)
27. Hasheminezhad, B., Shirzad, S., Wu, N., Diehl, P., Schulz, H., Kaiser, H.: Towards a scalable and distributed infrastructure for deep learning applications. In: 2020 IEEE/ACM Fourth Workshop on Deep Learning on Supercomputers (DLS), pp. 20–30. IEEE (2020)
28. Brandt, S.R., et al.: Distributed asynchronous array computing with the jetlag environment. In: 2020 IEEE/ACM 9th Workshop on Python for High-Performance and Scientific Computing (PyHPC), pp. 49–57. IEEE (2020)
29. Gupta, N., et al.: Deploying a task-based runtime system on raspberry pi clusters. In: 2020 IEEE/ACM 5th International Workshop on Extreme Scale Programming Models and Middleware (ESPM2), pp. 11–20. IEEE (2020)
30. Kurtzer, G.M., Sochat, V., Bauer, M.W.: Singularity: scientific containers for mobility of compute. PLoS ONE **12**(5), e0177459 (2017)
31. Merkel, D., et al.: Docker: lightweight linux containers for consistent development and deployment. Linux J. **2014**(239), 2 (2014)
32. Dooley, R., Brandt, S.R., Fonner, J.: The agave platform: an open, science-as-a-service platform for digital science. In: Proceedings of the Practice and Experience on Advanced Research Computing, pp. 1–8 (2018)
33. Brandt, S.R., et al.: Jetlag: an interactive, asynchronous array computing environment. In: Practice and Experience in Advanced Research Computing, pp. 8–12 (2020)
34. Blaze. https://bitbucket.org/blaze-lib/blaze/. Accessed 10 Sept 2021
35. Blaze tensor (2021). https://github.com/STEllAR-GROUP/blaze_tensor/
36. Van Der Walt, S., Colbert, S.C., Varoquaux, G.: The numpy array: a structure for efficient numerical computation. Comput. Sci. Eng. **13**(2), 22–30 (2011)
37. Sakin, S.A., et al.: Traveler: navigating task parallel traces for performance analysis. arXiv e-prints, pages arXiv-2208 (2022)
38. Rostam cluster, stellar group at cct (2021). https://wiki.rostam.cct.lsu.edu/

DSL-HPC

Workshop on Domain Specific Languages for High-Performance Computing (DSL-HPC)

Workshop Description

Domain Specific Languages (DSLs) have the potential to revolutionize the development of scientific high-performance software by providing scientists with abstractions that are tailored for their specific problem. By the programmer encoding rich domain knowledge, the compilation tool-chain is then able to make effective choices around parallelism. Furthermore, if designed correctly, then the programmer is able to express their workload in an architecture-independent fashion, thus making portability across architectures possible, with the compilation tool-chain doing much of the heavy lifting.

Many believe that DSLs have the potential to get us closer to achieving the three P's of parallel programming; productivity, performance, and performance portability. Whilst historically this objective has been often seen as a chimera, there is wide acceptance in the HPC community that we need to solve these programming challenges before we can fully exploit future exascale supercomputers. Consequently, there is a growing consensus that the benefits that DSLs can deliver are paramount to the HPC community.

However there are numerous hurdles that must be overcome if DSLs are to be widely accepted, and this workshop aimed to explore such facets and enable a conversation between different communities to reduce barriers and help promote DSL adoption.

The first International Workshop on Domain Specific Languages for High-Performance Computing (DSL-HPC 2022) took place in Glasgow, Scotland, organized in conjunction with the Euro-Par annual international conference. The format of the workshop included two invited talks and three technical presentations, followed by a panel discussion. The workshop received good attendance of around 20 people on average throughout the day. This year, the workshop received three paper submissions from two countries. After a thorough peer-reviewing process that included discussion and agreement among reviewers whenever necessary, the program committee selected all three papers for presentation at the workshop. The review process focused on the quality of the papers, their novelty, and applicability to high-performance computing.

The accepted papers cover an interesting set of technologies and techniques associated with DSLs, including industry-standard languages like TensorFlow, popular frameworks such as MLIR, and more esoteric technologies that have been developed to solve specific problems. The program chair thanks all authors and the Program Committee for their support in making the workshop a successful event. Special thanks are due to the Euro-Par organizers for hosting the workshop, and especially to the workshop chairs Dora Blanco Heras and Jeremy Singer for their consistent support throughout the process.

Organization

Program Chair

Nick Brown   EPCC at the University of Edinburgh,
                                              Scotland

Program Committee

Gabriel Rodríguez-Canal   University of Edinburgh, Scotland
Maurice Jamieson   University of Edinburgh, Scotland
Mark Klaisoongnoen   EPCC, Scotland
Tobias Grosser   University of Edinburgh, Scotland
Michel Weber   ETH Zürich, Switzerland
Larisa Stoltzfus   EPCC, Scotland

Exploring the Suitability of the Cerebras Wafer Scale Engine for Stencil-Based Computation Codes

Nick Brown[1,2](✉) , Brandon Echols[1,2], Justs Zarins[1,2], and Tobias Grosser[2,3]

[1] EPCC, University of Edinburgh, Bayes Centre, Edinburgh, UK
nick.brown@ed.ac.uk
[2] Lawrence Livermore National Laboratory, Livermore, California, USA
[3] School of Informatics, University of Edinburgh, Informatics Forum, Edinburgh, UK

Abstract. The Cerebras Wafer Scale Engine (WSE) is an accelerator that combines hundreds of thousands of AI-cores onto a single chip. Whilst this technology has been designed for machine learning workloads, the significant amount of available raw compute means that it is also a very interesting potential target for accelerating traditional HPC computational codes. Many of these algorithms are stencil-based, where update operations involve contributions from neighbouring elements, and in this paper we explore the suitability of this technology for such codes from the perspective of an early adopter of the technology, compared to CPUs and GPUs. Running on a Cerebras CS-1 we explore the performance and describe in which programmers at the moment express their algorithms. We demonstrate that, whilst there is still work to be done around exposing the programming interface to users, performance of the WSE is impressive as it out performs four V100 GPUs by two and a half times and two Intel Xeon Platinum CPUs by around 114 times in our experiments. There is significant potential therefore for this technology to play an important role in accelerating HPC codes on future exascale supercomputers.

1 Introduction

Scientists and engineers are forever demanding the ability to model larger systems at reduced time to solution. This ambition is driving the HPC community towards exascale, and given the popularity of accelerators in current generation supercomputers it is safe to assume that they will form a major component of future exascale machines. Whilst GPUs have become dominant in HPC, an important question is the role that other more novel technologies might also play in increasing the capabilities of scientific simulation software. One such technology is Cerebras' Wafer Scale Engine (WSE) which is an accelerator containing hundreds of thousands of relatively simple, AI, cores. Whilst the major target for Cerebras to this point has been accelerating machine learning workloads, as the cores are optimised for processing sparse tensor operations this means they are capable of executing general purpose workloads, and furthermore combined with massive on-chip memory bandwidth and interconnect performance.

J. Singer et al. (Eds.): Euro-Par 2022 Workshops, LNCS 13835, pp. 51–65, 2023.
https://doi.org/10.1007/978-3-031-31209-0_4

Put simply, the WSE has significant potential for accelerating traditional HPC computational kernels in addition to machine learning models.

There are currently a handful of Cerebras machines which are publicly available, making testing and exploration of the architecture difficult. Furthermore, the software stack is optimised for machine learning workloads, and whilst Cerebras are making impressive progress in this regard, for instance the recent announcement of their SDK [6], at the time of writing machine interaction is mainly driven via high level machine learning tools. It is currently a very exciting time for the WSE, with Cerebras making numerous advances in both their software and future hardware offering. Consequently, whilst the technology is still in a relatively early state, at this stage understanding its overall suitability for HPC workloads compared with other hardware is worthwhile, especially as the Cerebras offering is set to mature and grow in coming years.

In this paper we explore the suitability of the Cerebras WSE for accelerating stencil-based computational algorithms. Section 2 introduces the background to this work by describing the WSE in more detail and how one interacts with the machine, along with other related work on the WSE. In Sect. 3 we explore how one must currently program the architecture for computational workloads and then, by running on a Cerebras CS-1, in Sect. 4 use a stencil-based benchmark to compare the performance properties of the WSE against four V100 GPUs and two 18-core Intel Xeon Platinum CPUs. In Sect. 5 we draw conclusions and then discuss further work.

2   Background and Related Work

The Cerebras WSE has been used by various organisations, including large global corporations, for accelerating machine learning. Already there have been numerous notable successes from running AI models on the WSE including new drug discovery [3], advancing treatments for fighting cancer [4], and helping to tackle the COVID-19 pandemic [7]. The benefits of accelerating machine learning workloads has been well proven, however there are far fewer studies concerned with using the WSE to run more traditional computational tasks.

One such study was undertaken in [5] where the authors ported the BiCGSTAB solver, a Krylov Subspace method for solving systems of linear equations, and also a simple CFD benchmark onto the Cerebras CS-1. Whilst their raw results were impressive, the authors used Cerebras' low level interface for this work, programming each individual core separately and manually configuring the on-chip network. This required a very deep understanding of the architecture, and furthermore as the work was undertaken in part by Cerebras employees they had access to this proprietary tooling which is not publicly available to users.

In this work we focus on stencil-based algorithms because of their suitability for mapping to the WSE architecture and TensorFlow programming interface (see Sect. 3). When calculating the value of a grid cell stencils represent a fixed pattern of contributions from neighbouring elements. Most commonly operating in iterations, at each iteration the value held in each grid cell will be updated based upon some weighted contribution of values held in neighbouring cells. This form of algorithm is widespread in scientific computing and hence represents the underlying computational pattern in use by a large number of HPC codes.

2.1 Cerebras Wafer Scale Engine

The Cerebras Wafer Scale Engine (WSE) is a MIMD accelerator and on the CS-1, the hardware used for this work, there are approximately 350000 processing cores running concurrently and able to executing different instructions on different data elements. The WSE provides more flexibility than a GPU, for instance, where on that accelerator groups of cores must operate in lock-step within a warp. At the physical level the WSE is composed of a wafer containing 84 dies, with each die comprising 4539 individual tiles. Each tile holds a single processing element, which is a computational core, a router, and 48KB of SRAM memory. In total there is approximately 18GB of SRAM memory on the CS-1 but this is distributed on a processing element by processing element basis. Each computational core supports operations on 16-bit integers, and both 16-bit and 32-bit floating point numbers, with the IEEE floating point standard supported for both floating point bit sizes and additionally Cerebras's own CB16. Each core provides 4-way SIMD for 16-bit floating point addition, multiplication, and fused multiply accumulate (FMAC) operations, 2-way SIMD for mixed precision (16-bit multiplications and 32-bit additions), and one operation per cycle is possible for 32-bit arithmetic. Therefore it is advantageous to embrace 16-bit operations where applicable, which corresponds to the overarching objective of Cerebras in targeting the acceleration of machine learning models.

The WSE is designed to accelerate computation involved in model training and inference, with numerous support functions undertaken by the host machine. The host is connected to the WSE via twelve 100 GbE network connections, and undertakes activities include model compilation, input data preprocessing, streaming input and output model data, and managing the overall model training. The Cerebras machine used for this work is a CS-1 hosted by EPCC and connected to a host Superdome Flex Server (containing twenty four Intel Xeon Platinum 8260 CPUs, with each CPU containing 24 physical cores and a total of 17TB RAM). There is a total of 1.2 Tbps network bandwidth between the host and CS-1 accelerator. Whilst Cerebras have recently announced their next generation CS-2 WSE [1], which contains approximately double the resources of the CS-1, the hardware used for experiments in this paper is still very relevant and popular with many Cerebras customers. Importantly, the CS-1 represents the first generation of Cerebras's architecture and consequently lessons learnt here apply more widely to later generations being or to be released.

2.2 Programming the Wafer Scale Engine

In [5] the authors programmed their kernels for the CS-1 using a bespoke low level interface, however this is proprietary and not exposed to users. Cerebras have recently announced the availability of their SDK [6] for general purpose programming of the WSE and whilst this is a very important step in widening the workloads that can be executed on the architecture, at the time of writing the SDK is not widespread installed across Cerebras machines including the CS-1 at EPCC. Furthermore, whilst the SDK is much higher level than the low level interfaced used in [5], it still requires an investment of time for programmers to gain the expertise in order to be able to write optimal code for the WSE using it. Consequently in this work we use the TensorFlow API, which is the only programming approach currently installed on the EPCC CS-1 at this time, which abstracts the tricky and low level details of decomposing the workload into tasks, mapping these to cores, and determining the appropriate routing strategy. Hence whilst our objective is to focus on stencil-based, rather than machine learning, codes, by encoding our algorithm via TensorFlow it enables us to undertake performance explorations for this workload, to understand whether it is worthwhile investing the time in using the Cerebras SDK as it becomes more commonly available, and also means that such algorithms can be ported to the WSE more quickly to undertake such evaluations.

The WSE supports a subset of TensorFlow functionality, and in this work we use two major building blocks to encode stencil-based algorithms. The first building block are dense layers, which are fully-connected meaning that every value provided as an input to the layer will have a connection to every output value of the layer. As such the operation performed by a dense layer is a matrix-matrix multiplication with a batch of input tensors and weight matrix resulting in, for every output value, each input value multiplied by a specific weight and intermediate values added together to form the result.

The second TensorFlow construct used in this work are convolution layers, where a kernel slides across the input tensor and performs a convolution product to calculate results. For each element of the output, the kernel weight values will be multiplied with a subset of the input values. In the 2D case, the filter can be thought of as sliding from left to right and up to down, and whilst TensorFlow includes convolution layers that operate in one, two, and three dimensions, at the time of writing the Cerebras software stack only supports the 2D convolution layer. In this *Conv2D* layer the data-structure is comprised of four dimensions which are the batch size, number of channels (the depth of the input tensor, for instance red, green, blue for an image), rows, and columns. Whilst the WSE provides single and half precision in hardware, the Cerebras software stack only supports mixed precision (single and half) at the TensorFlow API level.

3 TensorFlow for Encoding Stencil-Based Algorithms on the Wafer Scale Engine

In this work our objective has been to implement a stencil-based benchmark and for this we selected the Jacobi iterative method for solving Laplace's equation for diffusion in multiple dimensions. Whilst this is a fairly simplistic solver compared to the BiCGSTAB method explored on the CS-1 in [5], the limitation of having to encode the algorithm via TensorFlow imposes some limitations. Furthermore, the underlying computational pattern is similar and represents an important class of algorithms and solvers. Consequently insights obtained from this benchmark on the WSE are highly relevant and interesting to the wider HPC community. Other benchmarks, such as the Open Earth Compiler benchmark suite [2], were considered however they were not readily representable in TensorFlow in a form that would build with the Cerebras software stack.

The first approach we explored used a dense layer to undertake the Jacobi stencil computation. A sketch of this algorithm is illustrated in Algorithm 1, where x is the input tensor containing data being operated upon, and *stencil* is a matrix representing the stencil operation. The input tensor is first flattened and then, along with *stencil*, passed to the *Dense* TensorFlow layer which will undertake the calculation. This operation is repeated *iterations* times.

Algorithm 1: Stencil Calculation with Dense Layer

---

1   function model-function $(x, stencil, iterations, N)$;

    Input   : x - the input tensor for the stencil calculations

               stencil - matrix used by Dense layer to perform stencil calculation

               iterations - the number of times the calculation will be performed

               N - total number of elements per step

    Output: result of performing stencil calculation on input tensor

2   $values = Flatten(x)$;

3   **for** $i \leftarrow 0$ **to** *iterations* **do**

4 | $values = Dense(N, kernelInitializer = stencil)(values)$;

5   **end**

6   **return** *values*

N is the total size of the input tensor per step, x, which is of size equal to X in one dimension, $X * Y$ in two dimensions, and $X * Y * Z$ in three dimensions. TensorFlow drives the dense layer with inputs over many steps, and the overarching problem size being operated upon is $N * numberofsteps$. The problem is therefore decomposed into tiles each of size N, and overlapping is undertaken to ensure boundary neighbours from one tile are available to another. This decomposition of the problem into steps, each of size N, is required to fit the hardware's memory and compute limits.

There are several advantages to programming the WSE using dense layers such as the ability to readily handle any number of input dimensions because the input is flattened regardless. Furthermore, because we explicitly define the stencil calculation then special cases, such as non-zero boundary conditions, can be handled without the need for conditional statements or other operations. For instance in this example the stencil matrix value can be set to 1 in order to maintain boundary conditions throughout the calculation.

However, the major disadvantage of this approach is that the dense layer is of size N^2 (where N is the total size of the input tensor per step). Depending upon the equation being solved this can involve a significant amount of redundant storage and computation. Figure 1 provides an illustration for solving Laplace's equation for diffusion in 2D with $X = Y = 3$. This is first flattened into a vector of size $N = X * Y = 9$ and then a matrix-vector product undertaken to calculate the results. In this example all cells on the boundaries, which is every element apart the middle value, 5, remains unchanged which corresponds to 1 in the stencil matrix as it is a boundary condition. The 0.25 values in the stencil matrix average neighbouring values, with every other element a zero and not contributing to the result. However these zeros must still be stored in the matrix and computations undertaken with them on them regardless.

$$
flatten\left(\begin{bmatrix}1\,2\,3\\4\,5\,6\\7\,8\,9\end{bmatrix}\right) = \begin{bmatrix}1\\2\\3\\4\\5\\6\\7\\8\\9\end{bmatrix} \qquad output = \begin{bmatrix}1\\2\\3\\4\\5\\6\\7\\8\\9\end{bmatrix} * \begin{bmatrix}1&0&0&0&0&0&0&0&0\\0&1&0&0&0&0&0&0&0\\0&0&1&0&0&0&0&0&0\\0&0&0&1&0&0&0&0&0\\0&0.25&0&0.25&0&0.25&0&0.25&0\\0&0&0&0&0&1&0&0&0\\0&0&0&0&0&0&1&0&0\\0&0&0&0&0&0&0&1&0\\0&0&0&0&0&0&0&0&1\end{bmatrix}
$$

Fig. 1. Illustration of dense layer operations for solving Laplace's equation for diffusion in 2D with $X = Y = 3$

Another approach, as introduced in Sect. 2.2, is to use a convolution layer where the stencil is represented as a much smaller data window that slides across the input values. A sketch of the code for driving the convolution layer approach is illustrated in Algorithm 2 where, in contrast to the dense layer of Algorithm 1, input values are not flattened because the convolution layer is dimensioned. Furthermore, there are two additional arguments, *dataFormat* and *padding* provided to this layer at line 3. The former determines the ordering of the dimensions in the input and output tensors, and the CS-1 only supports *channelsFirst*. The second option ensures that the output is the same shape as the input by undertaking additional padding if required, where *same* results in padding with zeros evenly to the left/right or up/down of the input.

The major benefit of the convolution layer is that, because the defined filter slides across the input, it decouples the size of the stencil matrix from the input tensor size. The convolution layer stencil for the same Laplace's equation for diffusion in 2D is illustrated in Fig. 2, where irrespective of the input tensor size, N, nine values are required for the 2D case. Consequently, whilst there are some zeros still present, representing wasted storage and computation, their number is very significantly reduced in comparison to the dense layer approach.

However there are two disadvantages with using convolution layers as sketched in Algorithm 2, firstly stencil-based algorithms with non-zero boundary conditions are not possible because padding adds extra zero elements. To enable boundary condition values other than zero, the padding of the convolution layer must be changed to mode *valid*, with the algorithm then manually defining the padding of the input. The most convenient approach to do this would be to

---

Algorithm 2: Stencil Calculation with Convolution Layer

---

1 <u>function model-function</u> $(x, stencil, iterations, stencilShape)$;
   Input : x - the input tensor for the stencil calculations
               stencil - filter for the Conv2D layer performing stencil calculation
               iterations - the number of times the calculation will be performed
               stencilShape - the shape of the stencil
   Output: result of performing stencil calculation on input tensor
2 **for** $i \leftarrow 0$ **to** $iterations$ **do**
3    $x = Conv2D(1, stencil, kernelInitializer = stencilInit, dataFormat =' channelsFirst', padding =' same')(x)$;
4 **end**
5 **return** x

$$\begin{bmatrix} 0 & 0.25 & 0 \\ 0.25 & 0 & 0.25 \\ 0 & 0.25 & 0 \end{bmatrix}$$

Fig. 2. Illustration of convolution layer kernel for 2D Laplace's equation for diffusion

use the *tensorflow.pad* operation, which pads the outer edge with zeros, and boundary conditions could then be added around this padded input, driven by a concatenate layer. However, at the time of writing, both the pad operation and concatenate layer are not supported by the Cerebras software stack.

Instead a mask must be created that will zero out the edges that were updated by the convolution layer and then subsequently add the boundary conditions back in. The mask is a tensor of the same shape and size, N, as the input tensor and contains *1* in the internal values and *0* on the outer, boundary condition, locations. Multiplying the mask by the output zeros out the boundary conditions and then a further, *boundary conditions* tensor which holds zeros for inner elements and the boundary conditions themselves, is added to the masked intermediate result. Whilst this approach is not ideal, as it results in additional runtime overhead, it is required because the Cerebras software stack does not yet fully support the entire TensorFlow API which would enable better alternatives.

The other challenge with using the convolution layer is that only *Conv2D* is currently supported by the Cerebras software stack, meaning that other convolution layers such as *Conv3D* are not currently available for increased problem dimensions. Due to the ubiquity in HPC of PDEs in three dimensions, this omission would be a major limitation. To address this we increase the number of channels in the 2D convolution layer. Figure 3 illustrates the approach, where the number of channels in the convolution layer can be considered the depth of the stencil in the third dimension. Because the depth corresponds to the stencil size in the third dimension, as the filter slides across the input tensor in two dimensions each channel will undertake calculations on separate third dimension

58   N. Brown et al.

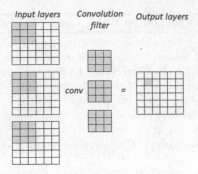

Fig. 3. Illustration of 3D convolution approach with the input in 3D but output in 2D

slices. However, as illustrated in Fig. 3 this only results in a 2D output layer. To expand the number of output dimensions then the number of filter channels needs to be further increased by the number of input channels as illustrated by Fig. 4. This supports the handling of three dimensions, within the limitations imposed by the Cerebras software stack, but does imposes additional storage and computation overhead.

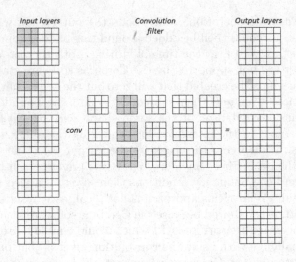

Fig. 4. Illustration of 3D convolution approach with the input and output in 3D

4   Results

In this section we conduct runs of our benchmark, a Jacobi method for solving Laplace's equation for diffusion in multiple dimensions, on the CS-1 which uses the latest version, 1.0.1, of Cerebras software. Performance is compared against **four** Nvidia Telsa V100-SXM2-16GB GPUs (CUDA toolkit version 10.1.243 and the CUDA library cuDNN version 7.6.5), and **two** 18-core Intel Xeon E5-2695 (Broadwell) CPUs. We use TensorFlow version 2.2.0 on the CS-1 and 2.3.0 on the GPUs and CPUs. Reported results are averaged over three runs.

To compare performance between the hardware we use the metric of *delivered performance* in FLOPS. This is defined in Eq. 1, where *stencilFLOP* is the total number of floating point operations involved in applying the stencil for each output element. From the perspective of the computational algorithm this is the number of FLOPS delivered and includes the unnecessary floating point operations highlighted in Sect. 3 which do not contribute to the final result. However there are additional internal operations being undertaken by the TensorFlow framework which are not readily discernible and these are not included in this metric. Consequently delivered performance can be thought of as a metric which is useful to compare the relative performance of hardware technologies, rather than able to provide an indication of absolute performance.

$$delivered\,performance = (problemSize * stencilFLOP * iterations)/time \quad (1)$$

As described in Sect. 3, the problem size is a product of N and the number of steps, where N is the size of the input tensor, for instance $X * Y$ in the 2D case. We set the batch size to be one, and the number of model iterations represents the number of solver iterations being undertaken, where an iteration operates on the data resulting from a previous iteration.

Table 1. Delivered performance for 2D Jacobi with a problem size of 2048 million elements ($X = Y = 64$) using dense (over 7 iterations) and convolution (3500 iterations) layers across hardware and different numeric precision configurations

Technology	Dense layer delivered performance (GFLOPS)	Convolution layer delivered performance (GFLOPS)
Two CPUs (single precision)	10.75	26.75
Two CPUs (mixed precision)	0.63	3.88
Four GPUs (single precision)	27.93	985.12
Four GPUs (mixed precision)	32.28	1255.74
CS-1 (mixed precision)	224.43	3054.89

Table 1 reports the delivered performance in GFLOPS across the CPUs, GPUs, and Cerebras CS-1. On the CPUs and GPUs we include results for single and mixed precision (the later is a combination of 32-bit and 16-bit operations), whereas the Cerebras software stack only supports mixed precision for TensorFlow. For each of these configurations we include results for the dense and convolution layer approaches, with the dense layer running in *training* mode and convolution layer in *predict* mode. It is important to stress that the numbers reported here are delivered performance, for instance the GPU is capable of far higher raw FLOPS and the CS-1 was demonstrated to reach 0.86 PFLOPS in [5], however representing this benchmark in TensorFlow induces additional overhead and-so whilst this does not give a measure of the raw performance it does enable us to compare relative performance between the technologies.

It can be seen from the relative performance comparison in Table 1 that the Cerebras CS-1 delivers around 2.5 times the performance of four V100 GPUs and around 114 times the performance of two 18-core Intel Xeon Platinum CPUs for this benchmark. Mixed precision is slightly more efficient on the GPU, but performs very poorly on the CPU which is because the CPU does not support half-precision floating point in hardware and-so must emulate it in software. Furthermore it can be seen that *predict* mode, used for the convolution layer, is beneficial as the weights are already provided by the user for our stencil-based algorithms and-so additional work involved by training is not required. However not all TensorFlow operations support *predict* mode on the WSE and consequently the dense layer experiments can be run in *train* mode only.

Whilst our *delivered performance* metric includes all stencil operations from the perspective of the algorithm, as described in Sect. 3, not all of these calculations are useful because not all contribute to the final result. For Laplace's equation for diffusion there are 7 useful calculations undertaken per input element, comprising four multiplications and three additions. However in the dense layer all input values contribute to each output element's calculation, resulting in $(N * 2) - 1$ operations for every output element. In the 2D case, with $X = Y = 64$ and therefore $N = 4096$, there are 8191 operations for each output element and 33550336 total calculations for the entire input tensor, per step, per iteration. The convolution layer by contrast undertakes 17 operations per output element, resulting in 69632 total operations for the 2D case where $X = Y = 64$. Whilst, as described in Sect. 3, there are $N * 2$ additional operations for applying the mask with non-zero boundary conditions after an iteration, this is still considerably less overhead than the dense layer. The dense layer approach has a further limitation which is that a separate dense layer, of size N^2, must be created for each iteration. This significantly limits the overall number of iterations possible with the dense layer, a maximum of 7 on the CS-1, whereas the convolution approach can run at thousands of iterations. This is the other reason for the large performance difference between the dense and convolution layer approaches seen in Table 1, as from our experiments we see performance improving as small numbers of iterations are increased because this keeps the CS-1 busy and helps ameliorates startup and shutdown overhead.

Consequently we now focus on the convolution layer approach as it is more flexible and delivers much better performance. We explored scaling of the problem size with different numbers of workers. Each worker runs on a node of the Superdome Flex over 12 cores, and in *predict* mode can drive the WSE independently by streaming in data concurrently to keep the fabric busy. Consequently multiple workers running concurrently can provide increased performance. This is illustrated in Fig. 5, where performance increases initially with the problem size and then plateaus. Increasing the number of workers significantly improves performance for smaller number of workers as they service the WSE fabric to keep it fed with data. However once we reach six workers, whilst there is still a small performance improvement when increasing to eight or twelve workers, the advantage is negligible. This is because at six workers the CS-1 is already being fed sufficiently well with data and beyond this the accelerator is saturated with data to process so there is no more capacity that requires filling.

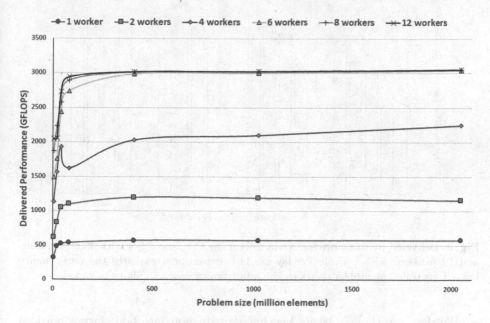

Fig. 5. Delivered performance for 2D Jacobi over 3500 iterations on the Cerebras CS-1 when changing the problem size and number of workers

To this point we have concentrated on the benchmark solving Laplace's equation for diffusion in two dimensions with input tensor shape $X = Y = 64$. Consequently in two dimensions we have an overall problem size of $N = 4096$ multiplied by the *number of steps*. To modify the problem size in Fig. 5 we changed the number of steps, however it is also possible to change the size and shape of the input tensor from $X = Y = 64$ too. Increasing the size and shape of the input tensor will result in a larger amount of input processed per step, consequently scaling the pipeline on the hardware to handle this and thus increasing the amount of fabric used on the WSE. Therefore it is interesting to see what difference this makes to performance, and Fig. 6 illustrates the delivered performance in GFLOPS for four different problem size configurations where we modify the size and shape of the input tensor and the number of steps appropriately. It can be seen that this configuration change has an impact on performance at smaller problem sizes, where performance favours a larger input tensor processed per step and fewer steps. However as the problem size is increased the difference becomes smaller until, at 2048 million elements there is no significant difference between the configurations. The 32×64 and 64×64 shapes utilised 27% of the CS-1 fabric, whereas the 128×64 used 45% and 128×128 67%, beyond this size the Cerebras compiler was unable to find a suitable placement.

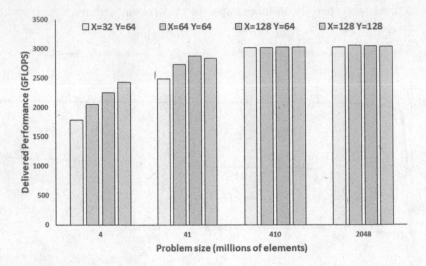

Fig. 6. Delivered performance for 2D Jacobi on the Cerebras CS-1 with 3500 iterations and 12 workers, with convolution layers. This experiment explores the performance impact for different problem sizes as the input tensor size and shape is varied

We then ran the 3D Jacobi benchmark with non-zero boundary conditions and an input tensor shape of $X = 64, Y = 64, Z = 10$, which is the largest supported shape on the CS-1, with non-zero boundary conditions over 3500 iterations and 12 workers. Figure 7 reports the speed up obtained against a baseline of two 24-core Intel Xeon Platinum CPUs executing the benchmark in single precision (which as per Table 1 is the best performing CPU configuration). We include results for four V100 GPUs at mixed precision, which is the highest performing GPU configuration, and the CS-1. It can be seen that the CS-1 significantly out-performs the CPUs and GPUs at all problem sizes, which broadly agrees with results reported for the 2D case in Table 1. It can be seen that speed up against the CPU is lower at smaller problem sizes for both the GPUs and Cerebras CS-1, although this is more pronounced for the CS-1, demonstrating that these accelerator technologies favour working on larger problem sizes and being fed with data to keep the fabric busy in the case of the CS-1.

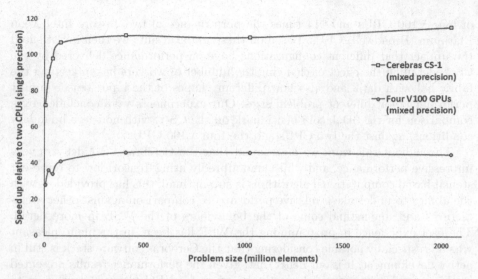

Fig. 7. Speed up relative to running single precision on two CPUs for 3D Jacobi. Using convolution layers, X=64, Y=64, Z=10, 3500 iterations, and 12 workers

5 Conclusions

The Cerebras Wafer Scale Engine (WSE) is a very exciting technology which has already delivered significant advantages for machine learning workloads. This makes it not only an important accelerator for AI, but also very interesting for traditional computational HPC applications. In this paper we have explored the suitability of accelerating stencil-based computational algorithms on the WSE via a benchmark which implements the Jacobi method for solving Laplace's equation for diffusion in multiple dimensions. This represents an important class of algorithm which are common place in HPC and-so insights gained from such experiments are interesting for high performance workloads more widely. The primary objective of the WSE has been to accelerate machine learning models, and whilst the Cerebras team are making significant progress in opening up the architecture for more general purpose codes, at the time of writing the only way for many users to interact with the WSE is via the TensorFlow API. Consequently, to undertake the early user exploration detailed in this paper we have encoded the stencil-based benchmark in TensorFlow using two approaches, dense and convolution layers. It was found that the later approach provides more flexibility and was able to deliver greater performance on the WSE.

We ran performance experiments on a Cerebras CS-1, and because the exact operations being undertaken by the TensorFlow API are somewhat of a black-box, the *delivered performance* metric was used which measures the performance delivered by the hardware from the perspective of the computational algorithm. This provides a relative, rather than absolute, measure of performance and enabled us to compare different hardware technologies. We found that, for this benchmark, the CS-1 delivered around two and a half times the performance of four V100 GPUs and 114 times the performance of two 18-core Intel Xeon Platinum (Broadwell) CPUs. Based on these initial results we then investigated the impact that different configurations have on performance delivered by the CS-1, detailing the effect of changing the number of workers has in keeping the fabric fed with data, and also how different shapes of the input tensor impact performance for different problem sizes. Our experiments were concluded by a comparison for the 3D Jacobi benchmark on the CS-1, with non-zero boundary conditions, against the two CPUs and the four V100 GPUs.

Throughout this work we have found that the Cerebras CS-1 delivers very impressive performance, and whilst undoubtedly using TensorFlow to represent stencil-based computational algorithms is sub-optimal, this has provided us with the ability to undertake a relative performance comparison against other architectures and understand some of the behaviours of the WSE in more detail. The user experience in programming the WSE has been, in the main, pleasant which is especially notable considering that the Cerebras software stack is still in active development. It is our belief that, given the performance results presented in this paper, it is very much worth the effort for HPC software developers to gain expertise with the Cerebras SDK [6] when it becomes more widely available in the coming months. It is expected that, whilst development using the SDK will inevitably require increased effort and architectural knowledge, this will help deliver significantly improved performance, and the user no longer limited to mixed precision only will also have more choice over numeric representation. Therefore a next step will be port our benchmark to use the Cerebras SDK and, with this work as a baseline, explore the increased performance that the WSE combined with the Cerebras SDK can deliver compared to other hardware technologies.

References

1. Cerebras: wafer-scale engine: the largest chip ever built. Technical Report, Cerebras (2021)
2. Gysi, T., et al.: Domain-specific multi-level IR rewriting for GPU: the open earth compiler for GPU-accelerated climate simulation. ACM Trans. Archit. Code Optim. (TACO) **18**(4), 1–23 (2021)
3. Hansen, L.L.: Accelerating drug discovery research with new AI models: a look at the astrazeneca cerebras collaboration. http://larslynnehansen.medium.com/accelerating-drug-discovery-research-with-new-ai-models-a-look-at-the-astrazeneca-cerebras-b72664d8783, April 2021, posted 26 April-2021
4. Pendse, M., Thangarasa, V., Chiley, V., Holmdahl, R., Hestness, J., DeCoste, D.: Memory efficient 3D U-net with reversible mobile inverted bottlenecks for brain tumor segmentation. In: Crimi, A., Bakas, S. (eds.) BrainLes 2020. LNCS, vol. 12659, pp. 388–397. Springer, Cham (2021). https://doi.org/10.1007/978-3-030-72087-2_34
5. Rocki, K., et al.: Fast stencil-code computation on a wafer-scale processor. In: SC20: International Conference for High Performance Computing, Networking, Storage and Analysis, pp. 1–14. IEEE (2020)

6. Selig, J.: The cerebras software development kit: A technical overview. Technical Report, Cerebras (2022)
7. Trifan, A., et al.: Intelligent resolution: Integrating cryo-em with ai-driven multi-resolution simulations to observe the sars-cov-2 replication-transcription machinery in action. bioRxiv (2021)

Performance of the Vipera Framework for DSLs on Micro-Core Architectures

Maurice Jamieson$^{(\boxtimes)}$ ⓘ and Nick Brown ⓘ

EPCC, The University of Edinburgh, Edinburgh, UK
maurice.jamieson@ed.ac.uk
https://www.epcc.ed.ac.uk

Abstract. Vipera provides a compiler and runtime framework for implementing dynamic Domain-Specific Languages on micro-core architectures. The performance and code size of the generated code is critical on these architectures. In this paper we present the results of our investigations into the efficiency of Vipera in terms of code performance and size.

Keywords: Domain-specific languages · Python · native code generation · RISC-V · micro-core architectures

1 Introduction

In order to reduce the power consumption of new High-Performance Computing (HPC) machines, the use of hybrid HPC architectures with graphics processing units (GPUs) as accelerators has increased, such as the 4:1 ratio of GPUs to central processing units (CPUs) per node of the new OLCF Frontier exascale supercomputer [1]. Other novel architectures for HPC have been introduced, including innovative *micro-core*[1] processor architectures that consist of many, low energy cores combined with small amounts of memory on a single chip, such as the 256 core Kalray MPPA, the 256 core Sunway SW26010, the 1024 Adapteva Epiphany-V and the 2048 core PEZY-SC2. These micro-core architectures have the promise of overcoming the power wall due to the high energy efficiency of their designs, for example, the class-leading 70 GFLOPS per Watt of the 64-core Adapteva Epiphany-IV [3]. Whilst these architectures provide the high energy efficiency and low overall power consumption levels, micro-cores are notoriously difficult to program and take advantage of; each technology is different with its own idiosyncrasies, such as the topology of the Network-on-Chip (NOC), and they each present a different low-level interface to the programmer. Although manufacturers have made great progress in developing the hardware, parallel programming and compilation techniques have not evolved

---

[1] Although the term *manycore* is commonly used, we define micro-cores as manycores with extremely small amounts of on-chip, scratchpad RAM (circa 32–64KB) without hardware cache support.

© The Author(s), under exclusive license to Springer Nature Switzerland AG 2023
J. Singer et al. (Eds.): Euro-Par 2022 Workshops, LNCS 13835, pp. 66–79, 2023.
https://doi.org/10.1007/978-3-031-31209-0_5

quickly enough to exploit this effectively [27]. Fundamentally, writing parallel, scalable code is difficult and requires the programmer to consider multiple levels of parallelism to get good performance [29]. However, to date, these technologies have tended to result in significant performance overheads, required the programmer to ensure their code fits within the limited on-chip memory, provided limited choices around data location and size, and provided little, if any, portability across architectures. As evidenced by ePython [16], a Python interpreter for the Epiphany-III, dynamic programming languages can significantly reduce the programming effort required to overcome these complexities in comparison to the provided, low-level C software development kits (SDKs) [26].

In this paper we present the investigations into the efficiency of our Vipera framework for dynamic programming languages, in terms of code performance and size, relative to handwritten (native) C, on a variety of micro-core and traditional CPU architectures.

2   Related Work

Whilst Python is currently the most popular programming language [2], its use of an interpreter results in performance significantly slower than statically compiled languages, such as C and Fortran. This has driven the need to overcome the performance overhead of the interpreter and the restrictions imposed by the global interpreter lock (GIL). This has resulted in technologies to increase the performance of existing Python codes through the compilation to native code, including Cython [15], MicroPython [11], Numba [28], Copperhead [18], Parakeet [30], ALPyNA [23] and PyCUDA [4]. The high-level approach of Numba, Copperhead and Parakeet is similar, whereby they define an embedded domain specific language (eDSL) and utilise Python *function decorators* (directives) to annotate the code to be compiled to native code or offloaded to GPUs. ALPyNA adopts a different technique to generating GPU code than the eDSL and function decorator approach. Rather than requiring the programmer to select and annotate the Python functions that will be generated as GPU kernels, ALPyNA analyses loop data dependencies and performs automatic loop parallelisation to generate CUDA kernels for GPUs. However, unlike Numba, Copperhead, Parakeet and ALPyNA, PyCUDA does not abstract the generation of GPU code but instead embeds CUDA C code directly within the Python source code. MicroPython performs the compilation of bytecode to native code on the device [10] similar to JIT except that the bytecode is not profiled as is common for JIT compilers, rather the bytecode is just lowered to native code. An alternative approach was taken for Vipera, similar to that employed by the Pallene/Titan compiler [21] for Lua [22]. Here, the source language compiler, running on the host, emits C source code that is then compiled to generate native binary executables.

2.1   Vipera Dynamic Language Framework

The Vipera [17] framework was created to support the development of dynamic languages on micro-core architectures. As shown in Fig. 1, the framework consists

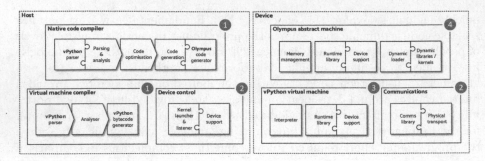

Fig. 1. Vipera dynamic language framework architecture

of a layered architecture with components running on the host and micro-core devices. Vipera manages the compilation of code ❶, the transfer and launch of kernels on the micro-core devices, and the transfer of data ❷. vPython is a development of ePython, a subset of the Python programming language specifically designed for micro-core architectures. Vipera provides two implementations of this; the first compiles down to bytecode that executes on a tiny virtual machine (c. 24KB on the Adapteva Epiphany-III [16]) running on the device ❸ and the second generates Olympus abstract machine code that is compiled to provide device native code ❹. The communications technology ❷ for the native code version of ePython is provided by the Eithne becnhmarking framework [24]. In this paper we will focus on the Olympus abstract machine version of vPython.

vPython can either be run *standalone* on the device or as a Domain-Specific Language (DSL) within Python running on the host, offloading kernels for execution to the device. More information on the parallel programming, offloading and dynamic code loading capabilities of the language can be found in [25,26].

3 Experimental Environment

3.1 CPU Selection

In order to support the assessment of the Vipera vPython compiler and Olympus abstract machine, a number of different platforms and processors were selected, including the Adapteva Epiphany-III , Xilinx MicroBlaze and PicoRV32 RISC-V micro-cores and the AMD64 (x64), ARM Cortex-A9 (ARM32), MIPS32, SPARCv9 and U740 RISC-V (RISCV64) traditional CPUs. As processor ISAs can have a significant impact on both the compiled kernel performance and binary size, the CPUs were selected to test the impact of the Olympus abstract machine design and to test the portability of Olympus between 32 bit and 64 bit processors with varying alignment constraints and byte ordering.

For the selected benchmarks, LINPACK [19] and the Sieve of Eratosthenes [20], the source vPython codes were compiled to Olympus abstract machine C source code and wrapped by Eithne API calls for execution on a single core of the CPUs. The benchmarks were executed 100 times on all of the CPUs at both GCC compiler optimisation levels -O2 and -O3.

3.2 LINPACK Overview

The LINPACK benchmark measures the floating point performance of a computer by solving a matrix problem using LU decomposition. It is a long-established benchmark, having been introduced in 1979, and is the standard benchmark used to rank supercomputer performance for the Top500 [13] list. LU factorisation is commonly used in scientific and industrial applications, such as design automation, machine learning and signal processing. The C version [12] was selected to compare the performance (MFLOPS[2]) of the Olympus abstract machine[3] against native C. For the Olympus abstract machine investigations, a serial version of the LINPACK code was run on a single core. Due to the extremely small memory available on the micro-core devices, the problem size n was 50 and for traditional CPUs $n = 1000$.

3.3 Sieve of Eratosthenes (Byte Sieve) Overview

The Sieve of Eratosthenes benchmark [20], often referred to as *Byte Sieve*, is an algorithm to finding all prime numbers up to a set limit ($SIZE$) and is commonly used to test compiler code generation performance and efficiency [5, 7]. The standard C and a new vPython version of the benchmark were used to determine the performance of integer array access and looping constructs of the Olympus abstract machine relative to native C, to augment the LINPACK benchmark that performs floating point array access and calculations. The standard Sieve benchmark is serial and both versions were run on a single core of all the CPUs. Like LINPACK, due to the limited memory on the micro-core devices, the flag array size was reduced ($SIZE = 4095$) on the Epiphany-III, MicroBlaze and PicoRV32 micro-cores, on the other CPUs, per the original benchmark, $SIZE = 8190$.

4 Results and Discussion

Table 1 details the mean MFLOPS attained by each CPU for Olympus and native C kernels at GCC optimisation levels -O2 and -O3. Table 2 lists the mean runtimes for the Byte Sieve Olympus and native C kernels at GCC optimisation levels -O2 and -O3. On the PicoRV32, the Olympus -O3 kernel froze and did not return a value to the host, even though the kernel successfully executed when compiled at optimisation level -Os. As the Byte Sieve (Sect. 4.3) PicoRV32 kernels also failed to execute correctly at -O3, it is likely that the version of the RISC-V compiler used (riscv32-unknown-elf-gcc 8.2.0) is generating code that is invalid for the PicoRV32 at this level of optimisation.

---

[2] Million Floating Point Operations per Second.
[3] A vPython version of LINPACK was written and compiled to Olympus abstract machine code.

Table 1. LINPACK kernel mean runtime performance (MFLOPS)

CPU	Olympus (-Os)	Olympus (-O3)	native C (-Os)	native C (-O3)
Epiphany-III	139.36	193.53	83.99	105.99
MicroBlaze	0.0604	0.0605	0.0611	0.0612
PicoRV32	0.0252	N/A	0.0256	N/A
ARM32	67.74	66.61	66.71	69.67
MIPS32	65.90	75.60	75.40	81.077
AMD64	520.98	563.03	652.46	695.57
SPARCv9	49.81	59.40	70.78	68.96
RISCV64	51.63	54.00	57.48	56.57

Table 2. Byte Sieve benchmark native C and Olympus kernel mean runtime (seconds)

CPU	Olympus (-Os)	Olympus (-O3)	native C (-Os)	native C (-O3)
Epiphany-III	4.972	3.475	2.760	1.996
MicroBlaze	48.23	32.70	17.78	14.94
PicoRV32	358.64	N/A	140.77	94.52
ARM32	12.53	9.135	4.629	3.443
MIPS32	13.79	9.211	3.683	2.858
AMD64	3.895	2.868	2.319	1.409
SPARCv9	30.93	18.80	6.763	5.060
RISCV64	14.61	11.12	2.676	2.755

4.1   LINPACK Runtime Performance

Figure 2 shows the single-core performance results for LINPACK on the target processor architectures, compiled using the -Os and -O3 compiler optimisation levels. Whilst the results vary widely across the architectures, the performance difference between the Olympus and native C kernels is very small. However, the Olympus LINPACK kernel compiled at -Os is 1.7 times faster than native C on the Epiphany-III and is marginally faster (1.5%) on the ARM32. Although the performance advantage of Olympus kernels on the ARM32 is reversed at -O3, where native C is 4.6% faster, the advantage is actually slightly increased at -O3 on the Epiphany-III to 1.8 times faster than native C. On the other architectures, native C is between about 1.2% on the MicroBlaze and 42% on the SPARC faster than Olympus at -Os and between about 7.2% on the MIPS32 and 24% on the AMD64 faster at -O3.

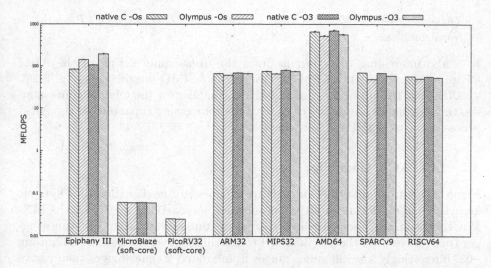

Fig. 2. LINPACK benchmark native C and Olympus kernel floating point performance, with error bars denoting standard deviation (log scale)

Analysing the performance advantage of Olympus kernels over native C on the Epiphany-III and at -Os on the ARM32 requires knowledge of the peculiarities of the Epiphany-III and looking at the assembly language generated by the C compiler. In the case of the Epiphany-III, there are four modes for the floating point unit (FPU) that can be specified at compile time [8]. The default FPU mode is *caller*, which results[4] in native C kernels being 1.7 times faster than Olympus. The *truncate* FPU mode does not provide a significant improvement (2.1%) of native C kernels over Olympus. The *round-nearest* mode provides a 2.1 times performance improvement of native C over the Olympus abstract machine. The *int* FPU mode, executing integer operations as well as floating point operations in the FPU, delivers a 1.66 and 1.83 times performance advantage of Olympus kernels over native C at for -Os and for -O3, respectively. This result is surprising but considering that the Epiphany-III is a superscalar design that can execute two floating point operations and one integer instruction per clock cycle [14], it is possible to surmise that the Olympus *mnemonics* can take advantage of the additional two integer operations per clock cycle afforded by the *int* FPU mode and prevent the pipeline from stalling.

The minor performance advantage of Olympus over native C on the ARM at the -Os compiler optimisation level can be explained by the additional 21 APSR_nzcv opcodes in the native C kernel. This opcode transfers the floating-point status flags to the ARM application program status register (APSR) and, as [9] state:

---

[4] The FPU mode comparisons were all performed using the -O3 compiler optimisation level.

These instructions stall the ARM until all current NEON or VFP operations complete.

It is also interesting to determine from the disassembly listing of the ARM Olympus kernel that the ARM NEON vector / SIMD instructions (e.g. VLDR, VLMUL and VSTR) are being issued by the C compiler for the Olympus mnemonics, thereby taking advantage of this parallel processing capability of the ARM processor for the LINPACK benchmark.

4.2   LINPACK Code Size

Figure 3 illustrates that the C kernels are significantly smaller than the Olympus kernels on all platforms, at GCC optimisation levels -Os and -O3, for the LIN-PACK benchmark. The difference in kernel size ranges from around 1.5 times bigger than native C on the Epiphany-III to 2.6 times bigger on the MIPS32, using -O3. Interestingly, the difference ranges from around 2 times bigger than native C on the Epiphany-III to around 3 times bigger on the MIPS32 and AMD64. This suggests that the Olympus mnemonics generate *wordy* C code, whereby a significantly larger number of underlying operations (machine opcodes) are generated by the C compiler in comparison to the equivalent native C operation. However, it should be noted that the Olympus kernels include a full compacting heap manager and other runtime functions required to support the dynamic features of ePython that are absent from the static native C LINPACK kernel.

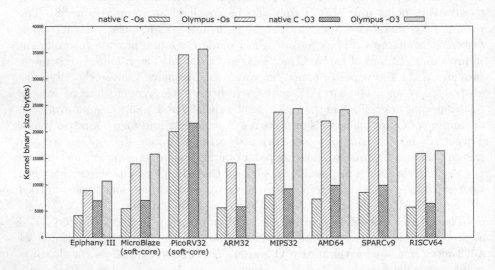

Fig. 3. LINPACK benchmark native C and Olympus kernel size

The figures for the MicroBlaze reflect the use of the floating-point emulation option for the LINPACK benchmark. Unsurprisingly, the code size difference is greater on the MicroBlaze in comparison to the Epiphany-III, at between 2 and 2.6 times larger (for both compiler optimisation levels), due to the increased number of operations generated by the Olympus mnemonics over native C, which is amplified by the floating-point emulation code required for the MicroBlaze LIN-PACK benchmark. There is up to a 20% advantage, on the Epiphany-III, in terms of code size in selecting -Os over -O3. However, for the SPARCv9 the advantage is minimal (0.048%) and is actually detrimental on the ARM32 (-1.67%). Overall, there is an average increase in code size of 7.5% selecting -O3 over -Os, which needs to be considered relative to any performance advantage gained by selecting the higher compiler optimisation level. For a micro-core architecture, such as the Epiphany-III, the code size saving of 20% (approximately 1.8KB) could be significant. Therefore, it is important to understand any performance differences between the two compiler optimisation levels.

4.3   Sieve of Eratosthenes Runtime Performance

The LINPACK benchmark tests the floating point performance of the Olympus abstract machine. Therefore, the Sieve of Eratosthenes[5] (Sieve) benchmark was selected to determine the size efficiency and integer performance of Olympus relative to handwritten (native) C. Figure 4 shows that, across compiler optimisation levels -Os and -O3, the Sieve benchmark displays a wider performance gap between the Olympus and native C kernels than was observed for the LIN-PACK benchmark, discussed in Sect. 4.1. The Olympus Sieve kernel performance ranges from approximately 1.4 times slower than native C on the Epiphany-III to over 5.5 times slower on the RISCV64. For all CPUs apart from the AMD64, the difference between Olympus and native C kernel performance is smaller at compiler optimisation level -O3 than at -Os. On the RISCV64, the native C Sieve kernel is 5.5 times faster than the Olympus kernel at -Os but is only 4 times faster at -O3.

Whilst the kernel performance difference between the -Os and -O3 GCC optimisation levels is greatest for the RISCV64, all of the RISC CPU Olympus kernels close the performance gap with the native C kernels at -O3. In comparison, the CISC AMD64 native C kernels are 1.7 times faster than Olympus at -Os and 2 times faster at -O3. This suggests that GCC is able to leverage the additional registers available on the RISCV64 over those available on the AMD64 to optimise the Olympus abstract machine code at -O3 optimisation level. However, the results for the Epiphany-III, MIPS32 and SPARCv9 suggest that the additional registers available on the Epiphany-III do not provide an advantage over the 32 available on the MIPS32 and SPARCv9.

---

[5] Due to the limited memory on the micro-core devices, the flag array size was reduced ($SIZE = 4095$) on the Epiphany-III, MicroBlaze and PicoRV32 micro-cores, on the other CPUs, per the original benchmark, $SIZE = 8190$.

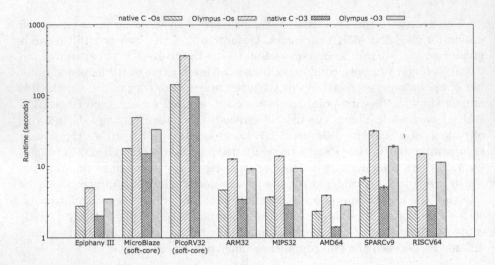

Fig. 4. Sieve benchmark native C and Olympus kernel runtimes, with error bars denoting standard deviation (log scale)

4.4 Sieve of Eratosthenes Code Size

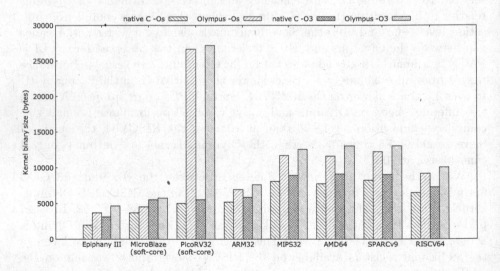

Fig. 5. Sieve benchmark native C and Olympus kernel size

Figure 5 shows the size of the Sieve kernels compiled with -Os and -O3 compiler optimisation levels for all CPUs. Whilst the Olympus kernel sizes are between near parity[6] and 1.9 times[7] that of the native C kernels for the other CPUs, the difference for the PicoRV32 is striking, with the Olympus kernel size around 5 times larger for both -Os and -O3. The Olympus kernel binary size for the PicoRV32 is explained by the fact that the GCC compiler allocates space in the kernel ELF file for the statically allocated C array used for the heap in the Olympus abstract machine. This is best illustrated by the size of the .bss segment reported by the GNU size utility for the Olympus Sieve kernel on the Epiphany-III, as shown in Listing 1.1, where the Olympus abstract machine heap is 24KB, and the 8MB default heap size of the RISCV64 desktop (threaded) kernel, as shown in Listing 1.2.

```
1    text      data       bss       dec      hex filename
2    4666      1208      25336     31210     79ea e_task.elf
```

Listing 1.1. Output of GNU size for Epiphany-III Olympus Sieve kernel

```
1    text      data       bss        dec      hex filename
2    9185       928    8001440    8011553    7a3f21 threaded_sieve.elf
```

Listing 1.2. Output of GNU size for RISCV64 Olympus Sieve kernel

```
1    text      data       bss       dec      hex filename
2   54668         0         0     54668     d58c rv_task.elf
```

Listing 1.3. Output of GNU size for PicoRV32 Olympus Sieve kernel

In contrast, for the PicoRV32, as shown in Listing 1.3, there is is only a single .text segment, containing the executable code, static values, strings and the Olympus heap array. This is due to the custom GNU *linker file* that is required to set up the memory map on the bare-metal PicoRV32 micro-core. The Epiphany-III and MicroBlaze micro-cores require similar custom linker files. However, the PicoRV32 file is unique in that the KEEP command is used to prevent the linker from performing *dead code removal* on the .text segment, which is vital to ensure that the PicoRV32 register initialisation is performed. As the register initialisation subroutine is not referenced in the C source code, it would be removed by the GCC linker when the kernel binary is created, if the KEEP command was not used. As all functions are placed in the .text segment and no dead code removal is performed, all unused library functions will also be kept in the final binary, unlike the binaries for other CPUs. Although this is an issue for PicoRV32 binaries, it impacts both Olympus and native C kernels. Therefore, a more detailed discussion of possible mitigations for this issue will not be provided, except to highlight the benefits of the Olympus dynamic code loading mechanism discussed in [25].

---

[6] MicroBlaze GCC optimisation level -Os.
[7] Epiphany-III GCC optimisation level -O3.

4.5   Optimising Loops

Whilst the performance of the Olympus abstract machine closes the gap with native C, the question remained as to whether the Olympus code generator could leverage the constrained vPython `for` loop to increase performance. Although it is considered *unpythonic* to use `range` to provide an index variable to iterate through the elements of a list [6], as shown in lines 2 and 3 of Listing 1.4, rather than accessing an iterator directly as shown in lines 5 and 6, the iterator is *immutable* and the list element cannot be updated, whereas the unpythonic approach allows the list element to be updated.

```
1  arr = [ "a", "b", "c"]
2  for i in range(0,len(arr)):
3    arr[i] = "x"
4
5  for i in arr:
6    i = "y"
```

Listing 1.4. *Unpythonic* and *Pythonic* list access

Although a `while` loop with a manual index variable is often used in this case, the unpythonic `for` loop approach provides a performance benefit in vPython. As the iterator is managed by the Olympus abstract machine and not the programmer, the vPython `for` loop can leverage a native C local loop index variable, for example $iter_i$ in Listing 1.5. This C variable not only controls the loop iteration but also is used to update the vPython list element, as shown in line 2 of Listing 1.5. In contrast, the `while` loop requires a lookup of the index variable in the Olympus environment for both loop control and list element updates, as shown in lines 5, 6 and 7 of Listing 1.5.

```
1  FOR($iter_i$,0,LDI(ADDRL(2)),1)
2  STAI(ADDRL(4),$iter_i$,TRUE);
3  END
4
5  WHILE((LDI(ADDRL(10))<LDI(ADDRL(2))))
6  STAI(ADDRL(4),LDI(ADDRL(10)),TRUE);
7  STI(ADDRL(10),(LDI(ADDRL(10))+1));
8  END
```

Listing 1.5. Example Olympus abstract machine code for vPython loop constructs

Two vPython variants[8] of the Sieve benchmark were used to determine the performance benefits of the `for` loop over the `while` loop alternative. These were compiled at GCC optimisation levels `-Os` and `-O3`, and run on the RISCV64. A native C version of the Byte Sieve benchmark was also compiled at both optimisation levels and run for comparison with the vPython variants. As detailed in

---

[8] Standalone versions, not run within the Eithne framework per Sect. 4.3.

Table 3, the `for` loop variant of the vPython Byte Sieve benchmark is approximately 3 times faster at both `-Os` and `-O3` GCC optimisation levels than the `while` loop variant. Furthermore, the `for` loop variant closes the performance gap with native C to around 1.5 times slower from approximately 5 times slower for the `while` loop variant (both at GGC optimisation level `-Os`).

Table 3. Byte Sieve benchmark runtime performance (seconds)

Code variant	GCC -Os	GCC -O3
vPython `while`	7.22	5.55
vPython `for`	2.33	1.92
Native C	1.33	1.20

The new version of the Olympus abstract machine for Vipera, that separates the object addressing from operation within the mnemonics, enables direct access to native C variables, as shown in Listing 1.5. This not only increases runtime performance but also simplifies the implementation of object references within the abstract machine , enabling the integration of Olympus applications with C frameworks, such as the Eithne benchmarking framework [24] and MPI (Message Passing Interface).

5 Conclusion

Whilst the vPython virtual machine provided a productive environment to deploy parallel codes written in a dynamic language to micro-core architectures, the performance overhead of the interpreter limited its use for real-world codes. However, the Olympus abstract machine approach resulted in kernel performance that was comparable to or, in some cases could exceed, native C kernels, as confirmed for the LINPACK benchmark in Sect. 4.1, and, at a worst-case, was around five times slower than native C for the Sieve of Eratosthenes benchmark (Sect. 4.3). Crucially, as shown in Sect. 4.5, this gap can be lowered to just over 1.5 times slower by leveraging the `for` loop's native C iterator. Furthermore, a single Python code is portable across these architectures, which is not the case for the standard C codes.

Vipera has also addressed the portability of user codes and underlying runtime support. All of the benchmarks run unmodified across all the supported platforms and the Olympus abstract machine builds from a single codebase, which results in significant programmer productivity gains. All device-specific code is managed within the mnemonics and runtime support functions, with the generated Olympus abstract machine code remaining the same across all platforms. Furthermore, the vPython virtual machine was also shown to be portable to a number of micro-core architectures with the minimum of effort.

Further work includes exploring automatic memory management for data and code, optimisation of the Olympus abstract machine, automatic dynamic function selection for the dynamic loading support discussed in [25], additional data types (byte arrays) to minimise the memory footprint of data and additional device support (GPUs and FPGAs) using OpenCL C and Xilinx HLS C.

Whilst this paper has focused on the assessment of the Olympus code generation model using vPython, we also believe that Vipera has a wider applicability to other dynamic programming languages targeting micro-core architectures.

References

1. Frontier to meet 20MW exascale power target set by DARPA in 2008. https://www.hpcwire.com/2021/07/14/frontier-to-meet-20mw-exascale-power-target-set-by-darpa-in-2008/
2. index — TIOBE - The software quality company. https://www.tiobe.com/tiobe-index/
3. June 2021 — TOP500. https://www.top500.org/lists/green500/2021/06/
4. PyCUDA 2021.1 documentation. https://documen.tician.de/pycuda/
5. The sieve of Eratosthenes benchmarks. https://www.keil.com/benchmarks/sieve.asp
6. Using an unpythonic loop - python anti-patterns documentation. https://docs.quantifiedcode.com/python-anti-patterns/readability/using_an_unpythonic_loop.html
7. Why you should benchmark your embedded system — SEGGER blog. https://testblog.segger.com/blog/2016/09/30/why-you-should-benchmark-your-embedded-system/
8. Epiphany SDK (ESDK) (2013), https://www.adapteva.com/epiphany-sdk/
9. NEON programmer's guide (2013). https://developer.arm.com/documentation/den0018/latest
10. Update 4: the 3 different code emitters · micro python: python for microcontrollers (2013), https://www.kickstarter.com/projects/214379695/micro-python-python-for-microcontrollers/posts/664832
11. MicroPython - python for microcontrollers (2018). http://micropython.org/
12. LINPACK_BENCH - The LINPACK benchmark (2019). https://people.sc.fsu.edu/~jburkardt/c_src/linpack_bench/linpack_bench.html
13. November 2019 — TOP500 supercomputer sites (2019). https://www.top500.org/lists/2019/11
14. Adapteva: E16G301 epiphany 16-core microprocessor. http://www.adapteva.com/docs/e16g301_datasheet.pdf (2013). Accessed 25 Jul 2018
15. Behnel, S., et al.: Cython: the best of both worlds. Comput. Sci. Eng. 13(2), 31–39 (2011)
16. Brown, N.: ePython: an implementation of python for the many-core epiphany co-processor. In: 2016 6th Workshop on Python for High-Performance and Scientific Computing (PyHPC), pp. 59–66, November 2016. https://doi.org/10.1109/PyHPC.2016.012
17. Brown, N., Jamieson, M.: Vipera. https://www.vipera.dev/
18. Catanzaro, B., Garland, M., Keutzer, K.: Copperhead: compiling an embedded data parallel language 46(8), 47–56. https://doi.org/10.1145/2038037.1941562

19. Dongarra, J.J., Luszczek, P., Petitet, A.: The LINPACK Benchmark: past, present and future. Concurrency Comput. Pract. Exp. **15**(9), 803–820 (2003)
20. Gilbreath, J.: A high-level language benchmark. In: BYTE Magazine Volume 06 Number 09 - Artificial Intelligence, pp. 180–198. https://archive.org/details/byte-magazine-1981-09/page/n181/mode/2up
21. Gualandi, H.M., Ierusalimschy, R.: Pallene: a statically typed companion language for lua. In: Proceedings of the XXII Brazilian Symposium on Programming Languages - SBLP 2018, pp. 19–26. ACM Press. https://doi.org/10.1145/3264637. 3264640, rlhttp://dl.acm.org/citation.cfm?doid=3264637.3264640
22. Ierusalimschy, R., de Figueiredo, L.H., Celes, W.: The Implementation of Lua 5.0 p. 18.https://www.lua.org/doc/jucs05.pdf
23. Jacob, D., Trinder, P., Singer, J.: Python programmers have GPUs too: automatic Python loop parallelization with staged dependence analysis. In: Proceedings of the 15th ACM SIGPLAN International Symposium on Dynamic Languages,pp. 42–54. DLS 2019, Association for Computing Machinery (2019). https://doi.org/ 10.1145/3359619.3359743
24. Jamieson, M.: Eithne micro-core benchmarking framework. https://gitlab.com/ mjamieson/eithne
25. Jamieson, M., Brown, N.: Compact native code generation for dynamic languages on micro-core architectures. In: Proceedings of the 30th ACM SIGPLAN International Conference on Compiler Construction, pp. 131–140. CC 2021, Association for Computing Machinery (2021). https://doi.org/10.1145/3446804.3446853
26. Jamieson, M., Brown, N., Liu, S.: Having your cake and eating it: exploiting python for programmer productivity and performance on micro-core architectures using ePython. In: Proceedings of the 19th Python in Science Conference : SciPy 2020, pp. 97–105 (2020). https://doi.org/10.25080/Majora-342d178e-00f, https:// conference.scipy.org/proceedings/scipy2020/pdfs/maurice_jamieson.pdf
27. Kudlur, M., Mahlke, S.: orchestrating the execution of stream programs on multicore platforms. In: Proceedings of the 29th ACM SIGPLAN Conference on Programming Language Design and Implementation, PLDI 2008, pp. 114–124. ACM (2008). https://doi.org/10.1145/1375581.1375596, http://doi.acm.org/ 10.1145/1375581.1375596
28. Lam, S.K., Pitrou, A., Seibert, S.: Numba: A LLVM-based Python JIT compiler. In: Proceedings of the Second Workshop on the LLVM Compiler Infrastructure in HPC, pp. 1–6 (2015). https://doi.org/10.1145/2833157.2833162
29. Lyberis, S., Pratikakis, P., Nikolopoulos, D.S., Schulz, M., Gamblin, T., de Supinski, B.R.: The Myrmics memory allocator: hierarchical, message-passing allocation for global address spaces. In: Proceedings of the 2012 International Symposium on Memory Management, ISMM 2012, pp. 15–24. ACM (2012). https://doi.org/10. 1145/2258996.2259001, http://doi.acm.org/10.1145/2258996.2259001
30. Rubinsteyn, A., Hielscher, E., Weinman, N., Shasha, D.: Parakeet: A Just-in-time parallel accelerator for python. In: Proceedings of the 4th USENIX conference on Hot Topics in Parallelism, p. 14. HotPar 2012, USENIX Association (2012). https://www.usenix.org/system/files/conference/hotpar12/hotpar12-final37.pdf

FFTc: An MLIR Dialect for Developing HPC Fast Fourier Transform Libraries

Yifei He[✉], Artur Podobas, Måns I. Andersson, and Stefano Markidis

KTH Royal Institute of Technology, Stockholm, Sweden
{yifeihe,podobas,mansande,markidis}@kth.se

Abstract. Discrete Fourier Transform (DFT) libraries are one of the most critical software components for scientific computing. Inspired by FFTW, a widely used library for DFT HPC calculations, we apply compiler technologies for the development of HPC Fourier transform libraries. In this work, we introduce FFTc, a domain-specific language, based on Multi-Level Intermediate Representation (MLIR), for expressing Fourier Transform algorithms. We present the initial design, implementation, and preliminary results of FFTc.

Keywords: MLIR · Fast Fourier Transform Compiler · DSL

1 Introduction

HPC libraries for computing Discrete Fourier Transforms (DFT) are critical computational building blocks for enabling signal processing, data analysis, and the solution of Partial Differential Equations (PDE). In particular, Fast Fourier Transform (FFT) algorithms solve DFT via $\mathcal{O}(n \log n)$ calculations, where n is the input size against the naive DFT implementation corresponding to a matrix-vector multiply with complex numbers requiring $\mathcal{O}(n^2)$ calculations.

Several algorithms for FFT have been designed, including the notorious Cooley-Tukey recursive scheme to the Stockham and Pease algorithms [11]. FFT algorithms can be expressed using a factorized formulation, e.g., the entire FFT operation is expressed as the multiplication of matrices, and different algorithms will correspond to various factorization forms. These matrices are largely sparse, and their final computation will still rely only on $\mathcal{O}(n \log n)$ operations. Therefore, from an abstraction point of view, we can express any FFT algorithms in terms of matrix multiplications. Most importantly for this work, different factorizations are better suited than others for achieving high-performance on a given system. For instance, Stockham FFT factorization is an excellent fit for accelerators while other factorizations containing block matrices are a good fit for hierarchical memory systems. For this reason, to be capable of expressing and generating automatically and optimizing different FFT algorithms for different architectures is critical for producing high-performance FFT libraries.

FFTW [8] is among the most successful implementations of FFT libraries. Inspired by the FFTW design and development, in this work, we propose a new

J. Singer et al. (Eds.): Euro-Par 2022 Workshops, LNCS 13835, pp. 80–92, 2023.
https://doi.org/10.1007/978-3-031-31209-0_6

framework, called FFTc (FFT compiler), for the automatic generation of FFT algorithms using the MLIR and LLVM compiler infrastructure. To achieve this, we design a new language to express FFT algorithms using different formulations. The major contributions of this paper are the following:

- We design and provide a first initial development of a domain-specific language for the automatic code generation of FFT algorithms, leveraging MLIR and LLVM infrastructure.
- We collect and analyze the preliminary performance results from small-size one-dimensional FFT and compare the performance with the FFTW performance.

2 Background

The goal of this work is to develop a DSL for FFT calculation. A direct computation of the Fourier transform is the multiplication of a DFT matrix by the input vector x. We can define the DFT_N matrix as:

$$\text{DFT}_{N_{m,n}} = (\omega_N)^{mn}, \quad \text{where} \quad \omega_N = \exp(-2\pi i/N) \quad \text{for} \quad 0 \leq m, n < N. \quad (1)$$

The most famous FFT algorithm was introduced in 1965 by Cooley and Tukey. This algorithm relies on the recursive nature of DFT i.e. several small DFTs can describe a large DFT. In this paper, we use a matrix-formalism to represent FFT algorithms where a matrix-factorization of the DFT matrix into sparse and structured matrices describes each FFT algorithm. For example the Cooley-Tukey factorization of DFT_4:

$$\text{DFT}_4 = \underbrace{\begin{bmatrix} 1 & & 1 & \\ & 1 & & 1 \\ 1 & & -1 & \\ & 1 & & -1 \end{bmatrix}}_{\text{DFT}_2 \otimes I_2} \begin{bmatrix} 1 & & & \\ & 1 & & \\ & & 1 & \\ & & & -i \end{bmatrix} \underbrace{\begin{bmatrix} 1 & 1 & & \\ 1 & -1 & & \\ & & 1 & 1 \\ & & 1 & -1 \end{bmatrix}}_{I_2 \otimes \text{DFT}_2} \begin{bmatrix} 1 & & & \\ & & 1 & \\ & 1 & & \\ & & & 1 \end{bmatrix}, \quad (2)$$

where the I is the identity matrix. Here, we see the use of DFT_2 in the formulation of DFT_4. In the example, we see the sparse (zeros in the matrices are omitted for clarity) and structured nature of the algorithm. The Cooley-Tukey general-radix decimation-in-time algorithm for N inputs can be written as:

$$\text{DFT}_N = (\text{DFT}_K \otimes I_M) \, D_M^N (I_K \otimes \text{DFT}_M) \Pi_K^N \quad \text{with} \quad N = MK, \quad (3)$$

where Π_K^N is a stride permute and D_M^N is a diagonal matrix of *twiddle*-factors. Different FFT algorithms, such as Stockham and Pease FFT can be expressed using different factorization schemes.

In this work, we use the LLVM (originally for Low-Level Virtual Machine) compiler infrastructure for the development of the FFT domain-specific language. LLVM is a collection of compiler and toolchain technologies: it consists of a set of modular compiler components, including the Clang front-ends, optimizer, code generator, debugger, linker, and OpenMP runtime. Particularly important for developing portable HPC code, the LLVM compiler technologies support many targets, including x86, Arm, and GPU systems [9].

The LLVM project also includes Multi-Level Intermediate Representation (MLIR), a project aiming at supporting the building of domain-specific compilers, and combining existing compiler infrastructure together. While MLIR (and the XLA compiler) was initially developed by Google for machine learning workloads, MLIR is widely used today for the development of domain-specific languages beyond machine and deep learning. To solve domain-specific problems, MLIR offers the infrastructure to define and introduce high-level abstractions and transforms [10]. The main mechanism to extend MLIR is the development of *dialects* that allow defining new operations, attributes, and types. In addition, MLIR allows using multiple dialects that can be used together within one module. Examples of existing MLIR dialects are the affine, LLVM, GPU, vector, SPIR-V dialects. In this work, we design and develop an MLIR dialect to express FFT libraries.

3   Related Work

Several efforts exist for the development of high-performance FFT libraries. The inspiration for developing an FFT DSL is FFTW [7], which is the most widely used open-source FFT library. At its heart, FFTW is an FFT compiler, based on Objective Caml, to generate Directed Acyclic Graphs (DAG) of FFT algorithms and performs algebraic optimization on them. FFTW uses a planner at runtime to recursively decompose the DFT problem into sub-problems. These sub-problems are solved directly by optimized, straight-line code that is automatically generated by a special-purpose compiler, called *genfft* [8]. An additional DSL for numerical kernels including FFT is SPIRAL. SPIRAL [6] is a program generation system for linear transforms and other mathematical functions that produces HPC code in C. SPIRAL also supports FFTs [5]: it applies pattern match and rewriting to generate optimal FFT formulation for different hardware, such as multicore systems. Then, SPIRAL maps the matrix formula to high-performance C code.

4   Methodology: A Domain-Specific Language for FFT

This section describes FFTc– a custom Domain-Specific Language (DSL) for describing Fast Fourier Transforms (FFT). Our aspiration with FFTc is to increase the productivity of algorithm developers without any loss in performance while at the same time being able to target multiple different backends (CPUs/GPUs/etc.) with the same input source code. In short, FFTc aims to increase *productivity*, *portability*, and (hopefully) *performance*.

The execution model and compilation pipeline are shown in Fig. 1. The current implementation supports the parts in dark color; the remaining parts will be the focus in the near future.

The FFTc compilation pipeline has five core parts: (a) is the translation from the DSL to the Abstract Syntax Tree (AST), (b) is generating the MLIR out of AST, (c) stands for progressive lowering from FFT dialect to LLVM dialect, going through different levels of abstraction represented by dialects, (d) emits LLVM IR out of the MLIR's LLVM dialect, (e) is the LLVM middle-end compilation and code generation.

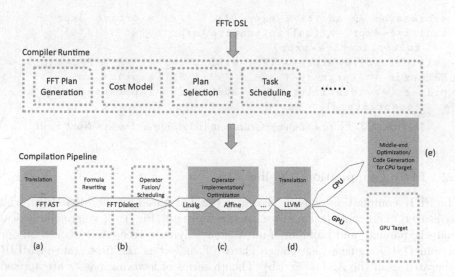

Fig. 1. Compilation Pipeline

4.1 The FFTc Language and Grammar

The goal of FFTc is to create an input language that resembles (as close as possible) that of mathematics, which we believe will help end-users in being more productive without losing familiarity with the code they are writing. An example source code of our is seen in Listing 1.1, where we have aimed to keep them as similar to abstract mathematical expressions as possible, such as Eq. (3). We support the *Kronecker product* through the binary operation '⊗', the matrix-matrix multiplication using '·', and the matrix multiplication with the twiddle matrix through the `twiddle`. Furthermore, we have a set of unary operations, such as creating the `identity` matrix, and calculating the `dft`. Finally, we have support for `permuting`. In short, we currently support all necessary language constructs to describe FFTs in a factorized form. Additionally, our grammar supports the correct right-associative binding of (e.g.,) matrix multiplication, which is different from the traditional left-associative binding of binary operators. A subset of the grammatical construct (in Backus-Naur form) is shown in

Listing 1.2. The grammatical construct is based on (and extended) from LLVM's
Kaleidoscope language tutorial [2].

```
1 var InputReal <4, 1> = [[1], [2], [3], [4]];
2 var InputImg  <4, 1> = [[1], [2], [3], [4]];
3 var InputComplex = createComplex(InputReal, InputImg);
4 var result =  (DFT(2) ⊗ I(2)) · twiddle(4,2) ·
5               (I(2) ⊗ DFT(2)) · Permute(4,2) · InputComplex
  ;
```

Listing 1.1. DSL FFT language

```
1 expression -> additive-expr ('+'| '-') additive-expr
2 additive-expr -> (multiplicative-expr ( '*' | '/' )
    multiplicative-expr)
3 multiplicative-expr -> (FFT-expr ( '*' | '/' ) FFT-expr) *
4 FFT-expr -> (primary ( '⊗' | '·' ) FFT-expr) *
5 primary -> identifierexpr | numberexpr | parenexpr |
    tensorliteral
```

Listing 1.2. FFTc Language Grammar Extension in Backus-Naur form

4.2 FFTc Compilation Pipeline

The FFTc compilation pipeline shown in Fig. 1 is based on the MLIR's tutorial
project [4]. The compilation starts at the frontend (Fig. 1:a), where the lexical
analysis, parsing, and building of an Abstract Syntax Tree (AST) based on our
custom DSL language take place. The FFT dialect is the first state of MLIR
generated from the AST (Fig. 1:b). Then a series of lowering passes are applied
(Fig. 1:c) on the FFT dialect in order to expand many of the custom operators
(e.g., the Kronecker product) into a lowered state. For example, a matrix multiplication, written in our language using "·", will be expanded to a three-level
nested loop implementing said matrix multiplication. Furthermore, we can apply
several existing MLIR optimization passes (such as Affine) in order to further
optimize the transformed kernels. Finally, near the end of the pipeline (Fig. 1:c),
we lower our representation to the LLVM Intermediate Representation (IR),
after which we inject the code into the LLVM backend for compilation towards
machine code (Fig. 1:d). We explain this pipeline in more detail next.

4.2.1 Phase 1: Translation The FFT dialect is the first dialect in the com-
pilation pipeline. The FFT dialect provides the basic building blocks for different
kinds of FFT algorithms and defines the complex tensor data type and operations.

- **FFT dialect data type:** The FFT dialect operates on the double tensor and
  complex tensor as well as scalar integer as attributes. There is `createComplex`
  to generate the complex tensor from the double tensor of real and imaginary
  parts.

- **FFT dialect operations:** We define the operations needed to implement various kinds of popular FFTs. Examples of such operators are the Kronecker product and matrix-matrix multiplication. We also define the DFT, Identity, and permute matrix generator. These make it a lot easier to construct the FFT algorithm with the similar notation and syntax in mathematics. The map of operations from FFTc DSL to MLIR FFT dialect is shown in Table 1.

With the FFT dialect implementation described above, we can generate MLIR out of AST, as shown in (a) to (b) in Fig. 1. Figure 2 shows an example of the FFT dialect IR that is translated from size 4 recursive FFT in Listing 1.1.

Table 1. From FFTc DSL to FFT Dialect MLIR

FFTc DSL	FFT Dialect
createComplex(A, B)	fft.createCT(a,b)
A · B	fft.matmul a, b :
A ⊗ B	fft.kroneckerproduct a, b
twiddle (a,b)	fft.twiddle (a , b)
I(size)	fft.identity (a)
DFT(size)	fft.dft(a)
Permute (a ,b)	fft.Permute(a, b)

4.2.2 Phase 2: Operator Implementation/Optimization MLIR supports different levels of abstraction through dialects. We lower the FFT dialect to a mix of dialects. Then, we can reuse the analysis/transform passes embedded in those dialects. We run shape inference to prepare for later transforms and perform progressive lowering to a mix of dialects to implement and optimize FFT operations.

- **Shape Inference:** In the FFTc DSL, all the operations operate on generic tensors. We do not need to explicitly specify the shape of tensor data. This reduces the efforts of the programmers. However, carrying shape information in the IR can simplify the workload of analysis and transform passes, as well as code generation. We can obtain the shape of input tensors during the initialization of constants. Later, we propagate the shapes through the computation to every operation involved. We implement a specific shape inference function for each operation based on the input augments, such as for the Kronecker product. All dimensions of the output tensor would be the multiplication of the corresponding dimensions of two input tensors.
- **Progressive Lowering:** The compilation pipeline generates the actual implementations of the operations, which we defined through progressive lowering. To reuse existing optimizations in MLIR's dialects, we lower the FFT dialect to a mix of dialects, comprising of Affine, Arithmetic, Complex and

MemRef dialects. The Affine dialect uses techniques from polyhedral compilation to provide a powerful abstraction for affine operations and analyses, such as dependence analysis and loop transformations. The Arithmetic dialect is intended to hold basic integer and floating-point mathematical operations, and the Complex dialect is intended to hold complex numbers creation and arithmetic operations. The MemRef dialect is intended to hold core memref creation and manipulation operations [3].

- **Affine Dialect:** We implement the computation-heavy part of the DSL in Affine dialect, by lowering from the tensor type that FFT dialect operates on to the MemRef type that is indexed via an affine loop-nest. Tensors represent an abstract value-typed sequence of data. By using tensor and tensor operations, we can increase the productivity of algorithm developers since it is similar to the notations used in mathematics. The MemRefs dialect, on the other hand, represents the lower level buffer access, builds a bridge to the actual computer memory.

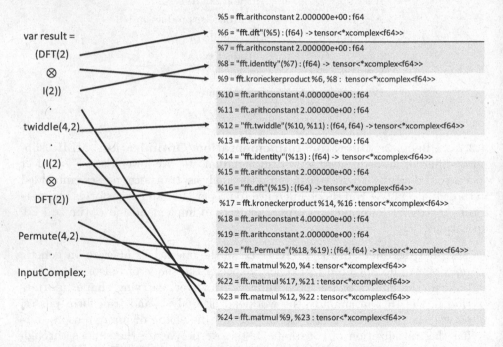

Fig. 2. Mapping from the Recursive FFT to MLIR.

To implement the operators, we allocate a chunk of memory for the output tensor, construct loops to compute each element of the output tensor, then store them to the corresponding index of the output memory. The scalarized tensor arithmetic operations are performed by corresponding operations in the Complex dialect. The lowering result of a matrix multiplication operator is shown in the Listing 1.3. We take advantage of the existing optimizations in the Affine dialect, such as loop fusion, AffineScalarReplacement and AffineLoopInvariantCodeMotion. These optimization passes can help perform operator fusion, eliminate redundant load/store and hoists loop invariant operations out of Affine loops.

```
1 From:
2     %10 = fft.matmul %9, %3 : (tensor<4x4xcomplex<f64>>,
3     tensor<4x1xcomplex<f64>>) ->
4     tensor<4x1xcomplex<f64>>
5 To:
6     affine.for %arg0 = 0 to 4 {
7       affine.for %arg1 = 0 to 1 {
8         affine.for %arg2 = 0 to 4 {
9           %18 = affine.load %9[%arg0, %arg2] :
10          memref<4x4xcomplex<f64>>
11          %19 = affine.load %3[%arg2, %arg1] :
12          memref<4x1xcomplex<f64>>
13          %20 = complex.mul %18, %19 : complex<f64>
14          %21 = affine.load %2[%arg0, %arg1] :
15          memref<4x1xcomplex<f64>>
16          %22 = complex.add %21, %20 : complex<f64>
17          affine.store %22, %2[%arg0, %arg1] :
18          memref<4x1xcomplex<f64>>
19        }
20      }
21    }
```

Listing 1.3. Affine Code Example for FFT.MatMul Operation

4.2.3   Phase 3: Translation There exist infrastructures in MLIR to perform a full conversion from the Affine, MemRef, and Complex dialects to the LLVM dialect. Then, we can emit the LLVM IR from the LLVM dialect.

4.2.4   Phase 4: Code Generation We set up a JIT compiler using the MLIR wrapper over LLVM OrcJit, and pass the optimization and debug flags to the JIT compiler. The pass manager is also populated by MLIR. Then, the JIT compiler will perform the LLVM's middle-end optimization and code generation.

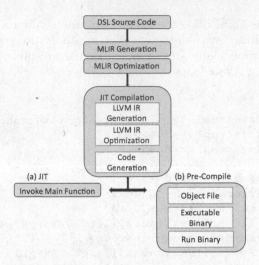

Fig. 3. Compilation modes.

4.2.4.1 Ahead-Of-Time vs Just-In-Time Compilation

We support two types of compilation modes in FFTc: Ahead-of-Time (AOT) and Just-in-Time (JIT) compilation. The compilation modes can be seen in Fig. 3, where they share multiple components and are in line with similar compilation flows (e.g., in OpenCL's Online/Offline compilation [1]). In short, both modes start by parsing the DSL source code and transforming/optimizing it using our MLIR intermediate representation. Next, we lower the MLIR down to LLVM IR. Once in LLVM IR, the two modes differ: using the JIT mode, we directly execute the main function of our compiled targets and exit afterward. The AOT mode, instead, transforms the LLVM IR representation to an object file, links with eventual standard libraries, and outputs a machine code binary file that can be invoked by the user.

Using either model has benefits and limitations. For example, the AOT mode can be faster and speed up the final execution significantly but has the limitation that the FFT size needs to be constant. The JIT model, on the other hand, is slower but allows the FFT size to be variable at runtime. In short, the AOT mode trades flexibility for performance, while the JIT mode honors flexibility over performance.

5   Experimental Setup

We evaluate our FFTc on the Kebnekaise supercomputer that is located at the HPC2N HPC center in Umeå, Sweden. Kebnekaise nodes have a dual-socket Intel Xeon Gold 6132 CPU, 192 GB of RAM. The operating system is Ubuntu 20.04.4 LTS. The version of LLVM we use to embed the FFTc is 15.0.0. We run the Ahead-of-Time compilation mode FFTc 1,000 times, and we calculate error computing the standard deviation for 30 execution rounds. We developed a Python script to generate the recursive implementation of the Cooley-Tukey FFT algorithm, using our FFTc DSL. An example of the output program is shown in Listing 1.1. Albeit our script can generate different FFT algorithm implementations, in this paper, we only present the results of the recursive Cooley-Tukey algorithm.

6   Results

As first step of our evaluation, we verify the correctness of DSL implementation. We test different random input vectors with different sizes: the input sizes are the powers of two, from 32 to 1024. We employ complex numbers in double-precision. We compare the results with the NumPy's FFT function, that is based on FFTW. The error is calculated as $\frac{|result_{DSL} - result_{Numpy}|}{FFT_{size}}$. The error is smaller than 1e-7 for each run.

For the next step, we evaluate the performance in the JIT mode. We measure the execution time of size 32 recursive FFT under JIT mode. The execution time is shown in Fig. 4. In the figure, the item Parser&MLIRGen stands for frontend compilation, 'builtin.func' stands for MLIR compilation pipeline, 'Jit' stands for both LLVM Jit compilation and running time. It is clear from analyzing the figure that the frontend takes a minor portion of the execution time. The MLIR pipeline takes the largest part of the execution time. Most of the time is spent in the optimization passes such as AffineLoopFusion and AffineScalarReplacement. We can choose whether to run these optimization passes or not by passing optimization flag to FFTc, currently there are O0/O2/O3 available. The Jit part takes much smaller portion compared with MLIR pipeline, under O3 optimization option for both LLVM middle-end compilation and code generation. In actual applications, FFT algorithms may run many times while only need to be compiled once, so the compilation time does not matter considerably. As a future plan, we intend to reduce the compilation time, such as multi-threading the compiler and remove redundant operations in Affine passes.

Under Pre-Compiled mode, we compare the FFTc pre-compiled binary with FFTW 3.3. We built FFTW with gcc compiler, enabled the SIMD instructions. The input size of the FFT are the powers of 2, we use single thread to run the program. The result is shown in Fig. 5, the standard deviation is shown as the black lines over bars.

We run four versions of FFT using FFTc: direct DFT implementation and Cooley-Tukey recursive FFT implementation with different optimization flags (O0/O2/O3). It is expected that the DFT performs much better than recursive implementations, because current implementation for FFT is computed through dense matrix multiplication, and to achieve the O(N log N) complexity FFT must be sparse matrix computation. The workload of the currently developed recursive FFT is much larger than DFT. However, we intend to use the current solution to showcase the functionality of FFTc and are planning to rewrite the

Total Execution Time Report

Wall Time / Seconds	Name
0.0034 (0.0%)	Parser & MLIRGen
0.0003 (0.0%)	Inliner
0.0000 (0.0%)	(A) CallGraph
0.0000 (0.0%)	'builtin.func' Pipeline
0.0002 (0.0%)	Canonicalizer
6.2268 (90.4%)	builtin.func' Pipeline
0.0001 (0.0%)	{anonymous}::ShapeInference
0.0001 (0.0%)	Canonicalizer
0.0000 (0.0%)	CSE
0.0000 (0.0%)	(A) DominanceInfo
0.0116 (0.2%)	{anonymous}::AffineToLLVMLoweringPass
0.0226 (0.4%)	Canonicalizer
0.0014 (0.0%)	CSE
0.0000 (0.0%)	(A) DominanceInfo
0.6238 (9.1%)	AffineLoopFusion
5.5622 (80.7%)	AffineScalarReplacement
0.0000 (0.0%)	(A) PostDominanceInfo
0.0000 (0.0%)	(A) DominanceInfo
0.0009 (0.0%)	AffineLoopInvariantCodeMotion
0.0384 (0.6%)	{anonymous}::FFTToLLVMLoweringPass
0.0000 (0.0%)	output
0.6154 (8.9%)	Jit
0.0057 (0.1%)	Rest
6.8903 (100%)	Total

Fig. 4. JIT Mode Performance for size 32 recursive FFT

computation in sparse form as a future work. The performance with optimization flag O3 is better that O2 and O0. The difference between O2 and O3 flag is that under O2, the AffineScalarReplacement pass will not be executed. For size

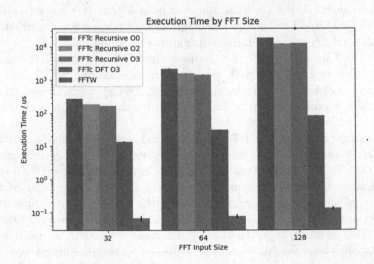

Fig. 5. FFTc Single Thread Performance Compared with FFTW

128 the O2 is slightly better than O3. Investigating the MLIR, the AffineScalar-Replacement performs memory access optimizations. In addition, there is also a similar optimization pass in LLVM pipeline. We plan to further investigate this issue in the future.

When comparing the performance between FFTc Cooley-Tukey code and FFTW, we note that here is still a significant performance gap. We believe that this gap can be attributed to (amongst others) the following reasons:

– The recursive factorized FFTs are computed through matrix-matrix multiplication where the matrices are not expressed as sparse matrices.
– We do not take full advantage of MLIR/LLVM infrastructure to generate high performance code. Examples of such a features are loop tiling, unrolling and jam and vectorization in the MLIR/LLVM pipeline.
– We do not support yet an autotuning mechanism, such as the FFTW *planner*, to decompose the FFT problem into simpler sub-problems, later solve the simpler sub-problems using codelets generated by genfft. Currently, our implementation is similar to genfft: for the FFTs with large-size input, the generated code is extremely large and introduces considerable compilation overhead.

7   Discussion and Conclusion

In this paper, we have introduced FFTc– an emerging, work-in-progress DSL for describing different FFTs variants. The goal of FFTc is to decouple algorithm description from hardware-specific details and ultimately provide higher productivity and better portability without sacrificing performance. To this end, we have chosen an abstract language representation that is not unlike the mathematical formulas we are used to describing FFTs. We show how such an abstract language design can be mapped down-to machine code by leveraging existing MLIR and LLVM infrastructure. The performance – while not a direct objective of this paper – of our DSL is not yet on par with state-of-the-art FFTW, but is never-the-less a good starting point to further build upon in future performance-focused studies, such as extending our compiler with support for OpenMP tasking or vectorization.

Acknowledgement. Funding for the work is received from the European High-Performance Computing Joint Undertaking (JU), Grant Agreement No. 3893 (IO-SEA). I want to thank Steven W. D. Chien (wdchien@kth.se) for his help with the proofread.

References

1. Intel   Online/Offline   Compilation.   https://www.intel.com/programmable/technical-pdfs/683521.pdf
2. Kaleidoscope: implementing a parser and AST. https://llvm.org/docs/tutorial/MyFirstLanguageFrontend/LangImpl02.html

3. MLIR dialects document. https://mlir.llvm.org/docs/Dialects/
4. MLIR toy language. https://mlir.llvm.org/docs/Tutorials/Toy/Ch-1/
5. Franchetti, F., al.: Discrete fourier transform on multicore. IEEE Sig. Process. Mag. **26**(6), 90–102 (2009)
6. Franchetti, F., al.: SPIRAL: extreme performance portability. From High Level Specification High Performance Code **106**(11), 1935–1968 (2018)
7. Frigo, M.: A fast fourier transform compiler. In: ACM SIGPLAN 1999 Conference on Programming Language Design and Implementation, pp. 169–180 (1999)
8. Frigo, M., Johnson, S.G.: The design and implementation of FFTW3. Proc. IEEE **93**(2), 216–231 (2005)
9. Lattner, C., Adve, V.: LLVM: a compilation framework for lifelong program analysis amp; transformation. In: CGO 2004, pp. 75–86 (2004)
10. Lattner, C., al.: MLIR: Scaling compiler infrastructure for domain specific computation. In: 2021 IEEE/ACM International Symposium on Code Generation and Optimization, pp. 2–14 (2021)
11. Van Loan, C.: Computational frameworks for the fast Fourier transform. In: SIAM (1992)

Hetero-Par

Workshop on Algorithms, Models and Tools for Parallel Computing on Heterogeneous Platforms (HeteroPar)

Workshop Description

HeteroPar is a forum for researchers working on algorithms, programming languages, tools, and theoretical models for efficiently solving complex problems on heterogeneous parallel platforms. Heterogeneity is emerging as one of the most profound and challenging characteristics of today's parallel environments. From the macro level, where heterogeneous networks interconnect distributed computers of diverse architectures, to the micro level, where ever deeper memory hierarchies and specialized accelerator architectures are increasingly common, the impact of heterogeneity on parallel processing is rapidly increasing. Traditional parallel algorithms, programming environments and tools designed for legacy homogeneous multiprocessors will at best achieve a small fraction of the efficiency and the performance expected from tomorrow's highly diverse parallel computing architectures. Therefore, efficiently using these new and multifarious parallel architectures requires innovative ideas, new models, novel algorithms, and other specialized or unified programming environments and tools.

The 20th International Workshop on Algorithms, Models and Tools for Parallel Computing on Heterogeneous Platforms (HeteroPar 2022) took place in Glasgow, Scotland, organized for the 14th time in conjunction with the Euro-Par annual international conference. The format of the workshop included one keynote and 11 technical presentations. The workshop received good attendance of around 25 people on average throughout the day. This year, the workshop received 22 paper submissions from 11 countries. After a thorough peer-reviewing process that included discussion and agreement among reviewers whenever necessary, the program chair selected 11 papers for presentation at the workshop. The review process focused on the quality of the papers, their innovation, and applicability to heterogeneous architectures. The quality and the relevance of the selected papers is high.

The accepted papers represent an interesting mix of topics, addressing the performance portability, programming models, dynamic task management, reconfigurable architectures, and applications of artificial intelligence oriented towards heterogeneous platforms, as the basis for upcoming exascale computers. The program chair thanks all authors, the Program Committee, and the Steering Committee for their support in making the workshop a successful event. Special thanks are due to the Euro-Par organizers for hosting the HeteroPar community, and especially to the workshop chairs Dora Blanco Heras and Jeremy Singer for their help and support.

Organization

Steering Committee

Rosa M. Badia — Barcelona Supercomputing Center, Spain
Anne Benoit — Ecole Normale Supérieure de Lyon, France
Alexey Lastovetsky — University College Dublin, Ireland
Leonel Sousa — INESC-ID/IST, University of Lisbon, Portugal
Denis Trystram — University Grenoble-Alpes, France
Roman Wyrzykowski — Czestochowa University of Technology, Poland

Program Chair

Aleksandar Ilic — INESC-ID/IST, University of Lisbon, Portugal

Program Committee

Giovanni Agosta — Politecnico di Milano, Italy
Hartwig Anzt — Karlsruhe Institute of Technology, Germany
Raja Appuswamy — EURECOM, France
Michael Bader — Technical University of Munich, Germany
Jorge Barbosa — Faculdade de Engenharia do Porto, Portugal
George Bosilca — University of Tennessee, USA
Xing Cai — Simula, Norway
Jorge Ejarque — Barcelona Supercomputing Center, Spain
Toshio Endo — Tokyo Institute of Technology, Japan
Brice Goglin — Inria & University of Bordeaux, France
Alfredo Goldman — São Paulo University, Brazil
Francisco Igual — Universidad Complutense de Madrid, Spain
Joanna Kolodziej — NASK, Warsaw, Poland
Hatem Ltaief — KAUST, Saudi Arabia
Maciej Malawski — AGH University of the Science and Technology, Poland
Ravi Reddy Manumachu — University College Dublin, Ireland
Raymond Namyst — University of Bordeaux & Inria, France

Ricardo Nobre   INESC-ID/IST, University of Lisbon,
                                       Portugal

Dana Petcu   University of Timisoara, Romania
Loic Pottier   University of Southern California, USA
Radu Prodan   University of Klagenfurt, Austria
Matei Ripeanu   The University of British Columbia,
                                       Canada
Paolo Romano   INESC-ID/IST, University of Lisbon,
                                       Portugal
Paolo Trunfio   University of Calabria, Italy
Pedro Tomás   INESC-ID/IST, University of Lisbon,
                                       Portugal
Didem Unat   Koç University, Turkey
Sebastien Varrette   University of Luxembourg

Programming Heterogeneous Architectures Using Hierarchical Tasks

Mathieu Faverge, Nathalie Furmento, Abdou Guermouche, Gwenolé Lucas[(✉)],
Raymond Namyst, Samuel Thibault, and Pierre-André Wacrenier

LaBRI/Inria/University of Bordeaux/CNRS/Bordeaux INP, Bordeaux, France
{mathieu.faverge,nathalie.furmento,abdou.guermouche,gwenole.lucas,
raymond.namyst,samuel.thibault,pierre-andre.wacrenier}@inria.fr

Abstract. Task-based systems have gained popularity as they promise
to exploit the computational power of complex heterogeneous systems. A
common programming model is the so-called *Sequential Task Flow* (STF)
model, which, unfortunately, has the intrinsic limitation of supporting
static task graphs only. This leads to potential submission overhead and
to a static task graph not necessarily adapted for execution on heterogeneous systems. A standard approach is to find a trade-off between
the granularity needed by accelerator devices and the one required by
CPU cores to achieve performance. To address these problems, we extend
the STF model of STARPU [5] to enable tasks subgraphs at runtime.
We refer to these tasks as *hierarchical tasks*. This approach allows for a
more dynamic task graph. Combined with an automatic data manager,
it allows to dynamically adapt the granularity to meet the optimal size
of the targeted computing resource. We show that the model is correct
and we provide an early evaluation on shared memory heterogeneous
systems, using the CHAMELEON [1] dense linear algebra library.

Keywords: Multicore · accelerator · GPU · heterogeneous
computing · task graph · programming model · runtime system · dense
linear algebra

1 Introduction

Due to the recent evolution of High Performance Computing systems toward
heterogeneous multicore architectures, many research efforts have recently been
devoted to the design of runtime systems that support portable programming
techniques and tools to exploit the complex hardware. Runtime systems with
mature implementations are now available both for regular homogeneous multi-
core systems and for complex heterogeneous systems. Standards like OPENMP
(since version 4.0) support the task-based paradigm with applications represented as direct acyclic graph (DAG) of tasks.

However, the task-based paradigm poses several problems when trying to
exploit heterogeneous platforms efficiently. First, the computing resources of

© The Author(s), under exclusive license to Springer Nature Switzerland AG 2023
J. Singer et al. (Eds.): Euro-Par 2022 Workshops, LNCS 13835, pp. 97–108, 2023.
https://doi.org/10.1007/978-3-031-31209-0_7

heterogeneous platforms have diverse characteristics and requirements. GPU devices typically favor large data sets, whereas conventional CPU cores reach peak performance with fine-grain kernels working on a reduced memory footprint. Systems usually have a much larger number of CPU units than GPUs, having more small tasks may lead to better performance. Several efforts have tried to tackle this problem either by finding the best trade-off between the optimal granularity of each device [1,7,17], or by aggregating CPU cores to process a task which was meant to be executed by an accelerator like a GPU [9,15]. Alternatively, some preliminary work has considered splitting the tasks on CPU cores [18]. Even though these approaches are efficient in specific contexts like dense linear algebra, they suffer from the fact that the task graph is static and does not allow to select an alternative granularity for a given operation at runtime. As an example, when designing linear algebra solvers based on low-rank approximation algorithms, it is almost impossible to statically predict the right DAG to ensure good numerical accuracy [2,6,8].

These runtime systems all use high-level descriptions of dependencies to build the task graph at runtime, and then schedule the corresponding computations on available resources. Several approaches are used to build the task graph. Most of the previously cited runtime systems rely on the so-called *Sequential Task-Flow* model (e.g. OPENMP, STARSS, STARPU) to build the task graph: by relying on data access-modes and a sequential submission order, dependencies between tasks can be inferred through data dependency analysis [3] ensuring the so-called *Sequential Consistency* at runtime. Other runtime systems such as PARSEC use the parameterized task-graph programming model (PTG) [10] where the task graph is unrolled at runtime using a high-level description of the dataflow corresponding to the computations. Alternatively, other runtime systems use a different paradigm for expressing computations. LEGION describes logical regions of data to express the data flow and dependencies between tasks. All these programming models differ with respect to usability and the overhead induced on the underlying runtime system.

In this paper, we propose a new type of task, namely the *hierarchical tasks*, which can transform themselves into a new task-graph dynamically at runtime. Programmers only need to provide hints stating which tasks can be transformed into a hierarchical task. The runtime system can then delay the submission of parts of the task graph to support dynamic implementation selection, to parallelize the task insertion process, and to strongly reduce the number of tasks in the runtime system. This approach is similar to what is done in OPENMP for the nested task-based parallelization scheme. However, we extend it to handle heterogeneous platforms while expressing fine grain dependencies. This is possible thanks to an advanced data manager which can dynamically and asynchronously change the data layout. The proposed model associated to these *hierarchical tasks* addresses the issues mentioned above: 1) How to make the task graph more dynamic? 2) How to reduce the overhead of the runtime system? 3) How to overcome the intrinsic limitation of the sequential task flow submission process? While this model is generic and targets distributed heterogeneous architectures, in this paper, we focus on an initial implementation for shared memory heterogeneous architectures. Our contribution is two-fold: 1) We present an advanced data management engine which supports asynchronous data layout modification, 2) We show how we extend the sequential task flow model to support hierarchical tasks and present our implementation within the STARPU runtime system.

2 Related Work

Several efforts have targeted the problem of reducing the overhead of task-based runtime systems (mainly for those based on the sequential task flow model) or enhancing the amount of parallelism provided by such systems. [4] analyzes the limiting factors in the scalability of a task-based runtime system and proposes individual solutions for each of the listed challenges, including a wait-free dependency system and a scalable scheduler design based on delegation instead of work-stealing. Alternative approaches consider advanced dependency management. For instance, [11] proposes an eager approach for releasing data dependencies. Following this approach, the execution of tasks will not be delayed until their predecessor tasks completely finish their execution. Instead, tasks will be launched for execution as soon as their data requirements are available. Alternatively, [15] introduces worksharing tasks. These are tasks that internally leverage worksharing techniques to exploit fine-grained structured loop-based parallelism without requiring a barrier.

The closest contribution to our proposition from the perspective of task dependencies was introduced in [16] as the concept of *weak dependencies*. It is an extension of the OPENMP task-nesting model which enhances the dataflow model of OPENMP by supporting fine-grained dependencies between any set of tasks. Our contribution is a generalization of the weak dependency concept to the heterogeneous case where memory consistency is not ensured by the underlying hardware, thus needing an advanced data manager (see Sect. 3). Alternatively, some preliminary work targeting heterogeneous architectures has considered splitting the tasks when assigned to CPU cores in the context of ParSEC [18] and XKaapi [12].

From the point of view of advanced/dynamic task management and generation, several efforts have been made to allow task-based runtime systems to have a more dynamic expressiveness. In TaskFlow [13], advanced tasking schemes are introduced including dynamic, composable and conditional tasking. Dynamic tasking, in particular, allows to dynamically generate a sub-DAG from a given task. However, a synchronization is added at the end of each hierarchical task to ease the dependencies management. Furthermore, data management must be handled by the programmers: it is their responsibility to change the layout of data when needed. [14] introduces the IRIS runtime which has the ability to perform dynamic task partitioning (either performed by the user or automatically via a polyhedral compiler). However, no details were provided to illustrate how dependencies are handled in this context. Finally, an advanced runtime system supporting hierarchical tasks in the context of low-rank linear algebra solvers is presented in [6]. In this work, hierarchical tasks are introduced and the dependencies are expressed at the finest level. However, the data management is straightforward since the partitioning of data is performed statically at the beginning of the execution.

3   Automatic Data Management

Data handling is at the heart of STARPU both to automatically infer dependencies between tasks in the STF model and to automatically manage data transfers between the different memory banks of a distributed/heterogeneous system. To benefit from these automation, applications must register the data that are handled by the tasks. To do so, STARPU provides an opaque data structure called *handle* which is an abstract view of a registered data. Handles are coupled with an access mode (read-only, read-write, ...) and are used as task parameters. It is mandatory for a task to access a piece of data through the associated handle. To ease data manipulation, STARPU brings the notion of *data filter*, a tool to partition data associated with a handle into subdata parts associated with new subhandles. Indeed, instead of registering all data subsets independently, it is often more convenient to register a large piece of data and to recursively partition it. Once a handle is partitioned, we can observe that the same piece of data can be designated simultaneously by several handles. Data in read-only access mode can advantageously be accessed simultaneously at different partitioning levels by several tasks. However, when a data is accessed in write access mode, this access must be exclusive for coherency purpose. This property is ensured by STARPU when a single partitioning is used for a data, but may be violated when several handles point to the same data. To deal with this problem, STARPU provides functions to invalidate other handles to ensure they cannot be used to access their underlying data, and to unpartition subhandles back into the main handle to gather the subdata.

We propose a mechanism to automate the management of several simultaneous partitions. This mechanism enhances STARPU such that it automatically inserts partition or unpartition tasks as needed. First, programmers need to define the partitioning scheme through the *plan* operation which declares the partitioning to STARPU, and can be seen as the declaration of a new set of subhandles. Once a plan is performed, it is possible to submit tasks using the initial handle or any of the subhandles even if the actual partitioning has not been done yet. Furthermore, several partitioning schemes can be planned simultaneously.

The data manager will then handle the actual partitioning tasks and data coherency. At runtime, STARPU will introduce coherency synchronization: when a task is ready to be executed, STARPU must ensure that the partition associated with each handle it uses is valid. If a data is accessed in read-only mode, STARPU will allow different partitioning to coexist. As soon as a data is accessed in read-write mode, STARPU will automatically (and recursively) unpartition subdata and activate only the partitioning leading to the handle being written to. Figure 1 shows a matrix on which two partition plans are defined. The matrix is first initialized through its root handle, then modified using the vertical partitioning, and finally checks are performed in both horizontal and vertical stripes.

Figure 1a shows the state of the DAG and the data-layout after the execution of the plan operations and the insertion of the initialization task. With the first task using a vertical stripe, STARPU will automatically insert the corresponding *partitioning* task (see Fig. 1b). The same scheme is then applied when submitting tasks working on the horizontal layout and vertical layout in read-mode. One should note that C_{v_1} and C_{v_2} share the same vertical layout as V_1 and V_2, so no partition operation is needed for these tasks. On the contrary, tasks C_{H_1} and C_{H_2} do not share any handles with those using the vertical layout. However the data manager knows that these handles share a common ancestor (the whole matrix) and thus it will insert as needed the unpartition/partition tasks to make the data available to the tasks using the horizontal layout. This is illustrated in Fig. 1c where the U_v and P_h tasks are inserted, making the tasks using the horizontal layout depend on them. Finally, when the partition needs to be cleaned, the final unpartition task is inserted (see Fig. 1d).

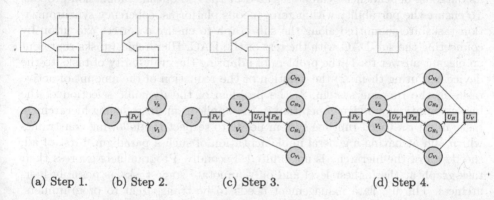

(a) Step 1.   (b) Step 2.   (c) Step 3.   (d) Step 4.

Fig. 1. Example of the behavior of the automatic data manager. Dotted border stands for *inactive*, solid border stands for *active*. Red border stands for *read-write partitioned*. Green border stands for *read-only partitioned* or *unpartitioned*. Step 1. Root handle initialization and partition plan, *Step 2.* Read-Write Vertical partitions, *Step 3.* 3 Read-Only active partitions, *Step 4.* Partition clean.

The previous example illustrates the general behavior of the data manager. More precisely, during the submission of tasks, each handle in the partitioning hierarchy can be either *inactive* (one cannot access the piece of data), *read-write-active* (one can read/write to the piece of data or a subpart of it), or *read-only-active* (one can only read from the piece of data or a subpart of it). The main handle at the root of the partitioning hierarchy is always *read-write-active*. Each handle in the hierarchy, when active, is additionally either *unpartitioned* (one can read/write the piece of data itself), *read-write-partitioned* (one can only write to the subpieces of data), or *read-only-partitioned* (one can read the piece of data or subpieces of data) ; when it is partitioned, its children subhandles in the hierarchy are active.

When submitting a task that accesses a handle within the hierarchy, STARPU will automatically ensure that the handle is active. This possibly requires recursively making its ancestors active by submitting partitioning tasks for them, possibly starting right from the root handle of the hierarchy. This also possibly requires recursively submitting unpartitioning tasks for some subhandles which were previously written to. In the case of the transition from Fig. 1b to Fig. 1c, STARPU indeed had to submit the unpartition task of the root handle, and repartition it.

4   The Hierarchical Task Paradigm

In a formal way, a hierarchical task is simply a regular task that can, at runtime, submit a sub-DAG instead of performing actual computations. Processing a hierarchical task consists in the submission of its corresponding task subgraph, its outgoing dependencies can be released at the end of that submission process. To ensure the portability with heterogeneous platforms, coherency synchronization tasks are submitted along the sub-graph to ensure a correct execution by connecting the sub-DAG with the rest of the DAG. Hierarchical tasks represent an elegant answer to: 1) the problem of adapting the granularity of tasks to the device executing them, 2) the question of the reduction of the amount of active tasks in the runtime system, 3) the problem of the dynamic selection of the implementation of a given operation in the application. Introducing hierarchical tasks in a task-based runtime system needs to respect the following constraints which aim at having a general implementation of such a paradigm. First of all, the depth of the hierarchy is not limited. Secondly, Programmers express their task-graph at the highest level and only annotate some tasks as possibly hierarchical. Thirdly, data management needs to be transparent to programmers. Finally, task dependencies always have to be inferred at the deepest level.

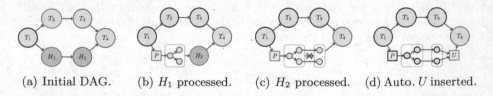

(a) Initial DAG.   (b) H_1 processed.   (c) H_2 processed.   (d) Auto. U inserted.

Fig. 2. Example of a DAG with 2 hierarchical tasks and 4 regular tasks. (Color figure online)

Figure 2a shows an execution scenario for a given task graph where **blue** tasks could be transformed into hierarchical tasks. The state of each task (i.e. node in the graph) is described by its border: 1) a ready task is green (all dependencies are met), 2) a not-ready task is red (some dependencies are unsatisfied), 3) an already executed task is **black**. Thus, we can see in Fig. 2a that T_1 has completed its execution making T_2 and H_1 ready for execution. T_2 and T_3 execute as normal tasks, while H_1 is processed, i.e. its corresponding subDAG is submitted, resulting to Fig. 2b. The dependency between H_1 and H_2 is then released, making H_2 ready for processing. Furthermore, we can see that after the processing of H_2 (see Fig. 2c) the dependencies between the resulting submitted tasks are inferred by the runtime system at the deepest level of the hierarchy.

We now have to consider how the data coherency will be achieved between the DAG and the subDAGs. Introducing hierarchical tasks in a task-based runtime system requires to change the granularity of data dynamically at runtime each time a hierarchical task has to be processed. We propose to automatically insert a data management task ahead of a task requiring data which are not in the correct layout by relying on the data manager introduced in Sect. 3. Figure 2b shows the insertion of the partitioning task P (resp. U) ahead of the subgraph produced by H_1 (resp. T_4). We can also notice that there is no data management task between the subgraphs produced by H_1 and H_2 since they share the same data layout. Finally, it is important to emphasize that hierarchical tasks are processed when their dependencies are fulfilled. However the actual computations tasks submitted by these hierarchical tasks are executed whenever they are ready. Thus we need to ensure a correct order of the actual computations.

4.1 Ensuring the Correctness of the DAG

We now show why the hierarchical task model to extend the STF model produces a correct DAG regardless of the depth of the hierarchy. First of all, as stated above, the STF model infers the dependencies from data access modes of individual tasks while relying on the sequential consistency. Introducing hierarchical tasks makes the submission process parallel while in the STF model, the submission is done by a single entity. We show that the dependencies respect the STF model by discussing four simple scenarios which are building blocks for any general DAG to show its correctness. The two first scenarios (T–T and T–H) will not be discussed since they inherently respect the sequential consistency.

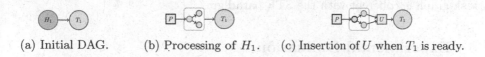

(a) Initial DAG.   (b) Processing of H_1.   (c) Insertion of U when T_1 is ready.

Fig. 3. Example of a scenario where a task follows a hierarchical task.

Task following hierarchical task. Figure 3 illustrates this scenario (H–T). The main problem is that the regular task is by construction submitted before the tasks resulting from the hierarchical task (H_1 in Fig. 3). This may violate the order required by the sequential consistency. However, the hierarchical task has changed the data layout before it starts its execution (see Fig. 3b). Thus the task following the hierarchical task (T_1 in Fig. 3) will request the data layout to be changed. The data manager will then automatically submit data management tasks to turn back data to their original layout. These data management tasks will be inserted ahead of the task in the DAG and will depend on the data produced by the DAG resulting from the execution of the hierarchical task (see Fig. 3c). Therefore, the data management tasks will ensure that the regular task T cannot start its execution before the completion of the DAG submitted by the hierarchical task.

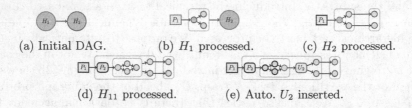

(a) Initial DAG.   (b) H_1 processed.   (c) H_2 processed.

(d) H_{11} processed.   (e) Auto. U_2 inserted.

Fig. 4. Example of a chain of two hierarchical tasks.

Hierarchical task following hierarchical task. Figure 4 illustrates this scenario (⊕—⊕). Since the dependency between the two hierarchical tasks is not released until the first one has completed its processing, the tasks resulting from the two hierarchical tasks are correctly ordered making the dependencies between these tasks coherent with the sequential consistency. This is illustrated in Fig. 4 where initially two hierarchical tasks H_1 and H_2 are submitted (see Fig. 4a). Then H_1 is processed (see Fig. 4b). Note that in the example, we assume that the data was previously unpartitioned, and thus a data partitioning task P_1 is needed before the DAG corresponding to H_1. Afterwards, H_2 is processed (see Fig. 4c) and it does not require any data layout modification. Note that, each individual task produced by a hierarchical task can itself be hierarchical, and the same rules can be applied recursively to ensure the correctness of the DAG. This is illustrated in Fig. 4d where the first task submitted by H_1, which will be referred to as H_{11}, is decided to be hierarchical and is processed. We can also see the partitioning task P_2 which was automatically inserted by the data manager. The resulting task-graph is coherent with the STF paradigm.

5   Experimental Evaluation

To illustrate the potential of hierarchical tasks for handling the coexistence of multiple levels of granularity, we apply them in a dense linear algebra context[1] using the CHAMELEON library [1]. To do so, we extended the matrix descriptors in order to describe a hierarchical partitioning of the matrix tiles. Note that as explained in Sect. 3, all these partitions are only planned and will be enforced, if needed, at runtime. The following experiments were conducted on an architecture

---

[1] https://gitlab.inria.fr/starpu/starpu-papers/heteropar2022 for replication.

composed of 2 INTEL XEON GOLD 6142 of 16 cores each running at 2.6 GHz, 2 NVIDIA V100, and 384 GB of memory. The tile sizes used are the ones providing the best asymptotic performance for CPUs only (960) and for hybrid CPU-GPU configuration (2880). Additionally, we provide results for tile size of 320 that provides the best performances on CPU configurations for small matrices. Concerning hierarchical variants we will use the following notation $x/y/z/...$ meaning that each initial tile is of size x and is partitioned into tiles of size y which are in turn split into tiles of size z etc. STARPU has been configured to use a single stream per GPU, to pipeline four events per stream and to use the DMDA scheduler.

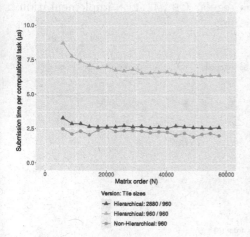

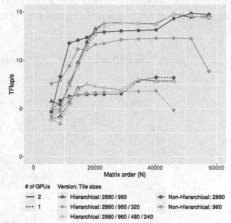

Fig. 5. Submission cost of computational tasks for DGEMM with all tiles partitioned.

Fig. 6. Performance evaluation of DGEMM with diagonal distribution of the hierarchical tasks

To evaluate the overhead induced by hierarchical tasks, we consider the graph of a matrix-matrix multiplication (GEMM) using a tile size of 960. Figure 5 compares the submission time per computational task for that graph in two configurations. The '960' curve represents the non-hierarchical case. The '960/960' curve shows the worst possible scenario: the DAG is composed only of hierarchical tasks and each one of them submits exactly one task when processed. This doubles the number of tasks submitted as well as heavily increasing the workload of the data manager making the submission time per computational task roughly 3.5 times slower. Finally, the '2880/960' curve is a more realistic scenario, where the graph is first submitted at coarse grain (with a tile size of 2880) and then refined down to the same granularity as the previous configurations (960). In this case, each individual hierarchical task submits $\lceil 2880/960 \rceil^3 = 27$ regular tasks when processed, thus amortizing the overhead induced by the management of hierarchical tasks.

In the following experiments we use a more realistic partitioning of the matrix where only the diagonal, subdiagonal and superdiagonal tiles are partitioned recursively. We evaluate the behavior of the GEMM operation on those matrices, using one and two GPUs (Fig. 6). In both cases, the hierarchical versions lag behind on small matrices, due to the overhead introduced. As the matrix size increases, the amount of kernels using smaller tiles becomes sufficient to feed the CPUs and compensates for that overhead. We can also observe that using more levels of partitioning does not have an impact on performance for this experiment. Eventually, the number of tasks needed for the computation becomes large enough that the '2880' curve can start affecting more work to the CPUs and catches up with the hierarchical curve. All in all, the hierarchical variants have a good behavior and outperform the regular CHAMELEON implementation while relying on simplistic matrix partitioning.

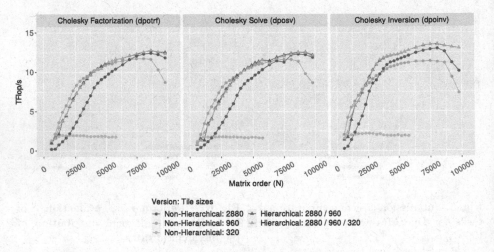

Fig. 7. Performance evaluation of Cholesky type operations (DPOTRF, DPOSV, DPOINV) with diagonal distribution of the hierarchical tasks.

To better illustrate the expressiveness of hierarchical tasks, Fig. 7 shows results of operations relying on Cholesky decomposition (POTRF): POSV (linear system solving, in this case of a single vector) and POINV (matrix inversion). These operations have complex task graphs, and in the case of POINV, validate the anti-dependency problem (*WRITE* after *READ*). We observe a similar behavior to the one observed for GEMM. A notable distinction however, is that we now benefit more from our partitioning scheme, because CHAMELEON places all POTRF kernels (which are on the critical path of the factorization) on CPU cores leading to moderate performance before $N \approx 75000$. On the other hand, thanks to hierarchical tasks, we can partition the tiles along the diagonal and split those large tasks into subgraphs with a smaller granularity allowing for better CPU utilization on the critical path. Similarly to the results on GEMM, the hierarchical tasks are sooner able to take advantage of the performance of both GPUs and CPUs resources. The sudden drop observed at the end of some non-hierarchical curves is explained by a conflict between the STARPU scheduler data prefetching and eviction in GPU memory. The experimental results illustrate the interest of hierarchical tasks for tackling the granularity problem of heterogeneous architectures.

6   Conclusion

In this paper, we propose an extension of the STF model together with an upgrade of the underlying runtime system in order to overcome the inherent limitations of the programming model. Our approach introduces a new type of tasks, the *hierarchical* tasks, which have the ability to submit at runtime a new sub-graph of tasks. In addition, to ensure that the parallel submission process still produces a valid DAG, we introduce a new automatic data manager whose goal is to handle data layout dynamically by submitting data management tasks at the right moment.

In the near future, we plan to extend this work in several ways. We first need to consider the hierarchical tasks from the scheduling point of view, and answer the question "when does a hierarchical task need to be processed?". This requires to consider the amount of tasks in the system and the work assigned to each resource. Additionally, we will consider the problem of choosing which subgraph has to be submitted when a hierarchical task is processed. Indeed, to be able to select the most adapted implementation, we need advanced performance models which have yet to be designed. Finally, the task graph resulting from the processing of a hierarchical task has to be efficiently scheduled. More generally, we want to investigate how this model can be used to implement advanced irregular algorithms like linear algebra solvers based on low-rank approximation or sparse solvers. We believe that extending the hierarchical task model to the distributed memory context will be an elegant answer to the scalability problem of task-based runtime systems.

Acknowledgment. This work is supported by the french ANR through the Solharis project under the grant (ANR-19-CE46-0009). Experiments presented in this paper were carried out using the PlaFRIM experimental testbed (https://www.plafrim.fr).

References

1. Agullo, E., Augonnet, C., Dongarra, J., Ltaief, H., Namyst, R., Thibault, S., Tomov, S.: A hybridization methodology for high-performance linear algebra software for GPUs. GPU Comput. Gems Jade Edition **2**, 473–484 (2011)
2. Akbudak, K., Ltaief, H., Mikhalev, A., Keyes, D.: Tile low rank cholesky factorization for climate/weather modeling applications on manycore architectures (2017)
3. Allen, R., Kennedy, K.: Optimizing Compilers for Modern Architectures: A Dependence-Based Approach. Morgan Kaufmann, Burlington (2002)

4. Álvarez, D., Sala, K., Maroñas, M., Roca, A., Beltran, V.: Advanced synchronization techniques for task-based runtime systems. In: Proceedings of PPoPP 2021, pp. 334–347 (2021)
5. Augonnet, C., Thibault, S., Namyst, R., Wacrenier, P.A.: StarPU: a unified platform for task scheduling on heterogeneous multicore architectures. Concurr. Comput. Pract. Exper. **23**, 187–198 (2011)
6. Augonnet, C., Goudin, D., Kuhn, M., Lacoste, X., Namyst, R., Ramet, P.: A hierarchical fast direct solver for distributed memory machines with manycore nodes. Technical Report, October 2019. https://hal-cea.archives-ouvertes.fr/cea-02304706
7. Bosilca, G., et al.: Flexible development of dense linear algebra algorithms on massively parallel architectures with DPLASMA. In: IEEE IPDPS Workshops and Phd Forum, pp. 1432–1441 (2011)
8. Carratala-Saez, R., Christophersen, S., Aliaga, J.I., Beltran, V., Borm, S., Quintana-Orti, E.S.: Exploiting nested task-parallelism in the H-LU factorization. J. Comput. Sci. **33**, 20–33 (2019)
9. Cojean, T., Guermouche, A., Hugo, A., Namyst, R., Wacrenier, P.: Resource aggregation for task-based Cholesky Factorization on top of modern architectures. Parallel Comput. **83**, 73–92 (2019)
10. Cosnard, M., Jeannot, E., Yang, T.: Slc: symbolic scheduling for executing parameterized task graphs on multiprocessors. In: Proceedings of ICPP 1999, pp. 413–421 (1999)
11. Elshazly, H., Lordan, F., Ejarque, J., Badia, R.M.: Accelerated execution via eager-release of dependencies in task-based workflows. Int. J. High Perform. Comput. Appl. **35**(4), 325–343 (2021)
12. Gautier, T., Lima, J.V.F., Maillard, N., Raffin, B.: Xkaapi: a runtime system for data-flow task programming on heterogeneous architectures. In: Proceedings of IPDPS 2013, pp. 1299–1308 (2013)
13. Huang, T.W., Lin, D.L., Lin, C.X., Lin, Y.: Taskflow: a lightweight parallel and heterogeneous task graph computing system. IEEE Trans. Parallel Distrib. Syst. **33**(6), 1303–1320 (2021)
14. Kim, J., Lee, S., Johnston, B., Vetter, J.S.: Iris: a portable runtime system exploiting multiple heterogeneous programming systems. In: Proceedings of HPEC 2021, pp. 1–8 (2021)
15. Maroñas, M., Sala, K., Mateo, S., Ayguadé, E., Beltran, V.: Worksharing tasks: an efficient way to exploit irregular and fine-grained loop parallelism. In: Proceedings of of HiPC 2019, pp. 383–394 (2019)
16. Perez, J.M., Beltran, V., Labarta, J., Ayguadé, E.: Improving the integration of task nesting and dependencies in OpenMP. In: Proceedings of IPDPS 2017, pp. 809–818 (2017)
17. Valero-Lara, P., Catalán, S., Martorell, X., Usui, T., Labarta, J.: sLASs: a fully automatic auto-tuned linear algebra library based on OpenMP extensions implemented in OmpSs. J. Parallel Distrib. Comput. **138**, 153–171 (2020)
18. Wu, W., Bouteiller, A., Bosilca, G., Faverge, M., Dongarra, J.: Hierarchical DAG scheduling for hybrid distributed systems. In: Proceedings of IPDPS 2015, pp. 156–165 (2015)

A C++ Library for Memory Layout and Performance Portability of Scientific Applications

Pietro Incardona[1,2,3], Aryaman Gupta[1,2,3], Serhii Yaskovets[1], and Ivo F. Sbalzarini[1,2,3,4(✉)] (iD)

[1] Technische Universität Dresden, Faculty of Computer Science, Dresden, Germany
{incardon,argupta,yaskovet,ivos}@mpi-cbg.de
[2] Max Planck Institute of Molecular Cell Biology and Genetics, Dresden, Germany
[3] Center for Systems Biology Dresden, 01307 Dresden, Germany
[4] Center for Scalable Data Analytics and Artificial Intelligence ScaDS.AI, Dresden/Leipzig, Germany
https://sbalzarini-lab.org

Abstract. We present a C++14 library for performance portability of scientific computing codes across CPU and GPU architectures. Our library combines generic data structures like vectors, multi-dimensional arrays, maps, graphs, and sparse grids with basic, reusable algorithms like convolutions, sorting, prefix sum, reductions, and scan. The memory layout of the data structures is adapted at compile-time using tuples with optional memory mirroring between CPU and GPU. We combine this transparent memory mapping with generic algorithms under two alternative programming interfaces: a CUDA-like kernel interface for multi-core CPUs, Nvidia GPUs, and AMD GPUs, as well as a lambda interface. We validate and benchmark the presented library using micro-benchmarks, showing that the abstractions introduce negligible performance overhead, and we compare performance against the current state of the art.

Keywords: performance portability · memory layout · generic algorithms · C++ tuples · multi-core · GPU

1 Introduction

Performance portability and programmability of scientific computing applications is gaining importance as hardware becomes more heterogeneous. With GPUs now commonplace in scientific computing, the landscape of multi-core CPUs is also diversifying with x86_64 and amd64 joined by POWER and ARM. Porting scientific codes to new hardware costs valuable developer time due to the large semantic gap between hardware-specific programming models.

Typically in High-Performance Computing (HPC), semantic gaps are addressed by abstraction [7]. This has been successfully demonstrated also for performance portability, for example by libraries like Kokkos [8], Alpaka [9],

© The Author(s), under exclusive license to Springer Nature Switzerland AG 2023
J. Singer et al. (Eds.): Euro-Par 2022 Workshops, LNCS 13835, pp. 109–120, 2023.
https://doi.org/10.1007/978-3-031-31209-0_8

and RAJA [1], as well as Intel's OneAPI built on top of SYCL [6], providing abstractions to execute code across hardware platforms. While providing a good variety of data structures as containers, these libraries have limited memory layout restructuring capabilities, in particular if an object is not a primitive type. Libraries like LLAMA [2] provide complex memory layout restructuring across hardware platforms, but are limited to multi-dimensional arrays as containers. Moreover, most of the existing libraries currently lack the capability of combining data structures with tuple-based layout switching, and all of them lack support for sparse data structures or the possibility to automatically serialize/deserialize arbitrarily nested data structures.

Here, we address this gap by providing an open-source memory- and compute-abstraction library that supports arbitrarily nested and sparse tuple data structures mapped to different memory layouts, as well as commonly used basic algorithms tuned for performance on a variety of hardware targets. Our library is implemented using C++ tuples (see Sect. 2) for compile-time code generation of generic scalar, vector, and tensor multi-dimensional arrays, in addition to more complex data structures like compressed-sparse-row graphs, cell lists, and arbitrary-dimensional sparse block grids [3]. Our library uses memory mirroring to support data structures that simultaneously exist on both device and host, enabling user codes to, e.g., have CPU and GPU sections share an abstract data structure simultaneously mapped to both memories. We provide optimized algorithms along with the data structures, e.g., for arbitrary-dimensional convolutions, sorting, prefix sum, reduction, and scan (Sect. 3).

The presented library, openfpm_data, is available as part of the OpenFPM scalable computing project [4]. It provides the shared-memory layer of OpenFPM, but can also be used as a stand-alone library. It provides two interfaces for user-implemented algorithms over abstract data structures: CUDA-like compute kernels and lambda functions. Since openfpm_data is able to shape pointers to external memory, zero-copy interfaces are possible with other libraries that provide algorithms or shape memory, like Kokkos [8] or LLAMA [2], supplementing them, e.g., with sparse grids, graphs, or neighborhood search.

We show in micro-benchmarks and in a real-world application that the flexibility afforded by openfpm_data does not impact performance (Sect. 4). Indeed, we find that combining memory layout restructuring of complex data structures with generic algorithms can benefit the performance optimizations of modern C++ compilers on multiple CPU and GPU architectures. We conclude the paper in Sect. 5.

2   From C++ Tuples to Compile-Time Data Structures

We construct memory-layout reconfigurable data structures with a common abstract programming interface by exploiting two features of the C++ programming language: The first is the existence of three types of brackets — <>, (), and []. We use them to cleanly separate the semantics of data structures. Angle braces are used to specify which property of a tuple/composite data structure one wants to access. Round parentheses are used to specify an element of a discrete set. Square brackets are used to access individual components of a vector or array. This three-brackets access semantic is common across all data structures and independent of the physical memory layout used.

The second C++ feature we use are tuples (and consequently variadic templates). We use the tuple data structure provided by the Boost library[1] to define properties or elements of a data structure. Using tuples instead of structs enables content parsing at compile-time using template meta-programming. The memory layout (or memory mapping) of a data structure is determined at compile-time by a layout restructuring algorithm implemented using meta-programming. We then construct an object that stores the information of a container with the specified layout and inject the access methods with layout-specific code required to overload the three parenthesis operators.

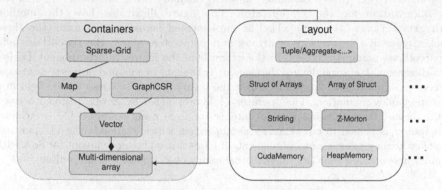

Fig. 1. Summary of the openfpm_data library: The UML diagram on the left lists the implemented containers and their composition, starting from multi-dimensional arrays, with template parameters as listed in the right box. The first template parameter (green) is the tuple defining the data type of the container. The memory layout is defined in the second parameter (red). The linearization of multi-dimensional indices is defined by the third template parameter (violet). The fourth template argument (yellow) defines the type of memory to be allocated: GPU device (Nvidia or AMD) or heap memory. The three dots outside the box indicate the possibility of the interface to be extended to user-defined layouts, linearizations, and memory types. (Color figure online)

The data structures and memory layouts available in openfpm_data are summarized in Fig. 1. The UML diagram on the left shows the composition of the available containers, starting from the base class "multi-dimensional array". A vector is a one-dimensional array, a Compressed Sparse Row (CSR) graph is stored in an encapsulated vector of vertices and edges, a map is a sorted vector, and a sparse grid is an n-dimensional map [3]. All sub-classes inherit the layout reconfigurability of the base class as defined by the four template parameters shown in the right box. Every container in the hierarchy can override every layout parameter, leading to a vast diversity of possible implementations.

---

[1] https://www.boost.org/.

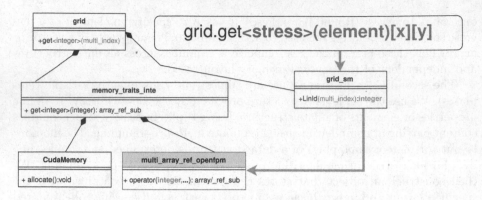

Fig. 2. Example to illustrate the classes involved in accessing an element of a Struct-of-Arrays (SoA) container in GPU memory with standard C++ striding linearization for the () operator. The figure illustrates how the method `grid.get<stress>(element)[x][y]` is implemented across classes using the three bracket types of C++. Colors of arrows and parameters match the parenthesis and in-parenthesis parameter colors. In the example of the figure, the component `[x][y]` (two-dimensional tensor index) of the element (`element`) of a named property `<stress>` is accessed. This is how one would access the components of a stress tensor field in a fluid mechanics simulation. The operator () is overloaded by `grid_sm` (green arrow), which converts the multi-index to an integer (orange) using standard C++ striding. This integer is passed to `multi_array_ref_openfpm`, which overloads the [] operator. The class `memory_traits_inte` implements the interleaved memory layout for SoA with memory allocated on the GPU in the `CudaMemory` object. (Color figure online)

Figure 2 illustrates the mechanism used for memory mapping and for abstract layout switching. In the example of the figure, the object `memory_traits_inte` implements the meta-algorithm to transform a tuple into a multi-dimensional container object with interleaved (i.e., SoA) memory layout, and it contains the code for the parentheses functions. In the figure, this is shown for the `get` method on a multi-dimensional array named `grid` to access tensor component $[x, y]$ of a certain element of a container called `stress` (e.g., the stress tensor field of a fluid mechanics simulation). All layout-specific code is encapsulated in the objects that overload the parenthesis operators, as indicated by the colors.

All `openfpm_data` data structures support memory mirroring to use host and device memory simultaneously. Mirrored data structures simplify code where some sections run, e.g., on a CPU and others on a GPU. However, `openfpm_data` does not provide any memory consistency model. Synchronization of a mirrored data structure needs to be triggered by the user when needed. Functions to transparently move data from device to host and vice versa are provided.

3   Generic Algorithms over Abstract Data Structures

We complement the hardware-independent data structures and memory layout capabilities of `openfpm_data` with generic algorithms, which are translated to optimized hardware-specific implementations at compile time. We further expose two different interfaces for user-implemented algorithms: a CUDA-like kernel interface and a lambda function interface.

In order for `openfpm_data` kernels to run on multiple hardware backends, we provide hardware-native implementations of the following algorithmic primitives: prefix sum, atomic add, stencils, n-dimensional convolution, adding and removing elements from maps, data structure copying and merging, sorting, segmented reduce, in-warp reduce, and cell lists. These implementations are encapsulated in switchable back-end objects that determine their implementation. At the time of writing, the following four backends are available: CUDA (Nvidia GPU), HIP (AMD GPU), SEQUENTIAL (CPU), and OpenMP (CPU). The backend is chosen by the user at compile time.

For the CUDA and HIP backends, the `openfpm_data` algorithms directly wrap the corresponding implementations in CUDA/HIP via the CUB/hipCUB API. The SEQUENTIAL backend executes each thread block sequentially on the CPU. Then, `__global__` and `__device__` map at preprocessor level to an empty string and an `inline`, respectively, and `blockIdx`, `blockDim`, `threadIdx`, and `gridDim` are global variables.

User-implemented algorithms can be written as CUDA-like compute kernels or using a lambda interface. Like in CUDA, `openfpm_data` kernels are labeled with the attribute `__global__`, and device functions are labeled with the attribute `__device__`. Also like in CUDA, computation is divided into a grid of blocks, where each block contains a user-defined number of threads. Within a kernel, `openfpm_data` provides the local variables `blockIdx`, `blockDim`, `threadIdx`, and `gridDim` that contain the thread block index, dimension, the thread index within the block, and the number of blocks in the grid. Static shared memory is available via `__shared__`, and `__syncthreads()` is implemented with lightweight threads (number of threads = size of the thread block; each thread has 8 KB stack, extensible via a compile-time parameter) and fast context switching. Every time `__syncthreads()` is encountered, execution is stopped and a context switch is performed, moving to the next lightweight thread. While this leads to suboptimal performance, it provides a direct mapping for user-defined kernels where no backend-native implementation is available to at least run (e.g., for debugging). When reaching the end of a block, the first lightweight thread in the block is resumed in a cyclic way.

For the SEQUENTIAL backend, lightweight threads are created internally, while fast context switching is performed using the Boost library's `boost::context`. Because lightweight threads are not concurrent, `atomicAdd` reduces to a regular addition operation. A block scan is implemented as a `__syncthreads()` followed by the calculation of the exclusive prefix sum for thread zero in the block and a final `__syncthreads()`.

In the OpenMP backend, `blockIdx` and `threadIdx` are marked `thread_local` and use thread-local storage (TLS) in order to have an independent copy for each thread. Blocks are distributed across OpenMP threads, with each thread of a block executed by one OpenMP thread. If blocks do not use __syncthreads(), the backend switches to non-lightweight threads to help vectorization.

To illustrate the similarity of the openfpm_data kernel programming interface with CUDA, List. 1.1 shows the first part (defining the shared memory and loading the fields) of the miniBUDE benchmark [5] implemented as an openfpm_data kernel that can run on both CPUs and GPUs.

```
template<typename vector_atom , ... >
__global__ void fasten_main( ...
    const vector_atom protein_molecule ,
    const vector_atom ligand_molecule , ...) {
    // Compute index of first TD
    int ix = blockIdx.x*blockDim.x*N_TD_PER_THR + threadIdx.x;
    int tid = threadIdx.x;
    ix = ix < numTransforms ? ix : numTransforms - N_TD_PER_THR
    
#ifdef USE_SHARED
    __shared__ FFParams forcefield [N_ATOM_TYPES];
    if(tid < num_atom_types) {
        forcefield [tid].hbtype = ...; forcefield [tid].radius =
            ...;
    }
    ...
}
```

Listing 1.1. Example of an openfpm_data compute kernel able to run on both GPU and CPU. The listing shows the first part of the miniBUDE benchmark [5].

For lambda-based computation, openfpm_data supports directly launching a lambda function similar to libraries like Kokkos [8], RAJA [1], and SYCL [6]. The blockIdx and threadIdx constants are passed to the function as arguments. This implies that TLS for the OpenMP backend is not required, because blockIdx and threadIdx are local function arguments rather than global variables.

4   Benchmarks

We profile the memory and compute performance of openfpm_data in microbenchmarks, and we demonstrate the use of the library in a real-world application from computational fluid dynamics. All benchmarks are performed on the hardware and using the compilers listed in Table 1. Benchmarks for sparse data structures are available elsewhere [3]. We only benchmark the OpenMP (on CPUs), CUDA (on Nvidia GPUs), and HIP (on AMD GPUs) backends of openfpm_data; SEQUENTIAL is always slower and only intended for debugging or porting purposes. Each measurement is repeated several million times to compute means and standard deviations.

Table 1. Hardware/compiler combinations considered for the benchmarks.

Hardware	Type	Vendor	Compiler
A100	GPU	Nvidia	NVCC 11.01
RTX 3090	GPU	Nvidia	NVCC 11.01
M1	CPU	Apple	clang 12.05
POWER 9	CPU	IBM	GCC 10.2
Ryzen 3990X	CPU	AMD	GCC 9.3
EPYC 7702	CPU	AMD	GCC 10.2
Xeon 8276	CPU	Intel	GCC 10.2
RXVega 64	GPU	AMD	clang 13

4.1 Memory Performance

We first analyze the memory performance. We do so using a micro-benchmark that moves data between aggregates/tuples containing scalars, vectors, and rank-two tensors. Because this benchmark is memory-bound, it assesses the memory performance portability of the openfpm_data aggregates/tuple data abstractions. We evaluate the results both absolutely and relatively. For the relative evaluation, we compare against a hand-tuned implementation in Kokkos [8] and a C++ plain-array implementation. For the absolute evaluation, we compare the memory bandwidth achieved by openfpm_data with the synthetic benchmarks babel-STREAM (for POWER 9, ARM, and dual-socket x86_64), pmbw (for single-socket x86_64—an optimized memory bandwidth benchmark written in assembly), and vendor-specific memory copy functions for the GPUs, as well as with the theoretical peak memory bandwidth reported in the data sheets.

We perform the benchmark on 67.1 million elements, each containing a scalar, two 2-vectors, and a tensor of rank two and size 2×2. We repeat each benchmark both for reading and for writing. The *write benchmark* reads one element from component 0 of the first vector and copies it into component 1 of the first vector, the scalar, all four components of the 2×2 tensor, and all components of the second 2-vector. This requires a total of nine memory accesses (counted from the generated assembly code): 8 write and 1 read. The *read benchmark* reads the values from the first 2-vector, the scalar, the tensor, and component 0 of the second vector, sums them, and writes the sum into component 1 of the second vector. This results in a total of 8 reads and 1 write. In this benchmark, we use lambda-based openfpm_data implementations compiled for the OpenMP backend on CPUs and for CUDA/HIP backends on GPUs. Memory bandwidth is calculated as the number of access operations divided by the runtime to complete all of them. The results are shown in Table 2.

On the x86_64 CPUs, the measured memory bandwidth when reading is significantly larger than when writing. This suggests the use of a cache policy of type write_allocate rather than write_around. In write_allocate, a write to a memory location out of cache generates a cache line that is filled from memory. Eventually the line is written back, causing double transfer of data compared to

Table 2. Memory performance (read/write) on different hardware in Gigabytes/second (GB/s) for the same memory transfer micro-benchmark (see main text) implemented in openfpm_data, Kokkos, and plain C++ arrays, compared with the synthetic memory benchmarks described in the text and the vendor-provided memory bandwidth from the data sheet, where available. All synthetic benchmarks except pmbw (for Ryzen 3990X) and data sheets only report composite read/write bandwidth. For all measurements, the standard deviation is < 3% and therefore not shown.

Hardware	openfpm_data	Kokkos	Plain C++	Synthetic	Data sheet
A100	(1390/1212)	(1375/1131)	(1394/1226)	1297	1555
RTX 3090	(868/818)	(860/810)	(868/818)	835	936
M1	(47.5/27.5)	(43.1/28.6)	(47.8/26.1)	61.8	N/A
POWER 9	(120.2/109.8)	(143.0/112.8)	(121.6/111.8)	250.0	340
Ryzen 3990X	(70.8/37.7)	(54.0/32.8)	(70.6/37.7)	(77.1/37.7)	96
EPYC 7702	(242.5/135.3)	(243.6/134.7)	(243.9/133.2)	214.0	384
Xeon 8276	(137.1/87.7)	(142.9/89.6)	(144.3/89.6)	150.0	216.8
RXVega 64	(359/358)	(323/293)	(359/360)	378	484

a read. The GPUs appear to implement a `write-through` cache policies. On all platforms, the memory performance of `openfpm_data` is comparable to that of plain C++ arrays (Table 2). With the exception of the M1 and the POWER 9, the numbers also match the synthetic benchmarks, confirming that the memory-mirrored tuple abstraction of `openfpm_data` incur low performance overhead.

To confirm that memory layout reordering does not interfere with the optimization stages of the compilers tested, but indeed helps the compilers vectorize the code, we check the generated assembly code. An example for an SoA memory layout is shown in Fig. 3 for clang 13. The analysis shows that even when combining tensor components of rank two with vector components, the compiler is able to understand the contiguity of the index for the parenthesis () and to generate AVX instructions without further hints. This shows that the `openfpm_data` abstractions do not interfere with the optimization stages of the compiler, and the thread model still allows for vectorization.

4.2 Compute Performance

In order to benchmark the compute performance of `openfpm_data`, we use the miniBUDE performance benchmark [5], which has previously been used to compare compute performance of programming models including OpenCL, Kokkos, CUDA, SYCL, OpenMP, and OpenACC. While this benchmark does not over-stress the data structures, it quantifies the performance portability of the algorithms provided by `openfpm_data`. We do so by running the miniBUDE CUDA benchmark kernel through `openfpm_data`'s kernel interface. The `openfpm_data` compute kernel remains the same across all benchmarks, but is compiled using different backends: CUDA on Nvidia GPUs, OpenMP on CPUs, and HIP on AMD GPUs.

In order to render the results reproducible and comparable across compilers, we manually enable DAZ (denormals are zero) and FTZ (flush to zero) on

```
for (int i = 0; i < 16777216; i++)
{
    out.get<2>(i)[0][1] = in.get<0>(i)[0];
}
```

18,53	be8:	movups	(%rcx,%rax,1),%xmm7
21,65		movups	%xmm7,(%rdx,%rax,1)
26,90		add	$0x10,%rax
		cmp	$0x4000000,%rax
1,50		↑ jne	be8

Fig. 3. C++ code reading from a vector component and writing to a rank-two tensor. As seen from the assembly code generated by clang 13, both the reads and writes are vectorized, processing 8 floats in one instruction. Then, the counter in the register %rax is incremented by 16 Bytes, the stop condition is checked, and the loop iterates to label be8. The numbers to the left of the vertical line indicate the percentages of profiling samples collected from each instruction.

all hardware. This does not affect significantly the values computed, but prevents compilers from using different SIMD mask flags with different compilation options.

Table 3 reports the relative performance of the same openfpm_data code on different hardware compared with the respective best performer from the miniBUDE test suite, as indicated in the last column. Despite the fact that the openfpm_data kernel was not manually changed or tuned for the different hardware targets, it mostly performs on par with the specialized CUDA or OpenMP implementations of miniBude. The only exception is the RXVega 64, where OpenCL is faster than openfpm_data with HIP backend. Code inspection shows that this is because the two compilers produce different code: HIP produces code with fewer registers and higher occupancy, while OpenCL does the opposite. While it is counter-intuitive that this explains the performance difference, it is what the measurements show, and it possibly hints at latencies or GPU stalling as the problem for openfpm_data on the RXVega 64.

4.3   Application Example: Smoothed Particle Hydrodynamics

We demonstrate the use of openfpm_data in a typical real-world application from scientific computing: a computational fluid dynamics simulation using the numerical method of Smoothed Particle Hydrodynamics (SPH). As a baseline, we use the CPU-only implementation of SPH from the original OpenFPM paper [4], which is freely available in the OpenFPM repository, albeit without the CPU-specific manual optimizations (like Verlet lists and symmetric interactions). We derive from this code a version implemented using the CUDA-like kernel interface of openfpm_data and the built-in algorithmic primitives cell-list, sort, and scan.

Table 3. Performance of the same miniBUDE-like `openfpm_data` kernel on different hardware compared with the respective best performer of the miniBude benchmark [5] as given in the last column. Values are given as relative performance (GFlops `openfpm_data`)/(GFlops best miniBude) as mean ± standard deviation over 30 independent trials. Values >1 (in bold) mean that `openfpm_data` was faster than the fastest miniBude implementation.

Hardware	openfpm_data/miniBude	best miniBude
A100	1.00 ± 0.07	CUDA
RTX 3090	1.00 ± 0.04	CUDA
M1	**1.05 ± 0.01**	OpenMP
POWER 9	0.80 ± 0.09	OpenMP
Ryzen 3990X	**1.08 ± 0.04**	OpenMP
EPYC 7702	1.01 ± 0.03	OpenMP
Xeon 8276	0.97 ± 0.03	OpenMP
RXVega 64	0.54 ± 0.01	OpenCL

We use both codes—the original MPI-only CPU code [4] and the code using `openfpm_data` kernels—to simulate the same "dam break" SPH test case [4].

Table 4 shows the measured relative performance of these two codes on different CPUs. Performance is reported as runtime ratio (original MPI code)/ (`openfpm_data` code) in percent for the OpenMP backend of `openfpm_data`. Therefore, numbers >100% (in bold) indicate speedup. The most expensive part of the simulation, the force calculation step, is also profiled separately.

The results show that the `openfpm_data` abstraction layer adds no detectable performance penalty in this complex real-world application. It actually being a few percent faster than the original MPI code is likely because the OpenMP backend has a lower communication overhead than MPI. The `openfpm_data` code also runs on GPUs. On a Nvidia A100, it runs 36 times faster than on all cores of an EPYC 7702 CPU, and on a RXVega 64 the speedup is 2.7. This difference in speedups is expected, as profiling shows the bottleneck for this application to be memory access and L2 cache. The Vega has slower memory than the A100 (484 GB/s vs. 1.5 TB/s) and 10x less L2 cache (4 MB vs. 40 MB). In addition, the Vega uses the old GCN architecture, known to be less efficient than AMD's new CDNA architecture.

Table 4. Performance of the `openfpm_data` SPH "dam break" simulation on different CPUs using all available cores, relative to the performance of the original MPI code [4] on the same CPUs (=100%). Numbers >100% (in bold) indicate speedups.

Hardware	Overall	Force calculation
M1	**109%**	113%
Ryzen 3990X	**105%**	98%
EPYC 7702	**115%**	121%
Xeon 8276	**122%**	97%

5   Conclusions

We have presented and benchmarked a C++14 memory and compute abstraction library for scientific computing applications on CPUs and GPUs. The presented library, called openfpm_data, combines shared-memory data structures with reusable algorithmic building blocks. Compared to the state of the art, openfpm_data provides more flexible memory layouts with tuples, memory mirroring, and advanced data structures like cell list, sparse grids, and graphs.

We have shown the benefits this brings for performance portability in both micro-benchmarks and a typical real-world numerical simulation application, comparing to the respective state of the art. The presented benchmarks have also shown that memory layout switching using memory-mirrored C++ tuples does not interfere with performance and does not distract compiler optimizations.

The algorithmic primitives provided by openfpm_data include n-dimensional convolution, merging, sorting, prefix sum, reduction, and scan. They are available in optimized implementations for CUDA, HIP, SEQUENTIAL, and OpenMP backends and can be used and extended in either a CUDA-like kernel programming interface or a lambda-based interface. This allows scientific codes to run on different hardware platforms without losing performance, as demonstrated in the SPH fluid-flow simulation example.

The abstract data structures provided by openfpm_data are composable and can be used as building blocks for more complex data structures, such as *distributed* sparse block grids [3], and for domain-specific data structures like those in OpenFPM [4]. The memory layout capabilities are inherited, as well as the memory mirroring capability, allowing the same data structure to simultaneously be mapped to host and device. Moreover, third-party libraries can be interfaced via external memory and pointer shaping.

The scalable scientific computing framework OpenFPM [4] is based on the openfpm_data abstraction layer presented here. The OpenFPM project composes the shared-memory openfpm_data abstractions to distributed-memory objects for multi-node and multi-GPU applications with transparent network communication. The portable openfpm_data data structures and kernels enable OpenFPM to transparently run simulation codes on multiple architectures.

Acknowledgments. We thank Christian Trott from the Kokkos project for his help and advise in tuning the Kokkos benchmarks for optimal performance. The authors are grateful to the Centre for Information Services and High Performance Computing (ZIH) of TU Dresden and the Scientific Computing Facility of MPI-CBG for providing their facilities for the benchmarks. This work was supported by the Federal Ministry of Education and Research (Bundesministerium für Bildung und Forschung, BMBF) under grants 01/S18026A-F (competence center for Big Data and AI "ScaDS.AI Dresden/Leipzig") and 031L0160 (project "SPlaT-DM – computer simulation platform for topology-driven morphogenesis").

Code availability. The source code of the presented library is available under the GPLv3 license as part of the OpenFPM project for scalable scientific computing (http://openfpm.mpi-cbg.de/) at: https://git.mpi-cbg.de/mosaic/software/parallel-computing/openfpm.

References

1. Beckingsale, D.A., et al.: RAJA: portable performance for large-scale scientific applications. In: 2019 IEEE/ACM International Workshop on Performance, Portability and Productivity in HPC (P3HPC), pp. 71–81 (2019). https://doi.org/10.1109/P3HPC49587.2019.00012
2. Gruber, B.M., Amadio, G., Blomer, J., Matthes, A., Widera, R., Bussmann, M.: LLAMA: the low-level abstraction for memory access. In: Software: Practice and Experience, pp. 1–27 (2022). https://doi.org/10.1002/spe.3077
3. Incardona, P., Bianucci, T., Sbalzarini, I.F.: Distributed sparse block grids on GPUs. In: Chamberlain, B.L., Varbanescu, A.-L., Ltaief, H., Luszczek, P. (eds.) ISC High Performance 2021. LNCS, vol. 12728, pp. 272–290. Springer, Cham (2021). https://doi.org/10.1007/978-3-030-78713-4_15
4. Incardona, P., Leo, A., Zaluzhnyi, Y., Ramaswamy, R., Sbalzarini, I.F.: OpenFPM: a scalable open framework for particle and particle-mesh codes on parallel computers. Comput. Phys. Commun. **241**, 155–177 (2019). https://doi.org/10.1016/j.cpc.2019.03.007
5. Poenaru, A., Lin, W.-C., McIntosh-Smith, S.: A performance analysis of modern parallel programming models using a compute-bound application. In: Chamberlain, B.L., Varbanescu, A.-L., Ltaief, H., Luszczek, P. (eds.) ISC High Performance 2021. LNCS, vol. 12728, pp. 332–350. Springer, Cham (2021). https://doi.org/10.1007/978-3-030-78713-4_18
6. Reyes, R., Lomüller, V.: SYCL: Single-source C++ accelerator programming. In: Parallel Computing: On the Road to Exascale, pp. 673–682. IOS Press (2016). https://doi.org/10.3233/978-1-61499-621-7-673
7. Sbalzarini, I.F.: Abstractions and middleware for petascale computing and beyond. Intl. J. Distr. Syst. Technol. **1**(2), 40–56 (2010). https://doi.org/10.4018/jdst.2010040103
8. Trott, C.R., et al.: Kokkos 3: programming model extensions for the exascale era. IEEE Trans. Parallel Distrib. Syst. **33**(4), 805–817 (2022). https://doi.org/10.1109/TPDS.2021.3097283
9. Zenker, E., et al.: Alpaka-an abstraction library for parallel kernel acceleration. In: 2016 IEEE International Parallel and Distributed Processing Symposium Workshops (IPDPSW), pp. 631–640. IEEE (2016). https://doi.org/10.1109/IPDPSW.2016.50

Implementation and Performance Evaluation of Memory System Using Addressable Cache for HPC Applications on HBM2 Equipped FPGAs

Norihisa Fujita[1,2(✉)], Ryohei Kobayashi[1,2], Yoshiki Yamaguchi[1,2], and Taisuke Boku[1,2]

[1] Center for Computational Sciences, University of Tsukuba, Tsukuba, Japan
[2] Degree Programs in Systems and Information Engineering,
Graduate School of Science and Technology, University of Tsukuba, Tsukuba, Japan
fujita@ccs.tsukuba.ac.jp

Abstract. When we apply field programmable gate arrays (FPGAs) as HPC accelerators, their memory bandwidth presents a significant challenge because it is not comparable to those of other HPC accelerators. In this paper, we propose a memory system for HBM2-equipped FPGAs and HPC applications that uses block RAMs as an addressable cache implemented between HBM2 and an application. This architecture enables data transfer between HBM2 and the cache bulk and allows an application to utilize fast random access on BRAMs. This study demonstrates the implementation and performance evaluation of our new memory system for HPC and HBM2 on an FPGA. Furthermore, we describe the API that can be used to control this system from the host. We implement RISC-V cores in an FPGA as controllers to realize fine-grain data transfer control and to prevent overheads derived from the PCI Express bus. The proposed system is implemented on eight memory channels and achieves 102.7 GB/s of the bandwidth. It overcomes the memory bandwidth of conventional FPGA boards with four channels of DDR4 memory despite using only 8 of 32 channels of the HBM2.

Keywords: FPGA · HBM2 · Memory System

1 Introduction

Field Programmable Gate Array (FPGA) have received attention as accelerators in the HPC field [9]. FPGAs have high-speed serial IO (HSSI) and can communicate with other devices directly between applications implemented in them. Other accelerators in high-performance computing lack this capability [4]. Hardware Description Language (HDL) has been used for programming in an FPGA. It is difficult for HPC programmers to use FPGAs because we have to describe clock cycle behavior in HDL. In recent years, development environments using High-Level Synthesis (HLS) have evolved. HLS uses C, C++, or

© The Author(s), under exclusive license to Springer Nature Switzerland AG 2023
J. Singer et al. (Eds.): Euro-Par 2022 Workshops, LNCS 13835, pp. 121–132, 2023.
https://doi.org/10.1007/978-3-031-31209-0_9

OpenCL as a programming language to describe hardware in an FPGA. Thus, expert-level knowledge is not required to use FPGAs.

However, the memory bandwidth of an FPGA is lower than that of other accelerators used in HPC clusters so far. It becomes the bottleneck when we implement HPC applications into an FPGA [15]. Conventional FPGAs are equipped with DDR4 memories as external memory. Four channels of DDR4-2400 have only 76.8 GB/s of bandwidth while NVIDIA A100 80 GB Graphics Processing Unit (GPU) has a memory bandwidth of 2 TB/s. There is an approximately 25 times memory performance gap between FPGAs and GPUs. High-performance FPGAs that are equipped with High Bandwidth Memory 2 (HBM2) have been developed. For example, the Intel Stratix 10 MX FPGA has up to 512 GB/s of HBM2 bandwidth. However, the architecture of HBM2 is different from that of conventional DDR4 memory. A new memory system optimized for HBM2 on an FPGA is urgently needed.

The purpose of this research is to propose and implement a new memory system optimized for HBM2. Our proposed system uses Block RAM (BRAM) embedded in an FPGA as the addressable-cache. Moreover, it has crossbars that connect HBM2 and caches. A crossbar can manage both high-performance and high-flexibility memory access. The contributions of this paper are as follows.

- We propose a memory system for HBM2-equipped FPGAs and show the implementation of the proposed system and the optimized API on an FPGA.
- The proposed system achieves near peak performance, and its performance is superior to that of DDR4-equipped FPGAs.

2   Related Works

Applications of FPGAs with HBM2 have been widely studied. [12] implemented HPCChallenge benchmarks what is memory bandwidth bound on an FPGA. [10,14] optimized the memory access of neural network applications using HBM2. In these papers, applications were connected to the HBM2 memory channels directly, and a client in an application could access only one channel. In [3], Y. Choi et al. proposed the interconnection network named "HBM Connect". They evaluated the network using bucket sort and merge sort on a Xilinx Alveo U280 Xilinx FPGA. They used half of the HBM2 on the FPGA board because of the limitation of the board development environment, but HBM Connect achieved 90% efficiency of the bandwidth. In [7], H. Philipp et al. proposed Memory Access Optimizer (MAO) for Xilinx FPGAs. They compared MAO performance with Xilinx's native switching fabric and achieved 3.8x and 40.6x performance improvements on random access and stride access, respectively.

HBM Connect and MAO are memory networks between the application and the HBM2. These systems do not have caches in the memory system. The novelty of this paper is that we propose a memory system with an addressable cache using embedded memory in an FPGA. Furthermore, we introduce an optimized API to manage the cache system efficiently.

3 Proposed Memory System

3.1 Overview

The fundamental design of the system is based on results of our previous study [5]. However, our previous system was a work-in-progress and supported only two channels; moreover, we did not propose APIs that could be used to control an FPGA from a host. In this paper, we propose not only advanced memory system hardware but also advanced software APIs for controlling an FPGA.

An Intel Stratix 10 MX FPGA has two HBM2 dies. Each die has 16 (pseudo) memory channels, and an FPGA has 32 channels in total. The maximum aggregated memory bandwidth is 512 GB/s if a −1 speed-grade FPGA is used. In this architecture, we have to use all the memory channels simultaneously to obtain a high performance from HBM2. Unlike CPUs or GPUs, FPGAs do not have high-performance caches or memory interconnections as dedicated functions. If we connect these channels with applications directly, the applications will not utilize the memory bandwidth efficiently. Moreover, HBM2 cannot handle random access efficiently because it is based on DRAM.

To address this issue, we implement addressable caches between the memory and the application. These caches are implemented by BRAMs inside an FPGA. Because BRAM is an embedded memory and SRAM, we can access it with high bandwidth and low latency. However, the capacity of BRAM is limited, which is only 20~30 MB in an FPGA.

In general processors, a cache is automatically managed by the hardware. However, an automatic cache system consumes a considerable amount of FPGA resources. We, therefore, decide to make the cache manually controllable. We have to describe data transfer between a cache and memory manually. This architecture makes the system simpler than that which uses automatic cache and reduces FPGA resource consumption. Manual data transfer is generally used in accelerator programming. For example, we call APIs manually to transfer data between the CPU's memory and the accelerator's memory. We consider that manual data management is acceptable for HPC applications.

3.2 System Design

Figure 1 shows an overview of our proposed memory system. This system comprises a group of eight memory channels. We call this group the "Memory Group" hereafter. A Memory Group has eight Local Stores (LSs), two crossbars, and eight memory controllers connected to HBM2 (eight channels). Crossbars tightly couple LSs and memory channels in the same Memory Group. They provide non-blocking data transfer between the LSs and the memory. In implementing this system on an FPGA, the complexity of the crossbars is the bottleneck. For this reason, the Memory Group supports only eight memory channels. In addition to Memory Groups, the system comprises a PCI express (PCIe) controller, global crossbar, and system management module (not shown in Fig. 1) The global crossbar provides system-wide communication.

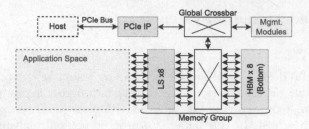

Fig. 1. Overview of the proposed system.

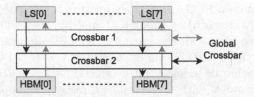

Fig. 2. Detail of the crossbars between LSs and HBM2. The red arrows and black arrows represent connections to crossbar 1 and connections to crossbar 2, respectively. (Color figure online)

Because the system described in this study is still a work in progress, we implement only one Memory Group that supports eight memory channels. To support all the memory channels, we would have to make three copies of the Memory Group and connect all the Memory Groups using the global crossbar. Inter Memory Group connections are sparse and will be blocking communication. This design is similar to Non-Uniform Memory Architecture (NUMA) on CPUs.

3.3   Crossbar

In Fig. 1, a crossbar between HBM2 and LSs has 17 ports, but the actual implementation is different because implementing such a large crossbar is not practical in an FPGA. Figure 2 shows the details of the crossbar. We implement two of the 9-port crossbars in that area. Crossbar 1 connects the HBM2 channels to the LSs. Crossbar 2 connects the LSs and HBM2 channels. LocalStore → HBM2 and HBM2 → LocalStore can use the full bandwidth and non-blocking communication. LocalStore → LocalStore and HBM2 → HBM2 are connected by the global crossbar indirectly, and their bandwidth is limited. However, such communication is only for management and is not important. Therefore, the indirect connection does not limit the system's performance.

The crossbars in the system have a 613bit width (101bit header + 512bit data). A Virtual Output Queue (VOQ) is implemented on each input port of a crossbar. It allows packets to pass other packets in the queue if two packets have different destinations. We use DRRM [2] as a scheduling algorithm in the arbiter. The scheduling happens every two cycles to achieve a high operation frequency.

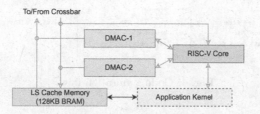

Fig. 3. Detail of a LS.

3.4 Design of LocalStore

Figure 3 shows the details of a LocalStore. Each LocalStore has the cache memory (128 KB of BRAM), Direct Memory Access Controllers (DMACs), and RISC-V [13] controller core. The cache memory is a 2-reads and 2-writes memory. Both the internal network and the application can access it simultaneously.

We have two DMACs in each LocalStore. Each DMAC has a fixed direction. One of them is only for LocalStore → HBM2, and the other is only for HBM2 → HBM2. The two DMACs are independent modules and can transfer data simultaneously.

We use the RISC-V core in a LocalStore as a system controller. We have the original RISC-V implementation that is tightly coupled with the memory system. Because we do not use the core for any computation, we optimize it for low resource utilization. It supports a subset of the RV32I instructions that we need and executes an instruction every two cycles.

The RISC-V core controls the memory system. It manages data transfer between HBM2 and a LS, and the kernel execution. In the proposed system, RISC-V instructions represent what the FPGA does. This design allows us to describe complicated behavior in the FPGA without changing the FPGA hardware implementation.

4 Design and Implementation of the API

4.1 Overview

In accelerator programming, we control accelerators by using APIs. When we use NVIDIA GPUs, we use CUDA API to control them. In these APIs, the host CPU controls all computations on the accelerators, as accelerators cannot start computation or data transfer themselves. On the other hand, FPGAs have different characteristics from these accelerators. We can configure them as self-contained accelerators. In such a design, they can start computation or data transfer without management from the host.

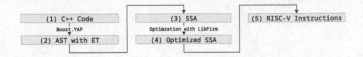

Fig. 4. Code generation flow.

For this system, before starting any computation, we transfer the data required for it between caches in the LocalStores and the HBM2. The capacity of a cache is limited because a cache uses BRAM, which is embedded memory in an FPGA. If we perform a large computation that does not fit into the cache in one step, we have to split it into small steps.

We estimate the time for each step is approximately $10\mu s$ if the computation is memory bandwidth bound. The estimation is calculated from the memory bandwidth and the operation frequency of the system. Moreover, we assume double-buffering is used to hide memory latency. We believe it is impossible for the host to issue control commands to an FPGA every $10\mu s$ through the PCIe bus. Therefore, in this system, we design the hardware and the software to allow FPGAs to operate themselves.

4.2 RISC-V Core and Code Generation

Each LocalStore has a RISC-V core to control its DMACs and kernel interface. A C++ API generates instructions executed by the core at runtime We transfer the generated instructions to the FPGA, and then the cores execute them.

In this system, we use double-buffering to hide memory latency and to improve performance. The RISC-V core supports the "Stream" mechanism to describe double-buffering behavior at a low cost. The core supports up to two Streams for double-buffering. The Stream mechanism is inspired by coroutine and CUDA Stream. Only one Stream can be active at a time, but we can switch the execution of the Stream with low overhead. When the core issues a command to DMACs or the kernel, the core enters the yield state and suspends the execution of a Stream. When a DMAC or a kernel executes a command, they emit an interruption. The interruption resumes the execution of the appropriate Stream that is waiting for the completed command.

The description of data transfer and kernel management is written in the code running on the host (Fig. 4-(1)). It has to be executed on the FPGA's RISC-V cores and not on the host CPU. We abstract API calls as an Abstract Syntax Tree (AST). The runtime library generates RISC-V instructions from the AST through optimizations on the Single Static Assignment (SSA) form.

We use the C++ Expression Template (ET) technique to make an AST (Fig. 4-(2)). The Boost.YAP [1] library from the Boost C++ Library uses C++ operator overloading and encodes C++ expressions as templated types. It has APIs that construct and evaluate expression templates. Next, we construct the SSA form from the AST (Fig. 4-(3)). We use LibFirm [11] to construct and optimize the SSA form. LibFirm's construction API allows us to construct the SSA as

Table 1. Evaluation Environment (PPX)

CPU	Intel Xeon E5-2690 v4 × 2
CPU Memory	DDR4 2400 MHz MHz 64 GB (8 GB × 8)
Host OS	CentOS 7.9
Host Compiler	gcc 9.1.0
FPGA Board	Intel Stratix 10 MX FPGA Development Kit
FPGA Memory	HBM2 16 GB (8 GB × 2)
FPGA Synthesis Tool	Quartus Prime Pro 20.4.0.72

a graph, including custom operators. We encode system management operations as custom operators and put them in the SSA graph. LibFirm supports various operations and optimizations on the SSA form including the Control Flow Graph (CFG) and data dependency analysis (Fig. 4-(4)). Finally, we develop RISC-V instructions from the optimized SSA graph (Fig. 4-(5)). We use the algorithm shown in [6]. We allocate registers in the order of the Perfect Elimination Order (PEO) of the dominator tree of the control flow. LibFirm computes the dominator tree from the SSA graph. Currently, the RISC-V core in the system does not support register spills. If the core does not have enough number of registers required by the allocator, the runtime library raises an error.

5   Performance Evaluation

5.1   Environment and Program for Evaluation

We use the Pre-PACS-X (PPX) cluster for performance evaluation in this study. It is a development cluster for accelerators operated by Center for Computational Sciences (CCS), University of Tsukuba, Japan. Table 1 shows the specification used in the evaluation. We use the Intel Stratix 10 MX FPGA development kit with the 1SM21CHU2F53E1VG FPGA, which is Speedgrade-1 SKU that has a 16GB HBM2 capacity.

In this evaluation, the HBM2 memory frequency, HBM2 controller, HBM2 FPGA IP, and other modules are run at 1000MHz, 500MHz, 400MHz, and 250MHz, respectively. The HBM2 memory and its controller are hardwired, and thus we operate them at the maximum frequency. The frequency of the HBM2 FPGA IP is the recommended frequency suggested by the Platform Designer. The bus width of the system is twice that of the memory bus and operates at 250MHz which is the 1:2 ratio of the controller frequency.

The evaluation program inverts all bits in the target array. This program intends to measure the data copy performance between the FPGA and HBM2, and to verify the transfer. First, the host writes random numbers to the array on the FPGA. Next, the FPGA flips all bits of the array. Finally, the host reads back data from the FPGA and verifies the result. We implement the application

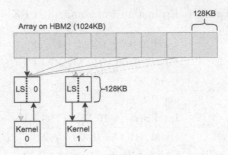

Fig. 5. Computation flow of the benchmark when the number of LSs is two and the size of the array is 1024KB. The dotted lines represent the sub regions for double buffering.

kernel in an FPGA in Verilog HDL, not in HLS, because this study focuses on the performance of the memory system.

Each LocalStore has DMACs and a computation kernel. We iterate multiple steps to solve a large part of the problem with double-buffering, as shown in Fig. 5. The figure shows the compute regions with double buffering for each LS when the number of LSs is 2 and the size of the array is 1024 KB. The actual number of LSs is 8, but it is reduced in the figure for simplification. DMAC copies data from HBM2, the kernel computes bitwise-not, and DMAC copies the result to HBM2.

Figure 6 shows a part of the host code using the API. Because the capacity of the cache in a LocalStore is 128 KB, we split it into two parts each with a 64KB (=16384 elements) size for double-buffering using two Streams. var variables and array_view variables are handles. They represent variables in the RISC-V core and regions of arrays, respectively. The location of each step is computed with the var variables. The assign statements using array_view variables invoke DMA transfers. A stream_for represents a loop on the RISC-V core like for statements on the host. Because it is implemented as a C preprocessor macro, we have to use commas as the separators of arguments.

5.2 Evaluation Result

The FPGA resource utilization is summarized in Table 2. Adaptive Logic Module (ALM), Registers, M20K, and Digital Signal Processor (DSP) contain Look Up Tables (LUTs), registers in ALMs, embedded RAM blocks, and 18bit integer multipliers, respectively. Table 2 shows that we consume 18% of the FPGA resources. This evaluation uses the small kernels that consume less than 0.1% of the FPGA resource. Therefore, we can assume Table 2 as the resource consumption for the memory system. The most consumed resource is M20K. A total of 18% of the M20Ks are used, but 6.5% of the M20Ks are used for the cache memory in LocalStores. Except for resources consumed by the cache memory, the most consumed FPGA resource is ALMs. The module for controlling memory and networking consumes 13.9% of the FPGA resources.

```
1   auto ctrl = device->open_control(id);
2   auto ls = device->open_ls(id);
3   device_array buffer1 = array_alloc_1d(ls, CHUNK_BYTE);
4   device_array buffer2 = array_alloc_1d(ls, CHUNK_BYTE);
5   ctrl->begin_config();
6   for (int s = 0; s < N_STREAMS; s++) {
7     define_stream(ctrl, s) {
8       var i;
9       var start;
10      array_view<uint32_t> buffer(s == 0 ? buffer1 : buffer2);
11      array_view<uint32_t> data(d_data);
12      i = 0;
13      start = NOC_LOCAL_STREAM_ID(id, s) * CHUNK_SIZE;
14      stream_for(i = 0, i < N_CHUNK / N_WORKERS, i = i + 1) {
15        buffer(0, CHUNK_SIZE) = data(start, start + CHUNK_SIZE);
16        if (s == 0) {
17          kernel(0, 0, LOOP_LEN);
18        } else {
19          kernel(LOOP_LEN, LOOP_LEN, LOOP_LEN);
20        }
21        data(start, start + CHUNK_SIZE) = buffer(0, CHUNK_SIZE);
22        start = start + N_STREAMS * NOC_GRP_SIZE(id) * CHUNK_SIZE;
23      }
24    }
25  }
26  ctrl->stream_start_and_sync();
27  ctrl->end_config();
```

Fig. 6. Part of the program using the proposed API. N_CHUNK and CHUNK_SIZE are constants decided by the problem size. N_WORKERS is a constant that represents the number of Streams in the system. d_data is a memory handle object on the HBM2.

Table 2. Resource consumption of FPGA resources.

ALM	Registers	M20K	DSP
97229 (13.84%)	174718 (6.22%)	1243 (18.15%)	120 (3.03%)

We implement performance counters on each memory channel from HBM2 running at 250MHz (4ns resolution). They measure the data transfer time from the start command from the host until all LocalStores complete the computation. LocalStores wait for completions of all issued memory transactions responded from the memory controller. Figure 7 shows the performance result. We change the size of the array from 1 MB to 64 MB, which is equivalent to changing the number of loops per LS from 2 ($1\times$ double-buffering) to 64 ($32\times$ double-buffering). We perform the measurement 10 times on every array size. The dots represent the median value, and error bars represent the minimum and the maximum performance of 10 runs.

We achieve 102.7 GB/s of the memory bandwidth at a maximum of 64 MB of array size. This performance is almost the same as the peak bandwidth of the FPGA side (256bit $\times$ 400MHz $\times$ 32 = 102.4 GB/s). We consider that this result reveals the proposed system works as expected. We will discuss the performance in detail in the next section.

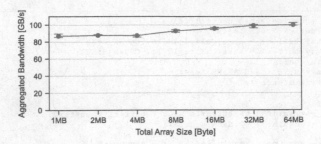

Fig. 7. Result of the performance evaluation.

6   Discussion

Except for the BRAMs used by the cache memory, the system consumes 13.9% of the FPGA resources as shown in the previous section. We implement the system to all of the memory channels from HBM2 here. This is equal to implementing four Memory Groups instead of one Memory Group in an FPGA. Therefore, we can estimate the resource utilization as being four times what it was with one memory group. We expect that approximately 56% of FPGA resources will be consumed if we have four Memory Groups. If we implement practical benchmarks or applications using our system in the future, this resource consumption might be the problem. Although our system achieves a high performance, it consumes too many resources, and we have to optimize and reduce resource consumption.

The most ALM-consuming modules are the crossbars between the LSs and HBM2 channels (6.33%). The multiplexers that select the output data require a considerable amount of ALMs. It is difficult to optimize resource consumption on them because they are essential and fundamental functions for crossbars. Optimization may be achieved by doubling the frequency and halving the width of the network. However, the congestion in the FPGA network makes increasing the frequency challenging. Other optimization approaches need to be explored.

Although HBM2 is DRAM and has a refresh interval to keep data in the memory cells, the evaluation achieves a 100.3% performance efficiency. We consider that the reason for this behavior is that the memory controller runs faster than the FPGA-side IP. The frequency of the controller is 500 MHz which is the maximum frequency allowed in the specification, but the frequency of the FPGA-side IP is 400MHz. The maximum throughput is limited by 256 bit *times* 400 MHz. However, the data refresh process is performed by the memory controller at 500 MHz. As a result, the FPGA cannot observe the time taken by the refresh process. In addition to the faster frequency of the controller, the bus between the FPGA and the controller is a full duplex. The bus enables us to make overlapping between write accesses and read accesses. We consider that this makes the 0.3% portion of the 100.3% efficiency. If the controller and the bus operate at the same frequency, the performance is limited by the HBM2 bandwidth, and the full-duplex bus will not offer any benefit.

The future Intel FPGA product, Agilex M series FPGA, has a Network on Chip (NOC) for memory access [8]. The details of the NOC have not been published yet, but the whitepaper indicates it is a hard-wired crossbar network. We can reduce the resource consumption significantly on Agilex FPGAs if we replace the crossbars with the NOC. We still need to implement an interconnection network in an FPGA because the NOC supports only allows transfers between the FPGA and memory. It does not support FPGA-to-FPGA or memory-to-memory transfers. However, we can use a network in an FPGA that is more lightweight than a crossbar network because the bandwidth of the network becomes trivial. Even if we were to use Agilex FPGAs, our research would still be important, as we also focus on important components such as caches, controllers, and software.

7 Conclusion and Future Work

We proposed and implemented a memory system for HBM2-equipped FPGAs using an addressable cache. Because this system uses BRAMs embedded in an FPGA, we need to consider the fine grain control of the FPGA. We implemented RISC-V cores as controller processors inside an FPGA to address this issue. We also proposed an API for this system so that RISC-V instructions can be made for the controllers. The API can describe complex operations on the FPGA, such as loops and branches. Using the RISC-V core allows an FPGA to operate itself without instructions from a host.

We evaluated the performance of the proposed system and achieved 100.3% efficiency of the memory bandwidth. This result revealed the system works as expected. Although all the memory channels were not implemented, the performance of the system was superior to that of DDR-4 equipped FPGAs (DDR4-2400 × 4 channels: 76.8 GB/s). The system supports eight channels, which is one-fourth of the total memory channels of the HBM2 in an FPGA. We estimated the resource consumption by the memory system as 56% if all memory channels are implemented. As a result, the system will limit the size of the application implemented in an FPGA. We have to optimize the system to improve operation frequency and reduce the width of the network in a future study.

Acknowledgments. This work was supported by JSPS KAKENHI Grant Number 21H04869. We also thank the Intel University Program for providing hardware and software.

References

1. Boost.YAP Library: https://www.boost.org/doc/libs/release/doc/html/yap.html
2. Chao, J.: Saturn: a terabit packet switch using dual round robin. IEEE Commun. Mag. **38**(12), 78–84 (2000). https://doi.org/10.1109/35.888261
3. kyu Choi, Y., Chi, Y., Qiao, W., Samardzic, N., Cong, J.: HBM connect: High-performance HLS interconnect for FPGA HBM. In: FPGA 2021 (2021)

4. De Matteis, T., de Fine Licht, J., Beránek, J., Hoefler, T.: Streaming message interface: High-performance distributed memory programming on reconfigurable hardware. In: Proceedings of the International Conference for High Performance Computing, Networking, Storage and Analysis, SC 201919, pp. 82:1–82:33. ACM New York (2019). https://doi.org/10.1145/3295500.3356201

5. Fujita, N., Kobayashi, R., Yamaguchi, Y., Boku, T.: Hbm2 memory system for HPC applications on an FPGA. In: 2021 IEEE International Conference on Cluster Computing (CLUSTER), pp. 783–786 (2021). https://doi.org/10.1109/Cluster48925.2021.00116

6. Hack, S., Grund, D., Goos, G.: Register allocation for programs in SSA-form. In: Mycroft, A., Zeller, A. (eds.) CC 2006. LNCS, vol. 3923, pp. 247–262. Springer, Heidelberg (2006). https://doi.org/10.1007/11688839_20

7. Holzinger, P., Reiser, D., Hahn, T., Reichenbach, M.: Fast HBM access with FPGAS: analysis, architectures, and applications. In: 2021 IEEE International Parallel and Distributed Processing Symposium Workshops (IPDPSW), pp. 152–159 (2021). https://doi.org/10.1109/IPDPSW52791.2021.00030

8. Intel: https://www.intel.co.jp/content/www/jp/ja/products/docs/programmable/agilex-m-series-memory-white-paper.html

9. Kenter, T., et al.: OpenCL-based FPGA design to accelerate the nodal discontinuous galerkin method for unstructured meshes. In: 2018 IEEE 26th Annual International Symposium on Field-Programmable Custom Computing Machines (FCCM), pp. 189–196, April 2018. https://doi.org/10.1109/FCCM.2018.00037

10. Kuramochi, R., Nakahara, H.: An FPGA-based low-latency accelerator for randomly wired neural networks. In: 2020 30th International Conference on Field-Programmable Logic and Applications (FPL), pp. 298–303 (2020). https://doi.org/10.1109/FPL50879.2020.00056

11. LibFirm: https://pp.ipd.kit.edu/firm/

12. Meyer, M., Kenter, T., Plessl, C.: Evaluating FPGA accelerator performance with a parameterized opencl adaptation of selected benchmarks of the hpcchallenge benchmark suite. In: 2020 IEEE/ACM International Workshop on Heterogeneous High-performance Reconfigurable Computing (H2RC), pp. 10–18 (2020). https://doi.org/10.1109/H2RC51942.2020.00007

13. RISC-V International: https://riscv.org/

14. Venkataramanaiah, S.K., et al.: FPGA-based low-batch training accelerator for modern CNNs featuring high bandwidth memory. In: 2020 IEEE/ACM International Conference On Computer Aided Design (ICCAD), pp. 1–8 (2020)

15. Zohouri, H.R., Podobas, A., Matsuoka, S.: Combined spatial and temporal blocking for high-performance stencil computation on FPGAS using OpenCL. In: Proceedings of the 2018 ACM/SIGDA International Symposium on Field-Programmable Gate Arrays, FPGA 2018, pp. 153–162. Association for Computing Machinery, New York, (2018). https://doi.org/10.1145/3174243.3174248

Programming Abstractions
for Preemptive Scheduling on FPGAs
Using Partial Reconfiguration

Gabriel Rodriguez-Canal[1]([✉]), Nick Brown[1], Yuri Torres[2],
and Arturo Gonzalez-Escribano[2]

[1] EPCC at The University of Edinburgh, EH8 9BT Edinburgh, UK
gabriel.rodcanal@ed.ac.uk, n.brown@epcc.ac.uk
[2] Escuela de Ingeniería Informática at Universidad de Valladolid,
47001 Valladolid, Spain
{yuri.torres,arturo}@infor.uva.es

Abstract. FPGAs are an attractive type of accelerator for all-purpose
HPC computing systems due to the possibility of deploying tailored hardware on demand. However, the common tools for programming and operating FPGAs are still complex to use, specially in scenarios where diverse
types of tasks should be dynamically executed. In this work we present
a programming abstraction with a simple interface that internally leverages High-Level Synthesis, Dynamic Partial Reconfiguration and synchronisation mechanisms to use an FPGA as a multi-tasking server with
preemptive scheduling and priority queues. This leads to a better use of
the FPGA resources, allowing the execution of several kernels at the same
time and deploying the most urgent ones as fast as possible. The results of
our experimental study show that our approach incurs only a 1.66% overhead when using only one Reconfigurable Region (RR), and 4.04% when
using two RRs, whilst presenting a significant performance improvement
over the traditional non-preemptive full reconfiguration approach.

Keywords: FPGA · Partial Reconfiguration · Heterogeneous
systems · Preemptive scheduling

1 Introduction

The end of Moore's law and loss of Dennard's scaling has motivated the search
of alternative ways of improving the performance of upcoming computational
systems. As a result, heterogeneous systems, primarily composed of CPUs and
GPUs [2], have become commonplace in HPC machines. However, these architectures are not ideally suited for all codes, and it has been found that when
HPC applications are bound by aspects other than compute, for instance memory bound codes, moving to a dataflow style and exploiting the specialisation of
FPGAs can be beneficial [3,8]. Nonetheless, FPGAs have not yet been adopted

© The Author(s), under exclusive license to Springer Nature Switzerland AG 2023
J. Singer et al. (Eds.): Euro-Par 2022 Workshops, LNCS 13835, pp. 133–144, 2023.
https://doi.org/10.1007/978-3-031-31209-0_10

by any of the large supercomputers, which is due to both the challenges of programmability and flexibility. The former has been partially addressed by High Level Synthesis (HLS) tooling, enabling the programmer to write their code in C or C++. However the latter has been less explored. The entire FPGA is often stalled during fabric reconfiguration which means that dynamic scheduling and preemptive execution of workloads is less common.

In this paper we propose a programming abstraction to easily use an FPGA as a multi-tasking server with preemptive scheduling and priority queues. It hides the complex low-level details of using Dynamic Partial Reconfiguration (DPR) and synchronisation mechanisms to support on-the-fly instantiation, stopping and resumming of kernels on parts of the FPGA fabric whilst the rest of the chip continues executing other workloads independently. The proposal includes, as a case study, the development of a full First-Come-First-Served (FCFS) preemptive scheduler with priority queues. The tasks are programmed as OpenCL kernels managed with the Controller model [4,7], a heterogeneous programming model implemented as a C99 library of functions. It is oriented to efficiently manage different types of devices with a portable interface. The Controller model has been extended to support multiple kernels and preemption on DPR capable FPGA systems. This solution brings all the benefits of task-based models to FPGAs, with a low programming effort. We also introduce an experimental study to show the efficiency of the proposed solution.

The rest of the paper is organised as follows: Sect. 2 describes related activities tackling flexible execution of kernels for FPGAs. Section 3 presents an overview of the original programming model that we use as a base to devise and implement our proposal. In Sect. 4 we present the techniques and extensions to support our approach, both on the management of the on-chip FPGA infrastructure and on the host code. Section 5 describes the programming level abstractions provided to the user. In Sect. 6 we present an experimental study to evaluate our approach. Section 7 concludes the paper and discusses further work.

2   Related Work

The integration of different types of architectures in heterogeneous systems can enable the execution of workloads more efficiently by using the most appropriate hardware for each part of a program. However, this also requires the user to master the programming models of these architectures. Programming abstractions have been introduced to simplify the management of different types of devices, targeting both functional and performance portability. Many approaches are devised as implementations of a heterogeneous task-based model. They present a common host-side API for orchestrating workloads/tasks, programmed as kernels, among the different accelerators present in the system. Approaches such as Kokkos [6], OpenCL [9], and OpenACC [1] have become popular for mixing CPUs and GPUs. Other approaches also support the FPGAs with a similar high-level approach. However, despite improving general programmability by supporting a common host-side API, these approaches fail to provide the high flexibility potential of FPGAs. For example, these frameworks lack the support to independently swap in and out tasks of varying sizes onto an FPGA accelerator. The FPGA is programmed with a full bitstream that contains the kernels that will be run during the program execution in a non-preemptive way.

The authors of [5] explore these issues. They present a task-based model targeting System on-a Chip (SoC) deployment based on OpenCL and using DPR. They support kernel preemption by enabling·checkpointing at the end of each OpenCL workgroup, and whilst this is a natural consistency point in the OpenCL model, the coarse-grained nature of the approach limits scheduling flexibility. For example, tasks of higher priority may need to wait until a previous workgroup with lower priority tasks finishes. Moreover, the user must write their kernel interfaces in a manner that are comformant to the interfaces of the Reconfigurable Regions (RR), causing a conflict between the high-level OpenCL description and the management of the lower-level on-chip infrastructure, which increases the overall development complexity.

3   The Controller Programming Model

Our proposal is devised as an extension of the Controller heterogeneous programming model. In this section we provide and overview of the original model and its features. Controller [4,7] is a heterogeneous task-based parallel programming model implemented as a C99 library. It provides an abstraction for programming using different types of devices, such as sets of CPU-cores, GPUs, and FPGAs.

As illustrated in Fig. 1, the model is based around the Controller entity. Each Controller entity is associated to a particular device on its creation and manages the execution or data-transfers with that device.

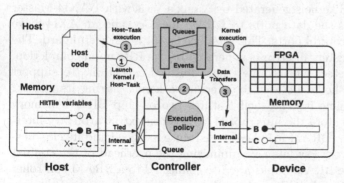

Fig. 1. The Controller programming model, generic FPGA backend. Extracted from [7].

The main program executes the coordination code in a main thread, using the Controller high-level API to enqueue computation tasks for the device. Each Controller entity has its own thread that dequeues and launches the execution of the kernels associated to the tasks. The model also provides an extra hidden device to execute host-tasks, which are managed through a separate thread. The Controller runtime resolves data dependencies between tasks automatically, performing data transfers in a transparent way. The requests of both kernel executions and data-transfers needed are derived to the internal queues or streams of the device driver, controlling the execution order of kernels, data-transfers and host-tasks with native events. It uses three queues for each device: one for kernel execution, one for host-to-device transfer, and one for device-to-host transfers. This enables a fast control operation and an efficient overlapping of computation and data transfers when it is possible. Portability is achieved using different runtime backends for different device technologies (such as CUDA or OpenCL), to implement the calls to manage the low-level device queues and events. The computations that can be launched as tasks are kernel codes written by the programmer. Controller supports generic codes, written in OpenCL and targeting any kind of device, or specialised kernels programmed in the native programming model of an accelerator such as CUDA for Nvidia GPUs.

4   Approach to Support Preemptive Scheduling on FPGAs

Our approach requires the use of new techniques in two areas, the on-chip FPGA infrastructure and the integration on the host-side of the Controller runtime.

4.1   On-chip Infrastructure

Figure 2 shows the architecture of the static part of the on-chip infrastructure, known as *shell*, that should be deployed in the FPGA to support the proposed control of Reconfigurable Regions (RR). The example shows two RRs, although this model is scalable to any number of RRs. The example shows details of a reference implementation of the proposal using Xilinx technology, although, these concepts can be easily ported to other FPGAs. This example shell implementation deploys HLS kernels generated by Xilinx's Vitis with 1 AXI4-Master interface which bundles the data ports to DRAM memory, and an AXI4-Slave interface bundling the control ports. This interface layout is fairly standard. The interrupt controller registers interrupts generated by the RRs upon completion. Thus, the CPU can detect when kernels have finished execution. To support preemption, the shell should be able to interrupt a kernel, saving its context and state, to later resume it. The shell features two on-chip BRAM memory banks (one per RR) to store the interrupted kernels context at arbitrary intervals, defined by the user. BRAM memory is used since its speed and its closeness to the RRs results in very low latency, minimizing the overhead of the context saving operation. These BRAM banks are also connected to a BRAM controller which enables access from the CPU, supporting overall book-keeping of the kernel context when they are being swapped in and out by the scheduler that controls the execution from the host.

Our approach needs support for resetting both the entire FPGA and individual RRs (to undertake partial reconfigurations). The former is achieved via the shell's *global reset* (see Fig. 2). The latter is supported by a specific reset functionality for each RR. It is implemented using the GPIO ports of the CPU, with the added complexity that HLS kernels by default contain a low active reset. We negate the GPIO signal and apply a logical *and* with the global reset signal. The application of the reset signal is asynchronous which means that the kernel might be interrupted unpredictably. The software abstractions described in Sect. 5.2 ensure that the task can be resumed later from a consistent state.

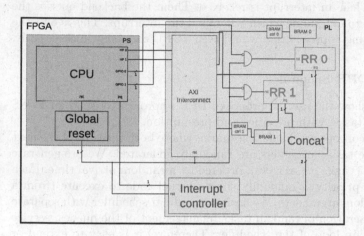

Fig. 2. Simplified architecture of the system.

This shell design is provided in *netlist* form with the RRs instantiated as black boxes. Consequently, to generate the shell's bitstream the number of RRs required is supplied to the associated TCL script. This generates a corresponding Vivado compatible DPR capable hardware design, which is built and deployed onto the FPGA. The programmer writes their HLS kernels using our proposed software abstractions (see Sect. 5.2), that effectively transform the C code into interface-compliant HLS code during the HLS synthesis.

4.2 Integration into the Controller Framework

A new backend has been written for the Controller framework. It supports interaction with our shell, targeting the Zynq-7020 FPGA in Pynq-Z2. To communicate with the FPGA, our backend uses the Pynq C API [10]. This API exposes low-level functionalities, such as the loading of both full and partial bitstreams, the interaction with design IP such as interrupt controllers or DMA engines through memory mapping, and host-device shared memory. Building on the C Pynq API means that this work is compatible with any other FPGA from the Zynq-7000 family with little modification required.

Each RR is treated as an independent accelerator by our backend to ensure that RR kernels can be executed in parallel. Thus, the Controller's queue is replicated as many times as the number of RRs, and each instance is managed by a separate thread. A request to reconfigure a region is implemented as an internal task, queued up and executed like any other task. This simplifies the backend structure and allows the scheduling of reconfigurations request before the associated task execution on the fabric. Zynq only provides a single Internal Configuration Access Port (ICAP) [12]. This means that only one RR can be partially reconfigured at a time. Thus, we need to implement a synchronisation between reconfiguration request in the Controller queues. The Zynq-7000 FPGA family architecture supports shared memory which can be accessed by both the FPGA fabric and host CPU. Thus, data-movement operations can be implemented with zero-copy. The backend utilises Userspace I/O (UIO) to interact with the shell's interrupt controller to detect the interrupts raised by the RRs to indicate kernel termination. We use the *select()* system call to activate the manager CPU thread when an interrupt is received. Then, the backend queries the interrupt controller to determine which RR raised the interrupt. This avoids the use of an active polling approach that would keep a CPU core busy unnecessarily.

4.3 Use Case: DPR Scheduler

In this section we show the use the proposed DPR approach to build an FCFS scheduler of kernel tasks, with priorities and preemption.

In this proof-of-concept we simulate scenarios where both the time of the next task arrival and the task parameters are randomly generated. We pre-generate a sequence of tasks (tasks_to_arrive), ordered by a random arrival time. Each task has a random priority, a randomly chosen kernel code to execute (from a given set), and random arguments. We design a modular scheduler with separate modules for the generation of random tasks, management of the queues, service of tasks and the main loop of the scheduler. Therefore, it is easy to extend or adapt. It is compatible with any number of RRs.

Algorithm 1. Main loop of the scheduler.

---
while *true* **do**
    $WaitForInterrupt(\&timeout)$
    if $has\_finished(N, R, \&tasks\_to\_arrive)$ **then**
        break
    end if
    if $tasks\_to\_arrive$ && $timeout == 0$ **then**
        $task = get\_arrived\_task()$
    else
        $task = get\_task\_from\_queue()$
    end if
    $serve\_task(task, R, P)$
    $update\_timeout(\&timeout)$
end while

The main loop of the scheduler is presented in Algorithm 1. The arrival of the next task is simulated with a timeout clock, used in the same `select()` function that detects the interrupts raised by the end of a kernel in a RR. Thus, the `WaitForInterrupt` function returns when a new task arrives or when a RR kernel finishes.

The process of serving a task consists of the following steps: (1) Find an available region, i.e., a region where the last task running has already finished. (2) In case no available region was found, if preemption is disabled enqueue the task. If preemption is enabled, check if there is a region executing a task with lower priority. In that case, stop the kernel execution in that region, save the context and state, enqueue the stopped task, and consider the region as available. (3) If the kernel loaded in the available region is distinct from the kernel of the incoming task, enqueue a swapping task to reconfigure the RR. (4) Launch the new task. If it was a previously stopped task, its context is copied back to the device before launching.

5 Programmer's Abstractions

This section describes the abstractions provided to the programmer to implement kernels and to use the proposed approach, without knowledge of the low-level details of the DPR technology.

5.1 Kernel Interface Abstraction

The generation of interfaces in technologies such as Vitis HLS is done adding pragmas that can be cumbersome and error prone to write. Moreover, a requirement of DPR is that HLS kernels to be deployed into a given RR must present the same external interface to the shell. They must conform to the same number of interface ports and port configurations, such as bus widths [12]. Thus, better abstractions are needed to hide these low-level details to the programmer.

```
1  CTRL_KERNEL_FUNCTION(
2    MedianBlur , PYNQ, DEFAULT,
3    KTILE_ARGS( KHitTile_int in_array ,
4                KHitTile_int out_array)
5    INT_ARGS(int H, int W, int iters),
6    FLOAT_ARGS(NO_FLOAT_ARG)) {
7    ...
8    int k, row, col;
9    context_vars(k, row, col);
10   ...
11   for_save(k, 0, iters , 1) {
12     for_save(row, 1, H+1, 1) {
13       for_save(col , 1, W+1, 1) {
14         window[0] = hit(
15         in_array , row-1, H_NCOL+col -1);
16         ...
17         checkpoint(col);
18       } checkpoint(row);
19     } checkpoint(k);
20   }
21 }
```

Listing 1.1. Sketch of a Median Blur kernel written with the Controller abstraction

The configuration of the interfaces is a parameter present in our TCL configuration script that generates the shell's hardware design, as discussed in Sect. 4.1. In the Controller model, the kernel codes are wrapped with curly brackets and preceded by a kernel signature. The kernel signature is provided with a macro-function named CTRL_KERNEL_FUNCTION. It specifies the kernel parameters in a form that is processed by the Controller library to generate the proper low-level interface. Listing 1.1 illustrates the definition of a Median Blur kernel, used in our evaluation in Sect. 6, preceded by its signature. In this work we extend the Controller kernel signature to generate code with a uniform interface, as required by the shell. The parameters of the kernel signature are the following:

CTRL_KERNEL_FUNCTION(K, T, S, A_p, A_i, A_f):

- K is the name of the kernel.
- T indicates the backend type that will be targeted. Supported types are: CPU, CUDA, OpenCL, FPGA.
- S is the subtype of backend that will be targeted, e.g. DEFAULT.
- A_p is a list of pointer non-scalar arguments defined with KTILE_ARGS.
- A_i is a list of integer scalar arguments defined with INT_ARGS.
- A_f is a list of floating point scalar arguments defined with FLOAT_ARGS.

Controller provides a wrapper structure for multi-dimensional arrays named *HitTile*. Any kind of non-scalar arguments are provided as *HitTile* arguments.

KTILE_ARGS function enables the use of *HitTile* accessors within the kernel, effectively providing input and output arrays to the kernel, as discussed in [7]. INT_ARGS and FLOAT_ARGS support passing integer and float scalar arguments, respectively. All these functions have variadic arguments to adapt the kernel interface to the number of arguments required by the programmer. The corresponding code generated by the kernel signature for the kernel shown in Listing 1.1 is shown in Listing 1.2. Three integer arguments are provided by the user and five extra dummy arguments i_args_ < n > are generated. Similarly, 8 dummy floating point and 1 dummy pointer arguments are generated to fill the argument count and provide a shell compliant interface. Finally, a pointer to a struct context is added for context book-keeping if the task is interrupted.

```
1  void MedianBlur(...,
2      int H, int W, int iters, int i_args_0, ..., int i_args_4,
3      ..., volatile struct context * context, int * return_var);
```

Listing 1.2. Code generation for the signature of the Median Blur kernel

5.2   Programmer Abstractions for Preemption

Preemption of a kernel whilst it is running requires saving its state so that it can be resumed in the future. Previous approaches, such as [5] only save the context at the end of an OpenCL workgroup. We also wanted to provide flexibility for the programmer to decide exactly where their code should be checkpointed. We propose a finer-grain and programmer-aware checkpointing approach, where the programmer has the flexibility to indicate when and what data should be checkpointed during the kernel execution. We provide several checkpointing macro-functions. The programmer declares which variables should be stored in the checkpoints using the context_vars macro-function. The checkpoint macro stores one or more of these variables at a given execution point. A for_save macro-function is used in-place of the normal *for* loop construct, to provide support for resumption on a specific loop iteration. These calls are expanded to the proper code at synthesis time.

An example of their use is shown in Listing 1.1. At line 11 the integer variables k, *row*, and *col* are selected to be checkpointed, with lines 11, 12, and 13 using the for_save macro to define loops and for these to be restarted as appropriate. The associated loop variables are checkpointed at lines 17, 18, and 19. This kernel saves the state at each iteration to be able to be resumed without discarding previously computed iterations.

```
1  struct context {
2    int var [N];
3    int init_var [N
     ];
4    int incr_var [N
     ];
5    int saved [N];
6    int valid;
7  };
```

Listing 1.3. Definition of struct context.

Context saving is done transparently storing the state in the struct context generated in BRAM (see Listing 1.3). In our prototype up to N integers can be nominated by the user to be saved, where N is a compile time parameter. It is trivial to extend the structure to support other data types. The field saved keeps information about whether the variables have already been saved through checkpoint and they should be restored in a resume operation. The valid field is used to indicate if the asynchronous preemption interrupted the kernel during a data saving operation. In that case, the resume operation will be done with the previously saved values.

6 Experimental Study

We present the results of an experimental study to evaluate the efficiency of our approach.

6.1 Use Case: Scheduler of Randomly Generated Image Filter Tasks

In this study we experiment with the scheduler described in Sect. 4.3. The kernels chosen for the experimentation are blur image filters applied to images pre-stored in memory. Tasks execute one of four possible kernels: Median Blur over one, two or three iterations or one iteration of Gaussian Blur. Tasks arrive at random times distributed over $\mathcal{U}(0, T)$ minutes. The scheduler features optional preemption and priorities. For these experiments we choose to use 5 different priorities, to generate enough preemptions, task switching and reconfigurations. The tasks, their arrival time, and the image on which it should be applied, are randomly generated before the scheduler starts.

6.2 Experimentation Environment

The experiments were conducted on a Xilinx PYNQ-Z2 FPGA. It features a ZYNQ XC7Z020-1CLG400C of the Zynq-7020 family, an ARM Cortex-A9 dual core at 650 MHz CPU and 512 MB DDR3. HLS kernels were compiled using Xilinx Vitis HLS version 2020.2 and the hardware design and corresponding bitstreams were generated with Xilinx Vivado v2020.2. Controller was compiled with GCC 9.3.0 and compilation scripts were generated with CMake 3.20.5.

Several random seeds for the task generation have been tested. We show the results for the value 15. The main observations can be extrapolated for other random sequences. The number of tasks generated was chosen to be 30. We enabled priorities both with and without preemption of tasks. We considered three different rate of arrivals T: busy (0.1), medium (0.5) and idle (0.8). We worked with image sizes 200×200, 300×300, 400×400, 500×500 and 600×600. In order to study the sequential vs. the parallel behaviour both one and two RRs were considered. Finally, each experiment was executed ten times to account for variability and the results presented are average times with standard deviation.

6.3 Results

In order to show the effectiveness of our approach we are presenting results for the following metrics: (i) service time, defined as the time it takes for a task to be served since it is generated until it starts execution on the FPGA and (ii) throughput, defined as the number of tasks executed per second. We also compare the use of partial reconfiguration with the more conventional full reconfiguration approach. Figure 3 reports the service time for tasks in every priority queue both with and without preemption for 30 tasks at size 600×600 accumulated by priority. We chose this number of tasks and image size as it provides enough workload and a sufficient number of tasks to study the behaviour of the scheduler. The results are presented both for one and two RRs. As can be seen, service times are longer for the busy rate of arrival than for medium and idle, as tasks have to wait a longer time until a RR becomes available than when they arrive later, giving the opportunity for kernels to finish. If the priority of an incoming task is higher than one of the tasks running, then its service time will be virtually zero. We can observe this by comparing the plots on the right with plots on the left. For this representative case, on average, preemption reduces service time substantially. This will be the case in general when incoming tasks present a higher priority than running tasks. These results show that our scheduler effectively reduces the total service time of tasks, thus increasing the flexibility, as preemption enables swapping in and out tasks upon a condition — priority in this case. The reduction in service time is heavily dependent on the structure of priorities of the generated tasks, both in terms of the number of tasks enqueued and the number of reconfigurations enforced by incoming kernels not loaded already in the fabric. Note that a task will have to wait until previous tasks of higher or the same priority have completed. Additionally, as shown in Fig. 3, the service time decreases with the number of RRs, as more opportunities are created for kernels of lower priorities to execute.

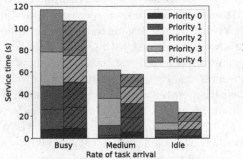 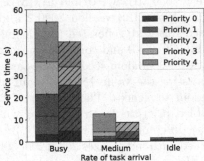

Fig. 3. Service times for 30 tasks at size 600×600. 1 RR (left), 2 RRs (right). Per bar group: Non-preemptive (left), preemptive (right).

Figure 4 shows the throughput of the scheduler with 30 tasks both with and without preemption over one and two RRs. As expected, the throughput increases with the rate of arrival of tasks. The lower the dimensions of the images the higher the throughput, as the kernels complete execution faster. It is also noticeable that the overheads incurred by preemption lead to a slightly lower throughput. These are most noticeable for a high rate of arrival of tasks, where throughput losses are 8.3% and 10.7% for the case with one and two RRs, respectively, at size 200 and busy arrival rate. For the rest of cases the loss ranges between 0–4%. Most of this overhead is explained by the time taken by the extra partial reconfigurations imposed by preemption. The dashed red lines show an upper bound of the throughput if full reconfiguration was used instead. This has been calculated from the throughput at busy rate of arrival adding the product of the number of reconfigurations by the average difference on time between full (0.22 s) and partial (0.07 s) reconfiguration. This is a highly optimistic upper bound, since it does not take into account the effects of stalling the FPGA, which impedes the concurrency of kernel execution and reconfiguration, and enforces a preemption of the rest of kernels that are to be kept in the FPGA. Finally, the average preemption overhead observed is 1.66% for one RR with standard deviation 2.60%, and 4.04% for two RRs with a standard deviation of 7.16%. The deviation is high due to a overhead peak of 23.40% for busy rate of arrival at size 200 × 200. This indicates that this technique might not be interesting for short tasks whose execution time is comparable to the reconfiguration time.

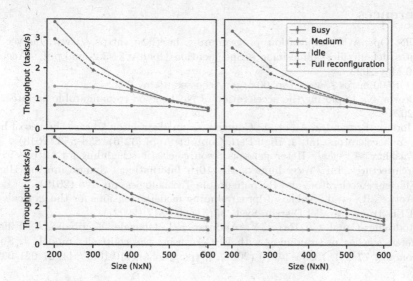

Fig. 4. Throughput for 30 tasks. 1 RR (first row) and 2 RRs (second row). Non-preemptive (first column) and preemptive (second column).

7   Conclusions

This work presents a task-based abstraction for programming FPGAs that enables task preemption using DPR. We abstract the low-level details of the generation of a DPR capable system and provide a high-level API for simple management of kernel launch, data transfer and transparent book-keeping for context preemption. We show that our approach enhances flexibility by reducing the service time of urgent tasks thanks to the ability to swap tasks in and out. The overhead of preemptive vs. non-preemptive scheduling with DPR is 1.66% on average for one RR and 4.04% for two RRs. Finally, our simulations show significant performance gains over the traditional use of full reconfiguration.

Future work includes, in no particular order:

1. Task migration between FPGA and other architectures e.g. GPU and CPU.
2. Extension to data-center FPGAs e.g. as Xilinx Versal and Xilinx Alveo.
3. Extension of the backend to leverage full reconfiguration to provide an accurate measure of the performance gain through the use of DPR.
4. Reduction of the overhead of this technique with a custom ICAP controller, as Xilinx's can only exploit up to 2.5% of the port bandwidth [11].

Acknowledgements. The authors acknowledge EPCC at the University of Edinburgh and EPSRC who have funded this work and provided the FPGA compute resource. This research has been partially funded by Junta de Castilla y León - FEDER Grants, project PROPHET-2 (VA226P20).

References

1. The OpenACC application programming interface. https://www.openacc.org/sites/default/files/inline-images/Specification/OpenACC-3.2-final.pdf. Accessed 19 May 2022
2. TOP500. https://www.top500.org/. Accessed 9 May 2022
3. Brown, N.: Exploring the acceleration of Nekbone on reconfigurable architectures (2020)
4. Moreton-Fernandez, A., et al.: Controllers: an abstraction to ease the use of hardware accelerators. Int. J. High Perf. Comput. Appl. **32**(6), 838–853 (2018)
5. Vaishnav, A., et al.: Heterogeneous resource-elastic scheduling for CPU+ FPGA architectures. In: Proceedings of the 10th International Symposium on Highly-Efficient Accelerators and Reconfigurable Technologies, pp. 1–6 (2019)
6. Trott, C.R., et al.: Kokkos 3: programming model extensions for the exascale era. IEEE Trans. Parallel Distrib. Syst. **33**(4), 805–817 (2022)
7. Rodriguez-Canal, G., Torres, Y., Andújar, F.J., Gonzalez-Escribano, A.: Efficient heterogeneous programming with FPGAs using the controller model. J. Supercomput. **77**(12), 13995–14010 (2021). https://doi.org/10.1007/s11227-021-03792-7
8. Brown, N., et al.: It's all about data movement: Optimising FPGA data access to boost performance. In: 2019 IEEE/ACM International Workshop on Heterogeneous High-performance Reconfigurable Computing (H2RC), pp. 1–10. IEEE (2019)
9. Munshi, A.: The OpenCL specification. In: 2009 IEEE Hot Chips 21 Symposium (HCS), pp. 1–314. IEEE (2009)
10. Brown, N.: PYNQ API: C API for PYNQ FPGA board. https://github.com/mesham/pynq_api (2019). Accessed 20 June 2021
11. Vipin, K., Fahmy, S.A.: FPGA dynamic and partial reconfiguration: a survey of architectures, methods, and applications. ACM Comput. Surv. (CSUR) **51**(4), 1–39 (2018)
12. Xilinx. Vivado design user suite guide - dynamic function eXchange. https://bit.ly/3MEDZTI. Accessed 9 May 2022

Modeling Task Mapping for Data-Intensive Applications in Heterogeneous Systems

Martin Wilhelm[✉], Hanna Geppert, Anna Drewes, and Thilo Pionteck

Otto-von-Guericke University, Magdeburg, Germany
`martin.wilhelm@ovgu.de`

Abstract. We introduce a new model for the task mapping problem to aid in the systematic design of algorithms for heterogeneous systems including, but not limited to, CPUs, GPUs and FPGAs. A special focus is set on the communication between the devices, its influence on parallel execution, as well as on device-specific differences regarding parallelizability and streamability. We show how this model can be utilized in different system design phases and present two novel mixed-integer linear programs to demonstrate the usage of the model.

Keywords: Heterogeneous computing · Task mapping · Resource allocation · Modeling · MILP · FPGA · Hardware/software partitioning · Design space exploration

1 Introduction

With Moore's Law declining, modern computing systems become increasingly heterogeneous, containing processing devices, such as CPUs, GPUs or FPGAs as well as associated memories with vastly different characteristics. A significant challenge lies in the mapping of application tasks to fitting devices. In general, a mapping should minimize the execution time of a task on a certain device, which is influenced by multiple factors, such as the parallelizability and streamability of a task. Nevertheless, a better suited device may be a suboptimal choice if the device is already highly contended. Moreover, even an unused device with a high processing speed may be avoided if the data transfer cost between devices exceeds the gain from the parallelization.

In this work, we develop an abstract model for the task mapping problem on heterogeneous devices for data-intensive applications, where communication cost plays a significant role. With this model we aim to support developers in the early design phases of a heterogeneous system and clear the path for theoretical evaluations and comparisons of task mapping algorithms. We demonstrate the capabilities of the model based on two linear programs in a sample environment, which can be used as a reference for future heuristics.

J. Singer et al. (Eds.): Euro-Par 2022 Workshops, LNCS 13835, pp. 145–157, 2023.
https://doi.org/10.1007/978-3-031-31209-0_11

2   State of the Art

The mapping of tasks to processing devices (also called resource/task allocation or workload partitioning) describes a central step in the design of heterogeneous systems. Much work exists for CPU-GPU task mapping [7]. Research in this field mainly focuses on (application-)specific algorithms without a reference to a general model or a common measure of cost. This makes it difficult to compare different approaches and to transfer insights to new problems. Some authors introduce a more detailed model [2,11]. However, the underlying parallelism of a heterogeneous system is seldom taken into account, especially with respect to the impact of data transfer. In the field of production research, a closely related problem is known as the *agent bottleneck generalized assignment problem* [1,5]. Here, the parallel execution through different agents is central, but communication cost between the agents are usually not present.

Few work is present that includes dataflow-based devices such as FPGAs. Works that include FPGAs frequently model them similar to software processing units [10]. Yet, FPGAs have special characteristics as they are area-bound and enable pipelining, leading to vastly different behavior. Modeling these differences is crucial for exploiting their full potential [3]. Owaida et al. discuss these differences in the context of designing OpenCL tasks for FPGAs [9]. Much work is done in the closely related field of hardware/software partitioning [6]. Models in this field better reflect hardware properties [8], but usually do not differentiate between software units e.g. in terms of parallelizability.

3   Modeling

In this section, we develop an abstract system model with a minimal set of interfaces that allows us to define a cost function to assess the quality of a given task mapping. We then show how this model can be utilized in different phases of a systematic design space exploration for a heterogeneous system.

3.1   Abstract Model

In different design phases, different knowledge about the system properties is present, therefore it is crucial to make single components of the model exchangeable without the need to adjust other components or the underlying algorithm. For this, we split the system model into an *application model*, which describes the properties of and relations between tasks, a *platform model* describing the characteristics of the available hardware, and an *implementation model*, defining the relation between the available hardware and the application model.

The **application model** is based on a task graph, i.e., a directed acyclic graph, where nodes represent tasks and edges represent data dependencies between these tasks. Similarly to Campeanu et al. [2], we differentiate between *computation nodes* and *memory nodes*. While computation nodes indicate that a certain computation must be executed, memory nodes indicate that data must be made available. More precisely, each task consists of three nodes: a memory node representing the input data, a computation node, and a memory node representing the output data. Furthermore, additional memory nodes may indicate data sources or sinks (Fig. 1). This representation is based on the assumption that a high amount of data needs to be computed, making memory access mandatory during the execution of each task. It allows us to accurately differentiate between the cost caused by the computation and the cost caused by the memory access. In particular, it allows us to consider different locations for the data. For example, a CPU could work on data provided by the System RAM and write it back directly into the GPU RAM.

In the **hardware model**, we assume that (1) each computation device is connected to (at least) one associated memory, (2) data transfer can only happen between memories (not between computation devices) and (3) the computation of a device is blocked by a memory transfer from or to the associated memory. Usually, the associated memory refers to a respective RAM unit, e.g. a GPU RAM for the GPU or the System RAM for the CPU. The model, however, is not limited to one memory unit per device. While the data transfer between different memories is usually done through DMA units, it is still reasonable to assume that computation units are affected by the memory transfer, since they cannot access their respective data. Excess data rate, however, can be used to start independent tasks. We elaborate on this in Sect. 3.3.

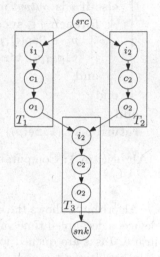

Fig. 1. Sample memory-augmented task graph with three tasks, one source and one sink.

The **(task) implementation model** represents the relation between the application and hardware model. Its main purpose is to work as an interface between those two models and to make parts of the modeling framework more interchangeable. Between each node of the application model and each device, a compatibility relation is defined that indicates which task can be mapped onto which device. Naturally, memory nodes can only be mapped onto memories and computation nodes must be mapped onto a processing device. However, there can be further restrictions. For example, a cache may only fit memory nodes that contain a small amount of data or a tensor processing unit can only execute a small subset of tasks. In addition to a compatibility function, the implementation model defines how much time is needed to execute a task on a certain device or to transport the output of a task from one device to another.

The overall advantage of the described modeling approach lies in the possibility to easily evaluate a given task mapping while abstracting from implementation and platform details. Consequently, we define a **cost function** based on a simple, but reasonably effective, evaluation algorithm.

> **Input**: Nodes, Devices, Map : Nodes $\mapsto$ Devices
> SortedNodes $\leftarrow$ topsort_bfs(Nodes)
> **foreach** $p \in$ Devices **do** time$(p) \leftarrow 0$
> **foreach** $i \in$ SortedNodes **do**
> > **if** i is *input memory node* **then**
> > > $j \leftarrow$ successor$(i), k \leftarrow$ successor(j)
> > > $p_i \leftarrow$ Map$(i), p_j \leftarrow$ Map$(j), p_k \leftarrow$ Map(k)
> > > t $\leftarrow$ max(time(p_i), time(p_j), time$(p_k)) + d_{i,p_i,p_j} + t_{j,p_j} + d_{j,p_j,p_k}$
> > > time(p_i), time(p_j), time$(p_k) \leftarrow$ t
> >
> > **else if** i is *output memory node* **or** *source* **then**
> > > **foreach** $j \in$ successors(i) **do**
> > > > $p_i \leftarrow$ Map$(i), p_j \leftarrow$ Map(j)
> > > > time(p_i), time$(p_j) \leftarrow$ max(time(p_i), time$(p_j)) + d_{i,p_i,p_j}$
> > >
> > > **end**
> >
> > **end**
>
> **end**
> **return** max$_p$(time(p))

Algorithm 1: Computation of the total cost of a given task-device mapping.

Algorithm 1 shows the computation of the cost of a given mapping. For each device, a decoupled time value is managed, which is increased when the device is in use. Tasks are queued for execution according to a topological sorting based on a breadth-first search. There are two main cost factors. The *transportation of data* from task i on device p to device q, denoted by d_{ipq}, and the *execution of a task* i on device p, denoted by t_{ip}. Transportation of data happens along the edge between two memory nodes. The time values of both memories are synchronized and increased according to the time given by the implementation model. The time for the execution of a task consists of the time for the read access to the input memory, the write access to the output memory and the computation time on the given device. The time values of all three involved devices are synchronized and the total time for the execution is added to each of them. Note that the input memory waits for the output memory and vice versa to account for the fact that data is processed in small chunks.

After all tasks have finished, the overall cost for the computation is given as the maximum time value over all devices. This value may depend on the used schedule, i.e. the order of tasks in the topological sorting. A potential bias can be circumvented by choosing the topological sorting at random.

3.2 Models for Different Design Stages

The high abstraction level of the model presented in Sect. 3.1 allows the designer to reuse optimization algorithms written for this model in different design stages.

In an early design stage, the time for task execution and data transport can be determined based on superficial characteristics of the given tasks and potential devices. This allows for a rapid estimate on the required characteristics for a performance gain and, in consequence, supports the designer in their hardware choice. In a later design stage, promising tasks may be implemented and measured on different devices. With these more precise values, the same algorithms can support the designer in finding the optimal configuration.

We present a simple realization of the abstract system model that can be used during an **early design stage**. In particular, we describe a more detailed hardware and application model that fulfills the specifications demanded by the abstraction. The model is primarily based on the *task sizes* of the given application and the processable *data rates* of the devices. The general idea is to get an estimate of the processing time of a certain amount of data based on device characteristics. Each task node is attributed with a *data processing function*, which computes the amount of output data generated from input data of a certain size, e.g. a simple sum of two values would have a 2:1 relation between input and output data. In addition, each node has a *complexity function*, which determines the amount of computations needed based on the input data. Finally, each computation node indicates which percentage of its execution time is *parallelizable*. For the sake of simplicity, we assume that the parallelizable part is fully parallelizable with an arbitrary amount of processors.

In the hardware model, we compute the data rate of a memory as the product of (1) the bus clock speed, (2) the bus width and (3) the number of memory channels. We set the *serial data rate* r_s of a processing device to the clock rate multiplied with a device-specific *overhead penalty*, describing the overhead caused by the microarchitecture. Note that a penalty is relevant only if the overhead is expected to be vastly different between devices. In the evaluation given in Sect. 5, we therefore do not apply penalties. In addition to the serial data rate, each processing device is assigned a *parallelization factor* r_p consisting of (1) the number of cores and (2) the potential data parallelism. For example, in case of a GPU, the second factor equals the number and width of SIMD units.

Finally, in the implementation model, we set the *execution time* of a task node on a device to 0 for a memory node and to $data_{in} /(r_s * (1 - p + pr_p))$ for a computation node, where $p \in [0, 1]$ denotes the parallelizability of the task. The *transport time* is determined by the minimum of the data rates of the two connected devices and a potential data rate limitation between them. It is set to infinity if no edge is present in a given hardware graph.

Using this model, an early assessment of the potential of a heterogeneous implementation can be made. In a **later design stage** a measure-based model should replace these rough estimates. For this, (time) complexity functions for both the execution and the transport time should be derived from the measured data, which can then be directly incorporated into the task implementation model. Using appropriate penalties, a mixture of both models can be used if measured data isn't available for all task-device combinations.

3.3   Extension: Full Usage of Data Busses

Data transport between two memories is usually done through DMAs, which are independent of the processing devices. Hence, processing devices are in principle able to execute tasks during the transport of (independent) data. In the presented abstract model, on the other hand, we wait until the input and output memories are unoccupied before we start another execution. The reasoning behind this decision is that during processing, data must be accessed by the processing device and therefore access to the memory bus is needed. However, a data transaction does not always use the full data rate of both memories. If, for example, memory is transferred between System RAM and GPU RAM, the transaction speed is usually limited by the bus of the GPU RAM. The remaining bus width of the System RAM can be used by a processing device to access data.

The resulting gain in performance can be incorporated into the model by adjusting the blocking time according to the used resources. Let r_1, r_2 be the data rate of two devices p_1, p_2 with $r_1 \leq r_2$. Then a data transport between these two devices that takes time t increases (after synchronization) the time value of p_1 by t and of p_2 by $\frac{r_1}{r_2}t$. The increase in the time value of p_2 represents the time that the device would work if it could use all of its resources for the task, i.e., the total delay that a parallel execution of other tasks accessing p_2 would experience. Note that the additional capabilities can only be used by independent computations. A task that is dependent on the data transport between p_1 and p_2 won't be able to make use of the free resources. Hence, the cost computation algorithm must assure that a dependent task waits the full time t until its computation is started.

3.4   Extension: Streamability and Virtual Memory

In the current model we write data back to the memory after each task execution. Depending on the granularity of the tasks, this may be inefficient if a subsequent task is executed on the same device. If a task works only locally on the given data, we may do several subsequent processing steps on the same data before writing it back to memory. These tasks are called *streamable*. We can model this behavior in two ways: (1) we modify the cost function to ignore memory accesses between subsequent tasks that are executed on the same device and do not produce intermediate data used by other devices or non-streamable tasks, or (2) we introduce *virtual memories* into the hardware model with zero access time from the chosen device and infinite data transfer time to other devices. Virtual memories can then be used in between operations on the same device to hide the memory access. The first variant increases the complexity of the cost function, whereas the second variant shifts the responsibility to the mapping algorithm.

A special case for streamability is the handling of dataflow-based devices such as FPGAs. Here, not only the memory access can be omitted, but also the execution of tasks can be pipelined, i.e., operations can be executed in parallel along the stream. Therefore, a subtree of streamable tasks on such a device will only take as long as the most expensive processing or memory node in the sub-tree. A limitation to this property is given by the limited area on such a device. To integrate this behavior into our model, we introduce an area requirement for all tasks and modify the cost function to compress subtrees up to the size of the respective device to one single task. Furthermore, bigger tasks that are streamable and fit on a single FPGA may also greatly benefit from pipelined processing. Regarding Sect. 3.2, the behavior can be modeled by a streamability factor for each task, indicating into how many pipelined steps the task can be split. If a computation node is mapped onto an FPGA and doesn't exceed the maximum area available on the FPGA, the execution time is reduced by this factor.

4   Mixed-Integer Linear Programs

The abstract model presented in Sect. 3.1 allows us to effectively develop and compare algorithms and heuristics for heterogeneous task assignments without regard for implementation details. In this section, we present two mixed-integer linear programs for heterogeneous task assignment based on the model.

4.1   Device-Based ILP

In the first MILP, we aim to minimize the maximum time on each device. In a system with n nodes and m devices, let t_{ip} be the time required to execute task i on device p and let d_{ipq} be the time required to transport the output data of task i from device p to device q. Let x_{ip} be a binary variable indicating that task i is executed on device p, and let E be the set of edges in the application graph. Then the times T_p, T_p^{in}, T_p^{out} reflecting the total time of execution on, transport to, and transport from device p, respectively, are given as:

$$T_p = \sum_{i=1}^{n} x_{ip}t_{ip} \qquad T_p^{in} = \sum_{q=1}^{m} \sum_{(i,j)\in E} d_{ipq}x_{ip}x_{jq} \qquad T_p^{out} = \sum_{q=1}^{m} \sum_{(i,j)\in E} d_{iqp}x_{iq}x_{jp}$$

Note that the quadratic terms $x_{ip}x_{jq}$ can be replaced by single variables using the McCormick inequalities $x_{ipjq} \leq x_{ip}$, $x_{ipjq} \leq x_{jq}$ and $x_{ipjq} + 1 \geq x_{ip} + x_{jq}$. Our goal is to minimize the term $\max_p(T_p + T_p^{in} + T_p^{out})$. To resolve the minmax formulation, we introduce another variable z with $z \geq T_p + T_p^{in} + T_p^{out}$ for all $p \in \{1, ..., m\}$, which is then minimized. As additional constraint we ensure that each task node is mapped to one device. Let C_i be the set of devices that are compatible to task i. Then we want to guarantee that $\sum_{p\in C_i} x_{ip} = 1$ for all $i \in \{1, ..., n\}$. Hence our final MILP is given as

$$\text{minimize } z$$
$$\text{subject to } z \geq T_p + T_p^{in} + T_p^{out} \qquad\qquad \forall p \in \{1, ..., m\}$$
$$\sum_{p\in C_i} x_{ip} = 1 \qquad\qquad\qquad \forall i \in \{1, ..., n\}$$

4.2   Time-Based ILP

While above MILP is reasonably simple, it does not consider execution order
and synchronization issues. In this section, we present a more exact, but also
more expensive time-based linear program. Here, the goal is to "simulate" an
execution, i.e., to assign start and end times to each task. For this, we introduce
variables $y_{i,0}, y_{i,1}$ representing the start and end of the execution of node i.

With the notation from the previous section, we guarantee that there is
sufficient time before the start and the end of the execution of a node and that
a node can only be started if all previous nodes have been processed. Hence,

$$y_{i,1} \geq y_{i,0} + \sum_{p=1}^{m} x_{ip}t_{ip} \quad \text{and} \quad y_{j,0} \geq y_{i,1} + \sum_{p=1}^{m}\sum_{q=1}^{m} d_{ipq}x_{ip}x_{jq}$$

for all tasks i and all edges (i,j), respectively. In contrast to the device-based
variant, we must assure that each device is used for only one task simultaneously.
For this, we sort the tasks topologically and assure that all tasks that are mapped
onto the same device are executed in topological order. Hence, we demand

$$y_{j,0} \geq \sum_{p=1}^{m} x_{ip}x_{jp}y_{i,1}$$

for all $j \in \{1, ..., n\}$ and all $i < j$. This equation can be linearized by replacing
it with $y_{j,0} - y_{i,1} \geq Mx_{ip}x_{jp} - M$ for all p with a sufficiently large constant
M and using the McCormick inequalities as before. We minimize the maximum
time z by demanding $z \geq y_{i,1}$ for all tasks. Adding, as before, the condition that
a device must be assigned to each task node, we get

minimize z

subject to $z \geq y_{i,1}$ $\hspace{4cm} \forall i \in \{1, ..., n\}$

$$y_{i,1} \geq y_{i,0} + \sum_{p=1}^{m} x_{ip}t_{ip} \hspace{3cm} \forall i \in \{1, ..., n\}$$

$$y_{j,0} \geq y_{i,1} + \sum_{p=1}^{m}\sum_{q=1}^{m} d_{ipq}x_{ip}x_{jq} \hspace{2cm} \forall (i,j) \in E$$

$$y_{j,0} \geq \sum_{p=1}^{m} x_{ip}x_{jp}y_{i,1} \hspace{2cm} \forall j \in \{1, ..., n\}, \forall i \in \{1, ..., j-1\}$$

$$\sum_{p \in C_i} x_{ip} = 1 \hspace{4cm} \forall i \in \{1, ..., n\}$$

4.3   Extension: Streamable Devices

The time-based linear program can be extended to reflect the pipelining behavior of dataflow-based devices such as FPGAs. For this, we modify the order

constraint to enable tasks on streamable devices to start simultaneously with a parent task executed on the same device. Let D be the set of all devices and D_p be the set of pairs of dataflow-based devices and their associated memories (including pairs with themselves). Then the modified constraint is given as

$$y_{j,0} \geq y_{i,1} + \sum_{(p,q) \in D^2 \setminus D_p} d_{ipq} x_{ip} x_{jq} - \sum_{(p,q) \in D_p} x_{ip} x_{jq} t_{ip}, \quad \forall (i,j) \in E$$

By this, we effectively reduce the constraint to $y_{j,0} \geq y_{i,0}$ if both tasks are on associated dataflow-based devices. Finally, to take the maximum of all operations in the pipeline, we ensure that a task cannot end before its parent ends, i.e., $y_{j,1} \geq y_{i,1} \ \forall (i,j) \in E$.

Since devices such as FPGAs have a maximum capacity, we must ensure that the total number of tasks added to the device does not exceed this capacity. Let s_i be the area requirement for task i and S_p' be the capacity of a device p. Then

$$\sum_{i=1}^{n} x_{ip} s_i \leq S_p \quad \forall p \in D_s$$

where D_s is the set of all streamable devices. This capacity constraint is added to the device-based approach as well to ensure a valid configuration, even though the pipelining capability can't be represented.

5 Evaluation

We demonstrate the usage of the model in an early design stage through several experiments in a sample environment. We determine the execution time and data transfer time based on the specifications of the given devices and the size of a virtual data load as described in Sect. 3.2. Our virtual test system contains an AMD Epyc 7531P with 16 cores (32 threads), a clock rate of 2.4 GHz and SIMD processing with 8×32B words, as well as a AMD Radeon RX Vega 56 with 1.6 GHz and 3584 SIMD units. Furthermore we assume a Xilinx XCZ7045 FPGA with a clock rate of 400 MHz and an equivalent of 350k logic cells, partitioned into 28 area units. We assume appropriate RAM units for CPU, GPU and FPGA with a calculated throughput of 170 GB/s, 410 GB/s and 11 GB/s, respectively.

For the application, we generate random series-parallel graphs with 30 edges. For this, we start with a connected source and sink node and subsequently add edges using either a series (split an edge into two by adding a node on it) or parallel (copy an edge) operation. The resulting graphs are stereotypical for data-intensive applications where you start with a common data set, process the data along different computation paths and combine the outputs to a common result. In order to avoid duplicate edges, we set the probability of a series operation to $0.5 + 0.5 \frac{i}{m}$, where m is the desired number of edges and i is the number of edges already added. That is, we start with a probability of 0.5 and continuously increase the probability to 1. After removing duplicate edges, we arrive at graphs with, on average, around 21 nodes and 22 edges. Each node, except for the source and sink, is then converted to a task with input, computation and output node, resulting in application graphs with on average slightly below 60 nodes.

We assign the same data load to each task, so the data processing function of each task is the identity function. We choose the parallelizability of a task uniformly between 0 and 1 and the complexity function as a linear function $f(x) = cx$, where the factor c is log-normal-distributed with $\mu = 3, \sigma = 0.5$. The parameters are chosen to create generally similar complexities with occasional outliers of significantly higher complexity. About 90% of the generated values for c lie in the interval $[10, 50]$ with a median of 20. For the FPGA extension, we assume that every task is streamable and that the area needed for a task as well as the possible gain through streaming is equal to its complexity factor. Through this, one used unit of area is equated to roughly one pipelining step. The linear programs are solved using Gurobi 9.1.2 [4] in Python on an AMD EPYC 7542 with 2TB RAM.

Table 1. Performance gain through task assignment strategies compared to assigning all tasks to the CPU for 100 graphs with on average 20 tasks and 100 MB input data. The fourth column indicates the number of cases in which the performance could be improved. Execution time is given in the last column.

	Avg	Min	Max	# impr.	Tme avg
CG					
Device-based	−10%	−19%	29%	8	0.06 s
Time-based	11%	−10%	66%	81	4.98 s
CGF					
Device-based	1%	−17%	54%	46	0.11 s
Time-based	17%	−8%	64%	92	18.95 s
CGFF					
Device-based	6%	−18%	40%	65	0.19 s
Time-based	19%	−5%	71%	94	47.54 s

In Table 1, results are listed for three different hardware configurations: A configuration with only CPU and GPU (**CG**), a configuration with CPU, GPU and one FPGA (**CGF**) and a configuration with CPU, GPU and two identical FPGAs (**CGFF**). It shows the average, minimum and maximum change of performance compared to an implementation where all tasks are mapped to the CPU. For our input data, mapping all tasks to the GPU makes the execution about 33% slower. Compared to the CPU, the higher parallelization factor of the GPU leads to an improvement only if close to 100% of the task is parallelizable. Consequently, potential improvements through the GPU are mainly enabled by the simultaneous execution of different tasks using uncontended memories.

As the results show, the time-based ILP is usually more effective than the device-based ILP in increasing the performance of the execution. Both the maximum performance gain and the frequency of getting an improved mapping is higher for the time-based ILP. Adding one or two FPGAs increases the size of the design space and consequently leads to more optimization opportunities, showing potential performance gains of up to 71%.

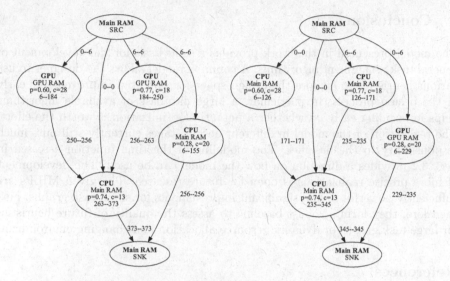

Fig. 2. Mappings found by the **device-based** (left) and the **time-based** (right) LP for a small sample graph. For each node, the parallelizability p and complexity factor c are given. At the edges and in the nodes, the time windows for transport and computation are annotated. For all tasks, the chosen input and output memory are identical, the corresponding nodes are omitted for readability.

An exemplary mapping of the two algorithms is shown in Fig. 2. Both depicted mappings improve on a pure CPU mapping (which has a cost of 423 time steps). The device-based approach chooses to put two moderately well parallelizable tasks on the GPU (with parallelizability 0.6 and 0.77, respectively). However it is not able to recognize that both nodes lie on the critical path of the task graph. The time-based approach is able to identify the critical path and therefore puts a badly parallelizable, but uncritical, task on the GPU, reducing the overall cost of the mapping. However, there are cases in which the device-based ILP finds a better mapping, since it is not restricted to follow a specific topological order. Furthermore, it is less complex to solve and therefore better suitable for very large task graphs. As shown in the last column of Table 1, the device-based approach is about two orders of magnitude faster than the time-based approach.

In the example shown in Fig. 2, the transfer cost between different memories has only a small impact on the mapping. This changes drastically if the complexity of the computations is reduced. If the complexity is set to 1 for all tasks, switching devices is much more costly compared to the computation itself. In this case, in each of the hardware configurations only about 40 out of 100 graphs with 30 edges could be improved using the time-based algorithm and about 2 out of 100 graphs with the device-based ILP. Furthermore, the tendency to map multiple connected tasks to the same device strongly increases.

6 Conclusion

The model presented in this work provides a solid basis for the development of general task assignment algorithms. A common model allows the designer to use various heuristics to explore the design space for potential improvements early in the design process. In particular, a large database of available algorithms helps in deciding early on whether a potential optimization is worth the effort. The realization of the model in different design stages currently still puts much responsibility to the designer. The modeling of the time function assessed in Sect. 3.2 provides a direction on how the model can be used. The development of more precise realizations is open for future research. The given MILPs are sufficiently powerful to find significant improvements for small task graphs. Furthermore, they form a robust baseline to assess the quality of future heuristics for large task graphs or dynamic resource allocation in a changing environment.

References

1. Bektur, G.: A multi-start iterated tabu search algorithm for the multi-resource agent bottleneck generalized assignment problem. Int. J. Opt. Contr. **10**(1), 37–46 (2019). https://doi.org/10.11121/ijocta.01.2020.00796
2. Campeanu, G., Carlson, J., Sentilles, S.: Component allocation optimization for heterogeneous CPU-GPU embedded systems. In: 40th EUROMICRO Conference on Software Engineering and Advanced Applications, SEAA 2014, Verona, Italy, 27–29 August 2014, pp. 229–236. IEEE Computer Society (2014). https://doi.org/10.1109/SEAA.2014.29
3. Che, S., Li, J., Sheaffer, J.W., Skadron, K., Lach, J.C.: Accelerating compute-intensive applications with GPUS and FPGAs. In: Proceedings of the IEEE Symposium on Application Specific Processors, SASP 2008, 8–9 June 2008, Anaheim, California, USA, pp. 101–107. IEEE Computer Society (2008). https://doi.org/10.1109/SASP.2008.4570793
4. Gurobi Optimization. LLC: Gurobi Optimizer Reference Manual (2022). https://www.gurobi.com
5. Özlem Karsu, Azizoğlu, M.: The multi-resource agent bottleneck generalised assignment problem. Int. J. Prod. Res. **50**(2), 309–324 (2012). https://doi.org/10.1080/00207543.2010.538745
6. Mhadhbi, I., Ben Othman, S., Ben Saoud, S.: A comprehensive survey on hardware/software partitioning process in co-design. Int. J. Comput. Sci. Inf. Secur. **14**, 263 (2016)

7. Mittal, S., Vetter, J.S.: A survey of CPU-GPU heterogeneous computing techniques. ACM Comput. Surv. **47**(4), 69:1–69:35 (2015). https://doi.org/10.1145/2788396
8. Niemann, R., Marwedel, P.: An algorithm for hardware/software partitioning using mixed integer linear programming. Des. Autom. Embed. Syst. **2**(2), 165–193 (1997). https://doi.org/10.1023/A:1008832202436
9. Owaida, M., Falcão, G., et al.: Enhancing design space exploration by extending CPU/GPU specifications onto fpgas. ACM Trans. Embed. Comput. Syst. **14**(2), 33:1–33:23 (2015). https://doi.org/10.1145/2656207
10. Wang, T., Chang, W., Srivastava, A., Kannan, R., Prasanna, V.K.: Monte carlo tree search for task mapping onto heterogeneous platforms. In: 28th IEEE International Conference on High Performance Computing, Data, and Analytics, HiPC 2021, Bengaluru, India, 17–20 December 2021, pp. 63–70. IEEE (2021). https://doi.org/10.1109/HiPC53243.2021.00020
11. Wang, T., Srivastava, A., Prasanna, V.K.: A framework for task mapping onto heterogeneous platforms. In: 2020 IEEE High Performance Extreme Computing Conference, HPEC 2020, Waltham, MA, USA, 22–24 September 2020, pp. 1–6. IEEE (2020). https://doi.org/10.1109/HPEC43674.2020.9286211

Mapping Tree-Shaped Workflows on Memory-Heterogeneous Architectures

Svetlana Kulagina[1]([✉]), Henning Meyerhenke[1], and Anne Benoit[2]

[1] Department of Computer Science, Humboldt-Universität zu Berlin,
Berlin, Germany
{kulagins,meyerhenke}@hu-berlin.de
[2] LIP Laboratory, ENS Lyon, Lyon, France
Anne.Benoit@ens-lyon.fr

Abstract. Directed acyclic graphs are commonly used to model scientific workflows, by expressing dependencies between tasks, as well as the resource requirements of the workflow. As a special case, rooted directed trees occur in several applications. Since typical workflows are modeled by huge trees, it is crucial to schedule them efficiently. We investigate the partitioning and mapping of tree-shaped workflows on target architectures where each processor can have a different memory size. Our three-step heuristic adapts and extends previous work for homogeneous clusters. In particular, we design a novel algorithm to assign subtrees to processors with different memory sizes, and we show how to select appropriate processors when splitting or merging subtrees. The experiments demonstrate that exploiting the heterogeneity reduces the makespan significantly compared to the state of the art for homogeneous memories.

Keywords: Tree partitioning · Mapping · Heterogeneous memory

1 Introduction

In many scientific disciplines, singular tasks revolving around the computation of one particular problem have made way to more complicated workflows that consist of many individual tasks. Such workflows are often represented as directed acyclic graphs (DAGs), with nodes of the graph representing the tasks and the edges their dependencies. One common form of such DAGs is the class of rooted directed trees, which we consider in this paper. These tree-shaped workflows occur in a variety of scientific applications, most notably as elimination trees for sparse matrix factorizations [10,13,17] or in computational physics [15].

Running such workflows efficiently in parallel, *e. g.*, on a compute cluster where processors have their own local memory and communicate via the network,

---

This work is partially supported by Collaborative Research Center (CRC) 1404 FONDA - Foundations of Workflows for Large-Scale Scientific Data Analysis, which is funded by German Research Foundation (DFG). Corresponding author: Svetlana Kulagina.

J. Singer et al. (Eds.): Euro-Par 2022 Workshops, LNCS 13835, pp. 158–170, 2023.
https://doi.org/10.1007/978-3-031-31209-0_12

requires a good scheduling strategy. Such a strategy would distribute singular tasks or whole subtrees to computing nodes in a way that fulfills a goal. Our focus regarding schedule quality is on the total execution time, expressed by the *makespan* of the schedule. To this end, we assume the workflow and its properties to be known before scheduling. Previous work [10] for completely homogeneous clusters (or other homogeneous platforms) showed the corresponding scheduling problem to be NP-complete and proposed several variants of a successful three-step heuristic: (i) partition the tree into subtrees, minimizing the makespan while not taking the memory limit into account, (ii) further partition subtrees too big for the memory limit, and finally (iii) ensure that the number of subtrees is less than or equal to the number of processors. Yet, more and more compute clusters are hetcrogeneous, *i. e.*, have variable memory sizes. This can happen due to hardware updates, a combination of clusters, or an intentional configuration with fat and light nodes. Thus, to adapt the scheduling algorithm to variable memory constraints is very relevant. Yet, maybe with the exception of He *et al.* [11], there are no scheduling algorithms in the literature tailored to tree-shaped workflows on memory-heterogeneous architectures. And while He *et al.* [11] design their algorithm with heterogeneity in mind, their experimental setup and results do not consider memory-heterogeneous architectures, which are our focus.

In this paper, we present a partitioning and mapping heuristic (called HET-PART – for *heterogeneous tree partitioning*) for tree-shaped workflows that exploits memory heterogeneity (*i. e.*, different memory sizes). Our algorithmic contribution, described in Sect. 4, consists of a three-step heuristic that builds upon the work by Gou *et al.* [10] for the homogeneous case. We adapt two of these steps: (i) the assignment of tasks to processors, which now considers the different memory sizes, and (ii) when splitting or merging subtrees, the selection of processors considers their memory size. For the experiments (Sect. 5), we choose the homogeneous state-of-the-art algorithm by Gou *et al.* [10] as standard of reference with different resource consumption scenarios. Our experimental results show that HETPART reduces the makespan by better exploiting the heterogeneous memories. The average improvement is 15.5% and 25.0%, respectively, compared to the two best homogeneous scenarios. Where the improvement by HETPART is only 15.5%, the corresponding homogeneous scenario does not produce a valid solution for more than 20% of the instances. Details omitted due to space constraints can be found in the companion research report [14].

2   Related Work

Scheduling and mapping collections of tasks on various types of computing platforms has been a focus of research interest since the 1990s. Many different kinds of applications have been considered over time, ranging from independent tasks to graphs of tasks, where tasks may have dependence constraints. Earlier works schedule various forms of workflows, such as pipeline workflows [5] and bags of tasks [4]. However, current consensus seems to be that a workflow is best described with a directed acyclic graph (DAG) [1,16], which is the most general representation of dependence constraints. Rooted task trees are a common special case of DAGs, where each task (except the root) has a single parent node. Such trees arise in particular from sparse linear algebra applications [7,17].

The goal is usually to be able to execute the whole application as fast as possible, hence minimizing the *makespan*, or total execution time. Several other objective functions have been studied, as for instance minimizing the throughput or latency of pipelined applications [5], focusing on fault tolerance [3], and also energy efficiency [2]. Recently, an important focus is put on memory optimization, since memory and I/O become a bottleneck [8,13]. Some of these optimization goals may be antagonistic, and one may want to consider several of them simultaneously. This can be done either by finding Pareto-optimal solutions aiming at optimizing all objectives, or by fixing constraints on some objectives and optimizing only one. This latter approach is particularly suitable when objectives are of different nature, as in [5].

In the current work, the main optimization objective is to minimize the makespan. As each processor has a limited amount of memory, one must ensure that a constraint on memory is not violated, by carefully mapping parts of the applications on each processor such that a processor can handle its part within its own memory limit. Hence, one must partition the tree, map each subtree on its own processor, and then schedule the subtrees without exceeding the processor's memory. Given a tree, an exact scheduling algorithm with minimum memory requirement was designed [13]. An algorithm was also designed to minimize the I/O volume when parts of data need to be evicted from memory (MINIO problem). We choose not to evict data from memory in our case, but rather we aim at using several processors to process the application. The focus of our work is hence on the partitioning of the tree, and mapping of subtrees onto processors. We then reuse, for each subtree, the optimal scheduling algorithm that minimizes the memory requirement.

The partitioning of various forms of graphs has been reviewed [6], and in particular, the partitioning of DAGs is difficult [12]. However, for the case when the strict condition of balanced weights of parts of the graph is relaxed, approaches to its partitioning were proposed [9].

Note that the problem of makespan minimization of a tree of tasks, by partitioning the tree so that each part fits (memory-wise) onto a processor, has already been tackled in the case of homogeneous processors [10]. As pointed out in Sect. 1, recent work by He *et al.* [11] has attempted to extend this approach to heterogeneous architectures. Their work leaves several important questions open, though: (i) the experiments seem to be on a system with homogeneous memories only, and (ii) the code is not available, but the descriptions regarding the subroutine FitMemory are not sufficient for a reimplementation. Our work differs from theirs in several respects. As an example, one of our main contributions is a new merging procedure accounting for heterogeneous memories, while He *et al.* use the homogeneous merge from [10].

3   Model

Application Model. We consider workflows that come in the form of rooted trees $\tau = (V, E)$, as in [10,13]. The tree vertices, numbered from 1 to n, correspond to the tasks, where each task is the smallest non-changeable workflow entity. Hence, each task $v_i \in V$ ($1 \leq i \leq n$) requires w_i operations to be performed. Vertex $v_r \in V$ ($1 \leq r \leq n$) is the root of the tree.

The edges, in turn, model precedence constraints between tasks. We assume all precedence constraints to be oriented towards the leaves, which is no limitation [10]. If $(v_j, v_i) \in E$ (i.e., $v_j \to v_i$), then task v_i cannot start before receiving an input file (or, more generally, input data) from its parent task v_j. The size of the (single) input file received by v_i is denoted as f_i (for the root, $f_r = 0$). The task also requires some memory to be executed; its size is denoted by m_i for task v_i (see [13] for a very similar way of modeling a workflow).

For each node, the memory requirement includes the size of all files to be sent to its children. Hence, given a tree workflow, $D_{\max}$ is the maximum memory requirement of a node in this tree: $D_{\max} = \max_{v_i \in V} \left\{ f_i + m_i + \sum_{j:(v_i,v_j) \in E} f_j \right\}$.

Platform Model. The target environment is a cluster consisting of a finite number l of processing units (processors), denoted by $p_1, \ldots, p_l$. Each pair of processors can communicate with each other via some network, and communication operations can happen in parallel. We assume that the system-specific bandwidth is always available for transferring input files to the responsible processor. All data generated during the execution of a task on processor p_u are stored on p_u, $1 \leq u \leq l$. Tasks are non-preemptive and atomic: a processor executes a single task at a time [13]. For $1 \leq u \leq l$, let M_u be the size of the main memory of processor p_u. Task v_i can be processed by p_u only if all the data required to execute the task fits into the processor's memory, i.e., $M_u \geq f_i + m_i + \sum_{j:(v_i,v_j) \in E} f_j$. While processors may have memories of different sizes, we consider a platform with processors computing at an identical speed s (number of operations per seconds), hence any processor can execute task v_i ($1 \leq i \leq n$) within time $\frac{w_i}{s}$.

For $(v_i, v_j) \in E$, if task v_i is mapped on processor p_u and task v_j is mapped on processor p_v, the input file for v_j is sent through the communication network, which has a bandwidth β. Hence, the time to send the file from v_i to v_j is $\frac{f_j}{\beta}$.

Constraints and Scheduling Objectives. In order to benefit from the parallel platform, the idea is to partition the tree τ into subtrees, and then map each subtree onto its own processor. Each subtree τ_ℓ is identified by its root $root(\tau_\ell) = v_i$, with $1 \leq i \leq n$. We denote by $tasks(i)$ the set of tasks included in the subtree with root v_i. The processor handling this subtree τ_ℓ with root v_i is denoted by $proc(i)$; it is a processor p_u that must be able to process the whole subtree within its own memory. Depending on the order in which tasks are processed, the required memory may differ. Yet, it is possible, given a subtree, to obtain its minimum memory requirement $M_{\min}$ and the corresponding traversal (in which order tasks should be executed), using the MINMEMORY algorithm [13].

Hence, we denote by $M_{\min}(i)$ the minimum memory required to execute the subtree τ_ℓ rooted in v_i. We can now express the **memory constraint**: for each subtree τ_ℓ rooted in v_i, $M_{\min}(i) \leq M_{proc(i)}$. Given a valid partitioning and mapping (i.e., a set of subtrees and a mapping of subtrees onto processors such that each subtree fits into the processor's memory), one can compute the corresponding execution time of the tree, or **makespan**. Let $desc(i) = \{j \mid v_j \notin tasks(i) \wedge (v_k, v_j) \in E \wedge v_k \in tasks(i)\}$ be the indices of tasks that are not in the subtree rooted in v_i, but that have a parent in this subtree τ_ℓ. These tasks are the root of subtrees that are descendants of τ_ℓ, and hence the processor in charge of τ_ℓ will need to send files to the processors in charge of these subtrees.

The makespan can then be computed recursively, where $MS(i)$ denotes the makespan of the subtree rooted in v_i. The makespan for the whole tree is then $MS(r)$. Note that for the subtree rooted in v_r, we have $f_r = 0$.

$$MS(i) = \frac{f_i}{\beta} + \sum_{k \in tasks(i)} \frac{w_k}{s} + \max_{j \in desc(i)} MS(j). \tag{1}$$

The first term corresponds to the incoming communication. The second term is the time to process all tasks on processor $proc(i)$ (no communication to be paid within the same processor). Finally, the last term corresponds to the longest makespan of descendant subtrees, which are processed in parallel (and hence the longest one determines the makespan).

Problem Statement and Its Complexity. The HETMEMPARTMAP problem targeted in this paper is the following. Given a task tree and a platform with **het**erogeneous **mem**ories, the goal is to **part**ition the tree into subtrees, to **map** each subtree onto a processor, such that the memory constraint on each processor is respected (for the subtree rooted in v_i, $M_{\min}(i) \leq M_{proc(i)}$), and the makespan $MS(r)$ is minimized. The problem was shown to be NP-complete for a fully homogeneous platform in [10], and considering platforms with heterogeneous memories only makes it more difficult. In the following, we focus on the design of an efficient heuristic for such platforms.

4   Heuristic Strategies

In this section, we describe HETPART, a polynomial-time heuristic for the HET-MEMPARTMAP problem. Following the idea of [10], the heuristic works in three steps: (1) partition the tree into subtrees to minimize the makespan; (2) assign the trees to fitting processors and further partition the subtrees that do not fit into memory; (3) adjust the number of subtrees to comply with the number of nodes in the target platform, and possibly reassign the new subtrees to different processors. Unlike the work of [10], we need to fix the assignment of each subtree to a specific processor, since processors have different memories. Furthermore, we need to consider which processors are still available when taking a partitioning decision in Step 2 or a merging decision in Step 3.

Minimizing Makespan. In the first step, we split the tree into a number of subtrees with the aim to minimize the overall makespan. Neither the memory constraint nor the number of resulting trees is the focus of this step. The splitting continues as long as a better makespan can be achieved. Several heuristics are designed for this case in [10] (also see Sect. 5.1 for details).

Fitting into Memory. After the tree has been partitioned with the aim to minimize the makespan, the subtrees need to be allocated to processors while respecting the memory constraints. Gou *et al.* [10] suggest three fitting methods that all cut the existing subtrees further until they reach the (unique) memory constraint. Building on the FIRSTFIT method, we propose the new BIGGESTFIT algorithm (shown in the report [14] as Algorithm 1), which additionally considers the memory size of each processor. We use a max-priority queue Q to keep the current set of subtrees, S, "ordered" according to their memory consumption. Moreover, we sort the processors by memory size (from largest to smallest) in a dynamic array M. Then, in a while loop that terminates if Q or M become empty, we iteratively fit the currently largest subtree s into the processor with currently biggest memory m. This is done using any memory fitting algorithm (referred to as MEMFIT in the pseudocode); we use FIRSTFIT [10]. This algorithm checks the memory required by subtree s, and if it does not fit entirely within memory m, it splits the subtree while increasing the makespan as little as possible. The result is a subtree that fits within m (denoted as S_{fitted}, which is never empty but possibly equal to s), and it may also generate new subtrees (denoted as S_{rem}) that are added to the set of subtrees still in need to be assigned to a processor (in the priority queue Q). If S_{rem} is empty (the original subtree fits within m, and hence $S_{fitted} = s$), then this step is ignored.

Thanks to this MEMFIT algorithm, S_{fitted} fits within memory m, and we assign it to the corresponding processor, which is then removed from the array of available processors. If all processors have been assigned a subtree but there still remain some subtrees in Q, we take care of these subtrees in a second while loop that terminates when Q is empty. In the loop, we further split the subtrees with the memory m of the smallest processor as a threshold. All these subtrees are left unassigned and will be merged in the next step below.

Adjusting the Number of Subtrees. After the tree has been partitioned into subtrees (for makespan minimization, Step 1) and after further splitting the subtrees to fit into the respective memories (Step 2), we need to adjust the number of the resulting subtrees to match the number of processors. This is mandatory if there are still unassigned subtrees after BIGGESTFIT has been applied on the tree: in this case, we need to decrease the number of subtrees so that each one can be assigned to a processor. However, note that this step may also increase the number of subtrees instead – in case all subtrees have been assigned and there remain some idle processors.

Algorithm 1. Merge for heterogeneous memories

```
 1: procedure HETERMERGE(τ, C, S, P)
 2:                              ▷ Input: tree τ, cut edges C, subtrees S, and set of processors P
 3:     T ← quotient tree according to τ and C;
 4:     A ← binary array of length |P|, initialized with 1s;   ▷ A[u] = 1 ↔ proc. u has
        been assigned a subtree
 5:     toMerge ← |S| − |P|;              ▷ Number of subtrees not yet assigned to a proc.
 6:     while toMerge > 0 do
 7:         Δ_min ← −∞;
 8:         for each node i ∈ T except the root do
 9:             j ← parent(i);
10:             if  i is a leaf and i has only one sibling k then          ▷ Case 1
11:                 p ← CHOOSEPROCESSOR(i, j, k, A);
12:                 Δ_i ← estimated increase in MS(r) if i, j and k are merged onto p;
13:             else                                                       ▷ Case 2
14:                 p ← CHOOSEPROCESSOR(i, j, 0, A);
15:                 Δ_i ← estimated increase in MS(r) if i and j are merged onto p;
16:             end if
17:             if p ≠ −1 and Δ_i < Δ_min then Δ_min ← Δ_i; p_min ← p; i_min ← i;
18:             end if
19:         end for
20:         if Δ_min = −∞ then break;              ▷ No further improvement possible
21:         end if
22:                 ▷ Now, i_min, p_min, Δ_min correspond to a possible merge, leading to the
           smallest increase in makespan
23:         if i_min is a leaf and i_min has only one sibling then          ▷ Case 1
24:             Merge i_min to its parent j and sibling k in τ; Update T and C;
25:             Assign the merged subtree to p_min;        ▷ And free other procs. next
26:             if 0 < proc(i) ≠ p_min then A[proc(i)] ← 0;
27:             else if 0 < proc(j) ≠ p_min then A[proc(j)] ← 0;
28:             else if 0 < proc(k) ≠ p_min then A[proc(k)] ← 0;
29:             end if
30:             toMerge ← toMerge − 2;
31:         else                                                           ▷ Case 2
32:             Merge i_min to its parent j in τ; Update T and C;
33:             Assign the merged subtree to p_min;        ▷ And free other proc. next
34:             if 0 < proc(i) ≠ p_min then A[proc(i)] ← 0;
35:             else if 0 < proc(j) ≠ p_min then A[proc(j)] ← 0;
36:             end if
37:             toMerge ← toMerge − 1;
38:         end if
39:     end while
40:     return (MS(r), C);
41: end procedure
```

Decreasing the Number of Subtrees. Should the previous step yield more trees than there are processors, some trees need to be merged. To this end, we propose the HETERMERGE heuristic (Algorithm 1). We first construct the quotient tree T of τ, where each subtree in τ becomes a vertex in T; there is an edge between two vertices $u \rightarrow v$ in T iff there is an edge from the corresponding subtree τ_u to τ_v in τ. The general idea now is similar to [10]: as candidate merge operations, we either try merging a leaf to its parent and only sibling (Case 1), or only to its parent (Case 2). The main difference to the homogeneous case is that we need to choose the processor on which the resulting merged tree is to be executed. This choice is done through the CHOOSEPROCESSOR procedure (see [14]). If at least one of the subtrees has been assigned already, then we select the processor with smallest memory that is able to hold the merged subtree. Otherwise, if we were not able to find a processor, we are looking for an available processor to handle the merged subtree. Such processors may have been released in a previous merge iteration. This processor must have enough memory to process the merged subtree, and if there are several candidates, we pick the one with the smallest memory to keep larger processors for further iterations. If no suitable processor can be found, we return -1 and this merge is not possible.

Since the processors have identical computing speeds (and only memories of different size), the makespan after a merge can be computed by applying Eq. (1). More precisely, we compute the difference Δ_i between the makespans before and after the merge of node i. Finally, in Lines 23 to 38 of Algorithm 1, we perform the merge that results in the smallest increase of the makespan (if there is at least one valid merge), and we iterate as long as merges are possible, until all subtrees have been successfully assigned to processors. When no further merges are possible, Algorithm 1 breaks in Line 20.

Increasing the Number of Subtrees. If all subtrees have already been assigned to processors but there are still some idle processors, some subtrees can be further broken down if it improves the makespan. We employ the SplitAgain algorithm from [10] with a single modification: we check if the resulting subtree fits into the memory of any free processor before assigning the subtree to this free processor.

5   Experimental Evaluation

We now describe the experimental settings and a representative subset of the results. Additional results can be found in the companion research report [14]. All results have been obtained via a simulation of the target cluster platforms.

5.1   Experimental Setup

All algorithms are implemented in C++ and compiled with g++ (v.11.2.0) with flags "-O2 -fopenmp". The code can be downloaded at this link: https://box. hu-berlin.de/d/fe55a68653c74809b14d/ with password "het-sched". The baseline algorithm from [10], which we call HOMPART, is also written in C++; it is compiled and executed with the same infrastructure.

Instances. We evaluate the algorithms on two general sets of trees: elimination trees generated from real-world sparse matrices, and randomly generated ones. The real-world tree workflows were provided by Jacquelin *et al.* [13]; we consider the set of 31 trees that were already used by Gou *et al.* [10] in the homogeneous setting. To avoid overfitting to one particular instance set, we also generate a set of random trees, derived from Prüfer sequences,see [14] for detailed parameters. We build eight categories, each containing 30 trees ranging in size from 2K to 50K nodes. The categories differ in the problem parameters (m_i, f_i, w_i) and the fanout, i.e., average number of children per node. By default, the fanout comes from a Prüfer sequence. For the "random" category, m_i, f_i, w_i all result from a uniform random distribution. For "large f_i, w_i, m_i", the expected values of these weights are all multiplied by 100, while for "small f_i, w_i, m_i", they are divided by 10. The categories "large m_i", "large w_i", and "large f_i" increase only one of these respective values. Finally, "large fanout" and "largest fanout" have an expected fanout of 3 (standard deviation 1) and 20 (standard deviation 4), respectively; their other weights are as in "random" in expectation. A detailed description of each tree category is given in [14].

Compute Platforms. For evaluation purposes, we create synthetic compute platforms that resemble heterogeneous real-world configurations. To make the algorithms' job difficult, we use a modest 4-fold cluster with a total of 36 nodes of four different kinds (9 nodes of each kind): "extra-light" nodes with memory $D_{\max}/2$, "light" nodes with a memory $D_{\max}$, "moderate" nodes with memory $1.5D_{\max}$, and "fat" nodes with memory $3D_{\max}$. Thus, the amount of memory given to a certain tree depends not only on the memory capacity of the cluster node, but also on the tree's requirements expressed by its $D_{\max}$. All processor speeds and bandwidths are assumed equal (normalized to 1 for speeds and to 500 for bandwidths).

Setup for Algorithmic Comparison. The two major criteria for comparing HetPart with the baseline HomPart are solution quality (makespan of the produced schedules) and running time. To account for fluctuations in the running time, we perform three runs of each experiment and use the arithmetic mean.

Since the homogeneous algorithm cannot exploit varying memory sizes, the heterogeneous clusters need to be represented in a homogeneous way for HomPart. The main differences stem from the memory limit imposed on each compute node (see [14]). The configurations of HomPart are suffixed with ML (*many light*, uses 27 nodes as "light"), SM (*some moderate*, uses 18 nodes as "moderate"), or FF (*few fat*, uses only the 9 "fat" nodes). Note that the memory would not suffice for the largest tasks if we took all 36 nodes and treated them as "extra-light".

We selected the best combinations of different heuristics in each phase (regarding solution quality, on average) for our setup, both for HetPart and for HomPart, in order to be as fair as possible (details in [14]). In the following, we use the combinations that respectively returned the best results. Detailed results supporting this claim can be found in the companion research report [14].

5.2   Results

We first study the increase of makespan when using HOMPART rather than HETPART. We report the percentage of increase in makespan when HOMPART is used in various configurations (ML, SM, FF). If HOMPART could not find a solution, no bar is reported. The geometric mean is used when aggregating several ratios. Lower values indicate a better quality.

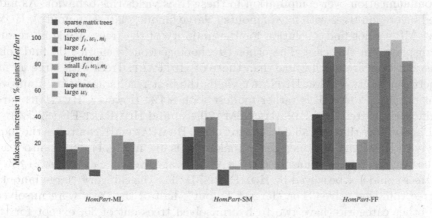

Fig. 1. Makespan increase of HOMPART in % compared to HETPART in different cluster configurations (higher means that HETPART is better). The two missing bars for HOMPART-ML indicate unsuccessful runs (no solution for HOMPART in this setting).

Makespan. Figure 1 displays the average increase of the makespan (in %) of the three HOMPART scenarios compared to HETPART. Each bar represents an instance group. As most bars are above 0, HETPART performs best overall: averaged over all instance groups, the best homogeneous variant HOMPART-ML still increases the makespan by 15.5%. At the same time, note that HOMPART-ML is not able to produce results for two instance groups (with fixed fanout). This robustness problem results from the fact that finding a valid solution can become more difficult if only light nodes are available. If we compare to the next best scenario, HOMPART-SM, which is able to solve all instances, HETPART is 25.1% better on average. Overall, HETPART achieves high improvements in most cases but two. In case of "large f_i" and "largest fanout", HOMPART-SM performs quite well – if it is able to find a solution.

In the following, we take a look at the respective instance groups. On sparse matrix trees, HETPART is 25.0% better than the best homogeneous scenario HOMPART-SM. HOMPART-ML fares comparably to HOMPART-SM (29.9% increase), while HOMPART-FF is clearly the worst (42.3% increase). On random trees, HETPART improves by at least 15.4% (against HOMPART-ML). The other two homogeneous variants perform significantly worse.

For the categories where only weights change (and not the tree topology – "large m_i, f_i, w_i" and "small m_i, f_i & w_i"), the improvement of HETPART compared to HOMPART-ML is significant (17.1% and 26.1% respectively). Similar results can be observed with "large m_i": HETPART improves on HOMPART-ML by 21.2%. HETPART works very well in these previous categories as the corresponding instances allow our heuristic to distribute the tasks across the whole cluster. The situation is somewhat different for the categories "largest fanout" and "large f_i". Here, all heuristics use only a subset of the cluster since the trees cannot be parallelized and distributed that well. Evidently, the dominance of communication over computation in these trees yields this behavior. As indicated before, on trees with fixed fanouts ("large fanout, "largest fanout"), HOM-PART-ML cannot find a solution for the majority of the trees, hence no results are displayed in this case. The other two homogeneous scenarios do find solutions, but they are much worse than those of HETPART. Trees with large w_i fall in between the two poles: HETPART yields the best results again; the improvement on HOMPART-ML is rather modest with 8.4%. However, HETPART fares significantly better than HOMPART-SM (29.4%) and HOMPART-FF (82.7%).

Finally, note that overall, for all categories, HOMPART-ML compares the most closely to HETPART (the increase in makespan is low in Fig. 1), but it also leads to the largest number of unsolved trees. On average over all categories, 21.8% of the trees could not be solved by HOMPART-ML. For the category "large fanout", no tree could be solved. For "largest fanout", half of the trees were unsolved. The other categories have two to five unsolved trees out of 30, except for the matrix trees, where all trees could be solved.

Comparison with a 2-Fold Cluster. We performed further experiments with a more homogeneous cluster with only "fat" and "light" nodes (18 nodes of each kind), and compared the results between the two clusters. Detailed results are available in [14], they are summarized below. With more heterogeneity to exploit in the 4-fold cluster, HETPART is able to provide a more tangible improvement. In the 2-fold cluster, HETPART wins by much smaller margins (2%-13%) and loses in 3 categories ("large f_i", "largest fanout", large "w_i"). For the sparse matrix trees (real-world instances), HETPART provides tangible improvements in both clusters (24.9% and 20.7%).

Running Times. Here again, a summary is presented while detailed results are available in the companion research report [14]. The running time of HETPART is comparable to that of HOMPART-SM and HOMPART-FF (averaged over all instance groups). More precisely, HETPART is 9.7% faster than HOMPART-SM but 7.3% slower than HOMPART-FF. At the same time, as we saw above, HET-PART provides a much better solution quality. The homogeneous scenario with the best quality, HOMPART-ML, is much slower. Its running time is 3.5× higher than HETPART's. Our experiments indicate that most time is spent merging.

Smaller memory sizes as in HOMPART-ML produce trees that require extensive merging, explaining the much longer running time. Note that we do not consider here the three largest matrix trees due to their very long runtime.

6   Conclusions and Future Work

We have studied the problem of tree partitioning for a heterogeneous multiprocessor computing system, where each processor can have a different memory size. Taking heterogeneity into account when partitioning these trees into subtrees pays off: our new heuristic HETPART clearly improves the makespan compared to the homogeneous state of the art. At the same time, the best homogeneous scenario, HOMPART-ML, fails to produce valid solutions in many cases due to its inability to exploit the full memory of the cluster and it is 3.5× slower.

Future work includes the increase of the heterogeneity level. This should include different processor speeds and different bandwidths in the cluster. Overall, we expect similar findings for such cases: when the compute platform is sufficiently heterogeneous, a heuristic taking this heterogeneity into account should pay off. However, integrating processor speeds and bandwidths makes a corresponding heuristic significantly more complicated.

References

1. Adhikari, M., Amgoth, T., Srirama, S.N.: A survey on scheduling strategies for workflows in cloud environment and emerging trends. ACM Comput. Surv. **52**(4), 1–36 (2019)
2. Aupy, G., Benoit, A., Renaud-Goud, P., Robert, Y.: Energy-aware algorithms for task graph scheduling, replica placement and checkpoint strategies. In: Khan, S.U., Zomaya, A.Y. (eds.) Handbook on Data Centers, pp. 37–80. Springer, New York (2015). https://doi.org/10.1007/978-1-4939-2092-1_2
3. Benoit, A., Le Fevre, V., Perotin, L., Raghavan, P., Robert, Y., Sun, H.: Resilient scheduling of moldable parallel jobs to cope with silent errors. IEEE Trans. Comput. **71**, 1696–1710 (2021)
4. Benoit, A., Marchal, L., Pineau, J.F., Robert, Y., Vivien, F.: Scheduling concurrent bag-of-tasks applications on heterogeneous platforms. IEEE Trans. Comput. **59**(2), 202–217 (2009)
5. Benoit, A., Rehn-Sonigo, V., Robert, Y.: Multi-criteria scheduling of pipeline workflows. In: 2007 IEEE International Conference on Cluster Computing, pp. 515–524. IEEE (2007)
6. Buluç, A., Meyerhenke, H., Safro, I., Sanders, P., Schulz, C.: Recent advances in graph partitioning. In: Kliemann, L., Sanders, P. (eds.) Algorithm Engineering. LNCS, vol. 9220, pp. 117–158. Springer, Cham (2016). https://doi.org/10.1007/978-3-319-49487-6_4
7. Davis, T.A.: Direct methods for sparse linear systems. In: Fundamentals of Algorithms. Society for Industrial and Applied Mathematics, Philadelphia (2006)
8. Eyraud-Dubois, L., Marchal, L., Sinnen, O., Vivien, F.: Parallel scheduling of task trees with limited memory. ACM Trans. on Par. Comput. **2**(2), 13 (2015)

9. Feldmann, A.E., Foschini, L.: Balanced partitions of trees and applications. Algorithmica **71**(2), 354–376 (2015)
10. Gou, C., Benoit, A., Marchal, L.: Partitioning tree-shaped task graphs for distributed platforms with limited memory. IEEE Trans. Par Distrib. Syst. **31**(7), 1533–1544 (2020)
11. He, S., Wu, J., Wei, B., Wu, J.: Task tree partition and subtree allocation for heterogeneous multiprocessors. In: 2021 IEEE International Conference on Parallel & Distributed Processing with Applications, Big Data & Cloud Computing, Sustainable Computing & Communications, Social Computing & Networking(ISPA/BDCloud/SocialCom/SustainCom), pp. 571–577 (2021)
12. Herrmann, J., Kho, J., Uçar, B., Kaya, K., Çatalyürek, Ü.V.: Acyclic partitioning of large directed acyclic graphs. In: 2017 17th IEEE/ACM International Symposium on Cluster, Cloud and Grid Computing (CCGRID), pp. 371–380. IEEE (2017)
13. Jacquelin, M., Marchal, L., Robert, Y., Uçar, B.: On optimal tree traversals for sparse matrix factorization. In: 2011 IEEE International Parallel & Distributed Processing Symposium, pp. 556–567. IEEE (2011)
14. Kulagina, S., Meyerhenke, H., Benoit, A.: Mapping tree-shaped workflows on memory-heterogeneous architectures. Research report 9458, Inria (2022). https://hal.inria.fr/hal-03581418
15. Lam, C., Rauber, T., Baumgartner, G., Cociorva, D., Sadayappan, P.: Memory-optimal evaluation of expression trees involving large objects. Comput. Lang. Syst. Struct. **37**(2), 63–75 (2011). https://doi.org/10.1016/j.cl.2010.09.003
16. Liu, J., Pacitti, E., Valduriez, P.: A survey of scheduling frameworks in big data systems. Int. J. Cloud Comput. **7** (2018)
17. Liu, J.W.H.: The role of elimination trees in sparse factorization. SIAM J. Matrix Anal. Appl. **11**(1), 134–172 (1990)

Hetero-Vis: A Framework for Latency Optimized Heterogeneous Deployment of Convolutional Neural Networks

Nupur Sumeet[(✉)], Karan Rawat, Manoj Nambiar, and Rekha Singhal

Tata Consultancy Services Research, Mumbai 400607, India
{nupur.sumeet,rawat.karan,m.nambiar,rekha.singhal}@tcs.com

Abstract. Convolutional Neural Network (CNN) models often comprise multiple layers varying in compute requirements. For deployment, a number of hardware accelerators are available that have subtle differences in compute architectures within the same family of platforms. A component (a set of layers) of a CNN model may perceive different performance in different compute architectures. Optimal mapping of the components of a CNN model across a given heterogeneous architecture can leverage underlying different compute architectures to deliver minimum inference latency[3]. In this paper, we present an optimal partitioning approach to map a CNN model across heterogeneous architectures by leveraging a repository of performance-measurement-benchmark (PerfLib) for different accelerators. Our proposed framework, Hetero-vis, decides optimal partitions and mapping of a CNN network across different accelerators to minimize the inference latency. Our experiments reveal up to 1.43× better performance with grouped layer deployment of CNN models on heterogeneous hardware compared to the entire model deployed on a single accelerator.[1] *Inference latency* and *latency* terms are used interchangeably in the rest of the paper.

Keywords: CNN deployments · Model partitioning · Heterogeneous deployment

1 Introduction

The need for performance-efficient Neural Network (NN) processing on resource-constrained devices has spurred the development of specialized hardware accelerators architect-ed to efficiently execute the kernels commonly found in deep neural networks. The accelerators have high variations in their architectural features including distinct micro-architectures, memory and compute capabilities.

NN models exert different computational intensity (computation/bit) requirements on the underlying hardware platforms as the processing progresses from one layer to another. For instance, in CNNs the convolutional layer are dominated by computational processing whereas the fully connected layers are heavy on memory access. Additionally, the amount of data parallelism, data

J. Singer et al. (Eds.): Euro-Par 2022 Workshops, LNCS 13835, pp. 171–183, 2023.
https://doi.org/10.1007/978-3-031-31209-0_13

transfer (dominating the execution time) and computation schedule in a CNN model may suggest suitability of different components of a CNN model to different compute architectures for minimizing inference latency.

Accelerators belonging to different paradigm have different <compute, memory> capability and consequently are not equally suitable for all kinds of workload. For instance, GPUs (Graphics Processing Units) support SIMD (Single Instruction Multiple Data) processing owing to large number of cores whereas FPGAs (Field Programmable Gate Arrays) have Block RAMs that provide quick memory access but limited number of compute units. Due to such varied hardware characteristics, matrix multiplication workloads are processed faster on GPUs whereas FPGAs provide performance benefits in moderate compute intensity workloads such as embedding fetch operation. With heterogeneous computing the computational efficiency of the workflow can be improved through acceleration for a subset of workflow tasks on the hardware that suits the computational requirement of the target task. The availability of parallel programming frameworks like OpenCL and SyCL across hardware platforms has further pushed the adoption of heterogeneous systems and accelerators for applications running in production data centers.

However, an efficient heterogeneous deployment requires optimal division and mapping of workload across hardware platforms. This necessitates multiple experiments and access to the set of hardware targeted for heterogeneous deployment. The engineering effort to deploy models on different accelerators (GPU, CPU and FPGA) can be bypassed by replacing performance measurement with estimates. Recently, the state-of-the-art includes BRP-NAS [8] and nn-meter [18], where BRP-NAS predict latency of the NASBench-201 [9] dataset on various accelerators and reports reasonable accuracy for NASBench-201 networks. However, the same level of accuracy can not be generalized for other untested networks. To address the problem of generalized latency prediction, we propose an automated and unified framework for CNN-based networks, called Hetero-Vis, that optimally partitions the CNN network and maps these partitions to heterogeneous accelerators to minimize te inference latency. We present a performance-measurement-benchmark library (PerfLib), consisting of processing time of NASBench-201 cells on different hardware accelerators. This library is used to estimate the execution time of the partitions/components (set of layers) of CNN model to identify the optimal <CNN partition, accelerator> pair for high-performance deployments. Additionally, we accommodate the communication cost for inter-accelerator communication. We observe, heterogeneous configurations generated by our framework offers a performance speed-up of upto 1.43× for CNN deployments, such as VGG, CRAFT and ResNet models, over homogeneous configurations.

The key contributions of this paper includes:

Hetero-Vis framework for low latency deployment of convolutional neural networks on heterogeneous architectures comprising the following.

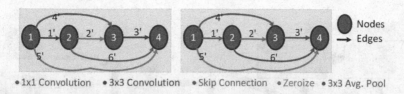

• 1x1 Convolution   • 3x3 Convolution   • Skip Connection   • Zeroize   • 3x3 Avg. Pool

Fig. 1. Examples of NASBench-201 [9] cell with 4 nodes. An edge is associated with an operation selected from a predefined operations set.

- Optimal partitioning of CNN for deployment on heterogeneous compute by searching network partition and hardware pair optimized for latency while including communication cost between hardware.
- Performance-measurement-benchmark library (PerfLib) comprising of NASBench-201 cell processing time for hardware accelerators such as multi-core Intel CPU platform, Xilinx Alveo U280 DPU, NVIDIA GPUs: A100 and V100.
- Heuristic-based approach to create performance-efficient network partitions.

The rest of the paper is organized as follows. Preliminaries and related work are presented in Sects. 2 and 3, respectively. We present details of Hetero-Vis in Sect. 4. The experimental results and performance is discussed in Sect. 5, which is followed by the proposed framework's limitations in Sect. 6. Finally, the paper is concluded in Sect. 7.

2   Preliminaries

Neural Architecture Search Benchmarks (NAS) for Vision Models: Researchers have addressed the NAS replication problem by providing NAS-Benchmark datasets [9,17] that have a fixed search space and provide a unified benchmark for NAS algorithms. NASBench-201 [9], in one of the NAS benchmarks, with a cell-based search space, results on multiple datasets, and more diagnostic information.

An Overview of Model Architectures in NASBench-201 [9]: NASBench-201 is a benchmark for NAS algorithms including all cell-based (sample cells shown in Fig. 1) NAS methods. The search space includes 15,625 neural cell candidates stacked 5 times in the selected macro skeleton to create model architectures. *Cell Structure:* Each cell in the search space is represented as a densely connected DAG, obtained by assigning a direction from the ith node to the jth node (i < j) for each edge in an un-directed complete graph. Each edge of DAG is associated with an operation transforming feature map from source node to the target node. The predefined operation set five representative operations: (1) zeroize, (2) skip connection, (3) 1×1 convolution, (4) 3 × 3 convolution, and (5) 3 × 3 average pooling layer. In this case, convolution is an abbreviation of an operation sequence of ReLU, convolution, and batch normalization. The DAG has V = 4 nodes, where each node represents sum of all feature maps transformed through the associated operations of the edges pointing to this node.

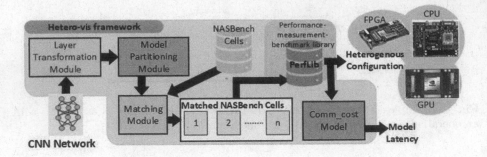

Fig. 2. The representative diagram of proposed Hetero-Vis framework.

3   Related Work

Previous works on latency estimators uses FLOPs as proxy for latency [11,14], which is simple but not a direct metric of latency. Recent works on latency predictions [6,16] use a layer-wise predictor which derives the latency by summing latency measured for each operation in the model individually. Recently, the state-of-the-art includes BRP-NAS [8] and nn-meter [18], where BRP-NAS uses graph convolutional networks (GCN) to predict latency of the NASBench-201 [9] dataset on various devices. It captures the runtime optimizations by learning the representation of model graphs and corresponding latency. However, this model-graph based approach heavily depends on the tested model structures and may not work for many unseen model structures. nn-meter on the other hand is a generalized framework for latency prediction for any arbitrary model. It opts for kernel level decomposition of the model since the kinds of operators and kernels are stable with a relative small set despite the increasing number of models. However, this approach has heavy dependency on inference backend and might loose its prediction accuracy when there are significant backend changes. Additionally, the latency prediction is limited to homogeneous implementation only. In this work, we provide latency estimations while optimally partitioning the workload across heterogeneous hardware devices. With our approach, we are able to leverage the benefits of inference backend optimizations at a partition level granularity.

4   Hetero-Vis Framework

Hetero-Vis, is an automated framework, that generates optimal deployment configuration for CNNs across hardware platforms. The framework accepts a CNN and presents the homogeneous latency on all target hardware platforms and heterogeneous deployment configuration optimized for latency as outputs.

4.1   Methodology

We leverage the structural properties of CNNs to build performance-measurement-benchmark library (PerfLib). We adopt CNN partitioning and optimal appropriation of partitions to candidate hardware that promises latency-efficient deployment. We estimate the overall network latency as sum of partition execution times and use cell structures available in NASBench-201 to build the PerfLib for CPU, GPU and FPGA. The cell-based granularity in PerfLib makes our approach modular as well as re-usable across networks since a partition can appear in many networks but the same is not true for a monolithic network.

4.2   Framework Components

The representative diagram of the framework is presented in Fig. 2. The framework components with their purpose is as follows:

- Layer Transformation Module: extend the support for layers and variations un-supported by NASBench-201.
- Model Partitioning Module: create partitions of the input model. This module use heuristics to make latency-efficient partitions.
- Matching Module: returns NASBench cells that match with the partitions created by model partitioning module.
- Performance-measurement-benchmark library (PerfLib): contains execution time of NASBench cells on target accelerators.
- Communication Cost Model: contains estimates of communication cost among accelerators.

The detailed discussion on the Hetero-vis framework components follows.

Performance-Measurement-Benchmark Library (PerfLib): We have considered four hardware platforms, namely A100 GPU [1], V100 GPU [2], Alveo U280 FPGA [3] and Intel Xeon CPU [4], in this work. The PerfLib contains measured execution time for 15,625 NASBench-201 cells with 40×8 combinations of *in* and *out* channels and image sizes ($2^3 \times 2^3$ to $2^{10} \times 2^{10}$). The *in* and *out* channels represent the feature depth of input and output of the cell, respectively. The <in,out> channels combinations are <n,n>, <n/2,n>, <n,n/2> and <3,n> with $n = 2^m$, with m varying from 1–10, since they are commonly seen at head, convolution and de-convolution parts of the network. The PerfLib returns cell execution time on all target hardware platforms upon query.

Layer Transformation Module: The NASBench-201 cells currently support convolution layer with filter sizes- 3×3 and 1×1 with unit stride, same padding (1 pixel padding on each side of input) and no dilation. This layer also includes batch normalization and ReLU. Other supported layers include average pooling (3×3) with support for skip connection and dropping an edge through zeroize. We extend support for upsampling, fully-connected layer, filter size 5×5 with variable stride, padding and dilation for convolution layers.

Algorithm 1. Layer Transformation Module

1: **Inputs:**CNN model,i mage size; **Outputs:**Transformed CNN model (TransModel)
2: NASBench_lay: set of NASBench supported layer
3: lay_db: set of layers having dedicated PerfLib (*e.g.* fully connected layer)
4: model_struct=model.read() *%returns net. struct., layer type, <in,out> ch.*
5: *Transform un-supported Layers.*
6: **for all** layers in model **do**
7:     **if** (model_struct.layer_typ[i] $\notin$ NASBench_lay) **then**
8:         eq_layer = **lat_eq** (model_struct.layer[i])
9:         **Replace** model_struct.layer[i] with eq_layer
10:    **else**
11:        **if** (model_struct.layer_typ[i] $\in$ lay_db **then** *%if dedicated PerfLib*
12:            **Retain** model_struct.layer[i]
13:        **else**
14:            **Advise:** Create PerfLib for model_struct.layer[i]
15:        **end if**
16:    **end if**
17: **end for**
18: **return** TransModel.write(model_struct)

We have established performance equivalences between NASBench-201 un-supported and supported layer. Performance equivalence denotes that two layers have approximately same execution time and can be used inter-changeably. By doing this, the NASBench-201 PerfLib can be used even for un-supported layer by considering its performance equivalent layer in its place. This approach can be extended to other layers in vision networks that are not addressed in this work. Our experiments suggest average pool and max pool layers are performance equivalent. We have created a dedicated PerfLib for upsampling and fully-connected layer since there were no direct performance equivalent layers for these operations.

The performance equivalence for two layers (*layer a* and *layer b*) is obtained using following steps:

1. Read *layer a*- type and parameters including filter size, stride, padding, dilation.
2. Measure its execution time on target hardware platforms (A100, V100, U280 and Xeon CPU) for different feature sizes.
3. Identify a NASBench supported layer with approximately same execution time across hardware and feature size. Say, *layer b* satisfies the requirements.
4. Record *layer b* as performance equivalent layer for *layer a*.

Algorithm 1 presents steps carried out by the layer transformation module. The module reads the input model structure and identifies the model structure with layer specifications such as layer name, layer type, filter size, stride, dilation, padding (Ln #4). As the next step, the module identifies the un-supported layers in input model (Ln #7) and replaces it with its performance equivalent layer (Ln #8–9). In case performance equivalent layer is not available, the module

---

Algorithm 2. Model Partitioning Module

1: **Inputs:**Transformed CNN Model (TransModel)
2: **Outputs:** Split configurations for Transformed CNN model
3: model_struct = TransModel.read()
4: *% Create all possible partitions for model.*
5: **for all** layers in model **do**
6:     Partn_1lay[j] = read(model_struct.layer[i]) *%1-layer partitions*
7:     Partn_2lay[j] = read(model_struct.layer[i:i+1]) *%2-layer partitions*
8:     Partn_3lay[j] = read(model_struct.layer[i:i+2]) *%3-layer partitions*
9:     i++
10: **end for**
11: all_com = combination(Partn_1lay, Partn_2lay, Partn_3lay) *%Combination of <1-layer, 2-layer, 3-layer> partitions*
12: **for all** combinations in all_com **do**
13:     **if** all_com[i] == len(model_struct.layer) **then**
14:         Splits.enqueue(all_com[i]) *%Combinations where all TransModel layer appear only once*
15:     **else**
16:         Dequeue all_com[i]
17:     **end if**
18: **end for**
19: **return** Splits

---

checks if un-supported layer has dedicated performance database (Ln #11). The layer is retained if its database is available (Ln #12) otherwise an advice to create database is issued (Ln #14) and layer performance is not modeled. The transformed model is returned as TransModel (Ln #18).

Model Partitioning Module: The task of the model partitioning module is diagrammatically shown in Fig. 3. The partitions are combined together to create splits that are representative of target model. A model, can be partitioned in many ways. For instance, considering each layer or group of two layers

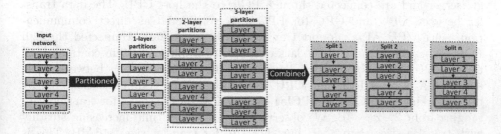

Fig. 3. The Model partitioning module partitioning a sample model into partitions (1-layer, 2-layer and 3 layer) that are later combined to form input network representatives called Splits.

as partitions are few ways of model splitting. Reducing the partition space is advantageous because it allows faster convergence on minimum latency model split. The NASBench-201 cells introduce partition constraint that reduces the partition space to a reasonable size. Additionally, we use some heuristics (discussed later in this section) from the PerfLib to further reduce the partition space. A NASBench-201 cell contains maximum of 4 nodes, out of which one node is considered as input node. This leaves three nodes for feature transformations thereby limiting the partition depth to ≤ 3 cascade layers. The Algorithm 2 captures the main steps carried out by partitioning module. The module takes the transformed network obtained from layer transformation block as input. It creates partitions for the network by taking layer groups of sizes 3, 2 and 1 (Ln #6–8). The combinations of partitions are created (Ln #11). The combination where all layers are considered only once are valid and queued into Splits (Ln #14) whereas other combinations are discarded (Ln #16). The retained combinations (or Splits) are returned (Ln #19).

Heuristics-Guided Partitioning: Based on our performance database, we tried to deduce the performance behaviours of multi-layer and single layer partitions. For this experiment, we selected a portion of the model with 3 cascade convolutions. This has 3 1-layer, 2 2-layer and 1 3-layer partitions that makes 4 split configurations. We estimated the execution time of all split options and observed that partition with 3 layers was the most performance-efficient. For example, split with 1-layer partitions takes 0.819 ms whereas the 3-layer split takes only 0.378 ms for A100. This behaviour is observed across all image sizes, <in,out> channels and hardware platforms. We used this finding as a guide to reduce the partition space.

Matching Module: The network partitions from partitioning block is passed to matching module. The matching module finds NASBench-201 cells that match the network partitions and returns the matched cells.

Communication Cost Modelling: For the purpose of modeling inter-hardware communication cost, we assume GPU and FPGA reside on a single server and are connected through PCIe to the host CPU. The data transfer between CPU and GPU (or FPGA) is considered as direct communication, since CPU APIs support transfers with accelerators connected through PCIe. Whereas, because of the lack of access to a unified system containing all three (CPU, FPGA and GPU) hardwares, the communication between GPU and FPGA is routed through CPU. We modelled the communication cost by benchmarking the PCIe3 and PCIe4 communication interfaces for transfer sizes ranging from 2^8–2^{32} MB. We observe that execution time increasing steadily with transfer sizes upto 8 MB but shots up for transfer size >16 MB. This is because the realised bandwidth peaks at 512k and a constant low bandwidth ($\approx 10\,\text{GB/s}$) is realize for transfers $\geq 32\,\text{MB}$.

Algorithm 3. Hetero-Vis Framework

1: **Inputs:** CNN model, Image size; **Outputs:** Latency on V100, A100, FPGA DPU and Xeon CPU, Heterogeneous deployment conf. optimized for latency
2: TransModel=Lay_tran(Model,Image size) *%from Algorithm 1*
3: Splits = Model_part(TransModel) *%from Algorithm 2*
4: prev_hetero = contains previous heterogeneous deployment conf. with min latency
5: prev_hetero_lat = contains heterogeneous latency for prev_hetero
6: prev_hw = hardware assigned with last partition of a model split
7: **for all** Splits **do**
8:     **for all** Partitions in Splits **do**
9:         **for all** NASBench cells **do** % *NASBench cells structure is available as string*
10:            **if** (**str_Match** (split[i].part[j], cells[k]) == 1) **then** % *string matching*
11:                {A100_lat, V100_lat, DPU_lat, CPU_lat} ¡- **Query** performance database for cells[k]
12:                hw_lat[0] += A100_lat
13:                hw_lat[1] += V100_lat
14:                hw_lat[2] += DPU_lat
15:                hw_lat[3] += CPU_lat
16:                {min_lat,hw} = min(A100_lat, V100_lat, DPU_lat, CPU_lat)
17:                **if** (prev_hw != hw) **then**%*comm cost*
18:                    Lat += min_lat + comm_lat[prev_hw, hw, tx_size]
19:                    hetero_config.add({hw, split[i].part[j]})
20:                **else**
21:                    Lat += min_lat
22:                **end if**
23:            **end if**
24:        **end for**
25:        tx_size = split[i].part[j].out_feat_size
26:    **end for**
27:    **if** (prev_hetero_lat ¿ Lat) **then**
28:        prev_hetero = hetero_config %*update heterogeneous conf.*
29:        prev_hetero_lat = Lat %*update heterogeneous conf. latency*
30:    **end if**
31:    **for all** hardware **do**
32:        **if** (prev_hw_lat[m] ¿ hw_lat[m]) **then**
33:            prev_hw_lat[m] = hw_lat[m] %*update homogeneous conf. latency*
34:        **end if**
35:    **end for**
36: **end for**
37: **return** prev_hw_lat, prev_hetero_lat, prev_hetero

4.3   Algorithm for Hetero-Vis Framework:

Algorithm 3 presents the Hetero-Vis framework. The framework takes target model, image size as user inputs and returns the latency on all target hardware (A100, V100, FPGA and CPU) along with heterogeneous deployment configuration optimized for latency. First two steps include layer transformation (Ln #2) and model partitioning (Ln #3), already explained as Algorithm 1 and 2. The network splits are iteratively accessed for heterogeneous deployments (Ln #7–37).

For a split, its partitions are matched with NASBench-201 cells and cell execution time is queried from performance database (Ln #10–11). The query returns the partition execution time for all hardware platforms that is accumulated for all partitions (Ln #12–15). The hardware with minimum latency is then recorded (Ln #16) and compared against the hardware selected for previous partition (Ln #17). In case both platforms are same, latency is updated with execution time for present partition (Ln #21) otherwise the communication cost is also accumulated in latency (Ln #18). The transfer size for communication cost is calculated using feature map dimensions from previous partition (Ln #25). At this point, the algorithm generates homogeneous (or hardware-wise) latency and heterogeneous configuration option. The algorithm checks and updates heterogeneous (Ln # 27–30) and homogeneous (Ln # 31–35) latency after comparing present latency with last minimum. The algorithm iterates over all splits and returns (Ln #37) the minimum latency achieved for homogeneous deployment on all target hardware platforms and heterogeneous deployment configuration across hardware platforms.

5   Results and Discussions

5.1   Experimental Setup

We have reported results on deployment configurations for four hardware platforms *i.e.* NVIDIA A100 [1] and V100 GPU [2], Xilinx FPGA Alveo U280 DPU [3] and Intel Xeon Gold CPU [4]. Broadly, we have analysed two deployments: homogeneous and heterogeneous where the former denotes single-hardware deployment. The Hetero-Vis framework takes CNN network model file (.pb or .pth), input image size, and an optional input of hardware platform for which latency estimation is required. The model file is converted from .pb or .pth to ONNX format for easy traversal. The latency database is available in a pickle format for quick access. We report measured and estimated (from Hetero-Vis) latency for following pre-trained networks: VGG16-bn [13], Resnet-18 [10], Resnet-50 [10] and text segmentation model CRAFT [5]. The latency is estimated for two image dimensions *i.e.* $1024 \times 1024 \times 3$ and $512 \times 512 \times 3$. The performance model accuracy (expressed in %) is derived from measured and estimated latency and is indicative of deviation of later with respect to former. For homogeneous deployment, latency is measured by running the model directly on the respective hardware. On the other hand, heterogeneous deployment measurements includes running the model across hardware by splitting and mapping partitions on suitable hardware platforms. For the communication cost, estimates are used instead of measurements since authors did not have access to a server housing A100, V100 an U280 FPGA at the time of this writing.

5.2   Experiment Outcomes

We present the latency for homogeneous deployment of target models in Table 1 for RGB images with dimensions 1024×1024 and 512×512, respectively. We observe our framework exhibits >90% accuracy for all target hardware.

Table 1. Homogeneous deployment: comparison of Hetero-Vis estimates and measured latency

Network	Image Size	A100			V100			FPGA DPU			Xeon CPU		
		M	E	% A	M	E	% A	M	E	% A	M	E	% A
VGG16-bn	1024	28	30.2	92.1	31	32.4	95.5	167	180.1	92.1	1950	1970	98.7
	512	9.7	10.1	95.9	10.5	11.2	93.5	33	35.4	92.5	500	537	92.5
CRAFT	1024	11.2	11.7	95.4	11.5	12.3	92.7	24.5	26.5	91.5	180	195	91.6
	512	6.1	6.3	95.7	6.8	7.1	95.5	8	8.5	92.6	55	56	96.7
ResNet-18	1024	8	8.7	91.2	9.5	10.3	90.8	11.5	12.3	92.7	430	450	95.3
	512	6.5	7.1	90.3	7.5	8.2	91.2	9.7	10.5	91.2	115	121	94.7
ResNet-50	1024	18	19.1	93.8	21.4	23.3	90.7	35	37.6	92.4	530	550	96.2
	512	9.6	10.2	93.2	12.6	13.3	94.6	19	20.9	90.1	220	235	93.1

M- Average Measured Latency (in ms), E- Estimated Latency (in ms), A- Accuracy,
Image- RGB, H=W

Table 2. Heterogeneous deployments: comparison of Hetero-Vis Estimates and measured latency

Network	Image Dimensions	# of Mapped Cells		Latency (in ms)		% A
		Total	#GPU-#FPGA	Measured	Estimated	
VGG16-bn	1024 × 1024 × 3	7	5A100-2FPGA	25 ± 1	26.93	92.28
	512 × 512 × 3	7	4A100-3FPGA	9.22 ± 0.5	9.51	95.86
CRAFT	1024 × 1024 × 3	13	6A100-3FPGA-4A100	10.87 ± 0.5	11.36	95.13
	512 × 512 × 3	14	6A100-6FPGA-2A100	4.25 ± 0.5	4.637	90.89
ResNet-18	1024 × 1024 × 3	10	5A100-5FPGA	7.05 ± 0.5	7.35	95.74
	512 × 512 × 3	10	4A100-6FPGA	5.28 ± 0.5	5.77	90.71
ResNet-50	1024 × 1024 × 3	18	13A100-5FPGA	16.55 ± 1.5	16.91	97.82
	512 × 512 × 3	18	8A100-10FPGA	8.54 ± 1	8.82	96.72

The heterogeneous implementation results are presented in Table 2. We observe that for VGG10-bn, CRAFT, ResNet-18 and ResNet-50, the heterogeneous deployments (measured latency) are marginally faster as compared to homogeneous. Higher improvements can be expected with faster communication links between the accelerators. The optimal latency heterogeneous deployment for VGG-16 network is obtained when it is split between GPU and FPGA. For a 1024 × 1024 × 3 image, the network is expressed as 7 NASBench-201 cells, out of which 5 are mapped on GPU and remaining on FPGA. However, we observe that for 512 × 512 × 3 image, the model split proportion between GPU and FPGA changes. Furthermore, in case of CRAFT, the # of matched NASBench cells changes from 13 to 14 for smaller image size. This captures the importance of image dimensions in performance modeling. The measured and estimated latency data presented in the Table are in good agreements. The overall accuracy for performance model is 90%–97%.

Comparison with State-of-the-Art: Performance model in [12] is conceptually similar to NASBench and has 90% accuracy while making estimation for

ResNet-50 on Mobile GPU. nn-Meter [18] works with mobile-CPU and mobile-GPU deployments with performance model accuracy of 85–95%. Heterogeneous implementation in [15] achieves $1.07\times$ reduction in latency for small CNNs and [7] shows 1.01–$1.3\times$ performance gain over homogeneous deployment. Our results indicate a performance gain of 1.07–$1.43\times$ in heterogeneous deployment over A100 GPU. Implementations in [7,15] have used fine-grained (layer-level) partitions, whereas, we have considered multi-layer partitions making better use of heuristics from the performance library. The performance models in [12,18], have used cell-based approach to predict latency but are limited to homogeneous deployments. In this work, we have focused on the datecenter devices (GPU, CPU and FPGA) and with performance model accuracy-90% to 98% as compared the state-of-the-art.

6   Limitations and Future Work

Handling In-parallel Layers: Models with skip connections over more than 3 layers does not have an equivalent NASBench cell. Additionally, the in-parallel layers of a model constitute data parallelism and can be mapped to parallel units in a hardware. Hetero-vis framework does not handle these model variations.

Limiting Performance Measurements: The performance library generation requires running 5 million test cases which needs to be repeated for every hardware considered for heterogeneity. An accurate performance mapping between hardwares can limit these measurements and is left as future work.

Latency Estimates for Batch Sizes > 1: The developed accelerator performance library contains cell latency for unit batch size. Techniques to extrapolate performance data for higher batch sizes is left as future work.

7   Conclusion

Increase in adoption of AI based models in enterprise applications with simultaneous growth of hardware accelerators suited to data-flow nature of AI workloads is ubiquitous. In order to utilize the underlying heterogeneous hardware architectures efficiently, we may need to deploy different components of an AI pipeline to their best performing hardware for an overall reduction in inference time. In this paper, we propose Hetero-Vis framework, to automatically deploy vision inference workloads and presented the evaluation results across CPU, GPU and FPGA heterogeneous architectures. The framework employs performance measurement benchmark library-based optimization algorithm to optimally deploy components of deep learning pipeline across right heterogeneous hardware for high performance. The performance model exhibit 90%–98% accuracy in latency prediction for CNN. Furthermore, we observe, heterogeneous configurations generated by our framework offers a performance speed-up of upto $1.43\times$ for CNN deployments over homogeneous deployments.

References

1. https://images.nvidia.com/aem-dam/en-zz/Solutions/data-center/nvidia-ampere-architecture-whitepaper.pdf
2. https://images.nvidia.com/content/technologies/volta/pdf/tesla-volta-v100-datasheet-letter-fnl-web.pdf
3. https://www.xilinx.com/support/documentation/data_sheets/ds963-u280.pdf
4. https://www.intel.com/content/www/us/en/products/sku/120473/intel-xeon-gold-5118-processor-16-5m-cache-2-30-ghz/specifications.html
5. Baek, Y., Lee, B., Han, D., Yun, S., Lee, H.: Character region awareness for text detection. In: Conference on Computer Vision and Pattern Recognition, pp. 9357–9366 (2019)
6. Cai, H., Zhu, L., Han, S.: Proxylessnas: direct neural architecture search on target task and hardware. ArXiv abs/1812.00332 (2019)
7. Carballo-Hernández, W., Pelcat, M., Berry, F.: Why is FPGA-GPU heterogeneity the best option for embedded deep neural networks? CoRR abs/2102.01343 (2021). https://arxiv.org/abs/2102.01343
8. Chau, T.C.P., Dudziak, L., Abdelfattah, M.S., Lee, R., Kim, H., Lane, N.D.: BRP-NAS: Prediction-based NAS using gcns. ArXiv abs/2007.08668 (2020)
9. Dong, X., Yang, Y.: NAS-bench-201: extending the scope of reproducible neural architecture search. ArXiv abs/2001.00326 (2020)
10. He, K., Zhang, X., Ren, S., Sun, J.: Deep residual learning for image recognition. In: IEEE Conference on Computer Vision and Pattern Recognition, pp. 770–778 (2016)
11. Liu, H., Simonyan, K., Yang, Y.: Darts: Differentiable architecture search. ArXiv abs/1806.09055 (2019)
12. Ponomarev, E., Matveev, S., Oseledets, I., Glukhov, V.: Latency estimation tool and investigation of neural networks inference on mobile GPU. Computers **10**(8) (2021). https://doi.org/10.3390/computers10080104, https://www.mdpi.com/2073-431X/10/8/104
13. Simonyan, K., Zisserman, A.: Very deep convolutional networks for large-scale image recognition. CoRR abs/1409.1556 (2015)
14. Tan, M., Chen, B., Pang, R., Vasudevan, V., Le, Q.V.: MnasNet: platform-aware neural architecture search for mobile. In: International Conference on Computer Vision and Pattern Recognition, pp. 2815–2823 (2019)
15. Tu, Y., Sadiq, S., Tao, Y., Shyu, M.L., Chen, S.: A power efficient neural network implementation on heterogeneous fPGA and GPU devices. In: International. Conference on Information Reuse and Integration for Data Science, pp. 193–199 (2019)
16. Wu, B., et al.: FbNet: Hardware-aware efficient convnet design via differentiable neural architecture search. In: International Conference on Computer Vision and Pattern Recognition, pp. 10726–10734 (2019)
17. Ying, C., Klein, A., Real, E., Christiansen, E., Murphy, K.P., Hutter, F.: Nas-bench-101: towards reproducible neural architecture search. In: ICML (2019)
18. Zhang, L.L., et al.: NN-meter: Towards accurate latency prediction of deep-learning model inference on diverse edge devices. In: International Conference on Mobile Systems, Applications, and Services (June 2021)

Rapid Development of OS Support with PMCSched for Scheduling on Asymmetric Multicore Systems

Carlos Bilbao$^{(\boxtimes)}$, Juan Carlos Saez , and Manuel Prieto-Matias

Facultad de Informática, Universidad Complutense de Madrid, Madrid, Spain
{cbilbao,jcsaezal,mpmatias}@ucm.es

Abstract. Asymmetric multicore processors (AMPs) couple high-performance big cores and power-efficient small ones, all exposing a shared instruction set architecture to software, but with different microarchitectural features. The energy efficiency benefits of AMPs together with the general-purpose nature of the various cores, have led hardware manufactures to build commercial AMP-based products, first for the mobile and embedded domains, and more recently for the desktop market segment, as with the Intel Alder Lake processor family. This indicates that AMPs may become a solid and more energy efficient replacement to symmetric multicores in a wide range of application domains.

Previous research has demonstrated that the system software can substantially improve scheduling –critical to get the most out of heterogeneous cores– by leveraging hardware facilities that are directly managed by the OS, such as performance monitoring counters, or the recently introduced Intel Thread Director technology. Unfortunately, the OS-level support enabling to access scheduling-relevant hardware support may take a long time to be adopted in operating systems, or may come in forms that make its utilization challenging from specific levels of the system software stack, especially in production systems. To fill this gap, we propose the PMCSched framework, which enables the creation of custom OS support on Linux to aid in the design of novel scheduling and resource-management policies for multicores implemented at different layers of the system software, but without requiring to patch the kernel. To demonstrate the potential of our framework, we implement a set of OS-level schedulers for AMPs, that make use of custom OS extensions to access scheduling-relevant hardware facilities in an x86 AMP processor.

Keywords: Asymmetric multicore processors · Scheduling · Operating systems · Runtime systems · Linux kernel · Intel alder lake

1 Introduction

Energy efficiency has become one of the most critical constraints of processor design [14]. The quest for improved energy efficiency substantially contributed

© The Author(s), under exclusive license to Springer Nature Switzerland AG 2023
J. Singer et al. (Eds.): Euro-Par 2022 Workshops, LNCS 13835, pp. 184–196, 2023.
https://doi.org/10.1007/978-3-031-31209-0_14

to the proliferation of heterogeneous architectures that combine within the same platform different types of cores and processing units for diverse and specialized uses [10]. Asymmetric multicore processors (AMPs) constitute an attractive type of heterogeneous architecture where high-performance big cores and power-efficient small ones –all exposing a shared ISA (instruction set architecture)– are combined on the same system. The common ISA in conjunction with the general-purpose nature of the AMP cores, allows the execution of legacy (unmodified) software. These facts, along with AMPs' energy efficiency benefits, have drawn the attention of major hardware players, leading to the massive release of commercial AMP products for mobile platforms, such as those based on the ARM big.LITTLE processor [28]. Today, the Intel Alder Lake processor family and the Apple M1 SoC, are clear examples of the expansion of AMPs toward the desktop market segment [31]. Moreover, in the high performance computing (HPC) domain, the combination of different core types with a shared ISA has also been explored; the Sunway TaihuLight supercomputer is a representative case [6,8].

Despite the remarkable benefits of AMPs [19], effectively scheduling diverse programs/tasks on heterogeneous cores poses a significant challenge to the various system software layers [5,6,10,21,25]. When a single multithreaded application runs alone on an AMP system, smart user-level scheduling within the runtime system is the key to making the most out of its heterogeneous cores [6,30]. However, in multi-application scenarios, and especially under the presence of legacy programs, the OS scheduler plays an essential role in transparently delivering the benefits of AMPs to the end user [10,16,18,25].

Previous research has demonstrated that the runtime system and the OS scheduler can perform optimizations on AMPs by leveraging hardware features that are directly controlled by the OS kernel and exposed to user space, such as Performance Monitoring Counters (PMCs) [10,18,36] or Dynamic Voltage and Frequency Scaling (DVFS) [7,35]. Often, the support to conveniently access new scheduling-relevant hardware features from the system software may take time to be adopted in operating systems [31], or it may come in the form of architecture-specific interfaces that limit application portability or make its utilization impossible from particular levels of the software stack [11,17]. Take for instance the Linux kernel, that does not currently feature support for the Intel Thread Director (TD) technology [31], unlike the proprietary Windows 11 kernel. TD is a set of scheduling-related hardware facilities –introduced with Alder Lake processors– that provide the system software with performance and energy efficiency hints to aid in carrying out effective thread-to-core mappings on Intel AMPs. Implementing custom mechanisms in the OS kernel to leverage these new –yet unsupported– features directly from the OS scheduler, or exposing them to user space involves a substantial development effort, due to the inherent challenges associated with kernel-level programming [11,26]. At the same time, custom OS-level extensions could be difficult to be adopted in production systems, where patching the OS kernel may be impractical.

To address these issues, we propose PMCSched, a framework for the Linux kernel that enables rapid development of the OS-level support required to create custom scheduling and resource-management schemes on both symmetric and asymmetric multicore systems. Unlike other existing frameworks that require patching the Linux kernel to function [4,20,26,39], PMCSched makes it possible to incorporate new scheduling-related OS-level support in Linux via a kernel module that can be loaded in unmodified kernels, making its adoption easier in production systems. Notably, the main focus of this framework is to simplify the creation of novel scheduling and resource-management strategies that are either implemented entirely in the OS kernel, or require changes in different layers of the system software, so as to benefit from coordinated decisions between the runtime system and the OS scheduler [10,13,30].

As a proof of concept of our framework, in this work we implement different asymmetry-aware OS-level schedulers on top of an unmodified Linux kernel v5.16, and evaluate their effectiveness by running different multi-application worloads on an Intel Alder Lake processor. These schedulers make use of PMCs and leverage the Intel Thread Director technology [15,16], by accessing such hardware facilities directly from kernel space.

The remainder of the paper is organized as follows. Section 2 discusses related work. Section 3 provides an overview of PMCSched design and introduces its main implementation challenges. Section 4 covers the experimental case study on scheduling for Alder Lake processors, and Sect. 5 concludes the paper.

2   Related Work

A large body of work has proposed asymmetry-aware scheduling strategies for adoption on either runtime systems [5,25,37] or OS kernels [10,18,31]. Frequently, such endeavors culminate in tools and frameworks that aim to ease the development and analysis of new scheduling algorithms; these are likewise some of the main goals of this paper.

Recent studies have shown that scheduling algorithms that come in stock general-purpose OSs exhibit suboptimal behavior for different workloads on a wide range of processor architectures [6,10,23]. At the same time, making the required changes in an OS kernel to build effective scheduling policies specifically tailored to custom workloads or microarchitectures may be a significant burden to the average developer [26,39]. On many monolithic kernels such as Linux, the development of new OS scheduling policies constitutes a labor intensive task, as the kernel itself needs to be modified. More specifically, testing any scheduling-related kernel modification requires compiling and reinstalling the kernel, and finally rebooting the machine for the changes to take effect. Testing an individual change in this way may as well take a full a coffee break, depending on the features and resources of the target platform and the development host.

To overcome these problems, some researchers have resorted to evaluating their proposed OS-level schedulers via simplistic user space prototypes [3,9,35]. Even though this approach may allow to draw interesting insights and also benefit from leveraging application-level metrics, strategies implemented in this way suffer from the limitations imposed to userland, such as the additional overhead of context switches and extra system calls required for dynamic thread affinity and performance monitoring [26], or the inability to quickly react to low-level scheduling-related events (e.g., a thread blocks due to I/O or a page fault), thus wasting CPU cycles [11]. In addition, user-level scheduling prototypes cannot access hardware extensions not currently exposed by the OS kernel.

Scheduling frameworks, such as those proposed in [4, 26, 39] or PMCSched itself, aim to overcome some of the aforementioned limitations. LUSH permits the creation of user-level schedulers for AMPs without special execution privileges, and introduces kernel-level changes to allow fine-grained access to PMCs from user space. Mvondo et al. [26] propose the extension of existing OS APIs, so as to allow the development of kernel-level schedulers programmable from user-space using a safe and controlled environment. LITMUS [4], by contrast, constitutes a substantial fork of the Linux kernel with extensions to facilitate programming of real-time kernel-level scheduling algorithms. Contrary to such solutions –some of them restricted to specific domains [4, 39]– PMCSched allows to create custom scheduling-related OS-level modifications without actually patching the kernel. This constitutes a major advantage, as getting profound modifications of the kernel accepted upstream is an arduous task; so much so that researchers tend to forget about that possibility altogether and treat their software as research prototypes with no hope of production integration in sight [26], even after conducting the required security audits. Conversely, the big effort required to maintain multiple project forks for various releases of the Linux kernel often shortens the lifespan of the associated projects [38].

Other studies explore the challenges of OS scheduling on highly heterogeneous architectures [25]. Of special attention is the case of Popcorn Linux [2], which targets heterogeneous systems consisting of nodes with different ISAs, opening the door to parallel ISA-heterogeneous runtime scheduling [24]. These efforts are orthogonal to ours, formulating a problem with several interconnected computing nodes with different processor architectures (e.g., x86 and ARM).

3   PMCSched: Implementation Challenges and Design

Motivation and challenges. PMCSched is implemented on top of PMCTrack, a performance monitoring tool [33] for Linux that was open sourced back in 2015 [32]. Unlike Perf Events [38] –the default Linux subsystem to access hardware facilities, such as performance monitoring counters (PMCs)– PMCTrack was not primarily designed to only expose hardware monitoring facilities to user space, but to assist the system software when performing runtime optimizations based on these hardware facilities. The operations for which the system software can benefit from PMCTrack include scheduling [10, 34] and resource management [11]. The main advantages of relying on PMCTrack for such tasks are its ability to foster new OS-level features as part of an extensible loadable kernel module, and its efficient architecture-independent API to access PMCs within the kernel on a wide range of architectures (x86, ARMv7, ARMv8, etc.). Figure 1 depicts the various components of PMCTrack and their relationship, described in detail in [33].

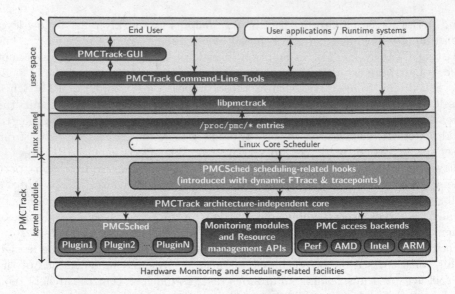

Fig. 1. PMCSched components (in green) inside PMCTrack's architecture. (Color figure online)

With the PMCSched framework we take PMCTrack's potential one step further by enabling rapid development of OS support for scheduling and resource management for Linux *within a loadable kernel module.* We need to highlight this because hitherto new scheduling policies could not be implemented as a kernel module [20,26], since no specific API exists for that purpose within the Linux scheduler. When creating novel OS-level schedulers for Linux without modifying the kernel, three main challenges have repeatedly appeared: (1) the inability to execute code in a kernel module in immediate response to the occurrence of key scheduling-relevant events –context switches, thread creation/destruction, etc.– (2) the lack of a standardized method to seamlessly extend the Linux task structure with new per-thread scheduling related fields that custom schedulers typically require to function, and (3) how to efficiently customize the behavior of the Linux load balancer. Notably, the first two barriers also arise when attempting to manage performance counters at the low level, and for that reason, most PMC tools require changes in the kernel; PMCTrack adds the associated functionality via a small portable kernel patch [33].

Our solution. PMCSched addresses the three aforementioned issues without patching the kernel as follows. First, to be aware of key scheduling events from a kernel module, PMCSched installs scheduling-related hooks (callbacks) leveraging two modern tracing facilities of the Linux kernel: *dynamic ftrace* [29] and *tracepoints* [22]. These two tracing technologies rely on dynamic and static kernel instrumentation, respectively. Noticeably, both are supported on a wide range of processor architectures, and can be found enabled by default on the most popular Linux distributions. Unlike other kernel instrumentation facilities (like

Kprobes), these technologies make it possible for a module to be notified when a kernel function is invoked or when a static tracepoint is reached with virtually no overhead [22,29]. Not only do PMCSched hooks –depicted in Fig. 1– enable the implementation of custom schedulers in a kernel module, but also allowed us to eliminate the need for the PMCTrack kernel patch entirely [27]. Secondly, PMCSched provides a seamless mechanism to extend the task structure with new thread-specific data without modifying the kernel. To this end, whenever a thread enters the system, PMCSched associates a *dummy* software event from the Perf Events subsystem to the thread, by inserting the event into the event list present in Linux's task structure (`perf_event_list` field). The structure of this dummy event (`struct perf_event`) contains a void pointer field (`pmu_private`) that can be utilized to point to any other structure. To simplify the integration of PMCSched in PMCTrack, we use the event's void pointer to point to PMC-Track's per-thread structure (`pmon_prof_t`). PMCSched scheduling fields can be seamlessly added without modifying the kernel, by extending the structures definition inside PMCTrack's kernel module sources.

To make it possible to implement custom load balancing policies, PMCSched introduces the *core group* abstraction. Essentially, cores in the system are organized into different sets (or *core groups*) based on their type (for AMP systems) or their hierarchical relationship in the platform's topology (e.g., cores sharing a last-level cache, or part of the same NUMA node). PMCSched automatically divides cores into different core groups based on system topology, but considering a configurable granularity (LLC, socket or NUMA domain). To implement custom and scalable OS-level load balancing policies or perform specific thread-to-core mappings, a scheduler implemented in PMCSched must assign threads to specific core-groups by using affinity masks. In using this approach, enforcing load balancing across cores within the same group is up to the Linux load balancer, which respects affinity masks. We should also highlight that PMCSched associates a set of linked lists to each core group (spin-lock protected), making it possible to keep track of active threads or multithreaded processes associated with each core group. This design approach allows to make scheduling decisions independently for threads assigned to different core groups, and favors scalable designs that reduce contention in accesses to core-group specific data structures.

A new scheduling or resource management algorithm can be implemented by creating a *scheduling plugin*, which –as illustrated in Fig. 1– becomes a part of the PMCSched subsystem within PMCTrack's kernel module. Building a plugin boils down to instantiating an interface of scheduling operations and implementing the corresponding interface functions in a separate ".c" file within the module sources. The various algorithm-specific operations are invoked from the core part of the scheduling framework when a key scheduling-related event occurs, such as when a threads enters the system, terminates, becomes runnable/non-runnable, or when tick processing is due to update statistics. The framework also provides a set of callbacks to carry out periodic scheduling activations from interrupt (timer) and process (kernel thread) context on each core group separately, thus making it possible to invoke a wide range of blocking and non-blocking scheduling-related kernel API calls, such as those to map a thread to a specific

CPU or core group. This modular approach to creating scheduling algorithms resembles the one used by *scheduling classes* (algorithms) inside the Linux kernel, but with a striking advantage: PMCSched scheduling plugins can be bundled in a kernel module that can be loaded on unmodified kernels. Moreover, plugin developers have access to a rich set of APIs available in PMCTrack, empowering them to configure performance counters seamlessly and retrieve PMC values in a per-thread fashion, to gather data from other hardware monitoring features [31,33], or to govern hardware facilities for shared-resource contention mitigation (e.g., LLC partitioning) available on Intel and AMD processors [1,11].

OS-runtime interaction and Future Work. As previously stated, PMC-Sched could also be used as a tool to perform system-software optimizations that exploit synergistic interactions between a user-level runtime system and the OS [13,30]. To allow different types of interaction between user space and the kernel, the current version of PMCSched exports a set of special files under the /proc filesystem. For example, the value of configurable parameters of the currently active scheduling plugin can be retrieved/altered by reading/writing from/to those special files. PMCSched also supports the creation of a per-thread page-sized memory region that can be shared between kernel and user space, so as to allow the runtime system to share critical application-level metrics with the OS (e.g., QoS metrics for throughput or latency constraints) and, at the same time, enable the OS to expose information not directly accessible from the runtime system, such as Thread Director performance and energy-efficiency estimates for the current core type where the thread runs [31]. As for future work, and by leveraging this or other communication features –such as netlink sockets–, we plan to implement an OS/runtime interaction scheme to enable efficient execution of multiple data-parallel OpenMP programs on an AMP system, where both layers of the system software play an essential role [6,30].

4   Experimental Case Study

To demonstrate the applicability of the PMCSched framework, we experimented with a system equipped with an Intel Core i9-12900K "Alder Lake" processor and 32 GB DDR4 SDRAM. This AMP processor combines 8 "Golden Cove" big (P) cores, and 8 "Gracemont" small (E) cores. E-cores are grouped into two 4-core clusters, each group sharing a 2 MiB L2 cache. P-cores, by contrast, have a private 1.25 MiB L2 cache. Every core in the platform integrates a private L1 cache, but shares a 30 MiB L3 (LLC) with the remaining E and P cores. With our experiments we evaluate how effectively an OS-level scheduler implemented with our framework can improve the overall system throughput on an Intel Alder Lake processor.

Maximizing Throughput on AMPs. Previous research has demonstrated that, to maximize throughput in the context of multi-program workloads, the scheduler needs to be able to (1) determine at runtime the performance benefit that each thread in the workload derives from running on a big core relative to a small one, and then (2) use big cores for running threads that exhibit a larger relative performance benefit from such cores, while possibly readjusting the mappings dynamically based on program-phase changes. Henceforth, we will refer to the big-to-small performance benefit as the thread's Speedup Factor (SF). Similarly, we will now use the acronym HSF (i.e., High SF) to refer to a dynamic scheduling strategy that aims to maximize throughput by mapping high-SF threads to big cores. While this experimental analysis focuses on workloads consisting of compute-intensive single-threaded applications, it is worth noting that other factors beyond the SF need to be considered for multi-threaded programs, such as latency constraints [12], load balancing and synchronization [6,30], along with other interdependencies among tasks/threads in the application [5].

Implementation of Scheduling Algorithms. One of the main deltas among the various HSF implementations [18,19,34] is the underlying method employed to determine the SF online. In this work we explore the effectiveness of two SF prediction methods: PMC-based estimation models [18,28,34], and reliance on specific hardware support for SF estimation [15,16]. Regarding the first prediction method, we use the two SF-estimation models proposed in our earlier work [31], which were specifically built for SF prediction from the big and small cores of an Intel Alder Lake processor. The methodology used to build these estimation models [34], the specific performance events they depend upon, and a detailed discussion on their accuracy can be found in [31]. For the hardware-aided SF prediction we leverage the Intel Thread Director (TD) technology, a set of hardware facilities –first introduced in Alder Lake processors– enabling to guide the OS in making thread scheduling decisions on Intel hybrid multi-cores [15,16]. To predict a thread's current SF with TD, the OS must retrieve its TD class (i.e., an integer in {0..3} in the Alder Lake processor we used) by reading a model-specific register, and then calculate the ratio of two performance estimates (for big and small cores) associated with the current TD class; these performance estimates are stored in a memory-resident table that the hardware maintains, which is directly readable from the OS kernel alone.

We experimented with several asymmetry-aware schedulers implemented in PMCSched: an Asymmetry-Aware Round-Robin (AARR) scheduler [21] that equally shares big and small cores among applications; and three variants of the HSF scheduler, which optimize throughput. The first variant of HSF –referred to as HSF/TD– employs Thread Director (TD) to obtain SF estimates. Because in the Alder Lake processor we used such estimates are only accessible directly when the thread runs on a big core (i.e., a valid TD class is not reported from E-cores [31]), our implementation continuously stores TD-based big-core SF estimates on a per-thread history table for different program phases, making it possible to obtain SF predictions indirectly from small cores by accessing the history table. The utilization of history tables to observe patterns from previous samples and predict current and future performance has been widely explored by previous work [10,39]. To deal with frequent *phase misses* when accessing the history table from small cores, our implementation triggers migrations to

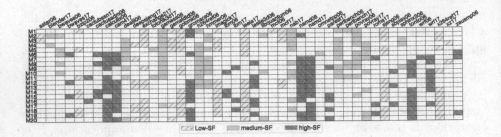

Fig. 2. Workloads used for our experiments. Each row M_i depicts the composition of the i-th workload. A blank cell indicates that the associated program is not included in the workload. Applications whose average SF is lower than 1.7 are considered low-SF programs in our platform, and those with an SF value greater than 2.05 are classified as high-SF. The remaining ones are labeled as medium-SF.

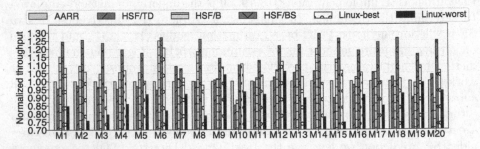

Fig. 3. Normalized throughput delivered by the various scheduling algorithms

big cores to gather new big-core estimates, and also implements a throttling mechanism to limit the number of profiling-related migrations, as in [10]. In the second HSF variant, denoted as HSF/BS, the OS continuously gathers a number of per-thread PMC metrics; an up-to-date SF prediction is obtained for a thread by using the metric values as input to the core-specific models proposed in [31] for the big and the small core (the model to use depends on the thread's current core type). Lastly, under the HSF/B variant, SF predictions on big cores are obtained via the same big-core model used by HSP/BS; however, on the small core, predictions are obtained indirectly by reading a history table, populated with past SF estimates retrieved on the big core. Note that this variant was implemented to conduct a fairer comparison with HSF/TD, where direct SF predictions on the small core are unavailable.

Experiments and discussion. For our experiments we randomly generate 20 diverse workloads, comprising of 16 single-threaded programs each. The composition of the various program mixes (Mi) is depicted in Fig. 2, and covers 46 different SPEC CPU applications in total. In launching each program mix, we follow a similar procedure to that of previous works [3,34], so as to ensure the machine's load is constant throughout the experiment. All applications in the workload are started simultaneously, and when one of them completes, the program is restarted repeatedly until the slowest application completes three times. We use the geometric mean of the completion times for each program to calculate the degree of throughput, by using the Aggregate Speedup metric [10,31,34]. All programs were compiled with GCC 11.2 with the -O3 and -mtune=alderlake compiler switches.

Figure 3 shows the normalized throughput for the various scheduling algorithms relative to AARR. As a reference, we also provide the best and worst results obtained by Linux default scheduler (CFS) across 10 runs of each experiment, referred to as Linux-best and Linux-worst, respectively. This scheduler is designed to minimize the number of thread migrations, but it is still largely asymmetry unaware [10], and provides highly variable completion times for the same application across multiple runs of the same experiment on Intel Alder Lake processors. Essentially CFS may map an application to a big core for a certain run, and then to a small core in another run, irrespective of its co-runners. This causes large throughput differences across runs, making CFS a misleading baseline [10].

These experimental results undoubtedly reveal that HSP/BS outperforms the other schedulers for most workloads, achieving up to a 30% throughput gain w.r.t. AARR, and providing a 22.9% average improvement against the TD variant. These numbers are tightly related to the superior SF-estimation accuracy provided by the PMC-based models for the big and small core, relative to that of Thread Director, as shown in [31]. Overall, a higher SF-prediction accuracy allows HSF to identify programs with a truly high SF better, and, as a result, the scheduler can grant more big-core cycles to them than to other threads. We further observe that using the big-core model in combination with the history table (HSF/B variant), provides substantially better throughout figures than HSP/TD (averaging 7.9% improvement). However, in a few workloads, such as M10 and M20, HSF/B fails to yield comparable performance to that of AARR. We found that this is caused by the extra thread migrations (and hence the overheads), triggered in response to frequent table phase misses, and aimed at refreshing the history table on big cores. Despite this fact, we conclude that the PMC-based big-core model alone provides superior accuracy than TD, and that the per-thread history table constitutes a reasonably effective method to deal with scenarios where direct SF estimation is not available on certain core types.

5   Conclusions and Future Work

In this paper we have presented PMCSched, a framework for Linux that enables to implement the custom OS kernel support required by new scheduling and resource-management policies for multicore systems. A key distinctive feature of our framework is that it empowers developers and researchers to add new kernel-level scheduling-related support via a loadable module that can be inserted in vanilla (unmodified) versions of the Linux kernel. This favors the adoption in production systems of custom, and potentially sophisticated, scheduling strategies implemented at one or multiple levels of the system software stack. To demonstrate the flexibility of the framework, we leveraged PMCSched's modular plugin-based design to implement several asymmetry-aware OS-level schedulers, and evaluated their ability to improve system throughput under multi-application workloads on an Intel Alder Lake (hybrid) multicore processor.

As for future work, we plan to design novel scheduling and resource management strategies to improve performance when both single-threaded and multithreaded programs are present on the system, making emphasis on potential optimizations that come from the synergistic cooperation between the runtime system and the OS. Lastly, we should highlight that part of the core functionality of PMCSched is already publicly available in PMCTrack's source code repository [27], but that the full framework will be open sourced with the next public release of PMCTrack, scheduled for late 2022.

Acknowledgements. Work supported by the EU (FEDER), the Spanish MINECO and CM, under grants RTI2018-093684-B-I00 and S2018/TCS-4423.

References

1. AMD: AMD64 Technology Platform QoS Extensions. https://developer.amd.com/wp-content/resources/56375.pdf
2. Barbalace, A., Lyerly, R., Jelesnianski, C., Carno, A., Chuang, H.R., Legout, V., Ravindran, B.: Breaking the boundaries in heterogeneous-ISA datacenters. In: ACM SIGPLAN Notices, vol. 52, pp. 645–659. ACM (2017)
3. Blagodurov, S., et al.: A case for NUMA-aware contention management on multicore systems. In: Proceedings of USENIX ATC 2011. USA (2011)
4. Calandrino, J.M., et al.: LITMUS-RT : a Testbed for empirically comparing real-time multiprocessor schedulers. In: 2006 27th IEEE International Real-Time Systems Symposium (RTSS'06), pp. 111–126 (2006)
5. Chronaki, K., et al.: Criticality-aware dynamic task scheduling for heterogeneous architectures. In: Proceedings of the 29th ACM on International Conference on Supercomputing, pp. 329–338. ICS 2015 (2015)
6. Chronaki, K., et al.: On the maturity of parallel applications for asymmetric multicore processors. J. Par. Distrib. Comput. **127**, 105–115 (2019)
7. Costero, L., et al.: Energy efficiency optimization of task-parallel codes on asymmetric architectures. In: Proceedings of HPCS 2017, pp. 402–409 (July 2017)
8. Dongarra, J.: Report on the sunway taihulight system. Tech Report University of Tennessee: UT-EECS-16-742 (2016)
9. Feliu, J., et al.: Perf&fair: a progress-aware scheduler to enhance performance and fairness in SMT multicores. IEEE Trans. Comput. **66**(5), 905–911 (2017)
10. Garcia-Garcia, A., et al.: Contention-aware fair scheduling for asymmetric single-ISA multicore systems. IEEE Trans. Comput. **67**(12) (2018)
11. Garcia-Garcia, A., et al.: LFOC: A lightweight fairness-oriented cache clustering policy for commodity multicores. In: Proceedings of ICPP 2019, pp. 14:1–14:10 (2019)
12. Haque, M.E., et al.: Exploiting heterogeneity for tail latency and energy efficiency. In: 50th Annual IEEE/ACM International Symposium on Microarchitecture, pp. 625–638 (2017)

13. Harris, T., Maas, M., Marathe, V.J.: Callisto: Co-scheduling parallel runtime systems. In: Proceedings of 9th European Conference on Computing Systems, EuroSys 2014 (2014)
14. Hennessy, J.L., Patterson, D.A.: A new golden age for computer architecture. Commun. ACM **62**(2), 48–60 (2019)
15. Intel: Intel® 64 and IA-32 Architectures Software Developer's Manual, Vol. 3: System Programming Guide (2021)
16. Intel: Optimizing software for x86 hybrid archiecture. Intel White Paper (Oct 2021)
17. Intel: User space software for Intel(R) Resource Director Technology. https://github.com/intel/intel-cmt-cat (2022)
18. Koufaty, D., Reddy, D., Hahn, S.: Bias Scheduling in Heterogeneous Multi-core Architectures. In: Eurosys 10, pp. 125–138 (2010)
19. Kumar, R., et al.: Single-ISA Heterogeneous Multi-Core Architectures for Multithreaded Workload Performance. In: 31st Annual International Symposium on Computer Architecture (ISCA 2004), pp. 64–75 (2004)
20. Lepers, B., et al.: Provable multicore schedulers with Ipanema: Application to work conservation. In: Proceedings of Eurosys 2020 (2020)
21. Li, T., et al.: Operating system support for overlapping-ISA heterogeneous multi-core architectures. In: Proceedings of HPCA 2010, pp. 1–12 (2010)
22. Linux: Using the linux kernel tracepoints. https://www.kernel.org/doc/html/latest/trace/tracepoints.html
23. Lozi, J.P., et al.: The linux scheduler: A decade of wasted cores. In: Proceedings of the 11th ACM European Conference on Computer Systems (Eurosys 2016) (2016)
24. Lyerly, R., et al.: An OpenMP Runtime for Transparent Work Sharing Across Cache-Incoherent Heterogeneous Nodes. ACM Trans. Comput. Syst. (dec 2021)
25. Lyerly, R., et al.: An Openmp runtime for transparent work sharing across cache-incoherent heterogeneous nodes. ACM Trans. Comput. Syst. (2021)
26. Mvondo, D., et al.: Towards user-programmable schedulers in the operating system kernel. In: Proceedings of the 11th Workshop on Systems for Post-Moore Architectures, SPMA 2022 (2022)
27. PMCTrack: Github repository. https://github.com/jcsaezal/pmctrack (2015)
28. Pricopi, M., et al.: Power-performance modeling on asymmetric multi-cores. In: Proceedings of CASES 2013., pp. 15:1–15:10 (2013)
29. Rostedt, S.: "ftrace: Where modifying a running kernel all started". https://kernel-recipes.org/en/2019/talks/ftrace-where-modifying-a-running-kernel-all-started/
30. Saez, J.C., Castro, F., Prieto-Matias, M.: Enabling performance portability of data-parallel openmp applications on asymmetric multicore processors. In: 49th International Conference on Parallel Processing. ICPP 2020 (2020)
31. Saez, J.C., Prieto-Matias, M.: Evaluation of the Intel Thread Director technology on an Alder Lake processor. In: 13th ACM SIGOPS Asia-Pacific Workshop on Systems (APSys 2022) (2022)
32. Saez, S.C., et al.: An OS-oriented performance monitoring tool for multicore systems. In: Hunold, S., et al. (eds.) Euro-Par 2015. LNCS, vol. 9523, pp. 697–709. Springer, Cham (2015). https://doi.org/10.1007/978-3-319-27308-2_56
33. Saez, J.C., et al.: PMCTrack: delivering performance monitoring counter support to the OS scheduler. Comput. J. **60**(1), 60–85 (2017)
34. Saez, J.C., et al.: Towards completely fair scheduling on asymmetric single-ISA multicore processors. J. Parallel Distrib. Comput. **102** (2017)
35. Salami, B., et al.: Online energy-efficient fair scheduling for heterogeneous multi-cores considering shared resource contention. J. Supercomput. **78**(6) (2022)

36. Servat, H., et al.: On the instrumentation of OpenMP and OmpSs tasking constructs. In: Euro-Par 2012: Parallel Processing Workshops, pp. 414–428 (2013)
37. Torng, C., Wang, M., Batten, C.: Asymmetry-aware work-stealing runtimes. In: Proceedings of ISCA 2016, pp. 40–52 (2016)
38. Weaver, V.M.: Linux perf event features and overhead. FastPath Workshop (2013)
39. Xu, V.M., et al.: Lush: Lightweight framework for user-level scheduling in heterogeneous multicores. In: 2021 IEEE 14th International Symposium on Embedded Multicore/Many-core Systems-on-Chip (MCSoC), pp. 396–404 (2021)

HIPLZ: Enabling Performance Portability for Exascale Systems

Jisheng Zhao[1(✉)], Colleen Bertoni[2], Jeffrey Young[1], Kevin Harms[2], Vivek Sarkar[1], and Brice Videau[2]

[1] Georgia Institute of Technology, Atlanta, GA, USA
jisheng.zhao@cc.gatech.edu, {jyoung9,vsarkar}@gatech.edu
[2] Argonne National Laboratory, Lemont, IL, USA
{bertoni,bvideau}@anl.gov, harms@alcf.anl.gov

Abstract. While heterogeneous computing has emerged as a dominant trend in current and future High-Performance Computing (HPC) systems, it is also widely recognized that this shift has led to increased software complexity due to a proliferation of programming systems for different heterogeneous processors. One such example is the Heterogeneous-Computing Interface for Portability from AMD (`HIP`), which is composed of a C Runtime API and C++ Kernel Language. Many HPC applications will likely use `HIP` on future exascale systems (e.g., Frontier and El Capitan), but `HIP` currently only targets AMD and NVIDIA processors. This limitation creates challenges for users who would also like to run their applications on exascale systems based on other architectures (e.g., Aurora, which is based on Intel hardware) that are currently not targeted by `HIP`.

In this paper, we introduce the design and implementation of `HIPLZ`, a compiler and runtime system that uses the Intel Level Zero API to support `HIP` on Intel GPU architectures. We discuss the design of `HIPLZ`, derived from `HIPCL` (an implementation of `HIP` on top of `OpenCL`), and portability issues that occur from using the Level Zero runtime as a back-end. We evaluate our implementation by running several performance benchmarks and mini-apps written in `HIP` on Intel architectures using `HIPLZ`. Our results show that this approach provides competitive performance relative to Intel's `OpenCL` implementations on Intel Gen9 GPUs, while providing good coverage of features needed by HPC applications. Overall, this approach is a promising demonstration of enabling performance portability for exascale systems.

1 Introduction

Modern High Performance Computing (HPC) has been defined as an era of extreme heterogeneity where an increasing number of accelerators support SIMD parallelism, spatial computing, or domain specific architectures. This is especially true as we move toward exascale, where the majority of pre-exascale and exascale systems are accelerator-based. For example, 7 of the top 10 systems in

J. Singer et al. (Eds.): Euro-Par 2022 Workshops, LNCS 13835, pp. 197–210, 2023.
https://doi.org/10.1007/978-3-031-31209-0_15

the Top 500 for November 2021 are GPU-based [1]. Recently, NVIDIA systems were the dominant accelerator which applications would target, but several next-generation systems will be based on accelerators from different vendors: Aurora and SuperMUC-NG Phase II, with Intel GPUs [2,3] and Frontier, El Capitan, and LUMI with AMD GPUs [4–6]. Each vendor generally develops its own programming model and implementation which is optimized for its hardware. This design poses a challenge for application developers who wish to create portable code for multiple systems. Often this programming model heterogeneity results in application developers maintaining multiple branches of code in each different vendor-specific programming model, which increases code complexity and developer time requirements.

Heterogeneous-compute Interface for Portability (HIP) from AMD is one example of such a programming system that targets AMD and NVIDIA architectures. In this paper, we introduce HIPLZ: a compilation and runtime system that supports HIP via Intel's Level Zero (L0) runtime [7] using the fat binary model for supporting multiple architectures and SPIR-V as an intermediate language (IL). To the best of our knowledge, HIPLZ is the first effort that bridges HIP to L0 which is the primary low level application programming interface (API) for Intel hardware.

In thispaper, we present the following contributions:

1. The prototype of HIPLZ, a library that allows applications using the HIP API to run on devices that support Intel Level Zero and OpenCL drivers. The source code is located at: https://github.com/jz10/anl-gt-gpu.
2. A test suite that covers the major functionality of HIP and that uses it as the validation of HIPLZ.
3. An evaluation of test coverage and code performance of HIPLZ on Intel Gen 9 GPUs. Our results show that HIPLZ supports the complete execution of 82% of tested applications and demonstrates performance parity with HIPCL and OpenCL for memory- and FLOP-focused benchmarks.

The paper is organized as follows: Sect. 2 gives background information about the HIP programming model, intermediate representation and the Intel L0 runtime. The details of the design and implementation are presented in Sect. 3. Section 4 discusses testing HIPLZ and evaluates the performance of HIPLZ. Section 5 discusses related work.

2   Background

2.1   Heterogeneous-compute Interface for Portability (HIP)

HIP [8] is a C++ 14 Runtime API and kernel language that is derived from CUDA [9] and that allows developers to create portable applications for AMD and NVIDIA GPUs from a single source code. It supports advanced C++ programming language features including templates, C++11 lambdas, and many other features.

2.2 Standard Portable Intermediate Representation (SPIR-V) and Fat Binary

SPIR-V [10] is an industry open standard intermediate language (IL) for shader and kernel language compilers used for expressing parallel computation and GPU-based graphics. SPIR-V provides a common language front-end compiler to developers for building computing kernels without needing to directly expose source code. This IL allows shipping compiled kernels in binary format while remaining portable on multiple hardware implementations.

The fat binary model integrates device code (kernel functions) into the host side executable binary via intermediate languages, and uses vendor APIs (driver compiler) to apply just-in-time compilation on kernel functions during runtime. SPIR-V and NVIDIA PTX are typical examples for fat binary.

2.3 OpenCL and HIPCL

OpenCL [11] is a widely used, open standard for programming heterogeneous platforms, and is supported by most of the major accelerator vendors, including NVIDIA, AMD, Xilinx, ARM, and Intel.

HIPCL [12] is an open-source compilation and runtime system that allows running HIP programs on OpenCL platforms with sufficient capabilities. HIPCL relies on SPIR-V as a target IL (i.e. fat binary embedded in ELF binary) and implements the HIP API on top of OpenCL calls.

2.4 Level Zero Runtime

Intel Level Zero (L0) [7] is a specification which is part of the Intel oneAPI suite which is a SYCL-based specification and set of APIs and tools targeting CPU, GPU and FPGA devices. The Intel L0 implementation provides a direct-to-metal access to accelerator devices and brings flexibility through the support of a broad set of language features, e.g. unified shared memory, synchronization primitives, and device function pointers. The aim of the L0 API is to provide a system level programming interface that easily allows higher level runtime APIs and libraries to target heterogeneous hardware. This is why we selected it for HIPLZ. The features of the L0 API include, but are not limited to: device partitioning, instrumentation, debugging, power managements, frequency control, and hardware diagnostics. The L0 specification does not define a kernel language, but relies on SPIR-V as an IL.

3 Design and Implementation

3.1 Design Goal

The main design goal of HIPLZ is to connect the Intel L0 runtime to the HIP programming model, thus enabling applications written using HIP to run on GPU devices driven by L0. Based on a survey of HPC application needs, we focused on supporting the following HIP features in HIPLZ: i) streams, including the command execution and callbacks (Sect. 3.4); ii) memory management, including host, device, shared memory, and texture memory (Sect. 3.5); iii) kernel and module management (Sect. 3.6); iv) device management (Sect. 3.7); and v) inter-operation with other parallel programming systems like Intel's DPC++ (Sect. 3.8). We ended up implementing 133 functions in HIPLZ out of 144 total HIP functions at the time HIPLZ was written. HIP now has 343 functions and the unincluded functions are mainly for graph operations.

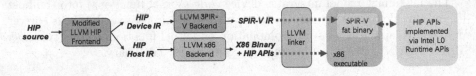

Fig. 1. The compilation workflow for HIPLZ.

3.2   The Compilation System

The workflow for the compilation of a HIP program by HIPLZ is shown in Fig. 1. The HIPLZ compilation workflow is based on that of HIPCL, which is a HIP-compatible compiler frontend based on the LLVM/Clang compiler. The HIPLZ compiler translates HIP source code to two parts of LLVM intermediate representation : host IR and device IR. The host part is processed via the legacy LLVM x86 backend to produce an x86 binary, and the device part is processed via the LLVM SPIR-V backend to produce SPIR-V IR. The x86 binary and the SPIR-V IR are then linked together to make an x86 executable binary (or shared library) that is embedded with SPIR-V (a fat binary).

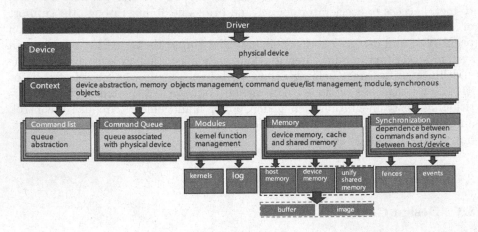

Fig. 2. The organization of Intel Level Zero runtime.

3.3   Runtime System

Before getting into the details of HIP feature support, here we introduce the basic structure of LO. Figure 2 presents the organization of LO APIs and objects in a top-down manner. On the top level, each Driver interacts with a collection of heterogeneous computing devices that share a given software stack. A physical device is presented as a Device that is associated with a Context that provides an interface for managing memory, modules, synchronization objects, command lists and queues. LO's memory management covers hosts, devices, shared memory, and image samplers.

The LO API is very similar to OpenCL's, especially in terms of the device data abstraction, execution model, and event driven synchronization. However, LO is at lower level and many features that are available in OpenCL are left to the application developer to implement. Such features include (but are not limited to) reference counting to handle object lifetime, callbacks on events state change, or host kernel enqueuing. HIPLZ wraps LO data structures in C++ classes in an object-oriented manner, similar to OpenCL's C++ bindings.

Table 1 gives some details about the mapping of data structures and similar objects for the different programming models we will use in the next sections HIP, HIPLZ, LO, OpenCL, and SYCL. The HIPLZ compiler translates a HIP object to its corresponding data structure in HIPLZ as in the first two columns in Table 1.

Table 1. The mapping among HIP, HIPLZ, LO, OpenCL, and SYCL objects.

HIP	HIPLZ	LO	OpenCL	SYCL
hipDevice	LZDevice	ze_device_t	cl_device_id	sycl::device
hipContext	LZContext	ze_context_t	cl_context	sycl::context
hipStream	LZQueue	ze_queue_t	cl_command_queue	sycl::queue
		ze_commandlist_t		
hipModule	LZModule	ze_module_t	cl_program	sycl::program
hipFunction	LZKernel	ze_kernel_t	cl_kernel	sycl::kernel
hipTextureObject	LZTexture	ze_image_t	cl_image	sycl::image
		ze_sampler_t	cl_sampler	sycl::sampler

3.4   Streams

A stream in HIP is presented as a sequence of tasks (e.g. kernels, memory copies, events) that execute in FIFO order. The tasks being executed in different streams are allowed to overlap and share device resources. Different streams may execute their commands out of order with respect to one another or concurrently. Three types of streams exist in HIP, the default stream (or NULL stream), blocking streams, and non-blocking streams. The last two types of streams can be created by the application programmer, and each differs in how they synchronize with the default stream. Tasks in the default stream will wait for all tasks previously submitted to blocking streams to be completed before executing. Similarly, tasks in blocking streams will wait for all tasks previously submitted to the default stream to be completed before executing. Non-blocking streams do not synchronize with the default stream.

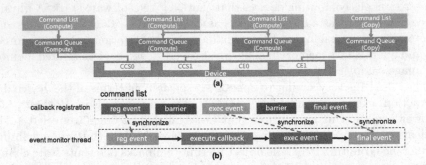

Fig. 3. a. The basic `HIPLZ` Command List and Command Queue (image source: https:// spec.oneapi.io/level-zero/latest/core/INTRO.html); b. The event order for executing callback

To be able to implement `HIP` streams with L0, L0 offers two possible modes of execution to dispatch tasks to a device. 1.) a command buffer abstraction (named command list), that will aggregate a series of tasks, and that can later be submitted to a command queue. The driver is free to optimize the execution of the command lists based on the synchronization expressed by the programmer; 2.)a low latency dispatch (named immediate command list) that will execute tasks as soon as they are ready (dependencies met) and able to be executed (available resources).

In `HIPLZ`, streams are implemented via `LZQueue` objects that wrap L0's immediate command lists (see Fig. 3(a)). This mode of execution is better suited to implement the FIFO behavior of `HIP` streams. Synchronization considerations are still important to ensure barriers between tasks within streams as well as to correctly implement the `HIP` default stream semantics and synchronization. Nonetheless, using the immediate command list greatly reduces the overhead of managing individual command lists that would need to be submitted to command queues and which would need to be freed or recycled once the tasks they contain have finished executing. This technique eliminates the need for dedicated event tracking for each command list, irrespective of synchronization with other streams, and it also reduces the latency between task submission and execution.

The commands executed by the streams include: kernel functions, memory copy operations, host callbacks, and `HIP` event operations. The synchronization among different streams is supported via L0 events and their wait and signal APIs. The event object in a command list acts as either a barrier or signal, so two tasks running on different streams can use events to synchronize their executions.

Stream Synchronization Example: We use the host callback implementation as an example of how synchronization between and within streams in HIPLZ is implemented with L0. Figure 3(b) presents the workflow of host callback registration and invocation in HIPLZ. The callback function pointer is registered by the callback registration API, and a synchronization scheme is set up to program the callback using L0 events. This implementation of host callbacks requires a three point synchronization scheme. For each callback three L0 events are created, here called reg event, exec event and final event. Three synchronization primitives are added to the L0 immediate command list: a barrier that will signal the reg event once it is reached, a barrier that will wait for the exec event to be signaled by the host, and lastly a signal to final event signifying that the synchronization is complete and that the events can be freed (or recycled). In parallel, the event (host) monitor thread waits on reg event to be signaled, executes the callback, signals callback termination via exec event and waits on final event before releasing the resources.

3.5 Memory Management

HIPLZ supports several HIP memory management APIs, including hipMalloc, hipMemcpy, hipMemcpyAsync, and hipFree. Users can specify the allocation site, i.e. host memory, device memory or shared memory. Shared memory is based on the underlying GPU's support, and its reference is presented as a raw pointer that can be referred on both the host and device side. As mentioned in Sect. 3.4, in L0 the memory copy operation is implemented as a command that is queued on the command list and is executed via command queue.

HIP texture objects are special memory objects, and their support is similar to as texture objects in CUDA; that is, the texture object is a first-class C++ object and can be passed as an argument just as if it is a pointer. HIPLZ provides hipCreateTextureObject and hipDestroyTextureObject to allocate and free texture objects.

The texture object is composed as an image buffer and a sampler object that operates on an image buffer. Since the image and sampler are defined as separate objects in L0 (i.e. ze_image_t and ze_sampler_t), we create the texture object as a C struct, as shown in Listing 1.1.

The ze_image_t and ze_sampler_t created via the L0 API are raw pointer values, thus they can be stored as intptr_t values. The actual texture operations are performed on reinterpreted structure fields, as shown in lines 6–9 of Listing 1.1, where a 2 dimensional texture of floating point values is sampled at coordinates x and y. This scheme relies on implementation specific behaviors of the Intel driver compiler.

Listing 1.1. HIP Texture Object Examples

```
1   typedef struct hipTextureObject_s {
2       intptr_t image;
3       intptr_t sampler;
4   } hipTextureObject_st, *hipTextureObject_t;
5
6   return read_imagef(
7       __builtin_astype(texObj->image, read_only image2d_t),
8       __builtin_astype(texObj->sampler, sampler_t),
9       (float2)(x, y)).x;
```

3.6   Kernel and Module Management

HIP defines three different attributes for functions: `__host__`, `__device__`, and `__global__`. A `__host__` decorated function is a function that is to be executed on the host, and functions without decorators will be considered host functions. A `__device__` function will be callable from the device, and this decorator can be combined with `__host__` to obtain a function that can execute on both the device and the host. A `__global__` decorated function or kernel is callable from the host. The HIPLZ compiler translates the kernel and device functions to SPIR-V IL, and they are translated to device binary via vendor compiler during runtime. Each kernel function is wrapped into a LZKernel object and managed by a LZProgram object that presents the L0 module. The kernel launch is based on the L0 API and issues a command to the immediate command list.

HIPLZ also supports device global variables that are used for exchanging values between kernels and host code. Device global variables are supported in SPIR-V, and they can be interacted with from the host using L0. They can also be supported in OpenCL using Intel extensions.

3.7   Device Management

The device management in HIPLZ focuses device selection (hipSetDevice and hipGetDevice) and device property queries (i.e. hipGetDeviceProperties). From L0 standpoint, this means creating a L0 context containing all the devices, and exposing those devices through the hipGetDeviceCount. This allows sharing memory between devices using USM, without needing to register USM allocations between different contexts. Setting the current active device in HIPLZ changes the values for the default devices and default stream. HIP device properties are derived from the different device properties available in L0.

3.8   SYCL Inter-operation

Interoperability between SYCL and HIP helps users maintain large heterogeneous code bases, and it also leverages the advantages of high performance libraries built by vendors (e.g. Intel oneMKL [13]). Both HIPLZ and DPC++ use L0 as the runtime driver for executing kernel functions on Intel GPUs, and use L0's driver object handles to maintain and exchange GPU device information, e.g. to pass an execution context object from HIPLZ to DPC++. To support data exchange, the unified shared memory (USM) mechanism is employed. Both HIPLZ and DPC++ use raw pointers to maintain the reference of the allocated memory from USM, and this simplifies memory reference passing between objects in each execution context.

https://www.overleaf.com/project/61854547ee0a74d0afa28679

3.9 Kernel Library

The implementation of the HIP math API in HIPLZ is based on OCML [14], which is a thin layer wrapping the OpenCL builtin math functions.

3.10 Discussion

Implementing HIP with LO comes with some challenges:

Program interface: The LO API organization is very similar to OpenCL, especially for the objects that abstract the GPU device. However, LO is a lower level API than OpenCL, as it lacks a kernel language, object lifetime management, and also requires finer grained control on tasks using queues and command lists. This requires careful management of objects lifetime in HIPLZ, and more involved synchronization schemes than in HIPCL.

Capacity of Conversion: Users could benefit from a conversion guide that would describe the potential pitfalls that can arise from migrating to the LO API from other heterogeneous programming models.

Lack of Thread Safety: There are many runtime objects and APIs that are not thread-safe in the LO specification, so mutual exclusion is employed for all relevant API call sites in HIPLZ using mutexes.

4 Evaluation

4.1 Employed GPU System

In this study we evaluated HIPLZ on an Intel Gen9 [15] on the JLSE cluster [16]. The Gen9 is an integrated GPU which is available in commercial Intel products such as laptops. Although Intel plans to release high-performance discrete GPUs [2], these are not publicly available at the time of writing, so we focus on the Gen9 GPUs.

The Gen9 GPU has a peak theoretical double (single) precision performance of 331.2 GFlop/s (1324.8 GFlop/s). With 2 channels of DDR4-2133, the peak theoretical DRAM bandwidth is 34.1 GB/s.

4.2 Overview of Tests

To evaluate HIPLZ we collected a repository of HPC-relevant benchmarks, mini-apps, frameworks, and applications hosted on GitHub [17]. The 50 selected codes include 2 benchmarks, 7 mini-apps (2 for BerkeleyGW), 1 application, and 40 HIP examples. The codes are listed in Table 4.

4.3 Results

We first discuss the performance results of the benchmarks and then the overall build/run/pass rate for the tests. For the measurements presented here we used:

- HIPLZ version: From HIPLZ, branch launch_bounds, commit cbf2260
- HIPCL version: From a fork of HIPCL, https://github.com/Kerilk/hipcl, in branch fence, commit dd39656
- OpenCL version: Intel OpenCL 3.0 NEO, driver version 22.02.0
- hip-test-suite [17], commit 3b19290

We note that HIPLZ has a differently named compiler driver than AMD HIP. HIPLZ uses clang++, while HIP uses hipcc.

Benchmark and Performance Results. To evaluate the performance of the HIPLZ implementation, we consider the tests in the hip-test-suite benchmarks subdirectory. The two tests in this subdirectory (ERT and BabelStream) measure the memory bandwidth and/or the peak performance of the system. The results are summarized in Table 2. By comparing the memory bandwidth and floating point performance, HIPLZ performs similarly to the OpenCL port, near the theoretical peaks of the Gen9 device.

For the memory bandwidth measurements, we expect the code to be able to reach 80% of the theoretical memory bandwidth of the hardware. As shown in Table 2, with the HIPLZ implementation, the HIP BableStream port measures a bandwidth of 27.76 GB/s and the HIP ERT port measures 25.84 GB/s. These are both near 80% of the theoretical bandwidth of the employed hardware.

For the floating point performance measurements, with our HIPLZ implementation, ERT measured 303.22 Gflop/s double precision peak performance, and 1240.69 Gflop/s single precision peak performance. The measured double precision peak performance is about 91% of the theoretical value, and the measured single precision peak performance is about 94% of the theoretical value.

Table 2. Efficiency evaluation of HIPLZ with Comparable APIs.

	HIPCL	OpenCL	HIPLZ
DRAM Bandwidth (GB/s) (from Triad BabelStream)	26.13	26.07	27.42
DRAM Bandwidth (GB/s) (from ERT)	25.48	25.77	25.84
FP64 peak (Gflop/s) (from ERT)	301.66	299.12	303.22
FP32 peak (Gflop/s) (from ERT)	1235.39	1184.91	1240.69

Details about how this test was compiled and run can be found in Ref. [17].

Several of the tests in the proxies and HIP-Examples subfolders also have HIP and OpenCL ports and measure performance metrics. We also compare several of these performance metrics in Table 3. As shown in Table 3, the performance

Table 3. Performance metrics from additional tests

Test (measurement)	HIPLZ	OpenCL
su3_bench (Total GFLOP/s)	28.813	28.6
strided-access (Stride 2 bandwidth, GB/s)	21.573	22.0791
GPU-STREAM (Triad bandwidth GB/s)	27.8	26.5
mixbench (Compute iter 256, Read-only Iops/bytes)	413.55	414.55

achieved by HIPLZ on Intel Gen9 GPUs is similar to that achieved by the OpenCL port for additional tests.

We also note that although add4 and cuda-stream do not have OpenCL ports in the test suite, they measure memory bandwidth. The bandwidth reported is similar to that reported by the OpenCL and HIP ports of Babelstream in Table 2, so we can consider them achieving the expected performance.

Overall Results. The results are shown in Table 4. Out of 50 tests, 45/50 (90 %) compile without errors, 41/50 (82%) compile and run without crashing, and 38/50 (76%) compile, run to completion, and give the correct answer.

Table 4. Detailed results of building, running, and checking correctness for the tests

Test	Build	Run	Correct	Test	Build	Run	Correct
BabelStream	Y	Y	Y	mixbench	Y	Y	Y
cs-roofline-toolkit	Y	Y	Y	BinomialOption	Y	Y	Y
cholla	N			BitonicSort	Y	Y	Y
KokkosDslash	N			FastWalshTransform	Y	Y	Y
su3_bench	Y	Y	Y	FloydWarshall	Y	Y	Y
BerkeleyGW-FF	N			HelloWorld	Y	Y	Y
BerkeleyGW-GPP	Y	N		Histogram	Y	Y	Y
add4	Y	Y	Y	MatrixMultiplication	Y	Y	Y
Cuda-stream	Y	Y	Y	PrefixSum	Y	Y	Y
gpu-burn	Y	N		RecursiveGaussian	Y	Y	Y
Mini-nbody	Y	Y	Y	SimpleConvolution	Y	Y	Y
Reduction	Y	Y	Y	dct	Y	Y	Y
rodinia_3.0 (18 tests)	Y (18)	Y (15)	Y (14)	dwtHaar1D	Y	Y	Y
rtm8	Y	Y	Y	adept-proxy	N		
Strided-access	Y	Y	Y	RSBench	Y	Y	N
VectorAdd	Y	Y	Y	GridMini	N		
GPU-STREAM	Y	Y	Y				

Discussion of Results. We now discuss reasons for the failures shown in Table 4. For the tests which did not build, this was due to dependence on external libraries that are not currently supported by HIPLZ (cholla (dependence on hipfft), KokkosDslash (dependence on kokkos)), unimplemented functions (adept-proxy (three-argument shuffles)), and compiler errors (BerkeleyGW-FF, GridMini).

There were four tests that failed at runtime. In three tests, rodinia-backprop, rodinia-dwt2d, and rodinia-b+tree kernel creation failed, and are being investigated. The other test which failed at runtime was gpu-burn, which fails since it allocates a piece of memory larger than what is available on the hardware.

Three of the tests ran but did not give correct answers. BerkeleyGW-GPP, rodinia-heartwall, and RSBench all return output arrays that do not pass validation. Future work will investigate these issues.

5   Related Work

Many of the programming language systems that support GPU offloading translate high-level programming language constructs to heterogeneous programming model APIs. Typical examples are OpenMP [18] and OpenACC [19]. Compilers which support OpenMP or OpenACC translate high-level pragma-based abstractions to lower-level (for example, CUDA driver or OpenCL) calls. This allows code using OpenMP or OpenACC to target a wide variety of hardware as long as the compiler lowers the abstractions into lower-level representations that the underlying runtime can ingest. This representation is bundled in a fat binary-based executable, in which the same binary embeds both host and device code. This allows the device code to be recompiled or optimized when the driver is updated, without having to rebuild the application. The usage of fat binaries brings the advantage for application deployment, i.e. no need to maintain separated binary or source code (host and device) and link them together for execution. LLVM/-Clang [20] uses PTX as the intermediate language (IL) for the CUDA driver. Intel OpenMP compiler makes another choice and uses SPIR-V as IL in order to target their OpenCL or L0 based GPU backends [21,22]. The approach in HIPLZ is similar, although we implement the HIP API and not pragma-based approaches, and we use SPIR-V as the intermediary representation.

Different approaches exist to bridge programming models to L0: for example ZLUDA [23] is a demonstrator showcasing running unmodified CUDA applications on top of L0 by implementing the CUDA driver API in L0, and converting NVIDIA PTX [24] to SPIR-V. ZLUDA only supports a limited subset of applications, but it does showcase promising performance on those applications.

Another well known project bridging several programming models to OpenCL is pocl [25]. pocl implements OpenCL for NVIDIA GPUs on top of CUDA, AMD GPUs on top of HSA and supports CPU devices as well through the Posix Threads programming API.

hipSYCL [26] is a SYCL implementation that leverages existing heterogeneous programming model such as CUDA, HIP to support different GPU architectures. It also provides a work-in-progress support for Intel GPUs via oneAPI [21].

6   Conclusion

In this paper, we introduced the design and implementation of HIPLZ, a compilation and runtime system that allows HIP code to run on Intel GPUs. It uses the L0 API to implement the HIP API's functionalities and SPIR-V as the IL to represent the kernel functions. To the best of our knowledge, HIPLZ is the first compiler and runtime system that allows HIP code to run on Intel GPUs by using L0.

HIPLZ successfully compiled and produced correct results on an Intel Gen9 GPU for more than 35 HIP test cases and mini-apps. In terms of performance, we ran two performance benchmarks using HIPLZ and were able to achieve approximately the same peak values as OpenCL, demonstrating that HIPLZ produces code that can effectively use the Intel GPU hardware. Future work will focus on extending performance for more applications and interoperability with other programming models like DPC++ and OpenMP.

Acknowledgements. This work was supported by the Argonne Leadership Computing Facility, which is a DOE Office of Science User Facility supported under Contract DE-AC02-06CH11357, and by the Exascale Computing Project (17-SC-20-SC), a collaborative effort of two U.S. Department of Energy organizations (Office of Science and the National Nuclear Security Administration). We also gratefully acknowledge the computing resources provided and operated by the Joint Laboratory for System Evaluation (JLSE) at Argonne National Laboratory.

References

1. Top 500 List. https://www.top500.org/lists/top500/list/2021/11/
2. Aurora. https://www.alcf.anl.gov/aurora
3. SuperMUC-NG. https://www.hpcwire.com/2021/05/05/lrz-announces-new-phase-of-supermuc-ng-supercomputer-with-intels-ponte-vecchio-gpu/
4. Frontier. https://www.olcf.ornl.gov/frontier/
5. EL Captain Supercomputer. https://www.hpe.com/us/en/compute/hpc/cray/doe-el-capitan-press-release.html
6. LUMI Supercomputer. hhttps://www.csc.fi/en/-/lumi-one-of-the-worlds-mightiest-supercomputers
7. Intel Level Zero Spec. http://spec.oneapi.io/level-zero/latest/index.html
8. Heterogeneous compute Interface for Portability (HIP). https://rocmdocs.amd.com/en/latest/Programming_Guides/Programming-Guides.html
9. Nvidia CUDA Toolkit. https://developer.nvidia.com/cuda-toolkit
10. The Industry Open Standard Intermediate Language for Parallel Compute and Graphics. https://www.khronos.org/spir/
11. Open Standard for Parallel Programming of Heterogeneous Systems(OpenCL). https://www.khronos.org/opencl/
12. Michal Babej and Pekka Jääskeläinen. Hipcl: Tool for porting cuda applications to advanced opencl platforms through hip. IWOCL '20, 2020
13. oneMKL. https://www.intel.com/content/www/us/en/developer/tools/oneapi/onemkl.html

14. OCML. https://github.com/RadeonOpenCompute/ROCm-Device-Libs/blob/amd-stg-open/doc/OCML.md
15. The Compute Architecture of Intel Processor Graphics Gen9. https://software.intel.com/content/dam/develop/external/us/en/documents/the-compute-architecture-of-intel-processor-graphics-gen9-v1d0.pdf
16. Argonne Joint Lab for System Evaluation (JLSE). https://www.jlse.anl.gov
17. HIP Test Set. https://github.com/jz10/hip-test_suite
18. OpenMP. https://www.openmp.org/
19. OpenACC. https://www.openacc.org/
20. Clang Compiler. http://clang.llvm.org/
21. Intel oneAPI. https://www.intel.com/content/www/us/en/developer/tools/oneapi/overview.html
22. DPC++. https://www.intel.com/content/www/us/en/developer/tools/oneapi/data-parallel-c-plus-plus.html
23. ZLUDA: CUDA on Intel GPUs. https://github.com/vosen/ZLUDA
24. Parallel Thread Execution (PTX) and ISA. https://docs.nvidia.com/cuda/parallel-thread-execution/
25. Jääskeläinen, P., et al.: Pocl: A performance-portable opencl implementation. Int. J. Parallel Program. **43**(5), 752–785 (2015)
26. hipsycl. https://hipsycl.github.io/

StorAlloc: A Simulator for Job Scheduling on Heterogeneous Storage Resources

Julien Monniot[(✉)], François Tessier, Matthieu Robert, and Gabriel Antoniu

University of Rennes, Inria, CNRS, IRISA, Rennes, France
{julien.monniot,francois.tessier,matthieu.robert,
gabriel.antoniu}@inria.fr

Abstract. The ability of large-scale infrastructures to store and retrieve a massive amount of data is now decisive to scale up scientific applications. However, there is an ever-widening gap between I/O and computing performance. A way to mitigate this consists of deploying new intermediate storage tiers (node-local storage, burst-buffers, ...) between the compute nodes and the traditional global shared parallel file-system. Unfortunately, without advanced techniques to allocate and size these resources, they remain underutilized. In this paper, we investigate how heterogeneous storage resources can be allocated on an HPC platform, in a similar way as compute resources. In that regard, we introduce StorAlloc, a simulator used as a testbed for assessing storage-aware job scheduling algorithms and evaluating various storage infrastructures.

1 Introduction

Running scientific applications at scale requires the power of a large infrastructure such as a High-Performance Computing (HPC) system. For years, HPC systems have been designed with the main objective of improving computing power. However, nowadays the corpus of compute-centric applications has evolved towards complex data-centric workflows across the domains of modeling, simulation, AI and data analytics. The *data deluge* engendered by these workloads has been observed in major supercomputing centers: the National Energy Research Scientific Computing Center, USA, noticed that the volume of data stored by applications has been multiplied by 41 over the past ten years while the annual growth rate is estimated to 30% [12]. Yet, during the same period, we have observed a relative performance decrease of storage systems: a study of the top three supercomputers from the Top500 ranking between 2011 and 2021 shows that the ratio of I/O bandwidth to computing power has been divided by 9.6.

An attempt to mitigate this gap has led to the emergence of new tiers of intermediate storage, such as node-local disks or burst buffers [9], backed by diverse technologies (Flash memory, NVDIMM, NVMeoF, ...), and placed between the compute nodes and the global shared parallel file-system. Although this storage disaggregation offers new alternatives to a centralized storage system, advanced techniques for sizing and allocating these resources have yet to be devised to fully leverage them.

J. Singer et al. (Eds.): Euro-Par 2022 Workshops, LNCS 13835, pp. 211–222, 2023.
https://doi.org/10.1007/978-3-031-31209-0_16

Unfortunately, exploring methods for allocating storage resources on super-computers suffers from several limitations such as a difficult access to the hard-ware with enough privileges or a panel of technologies reduced to those deployed on the studied system. Simulation is one way to overcome these constraints. At the cost of a loss of accuracy, ideally as moderate as possible, simulation offers much better flexibility for representing a wide variety of storage architectures and can be used to evaluate storage infrastructures before they are deployed.

In this paper, we propose to explore how storage resources can be allocated on HPC systems, i.e. with which method (scheduling algorithm) and with which efficiency (metric) a set of I/O intensive jobs can be scheduled on a pool of heterogeneous storage resources. To do so, we introduce StorAlloc, a Discrete-Event Simulation-based (DES) simulator of a batch scheduler able to play (or replay) the scheduling of I/O intensive jobs on intermediate storage resources. We first present the architecture of StorAlloc, then we evaluate the tool on a set of basic scheduling algorithms and on multiple models of infrastructures featuring heterogeneous storage resources. From our simulations, we can conclude on the right sizing of intermediate storage resources among a set of architectures or analyze the utilization rate of the underlying disks.

2   Context and Motivation

For many years, supercomputers have followed a hyper-centralized paradigm regarding storage: a unique global shared parallel file-system such as Lustre [1] or Spectrum Scale (formerly GPFS [15]), used as a staging area from which data is read or written by applications or workflow components. These file-systems, although increasingly powerful, suffer the drawbacks of any highly centralized system: contention and interference make them very prone to performance vari-ability [10]. In order to overcome this problem, we have seen the emergence of new storage systems, closer to the computing nodes. Node-local SSDs, burst buffers or dedicated storage nodes with network-attached storage technology (NVMeoF), to name a few, are all technologies that provide fast storage, albeit with limited capacity, various data lifetime, cost and performance, and different means of access.

This last point in particular makes the use of these resources complicated. To illustrate this, Table 1 presents the multiple ways of accessing resources for a subset of storage tiers that tend to become popular on large-scale systems. The usual scope of the storage space and the commonly deployed data manager, if any, are also listed.

This variety, which would require working on new levels of abstraction, also raises another problem: how to preempt all or part of these storage resources so as to make them available for the duration of an I/O-intensive job's execution, as we do for compute nodes? Allocation methods exist for storage tiers but they are numerous and not interoperable: storage allocated at the same time as the compute node, dedicated APIs integrated or not into the job scheduler, complex low-level configurations. Thus, while it is common on HPC systems

Table 1. Type of access, scope and default data management system on a subset of storage resources that tend to be democratized on large-scale systems.

	Access	Scope	Data manager
Global storage system	Mount point	System-wide	Parallel file-system
Node-local disk	Mount point	Node	File-system
NVDIMM - FSDAX	Mount point	Node	DAX-enabled file-system
NVDIMM - DEVDAX	Direct access	Node	Raw persistent memory
Burst buffer	Middleware	Job	(Parallel) file-system
Network-attached storage	API	Node(s)	Raw storage space

to get access exclusively to compute nodes (usually though a job scheduler), the allocation of those intermediate levels of storage remains minor in practice and often limited to homogeneous resources. In order to use these new levels of storage to their full potential, new allocation techniques must be invented and deployed on supercomputers.

The development of such solutions would, however, require access to intermediate storage resources with enough rights to repurpose them, which is usually not possible on deployed infrastructures for various reasons such as security or maintenance efforts. In addition, such experimentation can easily disrupt other users' workloads on production systems. An alternative approach is to use simulations as a way to reproduce with a certain degree of accuracy the behavior of a system with a very low footprint. While experiments on real systems would be limited to the embedded technologies, a simulator can also evaluate new types of architectures combining existing and emerging storage tiers, for example to make decisions about their sizing or their design. Several simulators already exist for scheduling jobs on compute nodes or for optimizing I/O, yet very few has been done to model and allocate storage resources. Therefore, in this paper, we propose StorAlloc, a simulator of a storage-aware job scheduler whose main objective is to explore heterogeneous storage resource allocation on supercomputers.

3   Related Work

To the best of our knowledge, there is no tool whose goal is to simulate the scheduling of jobs on heterogeneous storage resources of a supercomputer. Simulators allowing to play or replay the execution of parallel and distributed applications on HPC systems exist and have been studied for many years. However, it is the computational aspect that is essentially addressed. SimGrid [4], for example, is a powerful framework for simulating the scheduling and execution of a large number of applications on real or made-up infrastructure models. The I/O aspect is limited to simulating data movement but, although preliminary work was started a few years ago [11], storage resource allocation is absent from the framework. A few SimGrid derived simulators also have job scheduling oriented approaches. This is the case of batsim [7] or Wrench [5] for example. However, the full support of heterogeneous storage levels as allocatable resources is not implemented (disk capacity is not modeled in batsim for example). Another difference between these solutions and StorAlloc concerns the design of the tool as described in Sect. 4. StorAlloc has all its components decoupled. Therefore, the servers can be distributed on multiple nodes while the simulator component can be disabled to turn StorAlloc into a real storage-aware job scheduler.

The world of Cloud Computing is more familiar with the allocation of storage tiers as well as compute or network resources. Work has been done to simulate the allocation of resources between different users [3,13] in virtualized environment but these works are outdated and have very limited storage support.

Finally, models for partitioning and sizing intermediate storage resources such as burst buffers have been studied [2,14]. These techniques are the basis of storage-aware job scheduling algorithms that could be evaluated in our simulator.

4   Architecture

StorAlloc is a tool able to simulate the scheduling of I/O-intensive jobs on heterogeneous storage resources available on a HPC system. In this section, we present its design and discuss implementation choices.

The objective of StorAlloc is to provide a simple way to develop and evaluate storage-aware job scheduling algorithms targeting heterogeneous storage resources (any kind of disk-based storage can be described). Therefore, StorAlloc has been designed following the basic principles of a job scheduler, *i.e.* a middleware allowing clients to request resources available on a supercomputer. Extending from the original architecture, we added the ability to run it as a simulator, using a single code base.

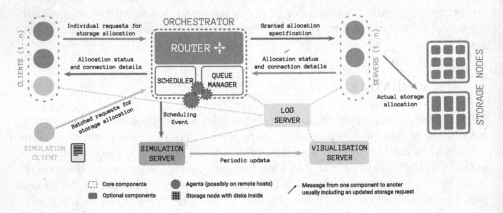

Fig. 1. StorAlloc Architecture

StorAlloc's design is based on the composability of several components, which can be run together and extended in order to provide the desired behavior. Figure 1 depicts the components already implemented and how they fit together. At the core, one or multiple *server* and *client* agents are communicating through a central *orchestrator*. The clients request storage allocations to the orchestrator and expect connection settings to the newly allocated storage space in return. The server components declare a pool of available resources under their responsibility to the orchestrator and perform the storage management operations when needed (partitioning, rights granting, exposure on the network, releasing). In between, the orchestrator handles routing messages between components, keeps track of running and pending allocations and hosts the scheduler process.

In addition to these core components, we have extended StorAlloc with two simulation units (client and server), a visualisation server for real time plotting during simulation and an external log aggregator. The architecture of the tool makes it possible to add additional elements if necessary. All of these components are interconnected using a message-based protocol we have defined. They can be deployed across a set of hosts, or run on a single machine. While the former case is intended to properly map clients and servers onto an actual HPC platform, the latter is sufficient for simulations. The current design only allows for one orchestrator component to be running at any time. This constraint creates a single point of failure when deployed as a middleware in a production setting, and will be addressed in further developments.

In the following sections, we detail design choices for StorAlloc. In particular, we explain the general functioning of the scheduler, a central component in our simulator. Then we describe the storage abstraction layer used to characterize the pool of resources. In Sect. 4.3, we present the simulation capability with a focus on the real-time collection of scheduling data. We end this section with some technical considerations about StorAlloc.

4.1 Scheduling of Storage Requests

We define a storage request as a triple consisting of a capacity in GB, an allocation time in minutes and a submission time in a *datetime* format. The scheduling of storage requests takes place in a *scheduler* sub-component of the *orchestrator*, as depicted in Fig. 1. This sub-component receives requests through messages from clients and process them asynchronously in the receiving order. The scheduler has access to both the entire list of available storage resources and the list of currently allocated requests. Any algorithm can thus make a resource allocation decision backed by a full view of the platform state. So far, four naive algorithms have been implemented in StorAlloc as listed below:

- *random*: storage resources are picked randomly with a chance of failure;
- *round-robin*: storage space is allocated in a round-robin manner;
- *worst-fit*: disks are filled until no more space is available;
- *best-bandwidth*: nodes and disks on nodes are selected according to the best remaining bandwidth, considering a permanent maximum I/O regime for the existing allocations.

At launch time, the scheduler chooses one of these algorithms through a user-defined parameter. The scheduling algorithms share a common interface which accepts a storage request and a list of available storage resources, and returns an identifier for the resource(s) on which the desired storage space will be allocated. A request can also be refused (no space left for instance). In this case, we assume that the job falls back to a traditional parallel file-system, instead of using the intermediate storage tiers available through StorAlloc.

The scheduling of storage requests can also be adjusted by leveraging two strategies presented in Table 2. They are meant to help allocate requests when resources are constrained. The impact of these strategies, independent of the scheduling algorithms, is evaluated in Sect. 5. Again, we make the assumption that in case of (possibly repeated) allocation failures, I/O will be performed on the global shared parallel file system.

Table 2. Optional scheduling strategies

	Default setting	Comment
Split	Threshold at 200 GB	Split requests with capacity over threshold and allocate the parts on multiples resources
Requeued	5 retries, one every 5 m	Postpone starting time and retry a failed allocation

4.2   Storage Abstraction

Because the available storage tiers can be extremely heterogeneous, an abstraction layer is needed to allow scheduling algorithms to accommodate the variety of technologies without needing to know the technical details of each level. In StorAlloc, storage platforms are represented through a hierarchy of three objects: *servers, nodes* and *disks*. Servers are top-level StorAlloc components which act as an interface between the orchestrator and one or many storage nodes. Nodes embed at least one disk. Nodes and disks may be of heterogeneous nature (number of disks, disk capacity, read and write bandwidth, node's network bandwidth). Whenever required by a parent server, a node should be able to setup and expose a specific partition of their storage resources, whose ownership will be transferred to a client. In simulation mode, servers passively accept requests without taking any action, but we still ensure that any allocation would be *legal* in terms of available resources.

It has to be noted that when defining a storage layout, we consider the network to be flat. This is motivated by the fact that dynamic routing policies are unpredictable, either because the vendor does not provide enough details (such as on the Cray XC40 Theta platform which provided the input data used in Sect. 5 [6]) or because there are too many factors involved in packet routing decisions to be accurately modeled. Hence we only define the bandwidth at the node and disk levels and let the scheduling algorithm model the impact of concurrent allocations on these resources.

4.3   Simulation

A longer-term goal of StorAlloc is to provide a single code base for a storage-aware job scheduler and its simulator. Therefore, we have designed our simulation server with a "component in the middle" approach. The core components run as if they were actually deployed on a real system except that, if the simulation mode is enabled, the requests are rerouted to the simulation server which stacks them until a specific message triggers the actual execution of the simulation. Then, the simulation is unrolled and go through the scheduler, using a discrete event simulation (DES) model [8]. During that phase, data measuring the impact of scheduling is collected and feeds a visualization server in real-time. In particular, we measure the following indicators:

- Total allocated (and deallocated) volume.
- Mean and max number of simultaneously allocated requests (global, per node and per disk).
- Mean and max percentage of non-free disk space for each disk over the simulation.
- Number of requeued requests and total delay time during the simulation.
- Number of split requests if any.
- Request's status: allocated or refused.

4.4   Implementation Details

The proof of concept presented in this paper is implemented using Python3. Our messaging protocol relies on ZeroMQ, while the DES model used for the simulation comes from the SimPy library[1]. The source code of StorAlloc can be found at https://github.com/hephtaicie/storalloc.

5   Evaluation

In this section, we evaluate the benefits of our simulator to assess storage-aware job scheduling algorithms on heterogeneous resources. To do so, we run multiple configurations and show their impact on the storage tiers thanks to metrics we have defined.

5.1   Simulation Setup

To simulate storage requests from clients representative of real applications, we used a dataset composed of one year of a Darshan[2] logs on Theta, a 11.7 PFlops

---

[1] Resp. https://zeromq.org/ and https://simpy.readthedocs.io/en/latest/.

[2] Darshan is a popular I/O monitoring tool. https://www.mcs.anl.gov/research/projects/darshan/.

Cray XC40 supercomputer at Argonne National Laboratory[3]. We extracted from these traces jobs spending at least 10% of their run time doing IO, and reading or writing at least 10 GB of data. It resulted in about 24 000 jobs out of approximately 624 000 jobs, each one translating into a storage request in StorAlloc: the requested capacity is based on the maximum of either read or write volume while the allocation time uses the initial job duration.

In order to have a good overview of what can be observed with our simulator, we have run 192 different simulation setups based on the settings presented in Table 3. The average simulation time is around 25 m 48 s per run, in a range of [5 m 40 s; 1 h 29 m 57 s] on a single core of a Intel Core i7-1185G7 processor. This variability is due to the difference in complexity of the algorithms and the activation or not of the requeuing and splitting systems.

Table 3. Simulation settings

Settings	Tested values	Comment
Algorithm	Random, round-robin worst-fit, best-bandwidth	See Sect. 4.1
Total capacity	8 TB, 16 TB, 64 TB	Disk sizes are 1, 2 and 8 TB respectively
Storage Layout	Single node, single disk (*1N1D*) Single node, multi disks (*1NnD*) Multi nodes, single disk (*nN1D*) Multi nodes, multi disks (*nNnD*)	*1N1D* serves as baseline
Requeued	Enabled or disabled	When enabled, new attempts every 5 m, until a 60 m delay
Split	200 GB or disabled	When disabled, some requests will be too large for any of the disks

5.2   Analysis

We present here results plotted from StorAlloc simulation data. From these figures, we can conclude on an approximation of a right sizing of the platform and we can compare the efficiency of the tested scheduling algorithms. For this analysis, platforms and algorithms have been chosen to reflect a variety of behavior.

Platform Sizing. In our dataset, the sum of all the storage capacities requested by clients, called *sum_cap*, reaches 1.6 PB. In Fig. 2, we plot the percentage of

---

[3] This data was generated from resources of the Argonne Leadership Computing Facility, which is a DOE Office of Science User Facility supported under Contract DE-AC02-06CH11357.

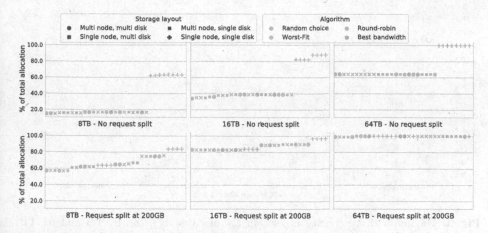

Fig. 2. Percentage of *sum_cap* (sum of the requested capacities in the entire dataset) per simulation run, grouped by capacity and split strategy.

this value achieved by each of the 192 runs of our simulation according to storage layouts and algorithms, grouped by platform capacity and split strategy.

On the top row (no request split), only the *1N1D* layout at 64 TB capacity reaches 100% of *sum_cap*. However this layout is merely a baseline which shouldn't be used, as it leads to a high concurrency and consequently a very low node bandwidth. From this result, we can also conclude that never more than 64 TB are needed at the same time in our dataset. This information must be balanced by the fact that we exclude from Theta's traces several hundreds of thousands of jobs that we do not consider I/O intensive. The best results with other layouts peak slightly above 60%, which hints towards an underprovisioning of storage resources. The bottom row depicts the same analysis with requests split in chunks of 200 GB. We see that all layouts reach a 100% of *sum_cap* at least once for 64 TB. More generally, the splitting of requests allows a better use of resources and requires less storage space (the 16 TB platform reaches 90% of *sum_cap* for half of the runs). These results give little information, however, about the use of the disks composing the modeled platform.

Figure 3 proposes to study this. Here, we plot the maximum disk utilization, called *max_disk_use*, for both 16 TB and 64 TB infrastructures (excluding *1N1D* layout). As expected, the disk utilization rate correlates with the ability to absorb split requests for storage space (Fig. 2). Nevertheless it is possible to quantify a potential underutilization, as seen for the 64 TB platform where no more than 65% of disk capacity is ever used. The worst-fit algorithm is specifically intended for maximising the use of a single disk from a single node, which explains that it reaches 100% of *max_disk_use* for several disks.

This first analysis shows that a platform slightly larger than 16 TB can handle all the I/O intensive jobs in our dataset, as long as the requests are split into 200 GB blocks. In that case, the targeted disks are mostly used at their full capacity at least once, leaving little flexibility in case of a sudden overload,

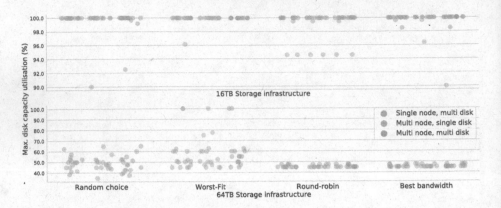

Fig. 3. Maximum disk capacity utilisation (% of capacity), for 16 TB and 64 TB platforms with request split threshold at 200G. The 1N1D layout has been removed.

while the average disk utilization rate is however very low (2.82%), which is explained by the sparsity of the jobs studied spread over a whole year. Finally, the different layouts tested (1NnD, nN1D, nNnD) behave in much the same way. Nevertheless, they have an impact on the available aggregated bandwidth as long as the scheduling algorithms can efficiently take advantage of the storage disaggregation, as shown in the rest of this paper.

Scheduling Algorithms Comparison. We have implemented four different storage-aware job scheduling algorithms in StorAlloc, as described in Sect. 4.1. To evaluate their efficiency, we propose to define a *fairness* metric that looks at the maximum and average number of concurrent allocations per disk allocated by each algorithm. This metric provides information on the balancing of the distribution of requests (split or not) and consequently on the potential bandwidth available for the allocations: in a permanent maximum I/O regime hypothesis (all jobs with continuous I/O operations), the less allocations are concurrent on resources, the more bandwidth will be available.

Figure 4 depicts this *fairness* for our four algorithms. First, we can see that the general variability (standard deviation) in both the mean and max numbers of allocations per disk are lower for round-robin and best-bandwidth than for random and worst-fit. As expected, worst-fit stands out, as its design clearly goes against fairness. We also observe that round-robin and best-bandwidth have quite similar fairness, with a slight advantage to best-bandwidth. This latter is the most advanced algorithm as it takes into account existing allocations on disks to make a decision. In terms of maximum number of allocations per disk, best-bandwidth is the most stable, and also usually leads to the smallest maximums. In other words, this algorithm can be expected to provide the best average bandwidth to jobs in the permanent regime case. Best-bandwidth behaves better than round-robin which, under the same conditions, tends to show more irregularities.

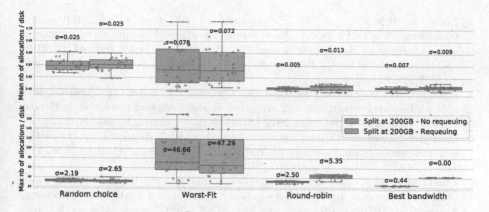

Fig. 4. Mean (top) and max (bottom) number of allocations per disk, grouped by algorithms, for 16 TB platform and split strategy. Storage layout 1N1D excluded. Dots plot the mean and max number of allocations of each disk separately.

Finally, we can see the impact of a queuing system on the number of allocations, i.e. fewer jobs are refused and have to fall back on the parallel file system.

6 Conclusion

In this paper, we have introduced StorAlloc, a DES-based simulator used to explore the scheduling of I/O intensive jobs on heterogeneous storage resources distributed across a HPC system. We have detailed its extensible design and configuration settings for modeling storage infrastructures and implementing various scheduling strategies. Our evaluation demonstrated how StorAlloc can ingest a large number of allocation requests generated from production traces and output storage-related metrics which provide valuable insights for storage platform sizing and scheduling algorithms evaluation. Building upon this preliminary work, we plan to extend this experimental campaign to more metrics, infrastructures and storage-aware scheduling algorithms. Another direction we want to take is to evaluate the benefits we could get from simulation frameworks such as Wrench [5] for the implementation of our simulation component. Finally, a longer term goal will be to explore how to combine computing and storage resources within the same request and provide suitable scheduling algorithms.

References

1. Lustre filesystem website. https://www.lustre.org/
2. Aupy, G., Beaumont, O., Eyraud-Dubois, L.: Sizing and partitioning strategies for burst-buffers to reduce IO contention. In: IPDPS 2019–33rd IEEE International Parallel and Distributed Processing Symposium, Rio de Janeiro, Brazil (2019). https://hal.inria.fr/hal-02141616

3. Calheiros, R.N., Ranjan, R., Beloglazov, A., De Rose, C.A.F., Buyya, R.: CloudSim: a toolkit for modeling and simulation of cloud computing environments and evaluation of resource provisioning algorithms. Softw. Pract. Exp. **41**(1), 23–50 (2011). https://doi.org/10.1002/spe.995. https://onlinelibrary.wiley.com/doi/abs/10.1002/spe.995

4. Casanova, H., Giersch, A., Legrand, A., Quinson, M., Suter, F.: Versatile, scalable, and accurate simulation of distributed applications and platforms. J. Parallel Distrib. Comput. **74**(10), 2899–2917 (2014). http://hal.inria.fr/hal-01017319

5. Casanova, H., et al.: Developing accurate and scalable simulators of production workflow management systems with WRENCH. Future Gener. Comput. Syst. **112**, 162–175 (2020). https://doi.org/10.1016/j.future.2020.05.030

6. Chunduri, S., et al.: Performance evaluation of adaptive routing on dragonfly-based production systems. In: IEEE International Parallel and Distributed Processing Symposium (IPDPS), USA, pp. 340–349. IEEE (2021). https://doi.org/10.1109/IPDPS49936.2021.00042

7. Dutot, P.-F., Mercier, M., Poquet, M., Richard, O.: Batsim: a realistic language-independent resources and jobs management systems simulator. In: Desai, N., Cirne, W. (eds.) JSSPP 2015-2016. LNCS, vol. 10353, pp. 178–197. Springer, Cham (2017). https://doi.org/10.1007/978-3-319-61756-5_10

8. Fishman, G.S.: Principles of Discrete Event Simulation (1978). [Book Review]. https://www.osti.gov/biblio/6893405

9. Henseler, D., Landsteiner, B., Petesch, D., Wright, C., Wright, N.J.: Architecture and design of cray DataWarp. In: Proceedings of 2016 Cray User Group (CUG) Meeting (2016)

10. Jay, L., et al.: Managing variability in the IO performance of petascale storage systems. In: 2010 ACM/IEEE International Conference for High Performance Computing, Networking, Storage and Analysis, New Orleans, pp. 1–12 (2010). https://doi.org/10.1109/SC.2010.32

11. Lebre, A., Legrand, A., Suter, F., Veyre, P.: Adding storage simulation capacities to the SimGrid toolkit: concepts, models, and API. In: 2015 15th IEEE/ACM International Symposium on Cluster, Cloud and Grid Computing, pp. 251–260 (2015). https://doi.org/10.1109/CCGrid.2015.134

12. Lockwood, G., Hazen, D., Koziol, Q., Canon, R., Antypas, K., Balewski, J.: Storage 2020: a vision for the future of HPC storage. Report: LBNL-2001072, Lawrence Berkeley National Laboratory (2017). https://escholarship.org/uc/item/744479dp

13. Núñez, A., Vázquez-Poletti, J., Caminero, A., Castañé, G., Carretero, J., Llorente, I.: iCanCloud: a flexible and scalable cloud infrastructure simulator. J. Grid Comput. **10**, 185–209 (2012). https://doi.org/10.1007/s10723-012-9208-5

14. Ruiu, P., Caragnano, G., Graglia, L.: Automatic dynamic allocation of cloud storage for scientific applications. In: 2015 Ninth International Conference on Complex, Intelligent, and Software Intensive Systems, pp. 209–216 (2015). https://doi.org/10.1109/CISIS.2015.30

15. Schmuck, F., Haskin, R.: GPFS: a shared-disk file system for large computing clusters. In: Proceedings of the 1st USENIX Conference on File and Storage Technologies, FAST 2002, USA, p. 19-es. USENIX Association (2002)

Performance and Scalability Analysis of AI-Accelerated CFD Simulations Across Various Computing Platforms

Krzysztof Rojek[(✉)] [iD] and Roman Wyrzykowski [iD]

Department of Computer Science, Czestochowa University of Technology,
Częstochowa, Poland
{krojek,roman}@icis.pcz.pl

Abstract. In this paper, we perform an extensive benchmarking and analysis of the performance and scalability of our software tool called CFD suite, which implements the AI-based domain-specific method for accelerating CFD (computation fluid dynamic) simulations proposed by us recently. By exploring various computing platforms containing both CPUs and GPUs, this analysis helps select suitable platforms for training and inference stages across heterogeneous execution environments. We propose and investigate two modes of utilizing the proposed decomposition of the AI model at the inference stage – either by calling each sub-model one by one (on GPUs) with reduced memory requirements or by performing pipeline predictions (on CPUs with large RAM) to improve the overall performance. It is shown that for the whole inference stage (including overheads), due to the pipeline execution and excluding overheads for data transfers through PCIe, the speedup provided by two Intel Xeon Gold CPUs (Skylake) is 2.4 times higher than for V100 GPU.

Keywords: AI-accelerated HPC · CPU/GPU/cluster computing · chemical mixing · CFD · OpenFOAM · performance · scalability

1 Introduction

Machine learning (ML) and artificial intelligence (AI) methods have become pervasive in recent years due to numerous algorithmic advances, and the accessibility of computational power [1]. In computational fluid dynamics (CFD) [21], these methods have been used to replace, accelerate or enhance existing solvers [13,22]. This work focuses on the AI-based acceleration of CFD tools used for chemical mixing simulations.

Chemical mixing [5] is a critical process used in various industries, such as pharmaceutical, cosmetic, food, mineral, and plastic ones. It can include dry

The authors are grateful to the byteLAKE company for their substantive support. The project financed under the program of the Minister of Science and Higher Education under the name "Regional Initiative of Excellence" in the years 2019–2022 project number 020/RID/2018/19 the amount of financing 12,000,000 PLN.

J. Singer et al. (Eds.): Euro-Par 2022 Workshops, LNCS 13835, pp. 223–234, 2023.
https://doi.org/10.1007/978-3-031-31209-0_17

blending, emulsification, particle size reduction, paste mixing, and homogenization to achieve the desired custom blend [5]. Recently we have proposed [20] the domain-specific method for accelerating CFD simulations by integrating the conventional CFD solver with AI models. The proposed workflow embraces the stirred tank mixing analysis tool called MixIT [10]. This tool utilizes the Open-FOAM toolbox [14] for meshing, simulation, and data generation allowing users to design, simulate and visualize phenomena of chemical mixing. MixIT provides geometry creation and performs 3D CFD simulations for stirred reactors, including tracer simulations and heat transfer analysis. Moreover, it allows users to get performance parameters: intensity, power per unit volume, blend time, critical suspension speed, gas hold-up, and mass transfer coefficients.

The goal is to provide an interaction between AI models and an OpenFOAM-based solver for much faster analysis. The scope of our research includes steady-state simulations, using an iterative scheme to progress to convergence. Steady-state models perform a mass and energy balance of a process in an equilibrium state, independent of time [3]. Our method is responsible for predicting the convergence state with the AI models based on a few initial iterations generated by the CFD solver. The time-to-solution is significantly reduced since we do not need to calculate intermediate iterations to produce the final result. The proposed approach makes it possible to run many more experiments and better explore the design space before decisions are made.

The contributions of this work are as follows:

- We provide an extensive benchmarking and analysis of the performance and scalability of our software tool called CFD suite, which implements the AI-based domain-specific method for accelerating CFD simulations proposed by us recently. By exploring various computing platforms containing both CPUs and GPUs, this analysis helps select suitable platforms for training and inference stages across heterogeneous execution environments.
- We propose and explore two modes of utilizing the proposed decomposition of the AI model at the inference stage - either by calling each sub-model one by one (on GPUs) with reduced memory requirements or by performing pipeline predictions (on CPUs with large RAM) to improve the performance.
- We show that CFD Suite is a scalable solution as we observe a stable efficiency when parallelizing the training process across cluster nodes (up to 64 nodes with 12-cores each). At the same time, for the whole inference stage (including overheads), due to the pipeline execution and excluding overheads for data transfers through PCIe, the speedup provided by two Gold CPUs is 2.4 times higher than for V100 GPU, and even for the desktop Core-i7 CPU, it is 1.47 times higher.

2   Related Work

Accelerating CFD simulations is an established problem in many domains, from industrial applications to fluid effects for computer graphics and animation.

Many works are focused on the adaptation of CFD codes to hardware architectures [21] exploring modern compute accelerators such as GPUs [12,17], Intel Xeon Phi [24] or FPGAs [19]. Developing a simulator can require years of engineering effort and often must trade off generality for accuracy in a given range of settings. Among the main disadvantages of such adaptations are the requirements for in-depth knowledge about complex CFD codes and the expensive and long-term process of providing portability across new hardware platforms. At the same time, relatively low-performance improvements against the original CFD solver are achieved. In many cases, only a small kernel of the solver is optimized.

Recent works [13,22] have addressed the increasing computation demand of CFD simulations by implementing generalized AI models to simulate various use cases. It gives the opportunity of achieving lower costs of experiments and faster prototyping/parametrization. Modern AI frameworks support multiple computing platforms providing code portability with minimum additional effort. Most related to this work, some authors have considered the fluid simulation process as a supervised regression problem. In [7], the authors present a novel generative model to synthesize fluid simulations from a set of reduced parameters. A convolutional neural network (CNN) is trained on a collection of discrete, parameterizable fluid simulation velocity fields. In work [25], J. Thompson et al. propose a data-driven approach using a CNN that leverages the approximation of deep learning to obtain fast and highly realistic simulations. The authors rephrase the learning task as an unsupervised learning problem. Work [8] introduces an ML framework for the acceleration of Reynolds-averaged Navier-Stokes modeling to predict steady-state turbulent eddy viscosities, given the initial conditions. In [23], the authors present a general framework for learning simulation and give a single model implementation that yields state-of-the-art performance across a variety of challenging physical domains.

Our method for AI-accelerated CFD simulations is based on utilizing a set of sub-models that are separately trained for each simulated quantity. This approach allows us to reduce memory requirements and operate on large CFD meshes. The proposed approach provides a low entry barrier for future researchers since the method can be easily tuned when the CFD solver evolves.

As the number of hardware and software systems for performing ML/AI computation increase so does the need for comprehensive performance analysis and benchmarking [9]. At the moment, the leading industry benchmark for ML/AI performance is MLperf [11]. The idea was [15] to allow decision-makers to determine what devices (from mobile devices to datacenter systems) to use for ML, for both training and inference [9,16]. MLPerf Training [11] consists of eight workloads covering a broad diversity of use cases, including vision, language, recommenders, and reinforcement learning. MLPerf Inference tests use seven cases across different kinds of neural networks - three use cases for computer vision, one for recommender systems, two for language processing, and one for medical imaging. Apart from difficulties with providing results obtained with MLPerf to be comparable [15], this benchmark does not cover an increasingly important domain of using ML/AI to accelerate key high-performance scientific computing problems such as CFD simulations.

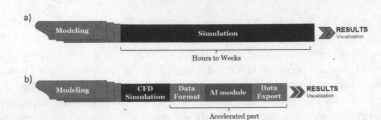

Fig. 1. AI-accelerated simulation (b) versus conventional non-AI approach (a)

3   AI-Based Acceleration of CFD Simulations for Chemical Mixing Using CFD Suite

The chemical mixing simulation is based on the standard k-ϵ model. The goal is to compute the converged state of the liquid mixture in a tank equipped with a single impeller. The simulation generates a set of quantities, including the velocity vector field U, pressure scalar field p, turbulent kinetic energy k of the substance, turbulent dynamic viscosity mut, and turbulent kinetic energy dissipation rate ϵ.

The OpenFOAM meshing tool *snappyHexMesh* is responsible for generating 3D meshes for considered domains. The conventional modeling with OpenFOAM involves several steps (Fig. 1a). The first step includes pre-processing, where the geometry and meshing are created. The next step is the simulation itself. It is the part that we mainly focus on in this paper by developing the AI-based acceleration. The third step is post-processing (visualization, result analysis).

The proposed method of acceleration [20] belongs to the group of data-driven methods where we use partial results returned by the CFD solver. Figure 1b presents the general scheme of the AI-accelerated simulation versus the conventional non-AI simulation. It includes the initial iterations computed by the CFD solver and the AI-accelerated part executed by the proposed AI module called CFD Suite. The CFD solver produces results sequentially iteration by iteration. The proposed method takes the results of initial iterations computed by this solver as input, sends them to the AI module, and generates the final results of the simulation. The AI module consists of three stages: (i) data formatting and normalization, (ii) prediction with AI model (inference), and (iii) data export.

The neural networks used in our AI models are based on the ResNet network [4] organized as residual blocks where each layer feeds into the next layer and directly into the layers about two hops away. To handle large meshes (about 1 million cells), we have to reduce the original ResNet network to 8–16 layers.

Pipeline Execution for AI Sub-models: Our AI model is responsible for getting results from 24 iterations (iterations $20, 40, 60, ..., 480$) as the input, feeding the network, and returning the final results. The number of required input iterations is estimated experimentally by searching the lowest value that allows us to achieve an accuracy of at least 90%. Using 3D meshes, we simulate five quantities

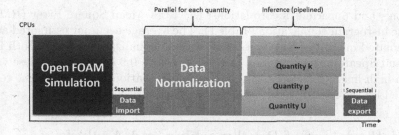

Fig. 2. Pipeline mode of executing CFD Suite

taken as the input and returned as the simulation output. For each quantity, we create a sub-model that predicts the results independently.

The proposed method is used in two scenarios (modes). The first one predicts the results by calling each sub-model one by one and allows us to reduce memory requirements. In the second scenario, we perform pipeline predictions for considered quantities to improve the overall performance. The created pipelines simultaneously call all sub-models, where each quantity is predicted independently (Fig. 2). Thus, our method is suitable both for GPU platforms to be executed in the one-by-one mode and CPU platforms with large RAM to be implemented in the pipeline mode.

Accuracy Analysis: Before exploring the performance, it is necessary to verify the accuracy of AI-accelerated simulations using the CFD suite. The selected scenario for chemical mixing includes the simulation of mixing the liquid mixture in a tank equipped with a single impeller and a set of baffles. For a 3D mesh with 40000 cells, 5000 iterations are required to converge into a final state.

We compare the simulation results for the converged state achieved with the OpenFOAM toolbox and our AI-based method. The outcomes calculated by MixIT include velocity magnitude, pressure torque, kinetic energy k, kinetic energy dissipation rate (ϵ), and dynamic viscosity mut. The observed deviation of results for the AI-based approach from the conventional CFD solver results is from 0.16% for the velocity magnitude to 1.5% for the parameter k. Results generated by both approaches are also compared using statistical metrics such as

Table 1. Statistical metrics of accuracy

Quantity	Pearson's corr.	Spearman's corr.	RMSE	Histogram equal. [%]
Velocity magnitude	0.990	0.935	0.016	89.1
Pressure torque	0.993	0.929	0.004	90.1
k	0.943	0.934	0.035	99.4
ϵ	0.983	0.973	0.023	90.3
mut	0.937	0.919	0.147	93.5
Average	0.969	0.938	0.045	92.5

Pearson's and Spearman's correlations, the Root Mean Square Error (RMSE), and the histogram equalization (Table 1). The average accuracy estimated across all simulated quantities based on the histogram equalization is 92%. Both Pearson's and Spearman's correlation factors are above 0.9 on average. These values show a high linear correlation and a monotonic relationship between the results obtained by the OpenFOAM solver and predicted using AI.

4   Methodology of Benchmarking and Analysis

4.1   Hardware and Software Environments

The CFD Suite performance is explored using the following computing platforms:

1. A single HPC node: two 20-core Intel Xeon Gold 6148 CPUs (Skylake architecture) clocked at 2.40 GHz and 2xNvidia V100 GPUs equipped with 16 GB of HBM and 400 GB of the host memory (abbreviated as Gold in case of CPU tests and V100 in case of GPU tests, respectively).
2. Intel CPU-only HPC cluster, BEM supercomputer [2] equipped with 12-core Intel Xeon E5-2670 v3 CPUs (Haswell) clocked at 2.30 GHz (abbreviated as BEM for cluster and E5-2670 or E5 for a single node).
3. Desktop platform with 4-core Intel Core i7-3770 CPU (Ivy Bridge architecture) clocked at 3.40 GHz (abbreviated Core-i7 or i7) with Nvidia GeForce GTX TITAN GPU (abbreviated TITAN) and 48 GB of host memory.

The software environment includes a set of the following tools: Python v3.8.2, TensorFlow v2.4.1, Horovod v0.21.3, OpenVINO v2021.2.200, NVIDIA Cuda v10.1, and cuDNN v7.6.5. The OpenVINO toolkit [18] is used to accelerate AI workloads for the inference part on CPUs, where the simulation is accelerated with the AI predictions. The Horovod framework [6] makes possible the distributed training across multiple GPUs and cluster nodes.

4.2   Benchmarking Scenarios

Training: Two configurations are used for benchmarking. The first one includes training AI models for a mesh with 400 cells (small mesh) and the second one is based on a mesh with 40000 cells (big mesh). The aim is to explore how scalable the training is for a relatively small dataset and how the training process is adaptable to the cluster platform with bigger meshes. The single-precision floating-point format FP32 is used for training (and then inferencing). The following benchmarking scenarios are explored: (i) validating performance improvements due to optimizing data access to the training dataset; (ii) exploring the scalability of the training module based on the Horovod distributed parallelization; (iii) performance comparison of training across the tested platforms.

Inferencing: The AI-accelerated simulation that uses inferencing with trained AI models is composed of a set of steps. First, we need to execute 10% of the conventional CFD solver. Then the remaining 90% are predicted by CFD Suite using the following steps: (i) data import from the conventional CFD solver, (ii) data normalization, (iii) inferencing with AI models, that is where we leverage trained AI models, and (iv) data export to the conventional solver format so that we output results ready for the analysis by existing CAE tools. When benchmarking inference, we utilize the mesh with 1,000,000 cells (relevant trained AI models are used).

5 Performance and Scalability Analysis: Training

Performance Improvements Due to Optimizing Data Access to the Training Dataset: Benchmarking the training stage includes three quantities, where the first and third represent scalar quantities (pressure – model1, turbulent kinetic energy – model3), while model2 corresponds to a vector quantity - velocity (only the big mesh configuration is considered). In this test, two versions are compared; (i) with data loaded from the disk to reduce as much as possible the host memory requirements, and (ii) the optimized version, where the data are stored in thread-safe structures in the host memory. This benchmark is executed using a single BEM node. Table 2 shows the normalized execution time for both versions and the achieved speedup. It can be concluded that the second version allows us to reduce the execution time by a factor of 1.5. Thus, the remaining experiments are based on the optimized version of the CFD Suite.

Scalability of Training Using the Horovod Distributed Parallelization: The results of these benchmarking scenarios executed on the BEM cluster are shown in Fig. 3 for both small and big mesh configurations.

For the small mesh, in spite of using the Infiniband FDR interconnect we observe the high negative impact of inter-nodes communications on the performance for more than 8 nodes. At the same time, a super efficiency with the speedup exceeding the number of nodes is observed in one case (8 nodes for model2). We conclude that there is not enough computation to saturate the platform and the cluster interconnect limits the scalability for small meshes.

For the big mesh, the execution time is reduced by a factor of 48 for 64 nodes. We can observe a stable efficiency of parallelization (>90% up to 8 nodes,

Table 2. Time normalized between 0 and 1 for training the models with datasets stored in hard disk and RAM with the corresponding speedup

	model1	model2	model3
Loading from disk	0.98	1.00	0.96
Loading from RAM	0.62	0.64	0.63
Speedup	1.56	1.57	1.52

Table 3. Execution time of training models on different compute platforms

Device	#devices	tasks	model1 [s]	model2 [s]	model3 [s]
Xeon E5-2670	1	12	1312.60	1324.13	1437.99
Xeon E5-2670	2	24	679.48	694.70	771.08
Xeon E5-2670	4	48	358.69	346.82	379.13
Xeon E5-2670	8	96	179.13	180.27	193.72
Xeon E5-2670	16	192	100.37	100.86	108.71
Xeon E5-2670	32	384	54.74	55.96	58.42
Xeon E5-2670	64	768	30.94	30.48	32.15
GeForce GTX TITAN	1	1	241.30	241.30	294.18
Tesla V100	1	1	209.68	210.29	255.81
Xeon Gold 6148	1	20	1108.96	1109.45	1193.04
Tesla V100	2	2	127.90	130.38	156.81
Xeon Gold 6148	2	40	991.91	991.71	1101.05

and ≈70% up to 64 nodes). The second model, which is the most compute-intensive since it feeds the neural network with the vector quantity, achieves the best efficiency, confirming that the more compute-intensive model, the better scalability is achieved. Thus, the Horovod-based implementation is well scalable for distributed training, being practical enough for our models on mesh sizes of at least 40000 cells.

Performance Comparison of Training Across Various Computing Platforms: Table 3 shows the execution time of training for the tested platforms, including both single- and dual-socket configurations with CPUs and GPUs, as well as CPU cluster. The achieved performance is also visualized in Fig. 4.

Typically, conventional CFD solvers belong to the group of memory-bound algorithms [21]. There is a relatively enormous amount of data for AI-based acceleration to feed the AI model. It enforces reduced model structures to make it

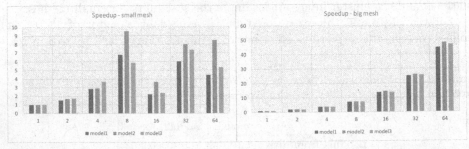

(a) Speedup of training for small mesh   (b) Speedup of training for big mesh

Fig. 3. Speedup of training on the BEM cluster using from 1 to 64 nodes

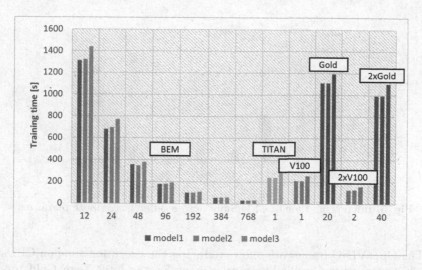

Fig. 4. Performance comparison across the cluster with 12–768 cores of E5-2670 v3 CPUs, GeForce GTX TITAN GPU, one and two NVIDIA Tesla V100 GPUs, one and two Intel Xeon Gold CPUs with 20 and 40 cores, respectively

possible to feed the neural network. Consequently, we have a lot of data processed by a relatively small network (up to 16 layers). As a result, there is no expected speedup across a single node when using two Gold CPUs (40 cores) instead of one CPU with 20 cores (speedup by a factor of about 1.1 times). The reason is that the training is not compute-intensive enough. Also, no significant difference is observed between a single V100 GPU and a single TITAN graphics card.

The performance improvement is much more promising in the case of distributed training on two V100 GPUs instead of a single one, and the BEM cluster with up to 64 nodes. The cluster implementation based on the Horovod framework allows us to overtake the performance of a single V100 GPU using 8 cluster nodes while using 16 nodes outperforms two V100 GPUs by a factor of 1.3. By comparing the results achieved for a single Intel Gold processor and a single cluster node (single E5-2670 v3 CPU), we can estimate that it is very likely that a cluster with 8 Gold CPUs would allow us to achieve execution time comparable to the time obtained on two V100 GPUs.

6 Performance Analysis: Inference

Table 4 presents the analysis of the AI-accelerated simulation across all steps fixed in Sect. 4.2. In the table, the total time of executing all steps required to predict results with AI models is included in the row named "CFD Suite", while the last row shows the total time of performing the AI-accelerated simulation.

First, we compare the performance (Fig. 5) of different computing platforms for the inference stage only - without any overhead related to data formatting ("Inferencing" row in Table 4). Also, the time of inferencing with the TensorFlow framework and inferencing optimized by the OpenVINO tool are compared.

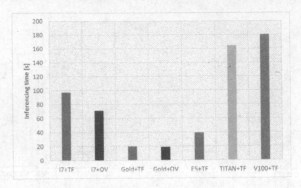

Fig. 5. Inferencing time of CFD Suite across different compute platforms

The OpenVINO framework allows reducing the execution time on CPUs up to 1.36 times, with a negligible improvement for the Intel Xeon Gold processors. CFD Suite uses a relatively small number of layers (up to 16), so there is a limited possibility to optimize the network by OpenVINO. The overall inference process within CFD Suite consists of a set of sub-model inferences that are pipelined across the CPU cores or executed one by one on the GPU with parallelization provided by cuDNN. Moreover, inferencing performed on the GPU has a much higher overhead than on the CPU. The overhead is related to the memory allocation and data transfers through PCIe from the host to the GPU global memory. As a result, GPU reaches a significantly lower performance for inferencing itself (without overheads), which is performed up to 9.5 times faster on two Intel Gold CPUs (CFD Suite optimized with OpenVINO) than on V100 GPU.

The performance analysis of inference across various platforms is summarized in Table 5 showing two kinds of achieved speedups. The first one (row "a") is the ratio of the time required for executing 90% of OpenFOAM iterations (performed on a CPU) to the time of inference, including overheads - data import, normalization, and data export. The second kind (row "b") compares the time of the conventional OpenFOAM simulation with the total time required by the

Table 4. Step-by-step analysis of the AI-accelerated simulation

Device	Core-i7	Core-i7	2xGold	2xGold	2xE5	TITAN	V100
Framework	TF	OV	TF	OV	TF	TF	TF
Data import [s]	25.29	25.48	22.42	22.87	40.78	25.32	22.21
Data norm. [s]	81.59	81.6	64.03	64	230.18	81.6	66.24
Inferencing [s]	97.41	71.1	19.66	18.91	39.39	164.38	180.31
Data export [s]	10.68	10.69	9.58	9.56	16.16	10.69	9.51
CFD Suite [s]	214.97	188.87	115.7	115.34	326.52	281.98	278.27
OpenFOAM+CFD Suite [s]	1639.09	1613	1539.82	1539.47	1750.64	1706.1	1702.39

Table 5. Speedup for (a) generating the steady-state with CFD Suite based on the initial 10% of OpenFOAM iterations versus using 90% of OpenFOAM iterations; (b) AI-accelerated simulation against conventional OpenFOAM simulation.

Device	Core-i7	Core-i7	2xGold	2xE5	TITAN	V100
Framework	TF	OV	TF	TF	TF	TF
a)	59.62	67.86	110.78	39.25	45.45	46.06
b)	8.69	8.83	9.25	8.13	8.35	8.37

AI-accelerated simulation. In particular, we conclude that on two Intel Gold CPUs, 90% of the OpenFOAM iterations are predicted about 110 times faster, while the entire simulation is executed 9.25 times faster.

Considerable interest represents the comparison of performance for CPUs and GPUs. All CPU-based configurations (except E5 CPUs) outperform GPU-based ones. In particular, regarding the execution of 90% iterations (row "a"), the speedup provided by two Gold CPUs is 2.4 times higher than for V100 GPU (even for Core-i7 with OpenVINO it is 1.47 times higher). This advantage is not so impressive for the whole simulation, but still, two Gold CPUs yield a speedup of about 1.1 times higher than V100.

7   Conclusions

The proposed AI-based method and its implementation by CFD Suite allow us to reduce the execution time of conventional OpenFOAM solver by a factor of 9 times and keep the accuracy at the level of at least 90%. The proposed tool can be used as an add-on to existing CAE/CFD environments, and its integration is a straightforward process.

CFD Suite is a scalable solution. We observe a stable efficiency when parallelizing training across cluster nodes - up to 64 nodes (12-cores each). It is shown that eight nodes of the tested HPC cluster are enough to overtake a single V100 GPU for training. At the same time, due to the pipeline execution of AI sub-models and excluding overheads for data transfers through PCIe, CPUs achieve significantly higher performance for the inferencing stage. In particular, inferencing itself (without overheads) is executed up to 9.5 times faster on two Gold CPUs than on V100 GPU. For the whole inference stage (including overheads), the speedup for two Gold CPUs is 2.4 times higher than for V100 GPU, and even for the desktop Core-i7 CPU, it is 1.47 times higher.

References

1. Archibald, R., et al.: Integrating deep learning in domain sciences at exascale. arXiv preprint arXiv:2011.11188v1 (2020)
2. BEM overview, September 2022. https://kdm.wcss.pl/wiki/Bem_overview

3. Bhatt, D., Zhang, B.W., Zuckerman, D.M.: Steady-state simulations using weighted ensemble path sampling. J. Chem. Phys. **133**(1), 014110 (2010)
4. Chen, D., Hu, F., Nian, G., Yang, T.: Deep residual learning for nonlinear regression. Entropy **22**(2), 193 (2020)
5. Paul, E.L., Atiemo-Obeng, V., Kresta, S.M. (eds.): Wiley, Hoboken (2004)
6. Horovod: Home, May 2022. https://horovod.ai/
7. Kim, B., et al.: Deep fluids: a generative network for parameterized fluid simulations. arXiv preprint arXiv:1806.02071v2 (2019)
8. Maulik, R., Sharma, H., Patel, S., Lusch, B., Jennings, E.: Accelerating RANS turbulence modeling using potential flow and machine learning. arXiv preprint arXiv:1910.10878 (2019)
9. Mattson, P., et al.: MLPerf training benchmark. arXiv preprint arXiv:1910.01500v3 (2020)
10. MixIT: the enterprise mixing analysis tool. https://mixing-solution.com/
11. MLPerf Benchmarks, April 2022. https://www.nvidia.com/en-us/data-center/resources/mlperf-benchmarks/
12. Mostafazadeh, B., et al.: Unsteady Navier-Stokes computations on GPU architectures. In: 23rd AIAA Computational Fluid Dynamics Conference (2017)
13. Obiols-Sales, O., Vishnu, A., Malaya, N., Chandramowlishwaran, A.: CFDNet: a deep learning-based accelerator for fluid simulations. In: Proceedings of the 34th ACM International Conference on Supercomputing (ICS 2020), pp. 1–12. ACM (2020)
14. OpenFOAM: the open source CFD toolbox, May 2022. https://www.openfoam.com
15. The Performance of MLPerf as a Ubiquitous Benchmark is Lacking, 8 April 2022. https://www.nextplatform.com/2022/04/08/the-performance-of-mlperf-as-a-ubiquitous-benchmark-is-lacking
16. Reddi, V.J., et al.: MLPerf inference benchmark. arXiv preprint arXiv:1911.02549v2 (2020)
17. Rojek, K., et al.: Adaptation of fluid model EULAG to graphics processing unit architecture. Concurr. Comput. Pract. Exp. **27**(4), 937–957 (2015)
18. OpenVINO, May 2022. https://docs.openvino.ai
19. Rojek, K., Halbiniak, K., Kuczynski, L.: CFD code adaptation to the FPGA architecture. Int. J. High Perform. Comput. Appl. **35**(1), 33–46 (2021)
20. Rojek, K., Wyrzykowski, R., Gepner, P.: AI-accelerated CFD simulation based on OpenFOAM and CPU/GPU computing. In: Paszynski, M., Kranzlmüller, D., Krzhizhanovskaya, V.V., Dongarra, J.J., Sloot, P.M.A. (eds.) ICCS 2021. LNCS, vol. 12743, pp. 373–385. Springer, Cham (2021). https://doi.org/10.1007/978-3-030-77964-1_29
21. Sadrehaghighi, I.: Basics of Computer Architecture as Relates to CFD, January 2022. https://www.researchgate.net/publication/339212886
22. Sadrehaghighi, I.: Artificial Intelligence (AI) and Deep Learning for CFD, January 2022. https://www.researchgate.net/publication/339795951
23. Sanchez-Gonzalez, A., et al.: Learning to simulate complex physics with graph networks. arXiv preprint arXiv:3394.45567 (2020)
24. Szustak, L., et al.: Adaptation of MPDATA heterogeneous stencil computation to Intel Xeon Phi coprocessor. Sci. Program. (2015). https://doi.org/10.1155/2015/642705
25. Tompson, J., Schlachter, K., Sprechmann, P., Perlin, K.H.: Accelerating eulerian fluid simulation with convolutional networks. In: ICML 2017: Proceedings of the 34th International Conference on Machine Learning, vol. 70, pp. 3424–3433 (2017)

Misc

Miscellaneous Workshops

Workshop Description

Two of the Euro-Par 2022 workshops were more informal and interactive in nature. These were:

1. Workshop on Distributed and Heterogeneous Programming in C and C++ (DHPCC++)
2. Workshop on Resiliency in High Performance Computing in Clouds, Grids, and Clusters (Resilience)

From each of these workshops, only a single full-length, peer-reviewed paper has been included in this post-proceedings volume. The DHPCC++ workshop had seven short paper submissions, six of which were presented at the workshop. However only one long-form paper has been accepted for publication.. The Resilience workshop had two long paper submissions, one of which was accepted for publication.

The workshop programs included keynotes and informal presentations along with panel discussions. The events were well-attended and there was excellent engagement throughout.

The two chairs thank all workshop participants and reviewers for their contributions to the successful events. Further, the chairs would like to thank the Euro-Par 2022 organizing committee, in particular Jeremy Singer for facilitating the workshop events and coordinating post-workshop publication of the accepted papers.

Organization

Workshop Chairs

Rod Burns   Codeplay Software, UK
Christian Engelmann   Oak Ridge National Laboratory, USA

Workshop Reviewers

Ferrol Aderholdt   NVIDIA, USA
David E. Bernholdt   Oak Ridge National Laboratory, USA
Wesley Bland   Meta, USA
Hans-Joachim Bungartz   Technical University of Munich, Germany
Marc Casas   Barcelona Supercomputer Center, Spain
Robert Clay   Sandia National Laboratories, USA
Zizhong Chen   University of California at Riverside, USA
Biagio Cosenza   University of Salerno, Italy
James Elliott   Sandia National Laboratories, USA
Kurt Ferreira   Sandia National Laboratories, USA
Kevin Harms   Argonne National Laboratory
Saurabh Hukerikar   NVIDIA, USA
Ignacio Laguna   Lawrence Livermore National Laboratory, USA
Scott Levy   Sandia National Laboratories, USA
Thomas Naughton   Oak Ridge National Laboratory, USA
Vincent R. Pascuzzi   IBM Research, USA
Rolf Riesen   Intel, USA
Yves Robert   ENS Lyon, France
Thomas Ropars   Universite Grenoble Alpes, France
Keita Teranishi   Sandia National Laboratories, USA

Performance Portability Assessment: Non-negative Matrix Factorization as a Case Study

Youssef Faqir-Rhazoui[1]([⊠]) [iD], Carlos García[1,2] [iD], and Francisco Tirado[1] [iD]

[1] Universidad Complutense Madrid, Madrid, Spain
{yelfaqir,garsanca,ptirado}@ucm.es
[2] Instituto de Tecnología del Conocimiento, Madrid, Spain

Abstract. SYCL standard has been released with the conviction to increase code portability in heterogeneous environments. On its side, Intel has launched the oneAPI toolkit, which includes the Data Parallel C++ language, the Intel implementation of SYCL. SYCL is designed to use a single source code to target multiple accelerators, such as multi-core CPUs, GPUs, or even FPGAs. Additionally, the C/C++ oneAPI compiler also supports OpenMP which also allows targeting CPU and GPU devices. In this paper, a performance evaluation of SYCL and OpenMP is carried out using the well-known, Non-negative Matrix Factorization (NMF) algorithm. Three different NMF implementations (baseline, SYCL and OpenMP) are developed to analyze the speedups on both CPU and GPU devices. Experimental results show that while on CPUs both programming models report almost the same performance, on GPUs, SYCL slightly outperforms OpenMP counterpart.

Keywords: OpenMP · SYCL · DPC++ · oneAPI · Non-Matrix Factorization · HPC

1 Introduction

Techniques related to machine learning have gained visibility because help to discover non-trivial and useful patterns in data sets in diverse areas such as genetics and genomics, consumption patterns, marketing and population opinion through social networks. These aspects joined with the demand for applying efficient computational techniques that accelerate the analysis of large volumes of data, is still a current challenge.

Matrix factorization and clustering algorithms are one of the most popular techniques in data science [14]. These methods allow to reduce the number of dimensions, or simply reveal certain patterns to facilitate data interpretation. Among them, the Non-negative Matrix Factorization (NMF) [3] can establish a correlation in experimental datasets, it is considered to be one of the most effective methods in biological disclosure. NMF's use and popularity have been

J. Singer et al. (Eds.): Euro-Par 2022 Workshops, LNCS 13835, pp. 239–250, 2023.
https://doi.org/10.1007/978-3-031-31209-0_18

spread in recent years motivated by its incorporation in well-known Machine Learning (ML) libraries, such as *scikit-learn* or *pytorch*. However, those libraries' implementations suffer from heterogeneous computing exploitation in the first case, while the *pytorch's* works on GPUs, but is limited to the CUDA proprietary software that constraints its adoption only on NVIDIA GPUs.

Facing that inconvenience, paradigms such as OpenCL, Kokkos or SYCL [20] abstract the vendor language (e.g. CUDA or HIP) and offer a transparent language targetable to any of those accelerators. However, while OpenCL was the main solution for many years, others have come to overcome the disadvantages of OpenCL. That is the case of SYCL, which could be considered the evolution of OpenCL, greatly simplifying the coding task for different accelerators. On the other way, traditional programming models, like OpenMP, have evolved from targeting CPU parallelization to also giving GPU support in recent versions with OpenMP offload.

This paper assesses a comparison of SYCL and OpenMP portability on CPU and GPU devices using the well-known NMF algorithm. The recent appearance of the oneAPI software suite allows this evaluation by using the Data Parallel C++ (DPC++) compiler [19] which supports either OpenMP or SYCL programming models.

The rest of the paper is organized as follows, Sect. 2 presents the new oneAPI software suite. Section 3 introduces the NMF algorithm and its key aspects. Section 4 contains the NMF implementations. Sections 5 and 6 focus on the experimental aspects. Finally, Sect. 7 discusses the main contributions and includes our remarks on this work.

2   Background and Related Work

Even though SYCL and OpenMP are cross-market specifications, not all the compilers support both models or the OpenMP offload feature. The Intel oneAPI, released in 2020, is one the market solution. It offers a unified programming API for different devices such as CPUs, GPUs, FPGAs or other chips developed to accelerate specific tasks. It is based both on a programming model using libraries that hide the particularities of each hardware from the programmer's point of view, as well as the so-called direct programming model supported by the DPC++ [19] compiler with support for SYCL [10]. oneAPI consists of a series of Toolkits for the specific application domain, which also includes the specialized libraries such as oneMKL for linear algebra, oneDNN for deep learning environments, oneDAL for machine learning or oneVLP for video processing, among others.

The novel Intel's compilers DPC++ and ICX also support the OpenMP 5.0/5.1 [11] standards which include the offloading feature. In addition, one of the advantage of using the DPC++ or ICX is the compatibility with the optimized libraries as oneMKL.

Motivated by the recent release of oneAPI, we found a reduced number of works in the literature coupled with the use of the suite. Most of them are

related to the migration from CUDA to DPC++ such as the tsunami simulation code *easyWave* [6] or the recent evaluation of the Intel's compatibility tool
with DPC++ [4] through the well-known Rodinia benchmarks. Focusing on a
comparative analysis of programming models, the paper [2] evaluates different
competing programming frameworks such as OpenMP, CUDA, OpenCL, and
SYCL in the context of PLSSVM library. Among the main conclusions, we can
summarise that there is no complete support of any framework for the accelerators exploitation either because backends do not support all devices without
the corresponding root permissions or some manufacturers no longer provide official support. Regarding portability aspects, Poenaru [17] compares the programming paradigms of OpenMP, native CUDA/OpenCL against the most promising
alternatives such as SYCL and Kokkos targeting both CPUs and GPUs using
miniBUDE application, highlighting that higher-level frameworks such as SYCL
can achieve OpenMP levels of performance while aiding productivity.

3   Non-negative Factorization

Non-negative factorization (NMF) was first proposed by Paataro and Tapper in
1994 [16] which was called *positive matrix factorization*. Later, Lee and Seung [13]
promoted it. The NMF decomposition can be seen as

$$V \approx WH, \tag{1}$$

where $V \in \mathbb{R}_+{}^{m \times n}$ corresponds to a positive matrix with m variables and n
objects, $W \in \mathbb{R}_+{}^{m \times k}$ is the reduced k vector or factor, and $H \in \mathbb{R}_+{}^{k \times n}$ contains the coefficients of linear combinations of the basis vectors. For the sake of
dimensional reduction of NMF, it is assumed that $k \ll min(n, m)$.

Particularly, for gene expression, the matrix V represents an experimental
biological matrix with m genes and n experimental conditions. For a specific
level, k, H and W represent metagenes (semantic features) and metagene expression patterns (gene semantic features), respectively.

In Lee and Seung's method, NMF repeatedly modifies W and H until their
product approximates V. Such modifications are derived from minimizing a cost
function that describes the distance between the product WH and V. For this
work we consider the well-known NMF factorization reformulated by Brunet et
al. [3] with the following update rules:

$$H_{\alpha\mu} \leftarrow H_{\alpha\mu} \frac{\sum_i W_{i\alpha} V_{i\mu}/(WH_{i\mu})}{\sum_k W_{k\alpha}} \tag{2}$$

$$W_{i\alpha} \leftarrow W_{i\alpha} \frac{\sum_\mu H_{\alpha\mu} V_{i\mu}/(WH_{i\mu})}{\sum_\nu H_{\alpha\nu}} \tag{3}$$

H and W are randomly generated, so this method does not always converge
to the same solution.

4 NMF Code Implementation

In a first instance, matrices W and H are initialized with positive random values. The number of iterations allows the matrix convergence at expense of a more demanding execution time. Algorithm 1 shows the main NMF code excerpts of each iteration of the refining process; although it is shown the necessary operations for updating H according to Eq. 2, analogous operations are applied to the W update.

Algorithm 1 NMF($V^{n\times m}$, $W^{n\times k}$, $H^{k\times m}$, $niters$)

1: **for** $iter \leq niters$ **do**
2:
3:        ▷ Get H as $H = H.*(W'*(V./(W*H)))./x_1$
4:
5:        $wh = W*H$
6:        $wh = V./wh$
7:
8:        ▷ Reduce to one column (x_1)
9:        $x_1 = repmat(sum(W,1)',1,m)$
10:
11:        $Haux = W*wh$
12:        $H = (H.*Haux)./x_1$
13:
14:        ▷ Get W as $W = W.*((V./(W*H))*H')./x_2$
15:        ...
16: **end for**

As seen, the matrix multiplication is performed twice (lines 5 and 11) for the computation of H. It is important to note that this operation is by far the most time-consuming stage on NMF, so the usage of BLAS libraries is highly recommended.

4.1 BLAS Baseline Implementation

The base version (coded in native C/C++) was optimized using the BLAS library, specifically using the Single-precision GEneral Matrix Multiply (SGEMM) operation. This implementation corresponds to the baseline version used in the rest of this paper.

Profiling the NMF (see Fig. 1), it is noticeable that the matrix multiplication takes most of the time. For this experiment, the $V^{n\times m}$ size selected is 5000×1000 with a factorization factor of $k = 4$ and ten iterations before the testing convergence. Regarding the non-optimized version, NMF takes 115 s, where the matrix multiplications account for 87% of the time, the division 12.9% and the remaining kernels 0.1%. On the contrary, the optimized version based on SGEMM accomplishes the task in 22.5 s, achieving an overall speedup of 5.1×. After this optimization, it is important to note that the most time-consuming kernel is now the point-by-point division (70%).

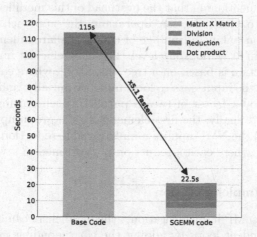

Fig. 1. NMF profiled time kernel by kernel. Non-optimized version (left bar) and a BLAS optimized version (right bar).

4.2   SYCL Implementation

Concerning the SYCL implementation,[1] it is pointing out that the oneMKL library API also supports SYCL, so its adaptation is immediate. For the rest of the kernels, it is necessary to rewrite the kernel code expressing the parallelism. Firstly, the basic data-parallelism is carried out with *parallel_for* constructions. We would like to notice that meanwhile, this parallelism scheme could achieve reasonable performance on a CPU, an important performance degradation has been observed on GPU devices, because the work-items do not cooperate, increasing the cache miss ratio and losing the data locality benefits in accordance with those indicated in [19].

However, the *nd_range* parallelism expression fits well on GPU, as several parallelism levels are available on Intel's GPUs: sub-slices, execution units (EU), and SIMD Units. A single work-group is mapped to a sub-slice (group of EUs) which allows sharing a cache memory and synchronization mechanisms. A single work-item usually cooperates with its analogous as part of a SIMD lane (subgroup) inside the EU. Hence, using this grade of parallelism to map the kernel over the GPU hardware will greatly increase the performance achieved.

In our own developed SYCL version, the point-by-point division is implemented using the *nd_range* parallelism feature. Nevertheless, it is important to take into account that the usage of *nd_range* feature forces to fix the number

---

[1] Available in: https://github.com/artecs-group/nmf-dpcpp.

of *work-groups* as a multiple of the *nd_range* parameter. To solve this aspect, the V matrix size was artificially increased to the closest pow two value in the same way that is performed in the padding technique for the memory alignment access. It is worth mentioning that the overhead of this modification is negligible.

With regard to the reduction operation, the approach is based on the *nd_range* expression, taking advantage of the local shared memory and synchronization mechanism at work-group level. The most efficient implementation of a classic array-reduction is based on a tree scheme [9], where each work item in a work-group copies the input data to local memory initially; and then, work-items reduce the input by a factor of two in parallel, synchronizing each stage with a local barrier; and finally, the first element of each group updates the original memory. However, the NMF applies a multivariable reduction of size k (see line 9 of Algorithm 1), where each k-reduction is performed in a working group.

4.3 OpenMP Implementation

Concerning to OpenMP implementation,[2] the parallelism can be exploited focusing on the independent loops by adding the corresponding *pragmas* directives. The for-loop parallel degree can be exploited on two levels: multithreading and vectorization. Traditionally, OpenMP was exploited on the multi-threading CPUs; however, newer OpenMP standards added support for target offloading since OpenMP v4.0. OpenMP API incorporates the multilevel parallelism expression through the *"teams distribute"* and *"parallel for"* directives, spreading the workload over the groups of EUs on the GPU.

Our implementation based on OpenMP defines a decouple version for CPU and GPU devices, where the main difference is found in the reduction kernel, and the memory management mandatory for the GPU devices (data copied from/to device).

The implementation of the point-by-point division kernel on GPUs is mapped using the above-mentioned keywords; nevertheless, in order to find the best fine-tuning performance, number of teams and the maximum number of threads per team should be specified. For this purpose, OpenMP provides the *"num_teams(EUs)"* and the *"thread_limit(gpu_threads)"* pragmas. It is worthy to indicate that the *"num_teams(EUs)"* directive set straightforward to the number of EUs of the GPU. We have observed that the optimal value of *"thread_limit(gpu_threads)"* corresponds with the number of hardware threads per EU [15]. We would like to point out that these values rely on the GPU features and OpenMP API provides no way to figure out at runtime, so unfortunately the setting up must be done manually at compiling phase in detriment of code portability.

On the other side, due to lack of support for the GPU local memory management through the OpenMP API, the efficient tree reduction scheme can not be implemented. Our OpenMP implementation is based on the classical *"reduction"* directive to spread the k reductions over the teams. This aspect supposes a

---

[2] Available in: https://github.com/artecs-group/nmf-openmp.

relevant increment in the number of cache miss (spatial locality is not exploited) with the corresponding scalability deterioration.

4.4   OpenMP and SYCL Common Ground

Both implementations (OpenMP and SYCL) also show common considerations due to the architecture target (CPU vs GPU).

Concerning the kernels, the parallel reduction kernel offers significantly lower performance on CPU-based systems compared to its sequential implementation. This fact is due to the reduction operation requires a high number of synchronizations and communications stages between CPU cores. Thus, we have coded a serial reduction kernel on the CPU version.

Another aspect to consider is the possible optimization of the point-to-point division operation by making use of oneMKL's native function div[3]. Although the experimental results show a poor performance in comparison with our custom implementation, we do not rule out that in future versions of oneMKL this aspect will turn if this operation is successfully optimized.

5   Experimental Conditions

This section describes the systems and datasets used for the experiment phase. In addition, we describe some experimental conditions, those are assessed to get the maximum performance.

5.1   Work Environment

The experiments were performed using two work environments: a retail desktop, and a more powerful node in the Intel's DevCloud. Table 1 summarizes the most interesting features. The desktop computer uses an integrated GPU (UHD 630) with 24 compute units, reaching a peak performance of 480 GFLOPS. On the other side, the chosen Intel DevCloud's node is equipped with a discrete Xe MAX DG1 GPU (2.5 TFLOPS) connected through PCIe. We would like to notice that all the experiments are carried out with the Intel's oneAPI 2022.0 version. The DPC++ and ICPX compiler used are set with the optimization flags -$O3$ -$xhost$ enabled. Experiments are performed 10 times to avoid time fluctuation discarding the worst execution.

5.2   Data Description

The datasets used in the experimentation are summarized below and include biological samples from two experiments. The main reason to choose those datasets is to evidence the differences between CPU and GPU architectures behaviour, for that we selected a relatively small dataset (Lung) in comparison to the bigger dataset (ExpO).

---

[3] https://spec.oneapi.io/versions/latest/elements/oneMKL/source/domains/vm/div.html#onemkl-vm-div.

Table 1. Work environment technical specifications used.

Parameter	Desktop	DevCloud
CPU	Intel Core i7-10700	Intel Core i9-10920X
Frequency	2.9 GHz (base) 4.8 GHz (boost)	3.5 GHz (base) 4.6 GHz (boost)
Cores	2×8	2×12
Performance (FP 32)	371.2 GFLOPS	672 GFLOPS
GPU	UHD 630	Iris Xe MAX DG1
Frequency	1050 MHz (base) 1250 MHz (boost)	300 MHz (base) 1650 MHz (boost)
Cores	24 execution units	96 execution units
Performance (FP 32)	480 GFLOPS	2.534 TFLOPS

– Lung (16063 × 280): Contains 16063 genes by Affymetrix Genechips of primary tumors tissues and poorly differentiated adenocarcinomas [5].
– ExpO (54675 × 1973): A set of 1973 tumor samples obtained by the expO project, which are available at Gene Expression Omnibus [1].

Concerning the experimentation aspect, the W and H matrices have been randomly initialized, fixing the seed to avoid variability in the convergence criterion. For the sake of simplicity, the results obtained were performed in single-precision. Despite in biological studies the factor k usually ranges from 2 to 10, we have noticed similar behaviour from the performance perspective, so for the sake of clarity, the k parameter is fixed to 4 in all the experimentation performed to avoid this redundancy.

5.3 Other Considerations

Multi-threading technology enables the CPU to keep two different contexts per physical core although there are certain resources that will remain shared [12]. Our experiments show that the use of two threads per core reports an average performance degradation of 22% in the SYCL paradigm versus 16% in OpenMP, motivated by competition between threads for shared resources such as hierarchy memory. Hence, *hyper-threading* has been disabled.

SYCL provides two host-device memory management mechanisms: the unified shared memory (USM) and the buffer model. USM is more transparent from the programmer perspective, meanwhile the programmer has fine-control at the expense an increment of code lines in buffer model. We would like to point out that in NMF most the variables can be stored in the device scope, except the W and H matrices, which are copied back periodically to evaluate the convergence criterion. Hence, testing both models, we found that the USM model runs 20% faster than its counterpart on the CPU, meanwhile, on the GPU USM exhibits 7.2% better rates.

One last consideration related to compiler choice is the use of the new Intel DPC++ and ICPX compilers. Both are based on LLVM technology [18] and supports OpenMP.

6   Discussion

We have grouped the results achieved for the Lung (16,063 × 280) dataset in Fig. 2, and the ExpO's (54,675 × 1,973) in Fig. 3. Both figures show the NMF time consumption split in stacked bars of each kernel varying the target device and the programming model. Besides, each bar represents the time achieved by the system (Desktop, DevCloud), device (CPU, GPU), and the implementation (BLAS base version, OpenMP, SYCL) used.

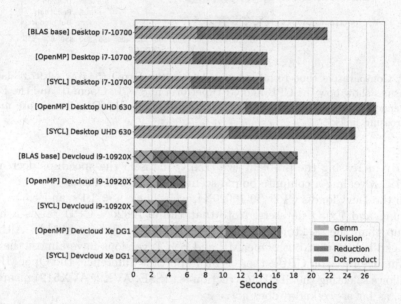

Fig. 2. Comparative time results obtained from the Lung (16,063 × 280) dataset. The results show how the CPU and GPU perform in SYCL, OpenMP and the BLAS-base version. The desktop executions are striped, while the DevCloud's are marked with crossing lines.

6.1   CPU Discussion

Regarding the Lung dataset, a speedup of ≈ 1.47× respect to the BLAS base version is achieved on the desktop CPU (i7-10700), either OpenMP or SYCL implementations give a slight similar performance. The boosted performance is mainly achieved by the division kernel, which reduces its time consumption by

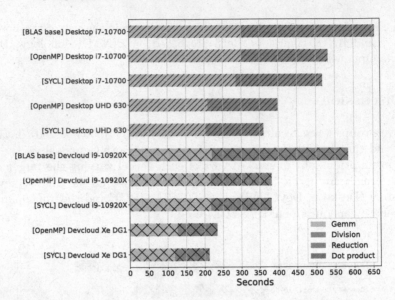

Fig. 3. Comparative time results obtained from the ExpO (54,675 × 1,973) dataset. The results show how the CPU and GPU perform in SYCL, OpenMP and the BLAS-base version. The desktop executions are striped, while the DevCloud's are marked with crossing lines.

43%. By increasing the problem size (ExpO dataset) the speedups decrease to $\approx 1.25\times$, revealing a compute bound scenario on CPU devices.

On the DevCloud's CPU (i9-10920X), we achieve a $\approx 3.1\times$ and $1.53\times$ using the Lung and ExpO datasets. Note that the i9-10920X CPU raises a higher speedup than the desktop's due to more parallel resource available. Although results still show that both OpenMP and SYCL versions have almost the same performance rates on CPUs, there is an important difference: the OpenMP version allows selecting the SIMD instruction-set (SSE, AVX2, AVX512) meanwhile SYCL, as far as we know, does not.

It is worth mentioning that although the i9-10920X supports the AVX512 SIMD-type, which theoretically should achieve even more performance, no effect is observed for the small dataset and in the large one the performance is even worse than choosing AVX2. This aspect is due to certain TDP restrictions and frequency downscaling when AVX512-SIMD is enabled [7,8].

6.2   GPU Discussion

Focusing on GPUs behaviour, we observed a poor performance in comparison to the baseline using the Lung dataset. The overhead of data offloading does not compensate by parallel gains for a small data set.

Nevertheless, the ExpO dataset achieves a relevant speedups, up to $1.64\times$ and $1.82\times$ with OpenMP and SYCL respectively on the UHD 630 GPU. The main performance differences appear in the SGEMM and reduction kernels. SGEMM runs a bit slower with OpenMP. The reduction kernel successfully scales with data size.

As expected, the discrete Xe DG1 GPU reports greater performance rates, achieving up-to 2.76× in the SYCL version. As a summary, we can indicate that the Xe DG1 device offers the highest throughput rates for huge problems.

7   Conclusion

High-Performance Computing benefits from the use of heterogeneous hardware to reduce computational times. Intel's SYCL implementation, DPC++, has reduced the gap between those accelerators and their specific programming model. To prove that, we developed three NMF implementations: an optimized version based on oneMKL library on the CPU (baseline version), as well as, SYCL and OpenMP versions, which run on both the CPU and GPU devices.

The experimental results reveal that all versions scale fine with small datasets on CPUs. As expected, for larger datasets, GPU devices report greater performance rates. Regarding the programming models, we found that although OpenMP and SYCL achieved almost the same performance on CPUs, SYCL slightly beats OpenMP on GPUs. However, focusing on portability/performance aspects we observe the main differences: (1) meanwhile SYCL allows to code once for both devices, OpenMP requires some customization coding to run on the CPU or GPU devices (memory management, and special directives on pragmas), and (2) the lack of expression of OpenMP to exploit EUs local group memory, and local group barriers make its implementation non-optimal.

Focusing on the SYCL, although the code was written once and executed on different target devices, sometimes, some extra hand-tuned coding is recommended to exploit the device's architecture advantages, which slightly introducing more code or even could require rewriting the entire kernel for a specific architecture.

This research aims to increase the number of studies that compare and evaluate SYCL against other programming models, such as OpenMP and OpenMP offload. It also examines the support with the well-known libraries as oneMKL. An extension of this analysis could target other GPUs such as NVIDIA or AMD, which is affordable for building a DPC++ toolchain with CUDA and HIP AMD support.

References

1. Barrett, T., Wilhite, S.E., et al.: NCBI GEO: archive for functional genomics data sets-update. Nucleic Acids Res. **41**(D1), D991–D995 (2012)
2. Breyer, M., Van Craen, A., Pflüger, D.: A comparison of SYCL, OpenCL, CUDA, and OpenMP for massively parallel support vector machine classification on multi-vendor hardware. In: International Workshop on OpenCL. IWOCL 2022. Association for Computing Machinery, New York (2022)

3. Brunet, J.P., Tamayo, P., Golub, T.R., Mesirov, J.P.: Metagenes and molecular pattern discovery using matrix factorization. Proc. Natl. Acad. Sci. **101**(12), 4164–4169 (2004)
4. Castaño, G., Faqir-Rhazoui, Y., García, C., Prieto-Matías, M.: Evaluation of Intel's DPC++ Compatibility Tool in heterogeneous computing. J. Parallel Distrib. Comput. **165**, 120–129 (2022)
5. Chopra, P., Lee, J., Kang, J., Lee, S.: Improving cancer classification accuracy using gene pairs. PLoS ONE **5**(12), e14305 (2010)
6. Christgau, S., Steinke, T.: Porting a legacy CUDA stencil code to oneAPI. In: 2020 IEEE International Parallel and Distributed Processing Symposium Workshops (IPDPSW), pp. 359–367 (2020)
7. Gottschlag, M., Brantsch, P., Bellosa, F.: Automatic core specialization for AVX-512 applications. In: Proceedings of the 13th ACM International Systems and Storage Conference, pp. 25–35. Association for Computing Machinery (2020)
8. Gottschlag, M., Schmidt, T., Bellosa, F.: AVX overhead profiling: how much does your fast code slow you down? In: Proceedings of the 11th ACM SIGOPS Asia-Pacific Workshop on Systems, pp. 59–66. Association for Computing Machinery (2020)
9. Intel: oneAPI GPU Optimization Guide (2021). https://software.intel.com/content/www/us/en/develop/documentation/oneapi-gpu-optimization-guide
10. Khronos SYCL working group: Sycl 1.2.1 specification (2020). https://www.khronos.org/registry/SYCL/specs/sycl-1.2.1.pdf
11. Konda, S.: OpenMP* features and extensions supported in Intel oneAPI DPC++/C++ compiler (2021). https://software.intel.com/content/www/us/en/develop/articles/openmp-features-and-extensions-supported-in-icx
12. Kwak, H., Lee, B., et al.: Effects of multithreading on cache performance. IEEE Trans. Comput. **48**(2), 176–184 (1999)
13. Lee, D.D., Seung, H.S.: Learning the parts of objects by non-negative matrix factorization. Nature **401**(6755), 788–791 (1999)
14. Lin, X., Boutros, P.C.: Optimization and expansion of non-negative matrix factorization. BMC Bioinform. **21**(1), 1–10 (2020)
15. Noudohouenou, J., Hariharan, N.: Using OpenMP accelerator offload for programming heterogeneous architectures (2021). https://techdecoded.intel.io/resources/using-openmp-accelerator-offload-for-programming-heterogeneous-architectures
16. Paatero, P., Tapper, U.: Positive matrix factorization: a non-negative factor model with optimal utilization of error estimates of data values. Environmetrics **5**(2), 111–126 (1994)
17. Poenaru, A., Lin, W.-C., McIntosh-Smith, S.: A performance analysis of modern parallel programming models using a compute-bound application. In: Chamberlain, B.L., Varbanescu, A.-L., Ltaief, H., Luszczek, P. (eds.) ISC High Performance 2021. LNCS, vol. 12728, pp. 332–350. Springer, Cham (2021). https://doi.org/10.1007/978-3-030-78713-4_18
18. Reinders, J.: Benefits of adopting LLVM (2021). https://software.intel.com/content/www/us/en/develop/blogs/adoption-of-llvm-complete-icx
19. Reinders, J., Ashbaugh, B., et al.: Data Parallel C++: Mastering DPC++ for Programming of Heterogeneous Systems Using C++ and SYCL. Springer, Cham (2021). https://doi.org/10.1007/978-1-4842-5574-2
20. Reyes, R., Lomüller, V.: SYCL: single-source C++ accelerator programming. In: Parallel Computing: On the Road to Exascale, Proceedings of the International Conference on Parallel Computing. Advances in Parallel Computing, vol. 27, pp. 673–682. IOS Press (2015)

Task-Level Checkpointing System for Task-Based Parallel Workflows

Pere Vergés(✉)📧, Francesc Lordan📧, Jorge Ejarque📧, and Rosa M. Badia📧

Department of Computer Sciences, Barcelona Supercomputing Center,
Barcelona, Spain
{pere.verges,francesc.lordan,jorge.ejarque,rosa.m.badia}@bsc.es

Abstract. Scientific applications are large and complex; task-based programming models are a popular approach to developing these applications due to their ease of programming and ability to handle complex workflows and distribute their workload across large infrastructures. In these environments, either the hardware or the software may lead to failures from a myriad of origins: application logic, system software, memory, network, or disk. Re-executing a failed application can take hours, days, or even weeks, thus, dragging out the research. This article proposes a recovery system for dynamic task-based models to reduce the re-execution time of failed runs. The design encapsulates in a checkpointing manager the automatic checkpointing of the execution, leveraging different mechanisms that can be arbitrarily defined and tuned to fit the needs of each performance. Additionally, it offers an API call to establish snapshots of the execution from the application code. The experiments executed on a prototype implementation have reached a speedup of 1.9× after re-execution and shown no overhead on the execution time on successful first runs of specific applications.

Keywords: High-Performance Computing · Checkpointing · Task-based programming model · Recovery System · Fault Tolerance

1 Introduction

Supercomputers and cloud computing have become essential tools for researchers to work on their investigations. The amount of data used in scientific applications has dramatically escalated and the computation time required to execute them. Parallelizing applications using multiple networked computers shortens its execution time, making research more manageable. Furthermore, distributing the workload across large infrastructures enables higher levels of parallelism, unreachable when using one single machine.

Using shared distributed infrastructures such as clusters, supercomputers, or the Cloud, usually entails execution time limits and resource quotas – e.g., disk –, increasing the probability of unexpected issues that makes the application unable to complete. There are myriad reasons for that: network disruptions, inability

© The Author(s), under exclusive license to Springer Nature Switzerland AG 2023
J. Singer et al. (Eds.): Euro-Par 2022 Workshops, LNCS 13835, pp. 251–262, 2023.
https://doi.org/10.1007/978-3-031-31209-0_19

to allocate memory, disk quota violations, issues with the shared file system, exceeding the allowed execution time, etc. Frequent solutions for these problems consist of retrying the failed computation on the same node or changing the host for that part upon failure detection. However, in most cases, the application fails due to the lack of resources. Therefore, either the crash affects the whole system or the queuing system ends the execution. A more complex solution to overcome these shortcomings consists of establishing checkpoints where the application saves its status and data values in persistent data space to avoid the re-computation of previous values on future re-executions of the application.

This article contributes to the current state of the art by proposing and evaluating a system that allows applications developed following a task-based programming model to recover from failures and reduce their re-execution time. Thus, application users will speed up significantly their research on their respective disciplines by avoiding computations that take hours, days, and even weeks while using extensive computing infrastructures.

The proposed system leverages the determinism of tasks to avoid re-executing non-failed tasks in case of breakdown by automatically copying their output as the execution goes on. Performing such copies entails a significant overhead on network and storage operations; the optimal balance for this trade-off between resilience and performance depends on each execution and the preferences of the end-user. To that end, the proposed system combines various mechanisms that systematically select which output values to checkpoint and envisages the customization of these decisions by incorporating mechanisms to define new policies. The user can define these policies by creating arbitrary checkpointing groups of tasks. Besides systematic copies, the system also provides application developers with a method to set up specific points in the application code to checkpoint the execution status.

The article continues by describing the baseline knowledge to understand the details of the presented work in Sect. 2. Section 3 discuss the design and implementation details of the solution. Section 4 evaluates and presents the performance measures that validate the solution's viability with a prototype, Sect. 5, casts a glance over the research already performed on the area. Finally, Sect. 6 concludes this work.

2   Checkpointing Task-Based Workflows

Task-based parallel programming models have become more popular and are a standard solution for creating parallel applications. This popularity is due to their higher development productivity due to their automatic exploitation of the inherent parallelism and, second, their ability to ease the implementation of scientific workflows by combining executions of different applications.

Such models build on the concept of task: a stateless logic executed asynchronously. It processes a specific set of input values to produce some output values. Applications are a combination of tasks where data establishes a dependency relation, defining a workflow. Often represented as a directed acyclic

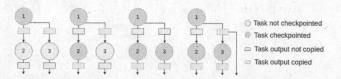

Fig. 1. Diagrams depicting four different situations where different output values are persisted to checkpoint Task 1.

graph, where nodes correspond to tasks, and edges illustrate data dependencies. Executing a task producing a data value will always precede the execution of a task consuming such value. A task will not start its execution until all its input data has been generated by its predecessor tasks.

Runtime systems supporting these programming models know which tasks are ready to execute and fully exploit the parallelism inherent to the application given the available infrastructure. Besides, they apply techniques to increase the application parallelism, such as data renaming to avoid false data dependencies. Instead of keeping a single value of the data, the runtime makes a new copy for each value computed for a datum, thus, enabling a task updating a datum to run ahead of others reading that value. Awareness of all the values that relate to the same data allows the system to consolidate a version and remove the preceding values that will no longer be used.

These runtime systems usually follow an architecture where one of the nodes hosts a process (the master) orchestrating the execution, and the other nodes run a middleware software (worker) that hosts the execution of the tasks. The worker can notice task failures when they terminate abruptly or an exception arises and notifies the failure to the master. When losing the connection with a worker, the master assumes that all the tasks offloaded to that node have failed. After unsuccessfully trying to recover from a task failure, the master terminates the execution, and the whole application fails. Errors on the master would end the execution abruptly. We aim to persist some data values so that the following re-executions recover them, avoiding a partial re-execution.

To that end, this work leverages the stateless, serverless, and determinism properties of deterministic tasks. A deterministic task always produces the same output values regardless of the node and moment it runs, given the same input values. Therefore, persisting all output values of the task beyond the run enables future executions of the application to skip the re-computation of the previous task. This technique is known in the bibliography as task-level checkpointing [10,12]; tasks that will not be re-executed in upcoming runs of the application are checkpointed tasks. Despite building on the task determinism, the presented solution is also valid for applications that exploit randomness in their computations – e.g., Monte Carlo simulations. Our solution design can execute stochastic algorithms. However, the seed of the pseudo-random generator must be treated as another application value to re-create the exact computation as it was in the previous execution and pass it in as another input value for each task.

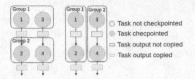

Fig. 2. Task diagram showing the output copies of a task workflow.

Being part of a workflow allows relaxing the conditions to consider a task as checkpointed from having all its output values persisted, to having each of the output values of the task, either persist or ensure that the value into consideration will no longer be used in the future – i.e., all tasks consuming the value have been checkpointed, and new tasks consuming the value cannot be created. Figure 1 depicts four different situations where Task 1, which produces two output values, is checkpointed by persisting different values. The first situation shows the original practice that persists all the output values to checkpoint the task. In the second case, it is unnecessary to persist one of the output values since checkpointing Task 2 ensures that the value will not be needed in the future. In this specific example, the second value persisted; however, as shown in the third situation, checkpointing Task 3 would have a similar effect and avoid persisting the value. The last case shows a slightly different situation, where the second output value is consumed by Task 3, but the output value could still create new tasks consuming the value. Therefore, the value needs to be saved despite Task 3 being checkpointed.

Whereas some task-based programming models define a static workflow before execution and, perhaps, scale the number of tasks according to the size of the processed data, some other models are more flexible and allow adapting the whole workflow depending on task results. In the latter case, the component spawning tasks require a mechanism to synchronize the results of some tasks to evaluate them and continue with the dynamic generation of tasks (e.g., to check convergence in a loop). These synchronization values need to be persisted and cannot be deleted even if future executions have no tasks consuming them to enable the re-creation of the same workflow.

Two essential aspects that automatically capture the progress of any application are the execution time and the amount of already finished tasks; hence, the proposed system implements two mechanisms building on them. The first mechanism, Periodic Checkpoint, registers the finished tasks and the produced data values and periodically triggers data operations to persist the output values computed until execution, avoiding unnecessary values as depicted in Fig. 1. The Finished Tasks mechanism behaves similarly, but the trigger is the completion of N tasks. The more frequent the checkpointing is, the fewer possibilities to avoid persisting values; however, the longer the checkpointing period is, the more tasks will need to be re-executed if the application fails.

Checkpointing can achieve an optimal balance between one execution performance and resilience by defining arbitrary checkpointing groups. The system persists only the final output values of each group and dismisses the values corresponding to intermediate versions or deleted data. Figure 2 illustrates an example of how arbitrarily grouping tasks impacts the amount of checkpointed values. The group distribution in the leftmost part of the figure depicts a case where groups are done according to the depth level in the graph. The group distribution shows that, for this specific workflow, creating groups according to data dependencies reduces the amount of persisted values from four to two by avoiding making persistent the intermediate value between them.

3   Solution Design and Implementation

Finding an optimal selection of values to checkpoint requires deep knowledge of the application workflow, the host infrastructure, the size of the problem solved with the application, and the current progress of each execution. The runtime system orchestrating the workflow execution is the only point where all this knowledge meets; therefore, there is the best place to select which values to persist. To that end, this article aims to provide the runtime system with a Checkpoint Manager (CM) component encapsulating the automatic management of the checkpointing for the execution. Figure 3 depicts an overview of the architecture of the proposed system.

The Runtime System (RS) notifies the CM of the different events required to checkpoint tasks. When the application generates a new task, the RS queries the CM whether the task was checkpointed in a previous execution. If it does, the task execution is skipped, and the checkpointed values are restored as if the task computed them for their later use in a non-checkpointed task or a synchronization point. Otherwise, if the task has not been checkpointed, the checkpoint manager registers its existence.

The RS also notifies the CM of other execution events such as finalizations of tasks, indicating the location of output values, accesses to synchronization values, and value deletions. With that information, the CM can know the values needed to recreate the workflow, request their persistence, or order their deletion when they will not be involved in future tasks or access synchronization points to minimize the I/O usage.

The CM component implements an engine supporting all the checkpointing mechanisms described in Sect. 2. Policymakers can combine them to create

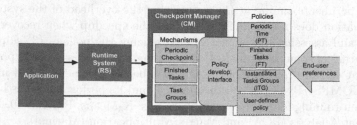

Fig. 3. Overview of the proposed checkpointing system

highly-efficient complex tactics to checkpoint applications fitting the specifics of each application. For that purpose, the CM offers an interface (Policy development interface) to customize each mechanism's behavior properly. The Periodic Time (PT) and Finished Tasks (FT) policies leverage the periodic checkpoint and finished tasks mechanisms while disabling the others. The application end-user can establish the period or the number of finished tasks to trigger them. Checkpointing some data values might have a cost higher than their re-computation; ignoring these values would improve the system's performance; similar to the period and the number of tasks, the system also allows indicating a set of tasks to be ignored by them.

As mentioned in the previous section, application-tailored policies rely on the task group mechanism. Upon task detection, the CM assigns the task to a group according to the selected checkpointing policy. To decide the group, the policy developer can use any information available at instantiation-time, e.g., the number of tasks, operation to perform, accessed data values, or preceding tasks. The Instantiated Tasks Groups (ITG) policy gathers tasks in N-sized groups according to their creation order. When the CM resolves a group closure – i.e., all tasks of the group have already been instantiated –, it determines the final output values of the group by analyzing the data accesses of all the tasks within the group. The RS requests the necessary operations to persist those values that have already been computed. For those that have not been generated, the RS monitors the task generation of each one of them. Upon its completion, requests the necessary operations to persist them.

Moreover, efficient checkpointing requires a deep understanding of the application. To ensure a certain quality of experience, application developers may not want to leave the end-user decisions about checkpointing in the hands of the end-user. To that end, the CM includes a mechanism to order snapshots of the current status of the execution from the application code. The runtime system will persist the useful output values of all the tasks until that point.

To affect the application execution minimally, the CM performs all the persistence operations asynchronously in a background thread with a lower priority and limits the maximum number of ongoing operations in parallel.

4   Evaluation

To validate the proposed design and evaluate its performance, we conducted several experiments aiming at (1) quantifying the overhead of the system when the application does not fail, (2) measuring the speedup when recovering from a failure, and assessing the impact of customizing the policies (3) skipping the checkpointing of some tasks and (4) developing application-tailored policies.

To that end, a prototype of the CM has been implemented and integrated into the COMPSs/PyCOMPSs runtime [4,5] and its performance has been evaluated when running four different applications: K-Means, PMXCV19, Principal Component Analysis (PCA) and Matrix Multiplication (Matmul).

Table 1. Execution time and relative overhead (baseline: NC) using different policies. The policy with the lowest overhead is highlighted with green background.

	NC	ITG	FT	PT
K-Means	220.12 s	222.56 s (1%)	229.34 s (4.5%)	228.44 s (4%)
PMXCV19	33 m	33.9 m (2.7%)	34.1 m (3.3%)	33.6 m (1.8%)
PCA	883.13 s	1075.13 s (21.7%)	1026.21 s (16.1%)	1284.07 s (45.4%)

K-Means[1] (2152 tasks) is a clustering algorithm that identifies K clusters within the input data. The algorithms start with K randomly generated centers. Iteratively, values are assigned to the closest center. These centers are recomputed using the data assigned to them. This process lasts until the centers converge, and their position is not updated. This application has two parts: data generation and center convergence.

PCA (see footnote 1) (685 tasks) is a dimensionality reduction algorithm that computes the principal components of a collection of points to use them to perform a change of data basis using only the first few principal components. It is often used to perform data analysis for predictive models.

PMXCV19[2] (2027 tasks) evaluates changes in the binding affinity between SARS-Cov-2 Spike protein and Human ACE2 (hACE2) receptor using the PMX algorithm [9]. It runs a large series of short Molecular Dynamic simulations executed using GROMACS.

Matmul (64 tasks) implements a blocked matrix multiplication. The resulting workflow consists of several chains of tasks corresponding to all tasks updating the same output block.

The presented results run using two nodes of the MareNostrum 4 supercomputer – each equipped with two 24-core Intel Xeon Platinum 8160 at 2.1 GHz. and 98 GB of main memory – interconnected with a Full-fat tree 100Gb Intel Omni-Path network.

4.1 Checkpointing Overhead

This experiment aims to measure the overhead induced by the checkpointing system when the application (K-Means, PMXCV19, and PCA) successfully finishes. To that end, a run with no checkpointing (NC) is compared to runs using different policies: PT (15-second interval), FT (every 10 finished tasks), and ITG (grouping every 10 instantiated tasks).

The results in Table 1 show the importance of adapting the checkpointing policy depending on the application being executed to minimize the time overhead. With the right policy, the checkpointing system overhead can be negligible depending on the application, with only a 1% of added time. However, picking the wrong policy may entail significant overheads, in the case of PCA, choosing PT over FT may add a 29.3% of overhead.

---

[1] Implementation with PyCOMPSs distributed within the dislib library [1].

[2] Implementation with PyCOMPSs offered as a BioExcel Building Blocks (BioBB) [3].

Regardless of the policy, picking the appropriate granularity for each policy has a significant impact. Table 2 shows the execution time and relative overhead of each application when running with the policy with a better result in Table 1, set up with different granularities: K-Means runs ITG with groups of 10, 50, and 100 tasks; PMXCV19, PT with 15, 30 and 60-second intervals; and PCA, FT triggering the checkpoint every 10, 50 and 100 completed tasks.

Table 2. Execution time and overhead (baseline: NC) using different granularities for the best policy in Table 1

	Fine-grain	Medium-grain	Coarse-grain
Kmeans (ITG)	222.56 s (1.1%)	244.25 s (11%)	264.36 s (20%)
PMXCV19 (PT)	33.6 m (1.8%)	33 m (0%)	33.1 m (0.3%)
PCA (FT)	1026.21 s (16.1%)	1016.20 s (15%)	1103.94 (24.9%)

Table 2 shows that balancing the checkpoint granularity is needed. Although coarser granularities reduce the number of copies, they can generate I/O-bandwidth peaks that may decrease performance.

4.2   Recovery Speedup

The second experiment aims to measure the speedup of an application when the application fails on the first execution and the checkpointing system recovers the state in a subsequent run. For that purpose, we forced an error when the application reached a certain point of the execution (For the Kmeans we chose the 8th iteration, PXMCV19 we make it fail at min 32 of the execution, finally at PCA we added an exception near the end of the fit function) and measured the duration of failed execution plus the time to finish the subsequent execution using different granularities – defined in Sect. 4.1 – for the best-performing policy for each application. Table 3 contains the obtained times and the speedup of the recovery compared to the same process when no checkpoint is enabled. The K-Means and PCA applications show that despite the overhead, more frequent checkpointing enables a faster recovery time due to the fewer tasks being recomputed on the recovery. The PMXCV19 application performs better with a medium granularity. However, the recovery difference with other granularities is insignificant.

Table 3. Failure, recovery execution time and speedup (baseline: No Checkpoint) using different granularities for the best policy in Table 1.

	No Checkpoint		Fine-grain			Medium-grain			Coarse-grain		
	1st Exec	2nd Exec	1st Exec	Recov.	SpeedUp	1st Exec	Recov.	SpeedUp	1st Exec	Recov.	SpeedUp
Kmeans (ITG) (s)	208.22	221.5	216.96	27.1	1.76x	232.38	25.83	1.39x	254.26	27.14	1.52x
PMXCV19 (PT) (m)	32	33	32	3.1	1.85x	32	2.3	1.89x	32	3.3	1.84x
PCA (FT) (s)	877.99	883.13	1026.21	187.30	1.45x	1016.20	861.26	0.93x	1103.94	855	0.89x

4.3   Avoid Checkpointing Tasks

This third experiment measures the impact of avoiding the persistence of the significant values computed by short tasks. The K-Means application has a pattern composed of two partially overlapped phases: the data set generation and the iterative center convergence. The experiment compares the behavior of a K-Means execution that fails on its 8th convergence iteration. Afterward, it is re-launched, disabling the checkpointing, enabling checkpointing with the FT policy (10-task granularity) for all the tasks and the same policy but disabling the checkpointing of those tasks corresponding to the data set generation phase.

Figure 4 depicts the traces of the failed (left) and recovery (right) executions for the no checkpointing (top), all-tasks checkpointing (middle) and generation-dismissed checkpointing (bottom) configurations. The blue tasks correspond to dataset-generating functions, and each batch of white tasks corresponds to a convergence iteration.

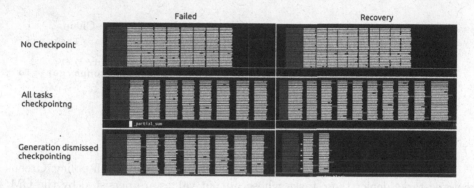

Fig. 4. K-Means execution traces without checkpointing (top), checkpointing all tasks (middle), and generation disabled checkpointing (bottom)

The traces of the first (failed) execution illustrate the effect of the I/O overhead due to the checkpointing. Limiting the number of concurrent checkpointing operations makes the overhead on both executions performing checkpointing similar regardless of the difference in the total number of checkpointed values. However, during the first part of the execution, the CM has no time to persist all the outputs of the generation phase. Thus, it must recompute part of them even if the checkpointing is enabled. The overall execution time grows from 222.99 s when checkpointing is disabled to 282.02 s (0.79× speedup) when the CM checkpoints all the tasks – 126.07 s on the first execution and 159.95 on the recovery. When disabling the checkpointing for the dataset generation tasks, the CM can keep up with the execution progress and avoid most of the tasks' re-execution in the recovery. In this case, the execution time shrinks to 175.75 s (1.27×) – 124.92 s on the initial run and 50.83 on the recovery.

4.4 Customized Policies

The last experiment aims to illustrate the impact of using customized policies leveraging the task groups mechanism on the number of persisted values. To that end, the experiment measures the number of persisted values when using the Matmul application to multiply two 4-by-4-block matrices, and the checkpointing system adopts two custom policies.

Each Matmul run generates a total of 64 tasks forming 16 chains – 1 per output block – of 4 tasks each. The algorithm iterates on all the blocks of the result matrix, instantiating all the tasks updating the block; from a graph point of view, the algorithm generates tasks in a depth-first manner. The custom policies used in the experiment create checkpointing groups of up to two tasks. The first policy (Same-depth policy) groups two tasks from the same depth level, and the second (Same-chain policy) groups two subsequent tasks from the same chain. Listings 1.1 and 1.2 respectively contain the implementation of the function assigning a task to a group for each policy.

Listing 1.1. Same-Depth

```
void assignTaskToGroup(Task t){
    int id = t.getId();
    int mod = id % 4;
    mod = mod == 0 ? 4 : mod % 4;
    int gId = 1+id/8+((mod-1)*8);
    TaskGroup group=groups.get(gId);
    group.addTask(t);
    if (group.size()==2){
      group.close();
    }
}
```

Listing 1.2. Same-Chain

```
void assignTaskToGroup(Task t){
    int id = t.getId();
    int gId = ((int) id/2)+1;
    TaskGroup group=groups.get(gId);
    group.addTask(t);
    if (group.size()==2){
      group.close();
    }
}
```

Figure 5a illustrates the graph of a run using the Same-Depth policy. Green-colored tasks depict those tasks whose output values are persisted by the CM; the output of white-colored tasks is not persisted. It is appreciated how all output data is saved except for two tasks, for which the checkpoint did not have time to copy the results before the execution finished. Thus, the Same-Depth policy persists in 62 data values. Creating groups that take into account the data dependency allows the Same-Chain policy to avoid persisting intermediate

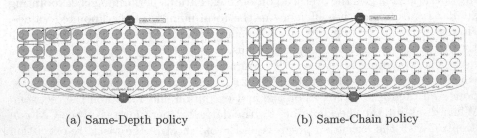

(a) Same-Depth policy   (b) Same-Chain policy

Fig. 5. Matmul's task graphs with both policies; tasks whose output is persisted by the CM are depicted in green. (Color figure online)

values (the output of tasks on the odd rows). Thus, the CM checkpoints 32 values, and there is time to persist as depicted in Fig. 5b.

Application-tailored policies persist fewer values and, thus, reduce the overhead. Avoiding the bottleneck of the concurrent operation allows checkpointing more advanced states of the execution and, therefore, faster recovery executions and lower disk usage.

5   Related Work

The most popular approach for facing failures using task-based parallel models, consists on re-executing the failed task several times, either in the failed node or in a different one. It does not have recovered in case the execution crashes. As instance we have Dask [11], when one node has network connection problems, it will reroute the computation to a different node. However, if the failed node is one with relevant results or the scheduling fails, all results previously executed will have to be re-computed again by other nodes. Additionally, there are PARSL [2], and COMPSs [8], which have some mechanism to retry tasks in case of failure, and even keep with the execution regardless of some tasks have failed. However, all these programming models do not have a recovery system that re-executes the application avoiding the computations performed in the failed execution.

Few workflow environments implement a recovery system that recovers a failed execution into a new one, avoiding re-computing the whole workflow. One of these systems is Pegasus [7]. In Pegasus, once one of the jobs surpasses the number of established failures, it will be marked as failed, and eventually, the whole application will crash. The recovery procedure is to mark nodes in the DAG that succeeded as finished. This allows the user to correct the problem by fixing the errors of ill-compiled nodes, incorrectly compiled codes, inaccessible clusters, etc. This way, the application can restart from the point of failure. Another environment with a recovery system is Legion [6], a data-centric task-based parallel programming system for distributed heterogeneous architectures. This system uses speculation, which allows them to discover non-predicated tasks while the system waits for predicates to finish. If there is a mis-speculation, the runtime must calculate the dependent operations that have been affected. Afterward will reset all operations impacted by it. This process is done recursively, so it could happen that when trying to recover from a failure, it would restart the whole execution from scratch. This checkpointing approach allows it to be performed independently on individual tasks without synchronization.

6   Conclusion

This article proposes a recovery system for task-based programming models. The introduced system copies task outputs to avoid re-executing the computed tasks in the previous execution run. The checkpointing system offers a checkpointing manager that, apart from encapsulating automatic checkpointing, has an interface that allows the end-user to create arbitrary tasks to checkpoint, enabling a specific checkpoint workflow formation to minimize the execution overhead. Moreover, the checkpointing implementation has been propounded to decrease the number of data copies by avoiding the copy of intermediate data values. The flexibility in creating different checkpointing workflows helps reduce the overhead, which can be as minimal as 0% of the execution time and allows for a faster recovery, achieving up to a 1.9× speedup. Additionally, the proposed solution offers an API call that establishes snapshots of the execution in the application code.

Acknowledgements. This work has been supported by the Spanish Government (PID2019-107255GB), by Generalitat de Catalunya (contract 2017-SGR-01414), and by the European Commission through the Horizon 2020 Research and Innovation program under Grant Agreement No. 955558 (eFlows4HPC-project). This work has partially been co-funded with 50% by the European Regional Development Fund under the framework of the ERFD Operative Programme for Catalunya 2014–2020.

References

1. Cid-Fuentes, J.Á., et al.: dislib: large scale high performance machine learning in python. In: 2019 15th International Conference on eScience (eScience) (2019)
2. Babuji, Y., et al.: Parsl: pervasive parallel programming in python. CoRR (2019)
3. Andrio, P., et al.: Bioexcel building blocks, a software library for interoperable biomolecular simulation workflows. Sci. Data **6**, 169 (2019)
4. Badia, R.M., et al.: Comp superscalar, an interoperable programming framework. SoftwareX **3**, 32–36 (2015)
5. Badia, R.M., et al.: Enabling python to execute efficiently in heterogeneous distributed infrastructures with pycompss. In: PyHPC 2017. Association for Computing Machinery, New York (2017)
6. Bauer, M., et al.: Legion: expressing locality and independence with logical regions. In: SC 2012: Proceedings of the International Conference on High Performance Computing, Networking, Storage and Analysis, pp. 1–11 (2012)
7. Deelman, E., et al.: Pegasus, a workflow management system for science automation. Future Gener. Comput. Syst. **46**, 17–35 (2014)
8. Ejarque, J., Bertran, M., Cid-Fuentes, J.Á., Conejero, J., Badia, R.M.: Managing failures in task-based parallel workflows in distributed computing environments. In: Malawski, M., Rzadca, K. (eds.) Euro-Par 2020. LNCS, vol. 12247, pp. 411–425. Springer, Cham (2020). https://doi.org/10.1007/978-3-030-57675-2_26
9. Quan, O., Xu, H.: The study of comparisons of three crossover operators in genetic algorithm for solving single machine scheduling problem (2015)
10. Qureshi, K., Khan, F., Manuel, P., Nazir, B.: A hybrid fault tolerance technique in grid computing system. J. Supercomput. **56**, 106–128 (2011)
11. Rocklin, M.: Dask: parallel computation with blocked algorithms and task scheduling, pp. 126–132 (2015)
12. Vanderster, D., Dimopoulos, N., Sobie, R.: Intelligent selection of fault tolerance techniques on the grid, pp. 69–76 (2007)

PhD Symposium

Euro-Par PhD Symposium

PhD Symposium Description

Euro-Par PhD Symposium aims at gathering students working toward a doctorate in broadly defined areas related to parallel and distributed processing. This event provides a unique opportunity for the students to present and discuss their ongoing dissertation research with the Euro-Par research community. The Euro-Par PhD Symposium strives at establishing itself as one of the premier European forums for graduate students in parallel and distributed computing. For this reason, it focuses on providing a productive platform where the students can get feedback on their research from some of the key players in the European scientific community, while also giving an opportunity for industry to get insights on academic work that is currently in progress.

The second Euro-Par PhD Symposium (2022) was held in-person in Glasgow, Scotland. The format of the PhD Symposium included seven student presentations and it received good attendance of around 30 people on average throughout the day, including at the evening poster session. This year, the Euro-Par PhD Symposium received ten submissions from five countries. The rigorous submission processes included an extended abstract and the endorsement letter from the official PhD adviser(s). A thorough peer-reviewing process coupled with in-depth discussions and agreement among reviewers (when applicable) resulted in seven extended abstracts being accepted for presentation at the Euro-Par PhD Symposium 2022, of which six are included in the following chapter. The review process focused on the quality of the submissions, their innovation, and applicability to the topics covered by the Euro-Par conference.

The accepted extended abstracts represent an interesting mix of topics, addressing novel algorithms, benchmarking, programming models and machine learning methods, all targeting large-scale parallel and distributed systems. The chair would like to thank all the Program Committee members, authors, presenters, attendees and the Euro-Par organizers for their help and support in making the second Euro-Par PhD Symposium a successful event.

Organization

Chair

Yehia Elkhatib   University of Glasgow, UK

Program Committee

Marco Aldinucci   University of Torino, Italy
Georgios Bouloukakis   Télécom Sud Paris, France
Thaleia-Dimitra Doudali   IMDEA Software, Spain
Maya G. Neytcheva   Uppsala University, Sweden
Pavlos Petoumenos   University of Manchester, UK
Sameer Shende   University of Oregon, USA
Zheng Wang   University of Leeds, UK

A Stochastic Programming Approach for an Enhanced Performance of a Multi-committees Byzantine Fault Tolerant Algorithm

Yifei Xie[1]([✉]), Btissam Er-Rahmadi[2], Xiao Chen[1], Tiejun Ma[1],
and Jane Hillston[1]

[1] School of Informatics, The University of Edinburgh, Edinburgh, UK
yifei.xie@ed.ac.uk
[2] Huawei Edinburgh Research Centre, Edinburgh, UK

Abstract. Byzantine fault-tolerance (BFT) algorithms enhance trust-worthiness of distributed systems by guaranteeing their resilience to Byzantine faults. Traditional BFT algorithms suffer from scalability issues, resulting in performance bottlenecks (e.g., low throughputs) in large-scale distributed systems. Moreover, distributed systems are generally deployed on geographically and/or logically distributed networks, which aggravates the performance-scalability issue. To tackle this challenge, existing works have proposed a number of new BFT algorithms (e.g., HotStuff, FastBFT). However, limited work has explored parallel BFT based on a partitioned set of connected subgroups. This is challenging due to 1) heterogeneous communications delays between different, potentially geographically distributed, peers, and 2) peers may have a random crash and/or Byzantine failures, which contribute to the failure of the BFT consensus. To address these issues, we propose a stochastic programming (SP) model to maximise the throughput, while considering communications delays and failure behaviors as constraints. The SP model solution provides the optimal multi-committee organisation. Evaluation results show 24% throughput enhancement with the SP model.

Keywords: Stochastic Programming · Byzantine Fault Tolerant
Algorithm · Parallel Consensus

1 Introduction

Blockchain is a technology that allows a group of peers to save the same records in a distributed ledger. Such a decentralised architecture releases the network peers from dependence on a trusted third party. However to perform their intended operations participating peers need to reach agreements. Consequently, reaching consensus becomes a critical problem, especially in Byzantine fault conditions. Moreover, scalability becomes the main bottleneck of classical consensus algorithms like the practical Byzantine Fault Tolerance (PBFT) [1] algorithm, as

© The Author(s), under exclusive license to Springer Nature Switzerland AG 2023
J. Singer et al. (Eds.): Euro-Par 2022 Workshops, LNCS 13835, pp. 267–273, 2023.
https://doi.org/10.1007/978-3-031-31209-0_20

they only support small peer sets (usually no more than 20). Small-scale peer networks do not meet the requirement of the current commercial blockchain applications. Thus, to address the scalability issue, researchers proposed a multi-committee-based consensus mechanism (e.g., Elastico [2]) to partition the large-scale peers set into several parallel consensus committees. However, most of these multi-committee solutions take a naive approach to peer set partitioning. They generally initialise the multi-committee peers set randomly without considering any optimization of the committee organization.

In this paper, we focus on finding an optimal partitioning scheme for a previously proposed multi-committee BFT algorithm, ParBFT [3], respecting that crucial algorithm parameters (e.g., network delay, failure behavior) are uncertain. Thus, our research explores the most performance optimal partitioning scheme by building a stochastic programming (SP) optimisation model. The SP model aims to maximise the transaction throughput, which allows us to optimally solve the number of committees and allocation of peers within the formed committees. The remainder of the paper is organized as follows: Sect. 2 describes the assumptions and the model. In Sect. 3 we present the performance evaluation results on the testbed. Section 4 concludes the work.

2   Stochastic Model

2.1   System Assumption

We consider a distributed system made up of geographically/logically distributed peers. Specifically, we seek to model the uncertainties of communications and failure behaviors in a previously proposed multi-committee BFT: ParBFT [3]. ParBFT achieves a parallel consensus via multi-committee scheme, and it includes three basic phases: *pre-prepare*, *prepare* and *commit*. In *pre-prepare*, each leader sends a message to the followers in its committee; follower peers then verify messages and reply to the leader peer in *prepare*; finally, leader peers send a message to the verification committee in *commit*. In the ParBFT algorithm, the peer set consists of 1) a verification committee which has at least one verification peer (*verifier*), and 2) multiple consensus committees, each of which consists of a leader peer (*leader*) and several follower peers (*followers*). We consider that the set of leaders and followers forms a set of N peers, denoted as $\mathcal{N}$. We assume that any two peers i and j are connected to each other via two unidirectional communication links (i, j) and (j, i). As peers in $\mathcal{N}$ are geographically distributed, their communications are subject to network condition changes, which leads to variable peer-to-peer (P2P) message delays. These delays substantially impact the BFT algorithm performance in terms of transaction throughput and latency as consensus messages may reach their destination peers later than expected.

We also consider that $\mathcal{N}$ peers are exposed to two types of failures: Crash and Byzantine failures. Crash failure happens when a peer stops working and does not resume. A Byzantine failure happens when a peer produces arbitrary, contradictory or conflicting responses at arbitrary times, with or without malicious intentions. The peers' failure behaviors considerably affect the BFT algorithm performance as allocating peers more prone to failures within the same committees will result in the failure of the consensus in these committees, and hence on the failure of the overall consensus. We use a failure detector (for e.g., [4,5]) to detect Crash failures. We record participating peers in previously failed consensus as Byzantine failures. The security of ParBFT is guaranteed by its Byzantine fault tolerant feature, which means each committee can tolerate no more than one third of faulty peers. In our model, for security reasons, each committee must be able to tolerate a certain number of Byzantine faulty peers [1]. We denote the number of faulty peers that can be tolerated in each committee as f_{min}. That is, for each committee, the system still works even if each committee has f_{min} Byzantine faulty peers. This requires us to ensure that the number of peers in each committee is guaranteed to be at least $3f_{min}+1$. In stochastic programming, there is the notion of "scenario", which represents the possible value of a random parameter. Hence, a "scenarios space" (or scenarios set) represents all possible values of a random parameter. We denote the network delay from j to i in scenario ω as $d_{ij}(\omega) \in R^{N \times N}$, $\forall i,j \in \mathcal{N}$. We define the failure rate of a peer i as the ratio of its failures over an observation time, denoted as $f_i(\omega)$ under scenario ω, We also introduce $b_i(\omega)$ to represent the status of peer i under scenario ω so $b_i(\omega) = 1$ if i fails under scenario ω and $b_i(\omega) = 0$ otherwise. We denote the total number of faulty peers under scenario ω as $B(\omega)$, where $B(\omega) = \sum_{i=1}^{N} b_i(\omega)$. In terms of consensus communication, we denote the available bandwidth at the verification committee as K^{bw}, and the required bandwidth by each consensus committee i as q_i^{bw}.

2.2   Decision Variables and Objective Function

To obtain an optimal configuration, we need to decide: the number of committees, the selection of leaders and the allocation of followers (remaining peers) to formed committees. Let p be an integer decision variable that represents the number of consensus committees (also the number of leaders). Let x_{ij} be a binary decision variable such that $x_{ij} = 1$ if i is the leader of j and $x_{ij} = 0$ otherwise, $\forall i,j \in \mathcal{N}, i \neq j$. For $i = j$, $x_{ii} = 1$ means i is selected as a leader of one of the formed committees and $x_{ii} = 0$ implies it is a follower.

The transaction throughput is a key metric to evaluate the performance of a consensus algorithm, and is defined as the number of successful transactions during an observation time period. Note that a higher transaction throughput implies that the time spent should be as short as possible for each single transaction. Let $T(\omega)$ be the time spent on processing a consensus under scenario ω. Similarly, we denote the time spent on *pre-prepare*, *prepare* and *commit* as $T_{p-pre}(\omega)$, $T_{pre}(\omega)$ and $T_{com}(\omega)$, respectively. The time spent in each phase depends on the communication defined in [3]. Consequently, the consensus time of one transaction could be represented as:

$$T(\omega) = T_{p-pre}(\omega) + T_{pre}(\omega) + T_{com}(\omega) \tag{1}$$

$$T_{p-pre}(\omega) = \max_{i,j} \left(x_{ij} \cdot d_{ij}(\omega) \right) \tag{2}$$

$$T_{pre}(\omega) = \max_{i,j} \left(x_{ij} \cdot (d_{ij}(\omega) + 2d_{ji})(\omega) \right) \tag{3}$$

$$T_{com}(\omega) = \max_{i} \left(x_{ii} \cdot 2d_{vi}(\omega) \right) \tag{4}$$

2.3   Performance Constraints

Partitioning of $\mathcal{N}$. Here we introduce the constraints related to the general formation of the multi-committees. Firstly, each committee should have exactly one leader. Consequently, the number of committees corresponds to the number of leaders, which implies:

$$\sum_{i=1}^{n} x_{ii} = p \tag{5}$$

Secondly, for each committee, the leader peer establishes links with all the follower peers to communicate messages; there is no communication between follower peers. This is expressed by the following constraint:

$$\forall i, j \in \mathcal{N} : \; x_{ij} \le x_{ii} \tag{6}$$

Thirdly, each peer only belongs to one committee. Consequently, a peer j can either be a follower to exactly one leader in its committee or the leader of this committee. Thus, we have the following constraint:

$$\forall j \in \mathcal{N} : \; \sum_{i=1}^{n} x_{ij} = 1 \tag{7}$$

Security and Stability. BFT algorithms require at least 2/3 of the peers to be honest to reach a consensus. To enhance the stability of the system, we need to ensure that there are at least $3f_{\min} + 1$ peers in each committee

$$\forall i \in \mathcal{N} : \; \sum_{j=1}^{n} x_{ij} + 1 \ge 3f_{\min} + 1 \tag{8}$$

Leaders play a critical role in the communications between their respective followers and between their respective committee and the verification committee. Consequently, leaders must be the most reliable peers in $\mathcal{N}$ and additionally meet system requirements in terms of reliability. Let F be a system parameter representing the upper bound of leaders failure rates. This is to prevent less reliable peers from leading the committees as expressed here:

$$\forall i \in \mathcal{N}, \forall \omega \in \Omega : \; x_{ii} \cdot f_i(\omega) \le F \tag{9}$$

Additionally, we need to prevent the grouping of peers susceptible to failures in the same committees. Thus, it is essential to distribute faulty peers evenly into committees. This constraint guarantees such a distribution:

$$\forall i \in \mathcal{N}, \forall \omega \in \Omega : \sum_{j=1}^{n} x_{ij} \cdot b_j(\omega) \leq \lceil \frac{B(\omega)}{p} \rceil \qquad (10)$$

Committee Number Optimisation. Constraint (8) states that the number of peers in each committee should be no less than $3f_{\min} + 1$, which implies that the number of formed committees p should respect such peer allocation:

$$1 \leq p \leq \lfloor \frac{N}{3f_{\min} + 1} \rfloor \qquad (11)$$

During consensus, committees' leaders simultaneously communicate with the verification committee, which consumes its available bandwidth. As a consequence, a high number of formed committees leads to a communication bottleneck in the verification committee communication resources. To avoid such situations, only peers that collectively respect the verification bandwidth are allowed to be the committee leaders

$$\sum_{i=1}^{p} x_{ii} \cdot q_i^{bw} \leq K^{bw} \qquad (12)$$

3   Performance Evaluation

To evaluate the performance of our proposed SP model, we apply the optimised committee configuration obtained by solving the SP model to the ParBFT algorithm. First, we apply the optimised committee organisation scheme driven by the SP model to the ParBFT algorithm and compare it to the non-optimised ParBFT algorithm that uses a random committee organisation scheme. Second, we compare with a recent BFT algorithm, FastBFT [6], that is considered one of the fastest BFT algorithm published recently. Third, we compare the performance of our SP model to a deterministic model, standard ParBFT, in which the parameters are set to constant values. This aims to verify the importance of adopting random parameters in the SP model. We developed a testbed using Java and composed of five Microsoft Azure cloud virtual machines (VMs). Each VM has eight v-CPUs and 32G RAM. We use the same transaction size and block size as in the Bitcoin system, where transaction size is 250 bytes and block size is 1 MB. Our settings are similar to FastBFT in [6], which allows a fair performance comparison. Also, we assume that each committee can tolerate $f_{\min} = 1$ faulty peer, and we vary the total number of peers from 40 to 200.

Figure 1 shows the throughput and latency of our proposed SP model and several BFT algorithms with a number of peers varying from 40 to 200, respectively. Compared to FastBFT, the ParBFT shows a stable throughput improvement when the number of peers increases as it benefits from the parallel consensus design. Moreover, the ParBFT achieves 220% improvements on throughput,

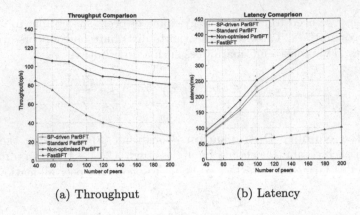

(a) Throughput   (b) Latency

Fig. 1. Performance comparison of various BFT algorithms

while the FastBFT has a significant decline when the number of peers increases from 40 to 200. The SP-driven ParBFT algorithm shows the best performance and can achieve around 20% throughput improvement compared with standard ParBFT optimised by deterministic model. When the number of peers increases to 200, the SP model can improve system throughput up to 24% (i.e. from 388K TPS to 480K TPS) compared to the non-optimised ParBFT algorithm. Hence, the SP model yields effective optimisation on consensus performance.

4 Conclusion

In this paper we presented a stochastic programming model for optimising the performance of our previously proposed multi-committee BFT algorithm, ParBFT. The experimental results show that the SP model can improve the throughput of ParBFT by around 24%. Such an improvement is vital for many domain applications including blockchain and traditional BFT replica services.

Acknowledgements. This project has also received funding from the EU Horizon 2020 research and innovation programme under the Marie Skłodowska-Curie grant agreement No. 801215 and the University of Edinburgh Data-Driven Innovation programme, part of the Edinburgh and SE Scotland City Region Deal.

References

1. Castro, M., Liskov, B., et al.: Practical Byzantine fault tolerance. In: OsDI, vol. 99, pp. 173–186 (1999)
2. Luu, L., et al.: A secure sharding protocol for open blockchains. In: Proceedings of the ACM Conference on Computer and Communications Security, pp. 17–30 (2016)
3. Chen, X., et al.: ParBFT: a high performance parallel Byzantine fault tolerance algorithm (2022). Manuscript submitted for publication

4. Er-Rahmadi, B., Ma, T.: Data-driven mixed-integer linear programming-based optimisation for efficient failure detection in large-scale distributed systems. Eur. J. Oper. Res. **303**(1), 337–353 (2022). ISSN: 0377-2217
5. Ma, T., Hillston, J., Anderson, S.: On the quality of service of crash-recovery failure detectors. IEEE Trans. Dependable Secure Comput. **7**(3), 271–283 (2010). ISSN: 1545-5971
6. Liu, J., et al.: Scalable Byzantine consensus via hardware-assisted secret sharing. IEEE Trans. Comput. **68**(1), 139–151 (2018)

Coupe: A Modular, Multi-threaded Mesh Partitioning Platform

Hubert Hirtz[1,2(✉)]

[1] LIHPC, CEA, Université Paris-Saclay, 91680 Bruyères-le-Châtel, France
`hubert.hirtz@cea.fr`
[2] CEA, DAM, DIF, 91297 Arpajon, France
`https://www.cea.fr/english`

Abstract. Mesh partitioning used for load balancing in distributed numerical simulations is typically managed with tools that are good enough but not optimal. Their use scope is not explicitly dedicated to load balancing, and they cannot make use of all available information. In this paper, the mesh partitioning problem and the context for its use are precisely defined. Then, existing tools are presented, along with their characteristics and features that are missing. Finally, a new partitioning platform – the subject of my PhD thesis – is presented: its architecture, software engineering choices made along the way, and how it can be the best fit for load balancing distributed simulations. The platform is open-source and is hosted on GitHub: https://github.com/LIHPC-Computational-Geometry/coupe.

Keywords: mesh partitioning · load balancing · shared memory · parallel algorithms

1 Introduction

Many numerical simulations are based on high-order finite elements or volume methods (FEM or FVM) and run on distributed-memory machines such as high-performance computing (HPC) architectures. The FEM and FVM approaches require the geometric domain of study to be discretized into basic elements, called cells, which form a *mesh*. Numerical and physical data is associated with each cell to model the physical phenomenon (e.g., pressure, temperature, speed). To run on HPC architectures, simulation codes tend to adopt the Bulk Synchronous Parallel (BSP) programming model: multiple computations phases are performed and, in between two successive computations steps, a synchronization step is carried out to exchange non-locally managed data in between processes. Therefore, to achieve efficient parallelism, one must balance data and workloads between processes.

To this end, we aim to solve a mesh partitioning problem: how to distribute the cells of a mesh across processing units while ensuring a fair amount of work on each and minimizing data exchange during the synchronization step.

Such a problem can be modeled and solved using geometric [5] or topological approaches, usually based on graph representations [12]. Finding high-quality solutions to these problems has received significant attention, and partitioning platforms have been developed during the last three decades [2,11]. My PhD's work defines a new mesh partitioning tool that fills the gaps between geometrical and topological approaches and adopts the Rust programming ecosystem to provide a safe, robust, multi-thread modular framework.

2   The Mesh Partitioning Problem

2.1   Topologic vs. Geometrical Mesh Partitioning

In the context of this work, mesh partitioning is a mean to balance computational work between process units in a numerical simulation. At a given step time of a simulation running on N process units, we associate each cell of a mesh $\mathcal{M}$ with both a computation and a communication cost. Additionally, cell connectivity[1] is chosen to define data dependencies since FEM and FVM require stencils of adjacent cells to compute numerical quantities. The mesh partitioning problem entails partitioning $\mathcal{M}$ in N parts such that the computational costs of the parts differ the least and the sum of communication costs of cells with neighbors in different parts is minimal.

A traditional approach to address the mesh partitioning problem is to consider only the mesh topology: most proposed solutions build the *dual* mesh structure, i.e., a graph where each vertex represents a cell and each edge links vertices that represent neighboring cells. Weights are defined on vertices to model the computational cost of the associated mesh cell and on edges to model the communication cost between the cells corresponding to its endpoints. Then the *edge cut* approximates the communication costs between different parts. The edge cut is the sum of the communication costs of all the edges (v_1, v_2) where v_1 and v_2 are in different parts.

Geometric approaches consist in partitioning the mesh using point coordinates. Each obtained part gathers cells having close coordinates. The advantage of geometric algorithms is that they are generally simple and efficiently implemented. However, the absence of topology may lead to partitions of arbitrary quality with respect to the communications. Handling weight on the vertices is also less flexible.

We illustrate some of the above concepts in Fig. 1, where a mesh (Fig. 1a) is first partitioned by a Recursive Coordinate Bisection (RCB) [1], a geometric algorithm that works on weighted points (Fig. 1b). Then, the partition is refined (Fig. 1c) using Fiduccia-Mattheyses [6] which works on a graph.

2.2   Current Partitioning Platforms and Features

There already exist partitioning platforms. METIS [11] and SCOTCH [2] for example use graphs primarily. They have the advantage of being able to work

---

[1] two cells share an edge or a vertex, for instance.

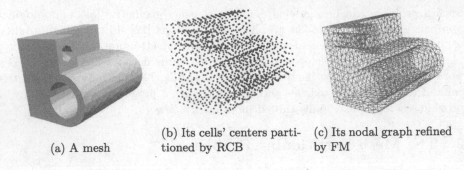

(a) A mesh | (b) Its cells' centers partitioned by RCB | (c) Its nodal graph refined by FM

Fig. 1. A composition of algorithms that work on different aspects of the same mesh

on any graph, be it the dual of a mesh or a social network graph, for example. Zoltan [5] uses a hypergraph representation. It can also work on geometrical information, such as the coordinates of the nodes that make up cells.

When dealing with large graphs, these tools use a method called *multilevel partitioning*, which relies on the fact that partitioning a reduced, *coarsened* version of a graph – where some vertices have been merged together – will produce a low-communication-cost partition on the original graph. This technique enables the use of sequential or otherwise non-scalable algorithms such as Fiduccia-Mattheyses [6] on arbitrarily large inputs. Multilevel partitioning is, however, geared toward graph and hypergraph algorithms. In the case of mesh partitioning for load balancing, geometrical information is also present, and algorithms that make use of it are known to scale better [1,4,14] than multilevel, where the partitioning is done sequentially. Additionally, all these tools sit above MPI for scalability. Mesh partitioners being mostly memory-bound, are typically not used with multiple MPI processes per node, leaving most computation power on the table.

Finally, a recent study [3] shows that memory constraints, not considered by existing partitioning tools, can fail some physics simulations where computation units need not only their own part's cells but also the neighbors of their part's border. Those cells are qualified as ghost cells. The traditional edge cut metric used to optimize partitions typically leads to memory overflow. Authors of [3] also claimed that integration trials of those extra constraints in SCOTCH have been difficult due to tight coupling between implementations and usages of its data structures.

3   Coupe: A Dedicated Mesh Partitioning Platform

The choice of starting from scratch first comes from a paradigm shift in how meshes are partitioned. Widely used partitioning tools, except for Zoltan, target arbitrary graphs or other topological structures. In our case, we want to partition meshes specifically to balance the workload of physics simulations. This means we can use the geometrical information absent in a dual graph. Furthermore, recent machines can host memory banks large enough to work on the whole mesh locally, using threading and GPU acceleration as a way to scale. Also, while the existing tools – built around MPI – do multilevel partitioning, we experiment with the use of inherently scalable algorithms, which have the potential to reach a higher threshold of concurrency [1,4,14]. Finally, this new platform must also consider the new metrics discovered since, and produce high-quality partitions that fit within the given constraints.

3.1 Software Choices and Architecture

Coupe hosts several partitioning algorithms, some geometrical, some topological, and some producing an initial partition, some optimizing an exiting one. In order to widen the range of possibilities, we should be able to compose any of these together. As such, their implementation should not interfere with others', and the source code, on the whole, must be highly modular.

Programming Language Choice. Building for distributed architectures inclined software developers to write code in C or Fortran whose support is required by the MPI standard. While Coupe is not bound to this interface, it still needs the low-level access to hardware these programming languages offer, so CPU cores and GPU accelerators can be fully made use of. The technological challenge induced by the modularity and the extensive use of multi-threading drove us to select Rust [15]. On the one hand, Rust compiles down to optimized machine code and has little to no runtime; on the other, it offers features worthy of high-level languages like iterators, closures, and generics. Its ability to detect data races and other memory errors at compile time significantly helps us build Coupe. Rust also has the advantage of having several collection types built into the standard library, such as hash maps and binary heaps.

Rust as a Choice of Ecosystem. All of these language features are also well integrated into Rust's ecosystem of libraries, seamlessly usable from the Cargo package manager:

- criterion [9] is a benchmark framework that runs statistical models on the performance results. It can work with add-ons to measure CPU cycles, assembly instructions, cache misses, and context switches. Post-processing is done to ensure measurements are stable and correct.
- iai [10] is another benchmark framework, though this one is designed to run in Continuous Integration environments. It runs benchmarks just once with CacheGrind and returns the number of instructions, CPU cache accesses, RAM accesses, and cycles.
- proptest [13] is a property testing framework. It picks random values within a given input domain and tests given properties. While it does not ensure all edge cases are covered, it allows for succinct unit testing.
- rayon [16] is a parallel processing library. It works mainly through iterators.

Integration with Other Languages. Code written in C can easily be called from other languages. Because this is not the case for Rust, Coupe has to offer a compatibility layer that exposes its features through the C ABI. This layer called *FFI* (for Foreign Function Interface) or *C bindings*, is the baseline for bindings to other languages. It must therefore be stable, low-level, and easy to understand. For these reasons, it has been written by hand.

Tooling. The modularity of the codebase and the fact that all the algorithms can be tested separately and composed together lead to a lack of tools to run relevant tests and benchmarks. Great care has been taken in making a set of tools around Coupe. These tools can test algorithms in different conditions and on different weight distributions. Visuals can be quickly produced through an SVG converter that optimizes the size of its output. A benchmarking tool built atop criterion allows for scalability measurements: it runs a list of algorithms on different numbers of threads and shows an efficiency graph. Finally, a mesh library for the simple MEDIT [7] file format has been written.

3.2   Example of Scaling Algorithm Under Development

As an example of how Coupe can be used to implement new algorithms, we will show the process of implementing a variant of the Fiduccia-Mattheyses [6] (FM) algorithm that can be used after the scalable geometrical algorithms for further reduction of the communication costs.

FM is a hypergraph partitioning algorithm, which, for simplicity here, is restricted to graphs. The algorithm minimizes the edge cut of a given bi-partition by moving vertices between parts, one by one, so that the edge cut decreases the most at every step. This decrease is called *gain*: a vertex has a positive gain if moving it to the other part decreases the edge cut. A gain table is used to retrieve in constant time a vertex that has the largest gain. Great care is taken to also enable constant time updates of gains each time a vertex is moved. The iteration stops when no more gain can be found. By its greedy nature, this algorithm is very much sequential and thus mainly used in multilevel partitioning, where the input size has been drastically reduced. Given our constraints, the idea is to drop the greedy requirement and the gain table and move any vertex with a positive gain.

Benchmarks have been run on a 128-thread machine. The mesh is 2D, triangular, and has 19 775 488 cells. RCB provides an initial partition which is then refined by the FM variant. RCB alone takes an average wall time of 321 ms (std.dev.: 15 ms), and the whole run takes 463 ms (std.dev.: 15 ms).

4   Outlook

Coupe is a partitioning platform geared towards mesh partitioning for load balancing in distributed physics simulations. Its codebase is made modular, and implemented algorithms can be composed together, so users can fine-tune how they partition their mesh. Although it is still a work in progress, the project is very much usable, and experiments are done at the order of the million of vertices. Multiple geometrical, topological, and number-partitioning algorithms have already been implemented. They can be used from Rust, C, and the command-line thanks to the bundled tooling. Shortly, Coupe will be integrated into the Arcane framework [8] and tested in real-life simulations. This will set performance goals to attain and deliver profiling data. It is also planned to support multi-criteria runs, i.e., runs where cells have multiple associated computation costs. In the meantime, sources of Coupe are available to the public on GitHub: https://github.com/LIHPC-Computational-Geometry/coupe.

Acknowledgements. Great thanks to my main advisor Franck Ledoux, and my supervisors Cédric Chevalier and Sébastien Morais for helping me both write this paper and throughout my PhD thesis so far.

References

1. Berger, M.J., Bokhari, S.H.: A partitioning strategy for nonuniform problems on multiprocessors. IEEE Trans. Comput. **C-36**(5), 570–580 (1987)
2. Chevalier, C., Pellegrini, F.: PT-Scotch: a tool for efficient parallel graph ordering. Parallel Comput. **34**(6), 318–331 (2008)
3. Chevalier, C., Ledoux, F., Morais, S.: A multilevel mesh partitioning algorithm driven by memory constraints. In: CSC (2020)
4. Deveci, M., Rajamanickam, S., Devine, K.D., Çatalyürek, Ü.V.: Multi-jagged: a scalable parallel spatial partitioning algorithm. IEEE Trans. Parallel Distrib. Syst. **27**(3), 803–817 (2016)
5. Devine, K., Boman, E., Heaphy, R., Hendrickson, B., Vaughan, C.: Zoltan data management services for parallel dynamic applications. Comput. Sci. Eng. **4**(2), 90–96 (2002)
6. Fiduccia, C.M., Mattheyses, R.M.: A linear-time heuristic for improving network partitions. In: Proceedings of the 19th Design Automation Conference, DAC 1982, pp. 175–181. IEEE Press, January 1982
7. Frey, P.: MEDIT: an interactive mesh visualization software, December 2001
8. Grospellier, G., Lelandais, B.: The arcane development framework. In: Proceedings of the 8th Workshop on Parallel/High-Performance Object-Oriented Scientific Computing (2009)
9. Heisler, B.: Criterion.rs, May 2022
10. Heisler, B.: Iai, May 2022
11. Karypis, G., Kumar, V.: A fast and high quality multilevel scheme for partitioning irregular graphs. SIAM J. Sci. Comput. **20**(1), 359–392 (1995)
12. Kernighan, B.W., Lin, S.: An efficient heuristic procedure for partitioning graphs. Bell Syst. Tech. J. **49**(2), 291–307 (1970)
13. Lingle, J.: Proptest, May 2022
14. von Looz, M., Tzovas, C., Meyerhenke, H.: Balanced k-means for parallel geometric partitioning. Technical report, May 2018. arXiv:1805.01208
15. Matsakis, N.D., Klock, F.S.: The rust language. Ada Lett. **34**(3), 103–104 (2014)
16. Stone, J., Matsakis, N.D.: Rayon, May 2022

Preliminary Study of Resource Allocation in Wireless Communications

Peace Ayegba[✉][iD] and Sofiat Olaosebikan[iD]

University of Glasgow, Glasgow, UK
p.ayegba.1@research.gla.ac.uk

Abstract. Wireless communications remain a vital part of our economy as it is a key enabler of information exchange between billions of people around the world. However, the current technology cannot meet the demands of the future (i.e., explosive growth in the number of devices, better coverage, and connection rate). For future wireless communications, the key technology that has the potential to enhance connectivity for billions of users is referred to as Cell-Free Massive Multiple-Input Multiple-Output (CF-mMIMO). One of the many challenges in CF-mMIMO is how to efficiently manage limited resources in a way that maximizes the performance of the network - the so-called resource allocation problem in wireless communications. This work explores computational and mathematical tools that will tackle some of the resource allocation problems in future wireless networks.

Keywords: Wireless communications · Resource allocation · Optimisation problems · Scheduling · Theory and Algorithms

1 Introduction

In recent years, there has been an explosive growth in the number of smartphones and other high-performance handheld devices which require high-speed wireless connectivity. In 2018, statistics showed that over 22 billion devices were connected around the world and it is predicted that in 2030, there would be over 50 billion connected devices [1]. This demand has necessitated the need for more efficient and scalable techniques for efficient communication. In the past, the main service for mobile networks was to cater for voice calls but presently transmission of data (internet connectivity) is the dominant service. Nowadays we have billions of smart devices used in critical sectors like healthcare and they require stable and reliable internet connections.

Unlike classical times when wired networks were dominant, wireless networks use radio waves as communication channels and signals are often transmitted in parallel across channels to improve the total spectral efficiency of the network. The *spectral efficiency* (SE) of a network can be viewed as a metric used to

Supported by University of Glasgow College of Science and Engineering scholarship.

J. Singer et al. (Eds.): Euro-Par 2022 Workshops, LNCS 13835, pp. 280–285, 2023.
https://doi.org/10.1007/978-3-031-31209-0_22

assess network performance and represents the total number of data (in bits) transmitted over a channel. Due to the variation of the wireless environment, the capacity of wireless links exhibits a dynamic nature. More so, signals are easily affected by interferences from other signals as they travel across the same channel. This stands in clear contrast to wired networks where the capacity of any channel is fixed and independent of the transmission rate on other channels. Furthermore, we often experience resource constraints (power, channels, bandwidth) that must be properly managed to maximise the network performance. As a result, strategies for resource allocation and interference management are usually necessary in wireless networks to provide acceptable data rates to the users.

In this work, we are concerned with optimisation problems for cell-free massive Mimo (CF-mMIMO) networks. The latest 5G network architecture follows a *cellular* model where the network is divided into *cells* and we have APs serving only users in their cells. With this, users far from the APs achieve low spectral efficiency and inter-cell interference occurs since APs have to handle several active users in their cells at the same time. On the other hand, there are no cells in CF-mMIMO and all APs can serve all users simultaneously as we see in Fig. 1. With this approach, it is envisaged that we can attain higher network speed, better reliability of connections and improved scalability [2].

1G to 5G : Cellular architecture   **6G: Cell Free architecture**

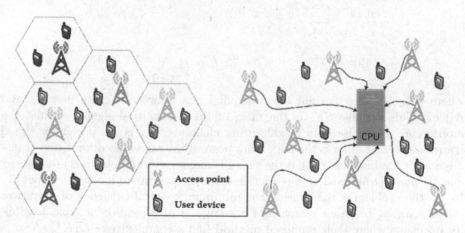

Fig. 1. Cellular networks vs Cell-free networks

2   System Model and Existing Work

A typical CF-mMIMO model contains a set of APs $\mathcal{A} = \{a_1, a_2, ..., a_M\}$ serving a set of users $\mathcal{U} = \{u_1, u_2, ..., u_K\}$ such that the number of APs $M \gg K$. We also have a channel g_{mk} between AP a_m and user u_k which is assumed to remain constant during a *coherence interval* and an upper bound on the achievable spectral efficiency attainable by each user can be calculated using Shannon sum capacity formula [5]. Different resource allocation problems exist in all stages of signal transmission which include an uplink training stage, a downlink data transmission stage (AP → user), and an uplink data transmission stage (User → AP). The uplink training stage typically involves the process of acquiring channel estimates for downlink (AP → user) data transmission to occur and for now we focus on the optimisation problems in this phase.

In downlink transmission, we have power constraints at each AP that determine the strength of transmitted signals. Therefore, resource allocation takes the form of optimising utility functions subject to these power constraints. These utility functions are sum spectral efficiency, proportional fairness, harmonic rate, and the minimum rate [5]. In this work, we focus on the problem of maximising the sum spectral efficiency (sum SE) under i) power constraints and ii) without power constraints i.e. assuming uniform power.

2.1 Sum SE Maximisation Under Power Constraints

Given a CF-mMIMO network of K users and M APs, the sum SE problem under power constraint is described as:

$$\max_{\eta_{mk} \geq 0} \sum_{k=1}^{K} SE_k \quad \forall m, k$$

$$\text{subject to} \sum_{k=1}^{K} 0 \leq \eta_{mk} \leq P_{\max}, \quad m = 1, \ldots, M.$$

where SE_k is the achievable spectral efficiency between a given user u_k and AP a_k. This variable SE_k is the ratio of the transmitted signals against the interference and noise from neighbouring channels. η_{mk} is the power for signal transmission and P_{max} is the maximum power that can be used for signal transmission. It has been shown that the sum-SE maximisation problem is non-convex and NP-hard [4,6] based on a reduction from the maximum independent set [3]. In [5], the problem of maximising the minimum spectral efficiency of users was solved using a bisection search and a sequence of second-order cone feasibility problems where their proposed method had a complexity of $O(K^4)$. Also, a concave-convex procedure (CCP) based fractional programming (FP) approach was proposed by [8] to solve the sum-SE problem. However, the algorithmic complexity of this method was not analysed.

2.2 Sum SE Maximisation Without Power Considerations

Under uniform power assumptions, a peculiarity in a cell-free network is that since all access points can jointly serve all users and we must further devise strategies to determine what set of APs serve users best. It has been shown that it is impractical for all APs to serve all users at the same time and constructing a serving cluster is more beneficial [4]. Here the problem is to allocate a set of serving APs to users in a way that maximises the overall spectral efficiency of the network. More formally, we define this as:

$$\max_{x_{ik} \in \{0,1\}} \sum_{i=1}^{R} \sum_{k=1}^{K} \text{SE}_{ik} x_{ik} \tag{1}$$

$$\text{s.t.} \quad \sum_{i=1}^{R} x_{ik} = 1, \text{for } i = 1, ..., R, \tag{2}$$

$$\sum_{k=1}^{K} x_{ik} = 1, \text{for } k = 1, ..., K. \tag{3}$$

where R is the number of AP clusters formed; and the objective function in (3) is presented by a reward matrix, where K rows represent K users and R columns are considered as the combinations (clusters) of the required number of APs to be selected for each user. In addition, SE_{ik} denotes the spectral efficiency of u_k assigned to a_i (selected AP) and x_{ik} equals 1 if there is an assignment between u_k and a_i, while x_{ik} equals 0 otherwise.

One of the earliest works in CF-mMIMO for optimal allocation of APs to users assumes that all users have equal power and adopted a hierarchical clustering algorithm whereby in the first instance we have K users in K different clusters that are merged into similar clusters iteratively based on channel similarities. The authors showed that the complexity of this technique is $O(M^2 log K)$ [7] where K is the number of users and M is the number of APs. Compared to using conventional methods of selecting APs with high SE which gives a complexity of $O(KM^2)$ [10], the authors in [9], introduce a preprocessing technique to eliminate access points that don't meet a required power threshold. After preprocessing, the complexity of the Hungarian algorithm order is significantly reduced such that we have a complexity of $O(K.M^2)$ to $O(K'.M'^2)$, where $K' \ll K$ and $M' \ll M$.

3   Our Contributions

Here, we describe some progress towards developing efficient algorithmic techniques that can be applied to solving the present challenges in CF-mMIMO networks, while maximising available resources. To better understand the model, we simulated an instance of the sum SE maximisation problem in (3) with an Integer programming model to see how it scales with respect to the input. We provided a fixed cluster size, such that a user can only be assigned to one cluster group. From the experiment, we observed that for smaller input sizes the IP model produces optimal results very quickly (≤60) s but begins to slow down considerably as the number of APs increases, $M \geq 40$. Furthermore, we compared the optimal solution shown by the model with the Hungarian matching algorithm and the random AP selection algorithm. We observe that although the IP model produces optimal solutions in general, as the input size n grows larger, the random and Hungarian algorithm produce their results in a faster time (Fig. 2).

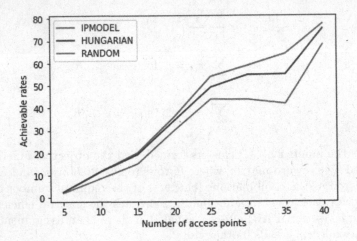

Fig. 2. Comparison of existing algorithms with IP model

4   Conclusion and Future Directions

The research on cell-free massive MIMO is still in its infancy and thus deserves more extensive studies on the complexities of algorithms used. CF-mMIMO is a type of wireless architecture that is receiving considerable attention for enhancing the efficiency of future wireless networks. However, several combinatorial optimisation problems exist with respect to resource allocation. In maximising the total spectral efficiency of the network, the challenge lies in allocating several users to wireless channels in an optimal way given power constraints and interferences that exist. Another distinct feature in CF-mMIMO networks is selecting the best subset of APs to serve users even under uniform power assumptions which is known to be NP-hard [11].

By exploring the connections that might exist between this type of wireless network and already existing graph techniques, we seek to design algorithms that produce feasible solutions for maximising the network performance. Some future directions include:

– Preprocessing the input graph and restricting the graph based on power thresholds and interference ratios to see how this affects the complexity of maximising the sum SE.

- Clustering approaches like hierarchical clustering has been used with a complexity of $O(M^2 \log K)$. However, this clustering technique is not specific to graph-like structures. Hence, we could try to obtain better complexity results by exploring advanced graph clustering algorithms.
- We could also focus on optimising other utility functions like fairness (Maxmin fairness) amongst users to improve network reliability. A bisection search algorithm was shown in [5] for optimising user fairness. We could explore load balancing approaches in graph theory that can be applied in our scenario.

Acknowledgements. We would like to thank the reviewers for their insightful comments.

References

1. Statista.   http://www.statista.com/statistics/802690/worldwide-connected-devices-by-access-technology/. Accessed 09 Mar 2022
2. Ngo, H., Tran, L., Duong, T.Q., Matthaiou, M., Larsson, E.: On the total energy efficiency of cell-free massive MIMO. IEEE Trans. Green Commun. Netw. **2**(1), 25–39 (2017)
3. Luo, Z., Zhang, S.: Dynamic spectrum management: complexity and duality. IEEE J. Sel. Top. Sig. Process. **2**(1), 57–73 (2008)
4. Björnson, E., Jorswieck, E.: Optimal resource allocation in coordinated multi-cell systems. Found. Trends Commun. Inf. Theory **9**(2–3), 113–381 (2013)
5. Ngo, H., Ashikhmin, A., Yang, H., Larsson, E., Marzetta, T.: Cell-free massive MIMO versus small cells. IEEE Trans. Wireless Commun. **16**(3), 1834–1850 (2017)
6. Chakraborty, S., Demir, Ö., Björnson, E., Giselsson, P.: Efficient downlink power allocation algorithms for cell-free massive MIMO systems. IEEE Open J. Commun. Soc. **2**, 168–186 (2020)
7. Wang, R., Shen, M., He, Y., Liu, X.: Performance of cell-free massive MIMO with joint user clustering and access point selection. IEEE Access **9**, 40860–40870 (2021)
8. Shen, K., Yu, W.: Fractional programming for communication systems-Part I: power control and beamforming. IEEE Trans. Sig. Process. **66**(10), 2616–2630 (2018)
9. Moghaddam, K.S., Moghaddam, S.S.: A fast sub-optimum access point selection in ultra-dense networks. In: 2021 IEEE International Conference on Communication, Networks and Satellite (COMNETSAT), vol. 2, no. 5, pp. 239–243 (2021)
10. Calabuig, D., et al.: Resource and mobility management in the network layer of 5G cellular ultra-dense network. IEEE Commun. Mag. **55**(6), 162–169 (2017)
11. Femenias, G., Lassoued, N., Riera-Palou, F.: Access point switch ON/OFF strategies for green cell-free massive MIMO networking. IEEE Access **8**, 21788–21803 (2020)

Benchmarking Parallelism in Unikernels

Akilan Selvacoumar(✉), Robert Stewart, Hans-Wolfgang Loidl,
and Ahmad Ryad Soobhany

Heriot-Watt University, Riccarton, Edinburgh EH14 4AS, UK
as251@hw.ac.uk

Abstract. Virtualisation technologies are widely used in Cloud computing infrastructures, because they can be provisioned cheaply and quickly to meet demand. The common approaches are either to package a Operating System (OS) as a Virtual Machine, or to containerise software with an OS kernel. An emerging alternative are unikernels, which are customised kernels to support just one application. Unikernels are lightweight and an applications has sole use of the kernel, which offers potential for fast, resource efficient and secure execution. For these reasons, unikernels may be idea for parallel computing in the Cloud. However, the parallel performance of unikernel-based Cloud applications has not been extensively studied. This paper presents an evaluation of the OSv unikernel using a parallelised Mandelbrot benchmark, comparing with Docker and a monolithic VM for runtime, parallel speedups and boot-up time. OSv has the fastest boot-up time, and is comparable with the parallel speedups of Docker and the monolithic VM.

Keywords: Unikernels · Parallel Computing

1 Introduction

1.1 Unikernels for the Cloud

The convention for running parallel programs is by executing them on multicore CPUs within standard Operating Systems (OS) with multithreading support. Security, on-demand elastic scalability and energy efficiency are the primary requirements when deploying parallel programs to the Cloud [19–21], which is why virtualisation technologies are widely used for Cloud deployments. The most widely used virtualisation technologies are application-specific containers e.g. Docker, and OS Virtual Machines e.g. VirtualBox and Qemu. These approaches package the full OS software stack along with compiled applications.

An emerging alternative approach is unikernels [2]. A unikernel is an executable image that can execute natively on a hypervisor, without the need for a separate operating system. A unikernel are application specific, i.e. they are customised to execute a single binary program. A unikernel is a lightweight OS kernel where the kernel modules are shared with the hypervisor e.g. Qemu. This

J. Singer et al. (Eds.): Euro-Par 2022 Workshops, LNCS 13835, pp. 286–293, 2023.
https://doi.org/10.1007/978-3-031-31209-0_23

results in quicker boot times because there are fewer modules to start, and additional security guarantees are provided because the compiled application is the only entry point.

Unikernels are designed to be fast, customisable and secure. Unikernels have a single address space, for the one application being executed. This minimises context switching only to kernel actions rather than to other OS processes. Unikernels have a single address space, for the one application being executed. This minimises context switching only to kernel actions rather than to other OS processes.

All components are modularised including operating system primitives, drivers, platform code and libraries should be easy to add and remove as needed, to generate a light weight and flexible operating system. This helps in terms of reducing overhead for the OS and provides the flexibility to switch between different OS modules. POSIX support provides the ability to run existing legacy applications. Exposure to external security threads is minimised because no other process is executed in the virtualised environment.

There are two distinct approaches to unikernel implementation. The first approach is to develop unikernels for specific programming languages, where the low-level kernel libraries are developed in one language and applications are developed in the same language. Examples include MirageOS [4] for OCaml programs and HaLVM [3] for Haskell programs. Any static security guarantees of the language, e.g. through its type system, are guaranteed for the complete software stack. The second approach is to develop unikernels that are compatible with standard binaries. That is, any programming language compiled to native code are supported by these kinds of unikernels. Examples include OSv [5] and Unikraft [6].

The experiments in Sect. 3 uses the language agnostic OSv unikernel. This is because it supports multiple programming languages with parallelism features, and is portable across both hypervisors (e.g. Qemu and Xen) and also CPU architectures (e.g. ARM and x86).

1.2   Parallel Performance of Unikernels

Existing unikernel benchmarks have focused on latency and boot-up time [4] and CPU performance [8]. Another metric is OS noise, which is benchmarked in [7] using FWQ (Fixed work Quanta), FTQ (Fixed time Quanta) and hourglass metrics. When compared with the Linux kernel, the Azalea Unikernel [7] had less kernel interference and scaled well to many-core CPUs. Other benchmarks focus on specific application domains, e.g. comparing boot-up times, file read/write latencies and memory allocation for the Sqlite and Redis databases [6].

The lightweight nature of unikernels, and the fact that programs have exclusive use of the kerne, may enable them to achieve good parallelism efficiency. To the best of the author's knowledge, there is little work on profiling the parallel performance of unikernels. This paper provides a systematic evaluation of a parallelised Mandelbrot implementation on three virtualised software stacks:

Docker, a virtualised Linux OS and the OSv unikernel. Section 3 compares boot-up times, wall-clock runtimes and parallel speedups.

The aim of this paper's experiments are to provide insights into the comparative performance of parallel computing with unikernels. The wider context of this PhD is to firstly discover parallel performance bottlenecks of emerging unikernels, to identify systems-level research opportunities and to find ideal use cases for parallel computing with unikernels.

2   Experimental Design

2.1   Benchmark Metrics

Wall Clock Run Times. The wall clock runtime measures in seconds the total time to execute the Mandelbrot [16] program. The wall clock runtime does not include the boot-up time. This metric shows the sequential runtime performance, as well as the parallel runtime performance on multiple CPU cores. The standard deviation, parallel speeds and parallel efficiency are calculated based on the wall clock runtimes.

Boot-Up Times. The boot-up times is the time taken to the start the Virtual Machine or Container as well as starting the application's execution. This metrics shows how fast it takes to start a parallel program, e.g. if deployed on-demand in the Cloud.

Parallel Speedups. The parallel speed up is defined as the ratio of serial execution time to the parallel execution time [17]. This metric shows how well Mandelbrot speeds up with multiple CPU cores versus the sequential runtime with the same virtualised software stack, e.g. OSv on 8 cores and OSv on 1 core.

2.2   The Mandelbrot Benchmark

Mandelbrot images are generated by applying a mathematical function to each complex number projected in the complex plane and determining for each whether they are bounded or escapes towards infinity. The experiments in Sect. 3 are ran with two sets of Mandelbrot parameters, image height and iterations.

These values are a height of 1000 with 3000 iterations, and then a height of 2000 with 6000 iterations. This is to evaluate the parallel performance of three virtualisation comparators when computational complexity increases.

The Mandelbrot algorithm is parallelised using Goroutines in Go. A Goroutine is spawned for each row to be generated in the Mandelbrot image. Inside each parallel Goroutine is a sequential loop which iterates through each image column. The loop executes the Mandelbrot iteration and Linear Interpolation. Once all go routines are executed the image is written from to disk (Fig. 1).

Fig. 1. A generated Mandelbrot image

2.3 Comparators

Existing unikernel benchmarks [6,8] use Docker and Monolithic kernels as their standard means of comparison. Docker is commonly used for Cloud deployment given its ability to rapidly spawn containers for elastic-scale computing.

There are three virtualisation comparators in the experiments (Sect. 3):

1. OSv running on a Qemu emulator. The Mandelbrot program (implemented in Go) is compiled using Cgo, and the generated shared object and header files are linked to the OSv kernel and then executed.
2. Docker running a Ubuntu 20.04 image. The Mandelbrot program is compiled with the Go compiler which is linked to the Docker file then executed.
3. A monolithic kernel (Ubuntu 20.04) running on a Qemu emulator. The Mandelbrot program is also compiled with the Go compiler, then executed in userspace as a binary file.

Both Qemu and Docker are ran on a host OS (i.e. type-2 hypervisor) in the experiments. The hardware specification of the machine is a Intel i7-1065G7 CPU with 8 cores and 16 GB of memory. For the experiments in Sect. 3, the type 2 hypervisors ensure a fair comparison between OSv, the monolithic kernel and Docker at the same layer of virtualized abstraction.

3 Results

3.1 Wall Clock Run Times

The wall clock runtime results for both parameters are in Figs. 3(a) and 3(b). The plots of the wall clock runtimes refer to the mean of run times. The x-axis refers to the number of cores used and the y-axis refers to seconds of the mean run time all measurements are the mean of 3 executions.

OSv on KVM	145ms
Ubuntu on KVM (Monolthic)	31 seconds
Docker	220ms

(a) Bootup Times

Fig. 2. Bootup times

Each experiment is executed 8 times to obtain the mean average and the standard deviation.

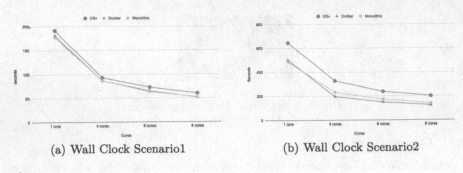

(a) Wall Clock Scenario1   (b) Wall Clock Scenario2

Fig. 3. Wall clock run times

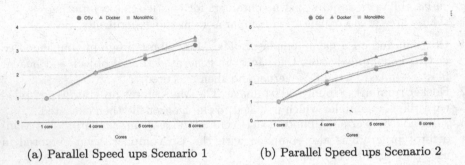

(a) Parallel Speed ups Scenario 1   (b) Parallel Speed ups Scenario 2

Fig. 4. Parallel Speed ups

Scenario 1: The result in scenario 1 in Fig. 3(a) shows that OSv is slower than Docker and the Monolithic kernel (i.e. Ubuntu). The Monolithic kernel and Docker have almost identical run times with a difference of 2 s (circa 1% of the single core runtime). OSv on the other-hand exhibits runtimes that are up to 8.5 s higher than Monolithic kernel and Docker. For Scenario 1 (Fig. 3(a)), OSv is the fastest system across all core numbers, 32 s faster than the Monolithic kernel and 29 s faster than Docker on 4 cores. On 6 and 8 cores OSv runs on average 19 s.

Across all parameters and core numbers, OSv was slower than the other 2 comparators by a difference on average of 17 s. With higher core numbers the differences in runtimes between the systems (both in absolute time and percentages) decreases. In Scenario 1 with one core OSv runs faster than Docker by 24 s and OSv is slower than the Monolithic Kernel (i.e. Ubuntu) by 3 s. In all other runs of Scenario 1 OSv is *slower* than the other 2 comparators by 20.5 s. In the case of OSv for Scenario 1 the first run of each core number delivered the fastest run time.

Scenario 2: In Scenario 2 in Fig. 3(b) OSv is slower than Docker and the Monolithic kernel. Docker consistently has the fastest mean wall clock run times compared to the other two systems: it is on average 23 s faster than the Monolithic kernel, and 102 s faster than OSv. In Scenario 2 (Fig. 3(b)), and in contrast to

Scenario 1, OSv is consistently *slower* than the other configurations: across all core numbers it runs by 82 s slower than Docker, and by 99 s slower than the Monolithic kernel. In a single core configuration, we observed the highest differences in runtime for OSv, by an average of 113 s slower than Docker and 130 s slower than the monolithic kernel. On a single core configuration OSv had the least stable results with a standard deviation of 57.84 s. In comparison Docker had a standard deviation of only 40 s and the Monolithic kernel had the lowest standard deviation of 16.4 s. Interestingly, for the multi cores runs OSv had more stable run times in comparison to Docker and the Monolithic kernel, with standard deviations of 0.4 for OSv, 1.45 for Monolithic kernel, and 9.61 for Docker. This means although Docker and Monolithic kernel had faster run times in the multi-core configurations, OSv delivers more predictable run times based on the standard deviation calculated across the 8 runs on different core numbers.

3.2   Boot up Times

Figure 2(a) shows the average boot times of OSv, Docker and monolithic kernel (i.e. Ubuntu). In terms of boot-up times OSv has faster than Docker by 25% and 99% faster than the monolithic Kernel (i.e. Ubuntu).

3.3   Parallel Speedups

The parallel speed ups are in Fig. 4(a) and Fig. 4(b). They show the parallel speed ups of all configurations, calculated based on the mean wall clock run times over 3 runs.

Scenario 1: The parallel speed ups for OSv multi core is respectively 2.05× times for 4 cores, 2.64× for 6 cores and 3.20× 8 cores. OSv achieves modest speedups of 2.05× on 4 cores, 2.64× on 6 cores, and 3.20× on 8 cores In comparison, Docker achieves initially higher but relatively dropping speedups of 2.10× on 4 cores, 2.79× on 6 cores. and 2.80× on 8 cores. Finally, the Monolithic kernel achieves similar speedups with the best high-end performance of 2.05× on 4 cores, 2.80× on 6 cores, and 3.40× on 8 cores. Based on these parallel speed ups for OSv the parallel efficiency is 51% on 4 cores, 45% on 6 cores, and 39% on 8 cores. The parallel efficiency for Docker is 52% on 4 cores, 46% on 6 cores, and 44% on 8 cores. The parallel efficiency for the Monolithic kernel is 51% for 4 cores, 46% for 6 cores and 43% for 8 cores. For this scenario Docker and the Monolithic kernel have a similar speed up compared to OSv with an average difference of 20%. Docker and the Monolithic kernel have a similar parallel efficiency compared to OSv with an average of 2% parallel efficiency difference.

Scenario 2 On Scenario 2, OSv achieves modest speedups of 1.96× on 4 cores, 2.70× on 6 cores, and 3.20× on 8 cores. In comparison, Docker achieves higher speedups of 2.54× on 4 cores, 3.35× on 6 cores, and 4× on 8 cores. Finally, the Monolithic kernel achieves speedups of 2.08× on 4 cores, 2.80× on 6 cores, and 3.49× on 8 cores.

3.4   Discussion

The boot-up time comparison shows that launching applications with OSv is slightly faster than doing so with Docker and significantly faster than with a monolithic VM. This is likely because Unikernels have fewer modules to launch compared to the other two. The more reproducible run times with Scenario 2 for OSv likely because there are fewer background processes and no other user-level applications running which results in less OS noise. The slightly longer runtimes for OSv may be due to the OS multi-threading scheduling implementation in OSv. As future work, will plan on investigating this.

4   Conclusion

This paper presents an experiment comparing the parallel and boot-up time performance of the OSv unikernel compared with a Docker container and a monolithic Linux VM. The results (Sect. 3) provides a better understanding on how Unikernels preform on parallel applications, and what needs deeper investigation. The unikernel achieved the fastest boot-up time. Moreover these experiments show that the OSv unikernel can achieve parallel speedups. Moreover these speedups are comparable with Docker and the Linux VM. This provides a starting point for deeper investigation in this PhD research. The future work will focus on benchmarking parallelised applications from a wider range of domains, using more metrics including memory profiling, energy consumption and OS noise.

References

1. Wu, S., et al.: Android unikernel: gearing mobile code offloading towards edge computing. Future Gener. Comput. Syst. **86**, 694–703 (2018). https://doi.org/10.1016/j.future.2018.04.069
2. Madhavapeddy, A., et al.: Unikernels: library operating systems for the cloud. ACM SIGARCH Comput. Archit. News **41**(1), 461–72 (2013). https://doi.org/10.1145/2490301.2451167
3. Cheon, J., Kim, Y., Hur, T., Byun, S., Woo, G.: An analysis of haskell parallel programming model in the HaLVM. J. Phys. Conf. Ser. **1566**, 012070 (2020). https://doi.org/10.1088/1742-6596/1566/1/012070
4. Madhavapeddy, A., Scott, D.: Unikernels: rise of the virtual library operating system: what if all the software layers in a virtual appliance were compiled within the same safe, high-level language framework? Queue **11**, 30–44 (2013). https://doi.org/10.1145/2557963.2566628
5. Kivity, A., et al.: OSv-optimizing the operating system for virtual machines. In: 2014 USENIX Annual Technical Conference (USENIX ATC 2014), pp. 61–72 (2014). https://www.usenix.org/conference/atc14/technical-sessions/presentation/kivity
6. Kuenzer S, et al.: Unikraft: fast, specialised Unikernels the easy way. In: Proceedings of the Sixteenth European Conference on Computer Systems, pp. 376–394. ACM, Online Event United Kingdom (2021)

7. Cha, S., Jeon, S., Jeong, Y., Kim, J., Jung, S.: OS noise analysis on Azalea-Unikernel. In: 2022 24th International Conference on Advanced Communication Technology (ICACT), pp. 81–84 (2022)
8. Xavier, B., Ferreto, T., Jersak, L.: Time provisioning evaluation of KVM, docker and unikernels in a cloud platform. In: 2016 16th IEEE/ACM International Symposium on Cluster, Cloud and Grid Computing (CCGrid), pp. 277–280 (2016)
9. What Is Rally? - Rally 3.3.1 dev7 Documentation. https://rally.readthedocs.io/en/latest/. Accessed 19 May 2022
10. OSProfiler (2022). https://github.com/stackforge/osprofiler
11. Projects — Unikernels. http://Unikernel.org/projects/. Accessed 14 May 2022
12. Tajbakhsh, M., Bagherzadeh, J.: Microblogging hash tag recommendation system based on semantic TF-IDF: Twitter use case. In: 2016 IEEE 4th International Conference on Future Internet of Things and Cloud Workshops (FiCloudW), pp. 252–257 (2016)
13. Boettiger, C.: An introduction to docker for reproducible research. SIGOPS Oper. Syst. Rev. **49**, 71–79 (2015). https://doi.org/10.1145/2723872.2723882
14. Prabhakar, R., Kumar, R.: Concurrent Programming in Go
15. Why Gleam · Chrislusf/Gleam Wiki. GitHub. https://github.com/chrislusf/gleam. Accessed 26 May 2022
16. Selvacoumar, A.: AKILAN1999/Mandelbrot-go-uni-kernel-. GitHub. https://github.com/Akilan1999/mandelbrot-go-uni-kernel-
17. El-Nashar, A.: arXiv e-print archive. To parallelize or not to parallelize, speed up issue. https://arxiv.org/pdf/1103.5616.pdf
18. Makkad, S.: Mandelbrot Set Basics. Fractal To Desktop (2018). https://fractaltodesktop.com/mandelbrot-set-basics/index.html
19. Bratterud, A.: Enhancing cloud security and privacy: The unikernel solution. https://aura.abdn.ac.uk/bitstream/handle/2164/8524/AAB02.pdf
20. Bratterud, A.: A framework for elastic execution of existing MPI programs. IEEE Xplore. https://ieeexplore.ieee.org/abstract/document/6008941
21. Fontana de Nardin, I., Da Rosa Righi, R., Lima Lopes, T., André da Costa, C., Yeom, H., Köstler, H.: On revisiting energy and performance in microservices applications: a cloud elasticity-driven approach. Parallel Comput. **108**, 102858 (2021). https://www.sciencedirect.com/science/article/pii/S0167819121001010

Machine Learning Methodologies to Support HPC Systems Operations: Anomaly Detection

Martin Molan[1]([⊠]) [iD], Andrea Borghesi[1] [iD], Luca Benini[1,2] [iD],
and Andrea Bartolini[1] [iD]

[1] DISI and DEI Department, University of Bologna, Bologna, Italy
{martin.molan2,andrea.borghesi3,luca.benini,a.bartolini}@unibo.it
[2] Institut für Integrierte Systeme, ETH, Zürich, Switzerland

Abstract. The increasing complexity of modern and future pre-exascale high-performance computing (HPC) systems necessitate the introduction of machine learning methodologies that support systems administrators. The key element of these monitoring and support systems is anomaly detection. This presentation discusses my current work - as part of my Ph.D. research - in developing anomaly detection systems for the HPC systems. Specifically, I discuss my ongoing work in improving upon the previous SoA anomaly detection system. The proposed approach is evaluated on the Maroni 100 supercomputer located in CIENCA. Based on a large-scale evaluation (on all 980 nodes), we see that the proposed approach outperforms the previous SoA.

Keywords: Anomaly detection · High-performance computing · Machine learning

1 Introduction

In the move towards exascale, modern High-performance computing (HPC) systems are becoming increasingly larger and more complex [9]. A typical modern HPC system consists of hundreds of compute nodes with future pre-exascale systems expending this number into thousands [6]. This increased complexity necessitates the introduction of monitoring systems supported by AI/ML methodologies that support system administrators in managing the HPC system.

The most critical application of AI tools in support of system administrators is the introduction of anomaly detection systems. Anmol detection systems are crucial as they allow system administrators to react to the downtime (or unavailability event) faster and thus reduce the time between the anomaly (evet) and their response. This faster response time severely reduces the time the compute nodes are unavailable and increases the overall availability of the HPC system [8]. This anomaly detection signal is then included in the dashboard presented to the system administrators as a part of a digital twin of the datacentre.

J. Singer et al. (Eds.): Euro-Par 2022 Workshops, LNCS 13835, pp. 294–298, 2023.
https://doi.org/10.1007/978-3-031-31209-0_24

The foundation for the creation of AI-augmented monitoring systems is the holistic monitoring infrastructure that combines out-of-band power monitoring, system monitoring, and historical availability data [3,7]. My Ph.D. thesis focuses on data collected by the ExaMon monitoring system developed by the University of Bologna [5]. I study the data collected from the Marconi 100, which is a Tier-0 HPC system located in CINECA Italy [2] (ranked 9th in Jun. 2020 Top500 list [1]).

The state-of-the-art (SoA) approach to anomaly detection is to deploy a semi-supervised approach [4,8]. This stems from the fact that the anomalies are rare events, and it would be impossible to collect a significant enough dataset for classical supervised classification methods [4]. The current SoA approach to anomaly detection proposed by Borghesi et al. [4] is a semi-supervised anomaly detection approach that takes minimal advantage of the temporal dependencies in the anomaly signal. Our current work - discussed in this paper - is thus how to extend this approach to include temporal dynamics. We propose to do this by deploying an encoder network consisting of Long Short-Term Memory (LSTM) cells.

1.1 Contributions

The key research question that this work discussed is how to extend our previous work [4] (which is the current SoA) with temporal dependency data. Specifically, we propose an LSTM-based approach that we evaluate in a very large scale experiment: we train two different models for each of the 980 nodes of Marconi 100; an extensive scale experiment thus supports the results (and the claim of the new SoA).

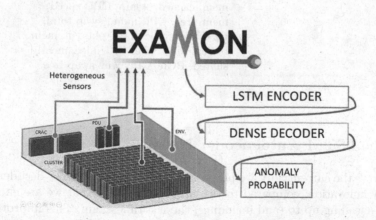

Fig. 1. Data collection schema of M100 HPC system. Data from various sensors is collected by ExaMon and then passed to the encoder/decoder network.

1.2   Anomalies and Dataset

The proposed methodology is evaluated on the complete first ten-month operation history of all 980 nodes of the Marconi 100 HPC system. The collected dataset contains out-of-bound hardware monitoring data and system data. The complete list of used features is presented in Table 1. The anomalies are determined as events where the nodes are unavailable to accept (or continue to execute) compute jobs. The dataset is prepared in collaboration between the University of Bologna and CINECA [2].

Table 1. An anomaly detection model is created only on hardware and application monitoring features. More granular information regarding individual jobs is not collected to ensure the privacy of the HPC system users.

Source	Features
Hardware monitoring	ambient temp., dimm[0-15] temp., fan[0-7] speed, fan disk power, GPU[0-3] core temp. ,GPU[0-3] mem temp. , gv100card[0-3], core[0-3] temp. , p[0-1] io power, p[0-1] mem power, p[0-1] power, p[0-1] vdd temp. ,part max used, ps[0-1] input power, ps[0-1] input voltage, ps[0-1] output current, ps[0-1] output voltage, total power
System monitoring	CPU system, bytes out, CPU idle, proc. run, mem. total, pkts. out, bytes in, boot time, CPU steal, mem. cached, stamp, CPU speed, mem. free, CPU num., swap total, CPU user, proc. total, pkts. in, mem. buffers, CPU idle, CPU nice, mem. shared, PCIe, CPU wio, swap free

2   The LSTM Autoencoder Network

To improve the current SoA, we propose an LSTM encoder-dense decoder model. The key innovation, compared to the current SoA [4] is that we are encoding a sequence leading up to (and including) the last timestamp. This improves upon the dense autoencoder as it better captures the temporal dependencies inherent in the dataset. The critical insight in this innovation is that while the data describing supercomputing nodes is composed of multi-variate time series, the state-of-the-art does not explicitly consider the temporal dimension – the dense autoencoder has no notion of time nor of *sequence* of data points. To overcome this limitation, our approach works by encoding the sequence of values *leading up to the anomaly*. The encoder network is composed of LSTM layers, which have often been proved to be well suited to the context where the temporal dimension is relevant. An LSTM layer consists of recurrent cells with input from the previous timestamp and the long-term memory. The latent layer (vector) output is passed into a dense decoder trained by reproducing the final vector in an input sequence. The decoder network is thus composed of fully connected dense layers.

The proposed LSTM encoder/dense decoder model takes as input a sequence of vectors of features x leading up to the current time t_0 and then tries to reconstruct only the last vector in the sequence $\hat{x}_{t_0}$:

$$M : x_{t_0-W}, \cdots , x_{t_0} \rightarrow \hat{x}_{t_0}. \tag{1}$$

The length of the input sequence W leading up to the current time t_0 is a tunable parameter. For experimental results, the length of the input sequence is set to 10. The proposed model M outputs the probability (estimated from the reconstruction error between x_{t_0} and $\hat{x}_{t_0}$) that the node is in an anomalous state at time t_0.

3   Experimental Results

To remove the potential for bias by setting up the decision threshold, we compare the proposed approach against the current SoA [4] by evaluating the area under the receiver-operator characteristic curve (AUC ROC). An exponential smoothing baseline is implemented as a sanity check - if the anomalies were simple jumps in value, the exponential smoothing would be able to catch them. As it is clear from the results, this is not the case - exponential smoothing performs even worse than the trivial classifier (AUC smaller than 0.5). As seen in the Table 2), the proposed model (combined results from 980 nodes) outperforms the current SoA. This confirms our hypothesis about the usefulness of considering temporal dependencies when modeling anomalies.

Table 2. AUC performance of different AD models. Proposed approach outperforms the current SoA for AD.

Anomaly detection method:	AUC:
Exponential smoothing	0.4276
Dense autoencoder (current SoA)	0.7470
LSTM autoencoder (proposed approach)	0.7582

M. Molan et al.

4 Conclusions

This work presents the genesis of developing anomaly detection systems on a Tier-0 supercomputer. It reevaluates our previous work [4] against a new proposed approach. This approach, based on LSTM cells, outperforms the old SoA approach.

Both deep learning-based approaches are evaluated on a very large-scale experiment consisting of the whole dataset collected from Marconi 100. Results from this large-scale experiment strongly support our claim that the proposed SoA approach sets a new SoA benchmark for anomaly detection in HPC systems.

Acknowledgments. All work discussed in the Ph.D. symposium is done in collaboration with and under the supervision of prof. Andrea Bartolini, prof. Luca Benini and prof. Andrea Borghesi.

This research was partly supported by the EuroHPC EU PILOT project (g.a. 1010-34126), the EuroHPC EU Regale project (g.a. 956560), EU H2020-ICT-11-2018-2019 IoTwins project (g.a. 857191), and EU Pilot for exascale EuroHPC EUPEX (g. a. 101033975). We also thank CINECA for the collaboration and access to their machines and Francesco Beneventi for maintaining Examon.

References

1. Top500list (2020). https://www.top500.org/lists/top500/2020/06/
2. Beske, N.: Ug3.2: Marconi100 userguide. https://wiki.u-gov.it/confluence/pages/viewpage.action?pageId=336727645. Accessed 17 Aug 2020
3. Borghesi, A., Bartolini, A., et al.: Anomaly detection using autoencoders in HPC systems. In: Proceedings of the AAAI Conference on Artificial Intelligence (2019)
4. Borghesi, A., Molan, M., Milano, M., Bartolini, A.: Anomaly detection and anticipation in high performance computing systems. IEEE Trans. Parallel Distrib. Syst. **33**(4), 739–750 (2022). https://doi.org/10.1109/TPDS.2021.3082802
5. Iuhasz, G., Petcu, D.: Monitoring of exascale data processing. In: 2019 IEEE International Conference on Advanced Scientific Computing (ICASC), pp. 1–5 (2019). https://doi.org/10.1109/ICASC48083.2019.8946279
6. Milojicic, D., Faraboschi, P., Dube, N., Roweth, D.: Future of HPC: diversifying heterogeneity. In: 2021 Design, Automation Test in Europe Conference Exhibition (DATE), pp. 276–281 (2021). https://doi.org/10.23919/DATE51398.2021.9474063
7. Netti, A., Kiziltan, Z., Babaoglu, O., Sîrbu, A., Bartolini, A., Borghesi, A.: A machine learning approach to online fault classification in HPC systems. Future Gener. Comput. Syst. **110**, 1009–1022 (2019)
8. Netti, A., Shin, W., Ott, M., Wilde, T., Bates, N.: A conceptual framework for HPC operational data analytics. In: 2021 IEEE International Conference on Cluster Computing (CLUSTER), pp. 596–603 (2021). https://doi.org/10.1109/Cluster48925.2021.00086
9. Shin, W., Oles, V., Karimi, A.M., Ellis, J.A., Wang, F.: Revealing power, energy and thermal dynamics of a 200pf pre-exascale supercomputer. In: Proceedings of the International Conference for High Performance Computing, Networking, Storage and Analysis, SC 2021. Association for Computing Machinery, New York (2021). https://doi.org/10.1145/3458817.3476188

FPGAs in Supercomputers: Performance Through Dataflow Programming and Flexibility

Gabriel Rodriguez-Canal[(✉)]

EPCC at The University of Edinburgh, Edinburgh EH8 9BT, UK
`gabriel.rodcanal@ed.ac.uk`

Abstract. In recent years heterogeneity become synonymous with supercomputing, and whilst GPUs are highly popular and demonstrated excellent computational performance, there are other options. One such option is that of Field Programmable Gate Arrays (FPGAs) which are reconfigurable at the electronics level to suit an application. Such tailoring means that programmers can directly connect with how the electronics is executing their code, rather than via the black-box microarchitecture of CPUs and GPUs. Consequently FPGAs can provide advantages, especially when codes are memory bound, however they are not yet mainstream due to the difficulty in gaining performance. The issue is that they require programming using the dataflow paradigm, whereas existing imperative languages are based on Von Neumann architectures. Furthermore, the FPGA tooling traditionally imposes usage patterns which lacks the flexibility expected by HPC programmers, especially around workload migration and preemptive scheduling. The overarching aim of this PhD is to improve accessibility of accelerating HPC codes on FPGAs, firstly by providing appropriate programming abstractions and secondly by enabling usage mechanisms which enable flexible interaction.

Keywords: FPGAs · Dataflow programming · Partial Reconfiguration

1 Research Problem

1.1 Dataflow Programming

FPGAs (Field Programmable Gate Arrays) are the most popular type of reconfigurable architectures, where their circuitry is not fixed during manufacture. Thus, the electronics can be adapted to the problem traditionally through Hardware Description Language (HDL) programming (usually written in Verilog or VHDL) and, most recently, through High Level Synthesis (HLS) codes (written in C or C++). Thanks to this flexibility, there is no predefined control logic as in CPUs or GPUs, as instead the architecture is bespoke for every problem. With Von Neumann based architectures, such as CPUs or GPUs, performance is drawn from a high clock frequency to issue a high number of operations per second (typically measured as FLOPS, floating operations per second) and parallelism.

© The Author(s), under exclusive license to Springer Nature Switzerland AG 2023
J. Singer et al. (Eds.): Euro-Par 2022 Workshops, LNCS 13835, pp. 299–304, 2023.
https://doi.org/10.1007/978-3-031-31209-0_25

FPGAs, without a predefined ISA or control logic provide reconfigurable fabric combined with hardened components, for example for undertaking floating point arithmetic, and memory. The hardware is created ad-hoc from the fundamental component parts of the FPGA, which, from a coarse-grained view, leads to a large pipeline of custom functional units. Dataflow is everything here, and for this reason, a traditional imperative program does not map well to this type of architecture and leads to poor performance. In addition, as already highlighted, Von Neumann architectures partially rely on a high clock frequency to deliver high performance, whereas FPGAs are powered by low-frequency clocks due to the higher underlying complexity of the reconfigurable building blocks — frequencies are typically around 250 to 350 MHz, however the ability to exploit massive parallelism when programmed properly provides the potential to ameliorate this and to outperform Von Neumann architectures.

Dataflow programming maps better to the FPGA architecture and unlocks massive parallelism. This paradigm assumes programs can be expressed as a Directed Graph (DG) with nodes being operations performed on input data, transforming it to output data. The nodes are connected by directed archs, that represent the data dependencies for the operations in the program. The data flow between nodes until all input has been exhausted. Essentially, these nodes could be mapped to the functional units synthesised in the FPGA and the whole program expressed as a DG could be mapped to the synthesised pipeline.

Opposed to the imperative paradigm, where a sequence of instructions would be fetched from memory sequentially as directed by the program counter and operate on data, dataflow programming unveils the data dependencies in the program thanks to its equivalence to a DG. This can prevent stalling on memory accesses between operations and increase parallelism. In dataflow the programmer's model is that the logic is laid out spatially across the chip.

Figure 1 shows a simple program both in an imperative fashion (left) and in a dataflow fashion as a DG (right). In the original work the following question is posed: What if Y is available before X? It turns out that, assuming no out-of-order execution, the imperative program will stall since, in order to execute the first instruction, it needs X. On the other hand, the division can be executed whilst X arrives in the dataflow program, thus not wasting computing cycles. This is possible thanks to the explicit expression

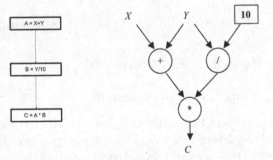

Fig. 1. Imperative vs Dataflow. Extracted from [5]

of data dependencies in dataflow programming. However, we know that nowadays CPUs have out-of-order execution capabilities. Even in that situation the dataflow approach would be advantageous as it would take only 2 cycles to complete when all the input data is available from the beginning, opposed to the imperative version whose best-case scenario is 3 cycles. These minor difference account for massive performance improvements at a larger scale. In words of J. Flynn [2], a pipeline is typically 500 deep, thus just by replicating the pipeline four times 2000 dataflow actions will be occurring every cycle. This ability to discover massive parallelism with dataflow in FPGAs renders them an attractive accelerator for HPC. Thus, tasks like data reordering whilst other parts of the chip consume different data concurrently can be undertaken. In combination with features such as the effective use of on-chip memory replacing generic L1/L2 CPU caches this allows to draw high performance from FPGAs.

Original works on the dataflow paradigm tried to find a general dataflow machine [3]. Unfortunately, this machine is not general enough and relies on overcomplicated constructs to keep track of the arrival of tokens to nodes which result in performance overhead and area occupancy. Our approach intends to ameliorate performance programming by enabling the user to implement bespoke dataflow machines entirely tuned to the application instead of programming a general one. This will be enabled by the dataflow programming language Lucid, originally designed to program general dataflow machines.

1.2 Flexibility

The reconfiguration of an FPGA takes place by downloading a pre-generated configuration file known as *bitstream*. This bitstream describes the contents of the configuration memory of the FPGA i.e., values held by the logic fabric and how the interconnect is wired. This configuration will remain static until a new bitstream is downloaded, completely erasing the old configuration to replace it with the new one. This process is time consuming, in the order of seconds for large FPGAs, and stalls the device, losing potential compute cycles. Furthermore, vendors do not provide a method for saving the context of running kernels, thus workload migration is not officially supported even within a same configuration. Widely adopted architectures in HPC such as CPUs and GPUs support preemptive scheduling, workload migration and the execution of new workloads does not include any performance penalty except for cache misses. Some works [1,8] on Dynamic Partial Reconfiguration (DPR), i.e. the ability to reconfigure one part of the FPGA fabric whilst the rest of it is running, address this issue of lack of flexibility. However, none of them deal with the use of this technology in a heterogeneous task-based model to potentially interact with other devices and they are limited in that they require the board to support OpenCL. Part of this PhD is focused on addressing this problem in a more technology agnostic way and with a focus on integrating FPGAs in heterogeneous systems.

2   Dataflow: Compiler Technology and DSLs

2.1   Vitis HLS Open Source Front-End

Xilinx released the frontend of Vitis HLS as open source, their framework for HLS, in 2021. This opens numerous research avenues, as it allows the manipulation of the IR to explore ideas for optimisation whilst still relying on the backend of Vitis HLS that will map the IR to the physical FPGA resources. The modifications at the IR level allow the developer to optimise aspects ranging from memory access patterns to the application of well-known optimisation techniques such as loop tiling manually if desired. Additionally, since the frontend is fully available, it is possible to modify the `clang` frontend to add new constructs such as pragmas that the user can utilise to indicate the compiler a given custom optimisation should be applied.

2.2   An Example: The Stencil Pragma

This example demonstrates the use of the recently released Xilinx technology and allows obtaining performance in a recurring method in computational science without further knowledge of the underlying technology. Stencil codes present a strided memory access that leads to poor performance. In FPGAs the pattern is transformed to the shift register pattern [4] that, supported by on-chip memory, provides the result of one cell per cycle. This is considered a low-level optimisation, and programmers will not generally be aware of this pattern or even that there is a performance problem.

To deliver performance transparently, the Xilinx's `clang` compiler was extended with a pragma that applies the shift register pattern to 1D/2D stencil codes. The user is just required to qualify the outer loop with `#pragma stencil`. The frontend was modified accordingly so that a metadata flag is added to the first instruction of the first basic block of the loop. This flag is later used in the LLVM optimiser to modify the IR accordingly to apply the shift register pattern.

2.3   DSLs and xDSL

Domain Specific Languages (DSLs) are programming abstractions specialised for a specific type of problem. As such, they provide an amenable user-facing interface for the domain scientist, thus allowing a straightforward mapping of the equations to the code. Additionally, DSLs provide builtin high-performant modules to solve the most common tasks for that particular type of problem, therefore improving code readability, performance and debugging. However, these languages present several hurdles:

1. Lack of uniformity: by the specificity nature of DSLs that renders them unusable for other problems apart from the one they were designed to target initially, the domain scientist that works on several different problems is forced to use more than one DSL should they opt for this approach. There is not a standard for the design of DSLs, which leads to non-uniform languages that have to be learnt separately by the user.

2. Code duplication: the development of every DSL has steps in common such as the definition of a new IR (Intermediate Representation). This is highly inefficient from the point of view of development and hinders maintainability.
3. Lack of support: DSLs are commonly developed by academic research groups that might or might not continue giving support to the language in the future, based on factors such as funding. This hinders its adoption, as users are reluctant to introduce a dependency in their software on an obsolete language.

The EPSRC funded xDSL project aims to address this by developing a common DSL ecosystem based on MLIR. Exposed via a Python toolkit, the idea is that DSL developers can write a thin layer on-top of this framework to then benefit from the underlying MLIR/LLVM ecosystem. I am working with xDSL to develop appropriate dataflow abstractions and compiler using this technology, effectively providing a dataflow DSL for efficient programming of FPGAs.

This will address the issues described above by providing the programmer with the appropriate set of dataflow abstractions to direct their code execution on the FPGA, whilst benefiting from an existing compilation stack. Because this is MLIR/LLVM we are able to generate LLVM IR which is compatible with the HLS tool as described above, or target other tools such as CIRCT.

3 Flexibility: Dynamic Partial Reconfiguration in Task-Based Models

Section 1.2 describes two issues regarding flexibility that affect FPGAs: (1) the stalling and the overhead derived from reconfiguration and (2) the lack of support for preemptive scheduling. DPR, unlike traditional full reconfiguration, does not require stalling the FPGA for loading new kernels and the reconfiguration time can be overlapped with computation. Additionally, since reconfiguration time is proportional to the size of the portion to be reconfigured, DPR is always faster than full reconfiguration. However, this

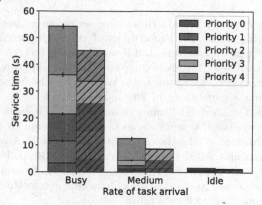

Fig. 2. Service times for 30 tasks at size 600×600 on 2 RRs. Per bar group: Non-preemptive (left), preemptive (right).

technology is not directly accessible to the programmer. It requires a compatible hardware design and awareness of multiple low-level details for the integration of HLS kernels.

To address the issues mentioned above, the author has integrated DPR alongside a checkpointing technique saving the kernel context in Controller [6,7], a mature heterogeneous task-based programming model based on C99 macros. This bridges the gap between the programmer and DPR through a software abstraction that allows swapping in and out kernels whilst the rest of the fabric keeps operating. Reconfiguration time is lower thanks to the use of partial bitstreams and it is hidden by overlapping with computation.

In summary, this work involved the implementation of a DPR-capable hardware design easily customisable by the user through TCL scripts, the extension of the Controller model with a new backend and the development of a modular preemptive scheduler that makes use of DPR. The work is proven with an application consisting of 4 image filters applied over images generated at random times drawn from $\mathcal{U}(0, T)$. Figure 2 shows the service time, defined as the time it takes for a task to be served since it is generated until it starts execution on the FPGA, for 30 tasks at size 600×600 on 2 RRs. Times T considered are Busy (0.1), Medium (0.5) and Idle (0.8). These results show that our scheduler effectively reduces the total service time of tasks, thus increasing the flexibility, as preemption enables swapping in and out tasks upon a condition — priority in this case. These results illustrate that the technique enables flexibility through preemptive scheduling, effectively reducing service time. This occurs at an overhead of only 4.04%. Furthermore, we know that the service time with preemptive scheduling can be further reduced by replacing the Xilinx's ICAP controller (used for DPR), as it only uses 2.5% of the maximum port bandwidth. This avenue will be explored in the future.

References

1. Vaishnav, A., et al.: Heterogeneous resource-elastic scheduling for CPU+ FPGA architectures. In: Proceedings of the 10th International Symposium on Highly-Efficient Accelerators and Reconfigurable Technologies, pp. 1–6 (2019)
2. Flynn, M.J.: Dataflow computing for data-intensive applications (2011)
3. Gurd, J.R., Kirkham, C.C., Watson, I.: The Manchester prototype dataflow computer. Commun. ACM **28**(1), 34–52 (1985)
4. Jia, Q., Zhou, H.: Tuning stencil codes in OpenCL for FPGAs. In: 2016 IEEE 34th International Conference on Computer Design (ICCD), pp. 249–256. IEEE (2016)
5. Johnston, W.M., Hanna, J.R.P., Millar, R.J.: Advances in dataflow programming languages. ACM Comput. Surv. (CSUR) **36**(1), 1–34 (2004)
6. Moreton-Fernandez, A., Ortega-Arranz, H., Gonzalez-Escribano, A.: Controllers: an abstraction to ease the use of hardware accelerators. Int. J. High Perform. Comput. Appl. **32**(6), 838–853 (2018)
7. Rodriguez-Canal, G., Torres, Y., Gonzalez-Escribano, A.: Integrating FPGAs in a heterogeneous and portable parallel programming model (2020)
8. Zamacola, R., Martínez, A.G., Mora, J., Otero, A., de La Torre, E.: IMPRESS: automated tool for the implementation of highly flexible partial reconfigurable systems with Xilinx Vivado. In: 2018 International Conference on ReConFigurable Computing and FPGAs (ReConFig), pp. 1–8. IEEE (2018)

Author Index

J. Singer et al. (Eds.): Euro-Par 2022 Workshops, LNCS 13835, pp. 305–306, 2023.
https://doi.org/10.1007/978-3-031-31209-0

Printed in the United States
by Baker & Taylor Publisher Services

Printed in the United States
by Baker & Taylor Publisher Services